Date Due

THE PHYSICAL EDUCATION CURRICULUM

Fifth Edition

THE PHYSICAL EDUCATION CURRICULUM

Jim L. Stillwell
Arkansas State University

Carl E. Willgoose
Boston University

Allyn and Bacon
Boston • London • Toronto • Sydney • Tokyo • Singapore

Senior Series Editor: Suzy Spivey
Editor in Chief, Social Sciences: Sean W. Wakely
Editorial Assistant: Lisa Davidson
Marketing Manager: Quinn Perkson
Editorial-Production Administrator: Donna Simons
Editorial-Production Service: Shepherd, Inc.
Composition and Prepress Buyer: Linda Cox
Manufacturing Buyer: Suzanne Lareau
Cover Administrator: Suzanne Harbison

Copyright © 1997, 1984 by Allyn & Bacon
A Viacom Company
160 Gould Street
Needham Heights, MA 02194

Internet: www.abacon.com
America Online: keyword: College Online

All rights reserved. No part of the material protected by this copyright notice may be reproduced or utilized in any form or by any means, electronic or mechanical, including photocopying, recording, or by and information storage and retrieval system, without written permission from the copyright owner.

Library of Congress Cataloging-in-Publication Data

Stillwell, Jim L.
   The physical education curriculum / Jim L. Stillwell, Carl E. Willgoose. — 5th ed.
     p. cm.
   Rev. ed. of: The curriculum in physical education / Carl E. Willgoose. 4th ed. © 1984.
   Includes bibliographical references and index.
   ISBN 0-13-296997-1
   1. Physical education and training—United States—Curricula.
I. Willgoose, Carl E. II. Willgoose, Carl E. Curriculum in physical education. III. Title.
GV365.S75   1996
375.6137'0973—dc20   96-27820
                                          CIP

Printed in the United States of America

10 9 8 7 6 5 4 3 2 1   01 00 99 98 97 96

CONTENTS IN BRIEF

1 Society and the Celebration of Life   1

2 Educational Foundations   30

3 The Student and Curriculum Objectives   49

4 Curriculum Planning in Physical Education   84

5 Research and Curriculum Change   110

6 Program Organization   127

7 The Curriculum Guide   166

8 The Elementary Physical Education Program, K–6   180

9 The Secondary Physical Education Program, 7–12   213

10 The Adapted Physical Education Program   237

11 The Extra-Class Program: Intramurals and Interscholastic Athletics   264

12 Curriculum Evaluation   290

CONTENTS

Preface xi

1 Society and the Celebration of Life 1
Direction in a Free Society 3
The Participation Philosophy 4
Our Technological Society 6
Our Multicultural Society 8
Population Density 9
Healthy People 2000 11
The Aging American 15
Leisure Pursuits 17
Leisure, Education, and Freedom 19
Sport as an Art Form 20
Dance in America 21
The Exercise Movement 22
International Physical Education and Sport 24
The Ultimate Endeavor 25

2 Educational Foundations 30
Defining the Ends 32
Lifestyles and Educational Objectives 35
Physical Education Objectives 36
Health-Related Fitness 37
Recreational Competency 40
Social Efficiency 41
Intellectual Competency 43

Culture   44
America 2000   45

3 The Student and Curriculum Objectives   49
The Student and the Times   51
The Physical Education Potential   53
From Philosophy to Objectives   53
Specific Objectives in Physical Education   58
Behavioral Objectives in Physical Education   58
Outcomes-Based Physical Education   60
The Nature of Curriculum   61
Curriculum Models   65
Physical Education Curriculum Models   69
The Hidden Curriculum   78
The Teaching Dimension   79

4 Curriculum Planning in Physical Education   84
Curriculum Development   87
Factors Affecting Program Planning   89
Personal Factors   89
School Factors   91
Non-School Factors   95
State Requirements for Physical Education   97
Title IX   97
Public Law 94.142   100
Liability   100
Concept Approach to Curriculum Development   102
Selection and Balance in Program Planning   104
The Broad and Varied Program   104
Structuring for Quality   106

5 Research and Curriculum Change   110
To Change or Not to Change   112
Curriculum Reform   112
Curriculum Research in Physical Education   113
Outside Influences   119
Local Assessment   124

6 Program Organization   127
Interaction and Reform   129
Scope and Sequence   130
Scheduling the Curriculum   138
Teaching Stations   146

Staff Organization 147
Paraprofessionals 149
The Selective Program 151
Ability Grouping 151
Performance Contracts 153
Programmed Instruction 153
Computer-Based Instruction 156
Instructional Strategies Using Students 161

7 The Curriculum Guide 166
Defining the Guide 168
Preliminary Considerations 168
The Administrator's Role 171
The Curriculum Coordinating Committee 171
Curriculum Subcommittees 172
Faculty Involvement 174
Constructing the Guide 174

8 The Elementary Physical Education Program, K–6 180
Children Moving 182
The Elementary School Child 183
Curriculum Content for the Elementary Grades 183
Time Allotment 208
The Middle School 209

9 The Secondary Physical Education Program, 7–12 213
Secondary School Organization 216
The Secondary School Student 216
Practical Considerations 219
Planning and Organizing the Content 220
A Closer Look at Content 224

10 The Adapted Physical Education Program 237
Definitions 239
Benefits of an Adapted Physical Education Program 240
The Mandate for Adapted Physical Education 241
Public Law 94.142 242
The Individualized Education Program 244
Cooperative Planning and the Coordination of Professionals 246
Classification and Organization 247
Inclusion 250
Additional Programming 253
Innovative Programs 254

Scheduling 258
Helpful Resources 258

11 The Extra-Class Program: Intramurals and Interscholastic Athletics 264
Moral and Ethical Behavior 267
Balance in Programming 268
The Need for Planning 270
The Intramural Program 271
The Interscholastic Athletic Program 276

12 Curriculum Evaluation 290
Definitions 292
The Intent of Measurement and Evaluation 293
Evaluation Guidelines 294
An Overview of Evaluation 294
Student Evaluation 299
Evaluation of Students with Disabilities 306
Portfolio Assessment 307
Teacher Evaluation 309
Program Evaluation 312

Appendix **Self-Appraisal Checklist for Physical Education in Idaho Elementary Schools** **321**

References **330**

Index **344**

PREFACE

Carl E. Willgoose began the preface of the first edition of this text by quoting second century Marcus Aurelius who said that one should always observe that everything is the result of change and get used to thinking that there is nothing nature loves so well as to change existing forms and to make new ones like them. This statement could have been made today by anyone involved in curriculum at any level since it embodies the essential truth that underlies program development in physical education. Societies change, as do the people within these societies. Schools change, as do the students within these schools. As a result, to better meet the ever-changing needs and interests of students, existing programs of physical education also must change.

The purpose of this book is to help awaken the readers to the genuine need for physical education in today's world and to assist them in the process of developing a curriculum for grades K–12. The primary thrust is directed toward curriculum improvement. The authors firmly believe that implementing sound curriculum development practices will contribute to quality programs that can meet the public outcry for educational accountability. The principles of curriculum development are pertinent in regard to the aims and objectives of physical education and attempt to better provide for an effective program.

As you may expect, with this edition comes change. The 12-chapter, linear approach has not changed because it provides an easy-to-follow format that heightens the reader's understanding of (a) what curriculum is; and (b) how curriculum should be developed, implemented, and evaluated. In addition to complete updating since the last edition, specific changes include:

- A discussion of our multicultural society.
- A clearly defined presentation of general, specific, and behavioral objectives.
- A presentation of the ten most common physical education curriculum models and discussion of outcome-based curriculum.

- A complete chapter on children with disabilities with up-to-date coverage of federal legislation.
- An update on factors affecting program organization including computer-based instruction, instructional strategies using students, and paraprofessionals.
- Greatly expanded content in Chapters 8 and 9, with activity examples in each category.
- A discussion of inclusion.
- A presentation of selected issues in today's interscholastic athletic programs.
- A broader discussion, with examples, of student, teacher, and program evaluation in both elementary and secondary settings.

Developing and implementing a sound physical education curriculum presents a challenge to each educator. The public concern for educational accountability is reason enough to strive for meeting this challenge. To do less is to risk missing the opportunity of bringing students *the celebrated life,* a term that Dubos enthusiastically used. This concept refers to a life of direction, adaptation, excitement, and human awareness filled with fully spirited individuals who appreciate the complex relationship between being able and being well.

ACKNOWLEDGMENTS

As in the case with any text, many individuals who have contributed to the development and completion of this volume should be recognized. First, a professional thanks goes to Dr. Carl E. Willgoose for having written the first four editions. From his foundation, this updated fifth edition was made possible.

To the many students and colleagues who brought me to a stage and place in my professional career where I felt comfortable sharing my beliefs in what it is I do, I extend a sincere thank you.

For preparation of the manuscript, my thanks go to Pat Cathcart for her diligence.

Thanks goes to the following four reviewers who (a) made me rethink, rework, and rewrite some parts of the text; and (b) gave me conviction not to rethink others: Dr. John Cheffers, Boston University; Dr. Linda McElroy, Oklahoma Baptist University; Professor Lynne Knell, Southern Connecticut State University; and Professor Stephen Sanders, Auburn University.

Finally, I extend a very special thanks to my wife, Nita, for her understanding, acceptance, and support during my hours at the computer.

THE PHYSICAL EDUCATION CURRICULUM

1
SOCIETY AND THE CELEBRATION OF LIFE

Outline

Direction in a Free Society

The Participation Philosophy

Our Technological Society

Our Multicultural Society

Population Density

Healthy People 2000

The Aging American

Leisure Pursuits

Leisure, Education, and Freedom

Sport as an Art Form

Dance in America

The Exercise Movement

International Physical Education and Sport

The Ultimate Endeavor

Outcomes

After reading and studying this chapter, you should be able to:
- Define
  The celebrated life
  Multicultural education
  Value illness
  Well-being
  Wellness
- Provide a sound philosophy of physical education.
- Identify changes that affect our society, including cultural diversity, longevity, and technology, as well as the implications arising from these changes.
- Develop a strategy to combat value-illness.
- Discuss the relationship among leisure, education, and freedom.
- Describe the place and importance of sport in our society.
- Justify the need for living a healthy lifestyle.
- Describe the wellness approach to living.
- Explain how sport can be viewed as an art form.

From the classical Indian Sanskrit, there is an enlightening expression indicating that a day well lived is what determines all tomorrows. This concept has been around a long time. A specific example is that optimum health and human functioning have always depended on the intricacies of one's way of life. Dubos (1981) writes enthusiastically about the celebrated life, a life of direction, adaptation, excitement, dynamism, and human awareness; a life of fully spirited men and women who acknowledge their fragilities and sensitivities and appreciate, beyond a doubt, the complex relationship between being able and being well.

Unfortunately, society has not always defined well-being in terms of human vitality and productivity. Historically, well-being has been defined as freedom from disease, discussed in terms of infectious organisms, degenerative conditions, and defective organs. In recent years, disease has been more broadly considered as an organism's total lack of ease, a dis-ease with numerous behavioral overtones of a psychosomatic nature, a dis-ease relating to such significant human movement deficiencies as chronic fatigue, obesity, hypertension, backache, and reduced muscular strength and endurance. It is this shortcoming in functional ability and the physical means to perform that has been a major deterrent to the advancement of our civilization.

With this celebration of life concept, one can be reasonably optimistic about supporting the objective of a fully awakened, enlightened, and able individual who has a beyond-the-self contribution to make in advancing human welfare.

DIRECTION IN A FREE SOCIETY

The ultimate health of Americans, and the inhabitants of the rest of the world as well, depends on informed citizens who understand the benefits and responsibilities of living in a free society—individuals preparing to join in seeking new and better solutions to the age-old problems confronting humanity. In terms of educational programs, there are problems pertaining to where the emphasis is placed. Has civilization become so organized, with an overspecialized development of the intellect, that it has separated from the senses and will soon be incapable of continued functioning? Have intellectual pursuits been carried to such an extreme that they overshadow our cultural and physical aspirations that are so much a part of the rich and full life?

When the American Alliance for Health, Physical Education, Recreation, and Dance (AAHPERD) joined with the governing boards of twenty-three professional education associations to express a sense of direction and renewed commitment to a more complete and balanced education for all, two objectives of significance to physical education clearly highlighted:

- To express oneself through the arts and understand the artistic expression of others.
- To apply knowledge about health, nutrition, and physical activity.

This kind of awareness for human potential was highly elevated by May (1953) in *Man's Search for Himself*. May discussed the need for this awareness and asked that men and women look at themselves in the total scheme of things. In doing so, the pattern of life, as influenced by physical education, takes on considerable meaning. Civilization can easily stagnate due to the cumulative effect of the forces around it, especially if the individual citizen remains rigid. This is particularly true when the practices of leaders in the many specialized fields of education are involved. The task of formulating a new culture, with new goals, sanctions, patterns, and group responsibilities is an issue for these leaders.

Although the Romans had a standard of living unparalleled in the history of the world, they did not choose to think beyond their materialistic desires. Because Romans were too resistant to change, the Roman culture slowly dissolved. Soft in mind, spirit, and flesh, they became viewers of the passing scene rather than participants in its evolution. The Romans chose to be smug, complacent, and satisfied at a time when the world demanded sensitivity, change, and struggle.

The true worth of physical education, or any education for that matter, is determined by how it affects the values, judgments, and commitments of the individual members of the society in which it is taught. In terms of physical well-being, people who understand themselves have fewer accidental injuries and diseases and recover sooner from illness than those who do not. They have what Abraham Maslow (1962) long ago characterized as an "appreciation of the body," which leads, by extension, to the personality. They are the healthy, self-actualizing individuals who not only know what to do but, more important, are moved to action. They are not indifferent to the consequences of their behaviors, but rather are sensitive to the delicacy and dearness of life. They share a profound awareness of the potentialities of a fully awakened human being. They perceive a clear relationship between their well-being and the healthy development of the well-being of the society in which they live.

THE PARTICIPATION PHILOSOPHY

The philosophical influence on the healthful practices of early Americans was substantial. During the first half of the twentieth century, physical education philosophers such as H. Harrison Clarke, Charles H. McCloy, R. Tait McKenzie, Jay B. Nash, Frederick R. Rogers, and Jesse Feiring Williams stressed the need to educate youth to be participants in their world, not merely spectators viewing the activity and accomplishments of others. This ancient educational philosophy is one path to a highly productive and rewarding life.

Although *spectatoritis* has long been a disease of western civilization—so much that "couch potato" has been included in Webster's dictionary—evidence shows it is lessening. More people now than ever are engaging in physical activity. Of course, as more people congregate in and about large, crowded, metropolitan areas, an ever-deepening danger exists that opportunities for full participation will be inadequate. To meet this concern, long-term planning becomes necessary in order to meet the recreational needs of all people, whether they be for outdoor pursuits or popular individual and group sports. Yet in this spectator spirit, people have found numerous ways of getting involved without necessarily being players. Sport has its coaches, trainers, and managers; its referees, scorekeepers, and judges; as well as its listeners, viewers, and readers. Sport has its entrepreneurs, among them artists, authors, and photographers. Ultimately, the quality of the participation is highest when the participant moves and has both the knowledge and skills pertaining to the various individual and group sports, dances, and other movement and fitness related activities.

Following World War II, one-time officer of the Austro-Hungarian army and dance choreographer, Rudolph Laban, urged his followers to study and focus attention on the value of human movement in the everyday lives of the citizenry. Ten years later Dwight D. Eisenhower, moved by research findings indicating a lack of concern for the physical capacity of both youth and adults, established the President's Council on Youth Fitness, now known as the President's Council on Physical Fitness and Sports. A short period later John F. Kennedy (1960) presided over a somewhat sedentary population and made his famous remark, "We do not want a nation of spectators, but a nation of participants in the vigorous life."

By 1973, after a year of nationwide hearings and studies, the President's Committee on Health Education cautioned that it was imperative to educate for health and well-being. The committee concluded that it was no longer possible to stem the tide of human illness, despair, and misery by merely improving medical and surgical techniques or by increasing the number of hospitals, social workers, clinical psychologists, and health care centers. The message called for prevention, the wellness approach.

Education of the public, relative to how to live, is mandatory in order to stay free from the various infirmities of mankind. Thus, the physical means to do, to move efficiently and understandably, is an indispensable quality that at last seems to warrant top priority.

In 1974 the Bureau of Health Education was established at the Centers for Disease Control and Prevention in Atlanta (Public Law 93.641) to be a focal point for illness prevention activities by the federal government. By 1977 preventive medicine and education efforts were becoming noticeable in society at large. The bureau described its educational function in terms of six concrete actions:

1. Informing people about health, illness, disability, and ways in which they could improve and protect their own health, including more efficient use of the health care delivery system.
2. Motivating people to want to change to more healthful practices.
3. Helping people learn the necessary skills to adopt and maintain healthful practices and lifestyles.
4. Fostering teaching and communication skills in all people engaged in teaching consumers about health.

5. Advocating changes in the environment that facilitate healthful conditions and healthful behavior.
6. Adding to knowledge through research and evaluation concerning the most effective ways of achieving the above objectives.

Note that the second and third actions direct attention to healthful skills, practices, and lifestyles. The implications relative to the role of physical activity and human movement programs in advancing health status and preventing illness are clear.

Although the general public supports physical education in the schools, many instances of nonexistent, limited, or inappropriate physical activity programs occur. Simply defining what is appropriate can be difficult. The American College of Sports Medicine (ACSM, 1993) considers appropriate physical activity to be that which involves large muscle groups in dynamic movement for periods of thirty minutes or longer, three or more days per week, performed at an intensity requiring sixty percent or greater of an individual's aerobic capacity.

In terms of participation, there is much to be done. School physical education programs are designed to provide physical activity for all children. As stated in *Healthy People 2000* (U.S. Department of Health and Human Services, 1992), this participation encourages extracurricular physical activity by children, leading to continued participation into adulthood. But only one-third of American children and adolescents in grades K-12 take part in daily school programs involving physical education. The Office of Disease Prevention and Health Promotion (1987) points out that even in the non-school sector only twenty-two percent of companies with more than fifty employees offer fitness programs for their employees. Furthermore, in today's society an inadequate level of physical activity is present among girls, women, older people, the physically and mentally handicapped, and inner city and rural residents.

OUR TECHNOLOGICAL SOCIETY

Computers and an array of manufacturing technology exist today that are creating robots to increase industrial production, drastically reducing the need for human workers. In a Pennsylvania factory, General Electric previously had sixty-eight skilled machinists working sixteen days to build a locomotive frame. Today the same frame can be turned out in one day with the sole use of robots.

The second industrial revolution, as it has been called, has had and will continue to have a profound social impact on men and women long associated with physical labor. The installation of an increasing number of robots in the workplace and the social costs of additional automation are of considerable significance to the educator. As automation continues to advance, the lifestyles of workers are subject to change. Are they prepared for less physical work on the job and possibly more leisure time?

With worker well-being becoming a national concern, a growing number of corporations are investing millions of dollars for the development and implementation of wellness programs. Major reasons for this investment include (a) diminished worker productivity, (b) increased absenteeism, and (c) increased health insurance and health care costs due to worker illness.

Wellness programs typically take one of two forms:

- Health promotion
- Work-site fitness

Health promotion programs primarily provide education and disease prevention services for employees. Services include health appraisal, health information, and behavior change programs. One of these programs is the Good Health Makes $ense (GHM$) Program designed by James M. Eddy from the University of Alabama for the Alabama Power Company. The GHM$ program includes:

- A mobile screening van for health appraisal, including assessments of total and HDL cholesterol, percent body fat, blood pressure, flexibility, height, and weight.
- Health and safety seminars provided upon request at all of the Alabama Power Company locations.
- Health education and behavior change programs including topics such as controlling stress and blood pressure, preventing low back pain and cancer, and developing a healthy lifestyle.
- A 1-800 health information hotline that provides employees an easy means to gather information on health and health promotion. Sample information includes results of personalized health assessments, a listing of GHM$ seminar sites, and printed information on a variety of health topics, including:
  - Exercise and physical activity
  - Prevention of injuries
  - Proper nutrition
  - Stress management
  - Consumer health and medical self care

Work-site fitness programs generally provide both facilities and services for employees. The CIGNA Corporation's Preventive Medical Program (Eddy & Beltz, 1989) in Philadelphia is an example. The objectives for this program are twofold:

- To identify risk factors.
- To educate and motivate employees to modify these risk factors.

Following the preliminary screening, an individualized exercise program is developed based on each employee's stress test results and exercise preference.

On site is a 7,000-square-foot corporate fitness center. Available equipment includes motorized treadmills for walking and running, stationary bicycles, rowing machines, cross-country skiers, Stairmasters, and Universal and Nautilus weight machines. The center is open twelve hours a day. The participants are closely monitored and receive feedback on a regular basis.

Although people should not worry that science and technology will create a sick and impersonal society while robbing people of their freedom and humanity, it is nevertheless true that the possibility exists especially if an educational effort to control them is not made. One task of both the school and community, involving more than a hundred million school children, is to prepare people for the world of automation and an increasing production-line way of life. The question raised by J. B. Nash (1965) more than thirty years ago is still germane—if approximately a fifteen percent of the nation's workers are in the so-called learned professions, what type of education should be advocated for the other eighty-five percent? How rich can we make the lives of the masses if the boredom of routinized automation is to be made bearable? How can we give people something to struggle for, master, and conquer so they can achieve and maintain their self-respect and dignity?

OUR MULTICULTURAL SOCIETY

Dante said that the worst place in hell is reserved for those who in times of great moral crisis take a neutral stand (Alighieri, 1948). Martin Luther King, Jr. (King, 1987) stated that injustice anywhere is a threat to justice everywhere. Both of these statements suggest a need for multicultural education.

The class, cultural, ethnic, and racial diversity that was long ago global and not-so-long ago national, has now reached our schools. Within the next twenty years, more than forty percent of public school students will be minorities (Knott, 1991). With this ever-expanding diversity among students, it is now essential that they come to know, accept, and respect the cultural heritages of all people. Cawelti (1990) states that the very survival of the human species has become more dependent on close communication and a better understanding of other cultures.

Such diversity poses a tremendous challenge for education as it strives to develop effective, productive members of society. As Butt and Pahnos (1995) state, providing excellence and equity in education is difficult when both teachers and students have different means of communication, patterns of participation, and views of the world in which they live. This situation is compounded by the social and cultural changes occurring in today's world. To meet this challenge we must help students not only to know, but also to care, and ultimately to act. Chepyator-Thomson (1994) explains that as educators, people need to learn about increasingly diverse groups of people and in turn, develop culturally sensitive programs to more effectively teach students from radically different cultural or social backgrounds. Educators need to provide all students with adequate knowledge to care about people and social issues and to be moved on improving society.

The foundation of multicultural education stems from the word culture and includes one's means of communication, language, beliefs, values, attitudes; in essence, one's behavior (Tiedt & Tiedt, 1990). Within the physical education curriculum, these characteristics are considered relative to program content, or the movement experiences provided. Through these movement experiences and the social and cultural interaction they provide, students develop the interpersonal skills that contribute to mutual understanding and acceptance by all (Chepyator-Thomson, 1994). The theoretical base for this is derived from Bennett's (1990) conception of multicultural education—an education including curricular experiences that:

- Focus on the development of equal opportunity among all groups,
- Advance the development of knowledge and understanding of cultural differences within the United States,
- Advance the development of appropriate skills to commit one to end all discriminatory practices,
- Allow students to become multiculturally competent.

This can be accomplished through multicultural education, a term that Banks (1992) calls a transformative curriculum—one designed to help students understand that knowledge is socially constructed. From this, students will be better equipped to view the human experience from the perspectives of a range of diverse groups. Baldwin (1989) explains that the purpose of education is to create individuals who have the ability to look at the world for themselves, to make their own decisions, to say that this is black or white, and to decide whether there is a god in heaven or not. Asking questions of the universe and then living to answer them, is the way a person achieves identity. Baldwin adds that no society is really eager to have these people around. What society wants is individuals that will obey the ruler. If a society succeeds with this, then it will surely perish.

POPULATION DENSITY

Social and public health planners, as well as leisure-time specialists, have numerous reports that the growth of a city threatens the welfare of its inhabitants. Major increases in population throughout the world, especially in metropolitan areas, tend to stifle individual and group mobility and expression. The question, then, is whether the 11.4 percent increase in U.S. population between 1970 and 1980 and the 18.3 percent increase between 1970 and 1990 has had a negative effect on human welfare. Is human welfare measurably affected by the more than thirty-one million Americans who are sixty-five years of age or older? Population, and population density to be meaningful, must be reviewed in terms of optimum population size, an expression attributed to Paul and Anne Ehrlich (1972) as they related optimum population to the quality of life or the pursuit of happiness. Such expressions are somewhat subjective until related, for example, to natural resource depletion, human nutrition, and psychosomatic illnesses, all of which are part of the stress syndrome. The question as to what population size a city can comfortably manage and the earth can adequately support will always exist.

Significant from an educational viewpoint will be the difficulty of crowding more people into smaller spaces, potentially causing increases in transportation, crime, air pollution, noise pollution, water pollution, drug addiction, and numerous other problems having implications for one's physical and mental well-being. Consequently, the needs of urbanites and suburbanites will have to be carefully reviewed. The educational implications are numerous, including the need for more schools, teachers, and other resources to better meet the necessities of children. The role of the physical education and recreation specialist is extremely relevant in bringing youth and adults together to find ways of enjoying forced proximity to each other. This is necessary if violence is to be reduced in cities.

As privacy is threatened, humans squabble and fight, frequently against unseen forces. People suffer from apprehension and anxiety, fear and anger, and either resign themselves or rebel. Aggression and violence are basic to an individual's human power. Moreover, people can be creative, permitting others to affirm or assert themselves. Individuals who know where they are going or are determined assert themselves in a number of socially accepted ways. However, when the need to be assertive is blocked, the stage is set for aggressive, antisocial behavior. When no outlet is available, violence often follows. Therefore, it is not surprising that physical activity through games, sport, and dance helps provide a wholesome outlet for these aggressive feelings.

James F. Conant (1961), a former president of Harvard University, wrote that if he were to name one educational program that potentially could do the most to reduce just one city problem—that of school dropouts—he would select physical education. Indeed, if quality physical education, intramural, and interscholastic athletic programs are available, the attention of young people will be occupied. This fact alone should lend support for such school programs.

As the need for recreation and physical education space increases, the city alone will be unable to meet this demand. The adjoining suburban areas will have to become involved. Often times, the middle class departs to the suburbs and leaves the central cities increasingly dominated by slum dwellers who require city services such as police, welfare, and education, but who can rarely contribute in terms of taxes. The problems of the city are no longer merely confined to just the city. They are suburban as well. It has become necessary to combine urban and suburban school boundaries, cutting across geographic, economic, and social boundaries.

HEALTHY PEOPLE 2000

In 1992, the U.S. Department of Health and Human Services updated its previous report with the publication of *Healthy People 2000,* calling again for a public health revolution. This long-term effort provides a national strategy for improving our nation's health. It is aimed squarely at the prevention of infectious diseases, injuries, and chronic diseases including heart attack, stroke, and cancer, all of which are linked to an unhealthy lifestyle. One strategy, in particular, is to combat the following five risk-producing behaviors:

- Poor diet
- Smoking
- Lack of exercise
- Alcohol abuse
- Failure to use antihypertensive medication

It is apparent that the general public is beginning to support this view, at least cognitively. People know the importance of illness prevention or leading a wellness lifestyle. Individuals know the negative effects resulting from a poor diet and not exercising regularly. They know the importance these risk-producing behaviors play in one's life expectancy. That is one of the reasons Americans are living longer.

Longevity has increased primarily because of sophisticated technology for both the diagnosis and the treatment of disease, but also in part because of the way people live today. This view is supported by research completed at the California Human Population Laboratory (California Department of Health, Alameda County) where studies were conducted dealing with seven personal health practices, as shown in Figure 1.1. The results show a direct and statistically significant association with age-adjusted mortality rates. Mortality declines with an increase in the number of health practices observed. For males, 8.8 times more men died among those with three or fewer of these seven favorable practices as compared to those who practiced all seven. For females, the rate was high, but lower than the rate for men—3.6 times as many women died.

Hippocrates taught that each disease of mind and spirit arises from a natural cause. Even one's values have much to do with both health building and health destroying activities. Unfortunately, large numbers of people suffer from *value illness,*—knowing what to do to get and stay well, but failing to do it. People know about the recovery power of proper relaxation, but they do not get adequate rest. They are aware of the link between tobacco smoking and lung cancer, but they continue to smoke. They know how alcohol affects the ability to drive, but they continue to drink and drive. They appreciate the role that regular exercise plays in weight control and maintaining a fit lifestyle, but they do little to alter their sedentary existence.

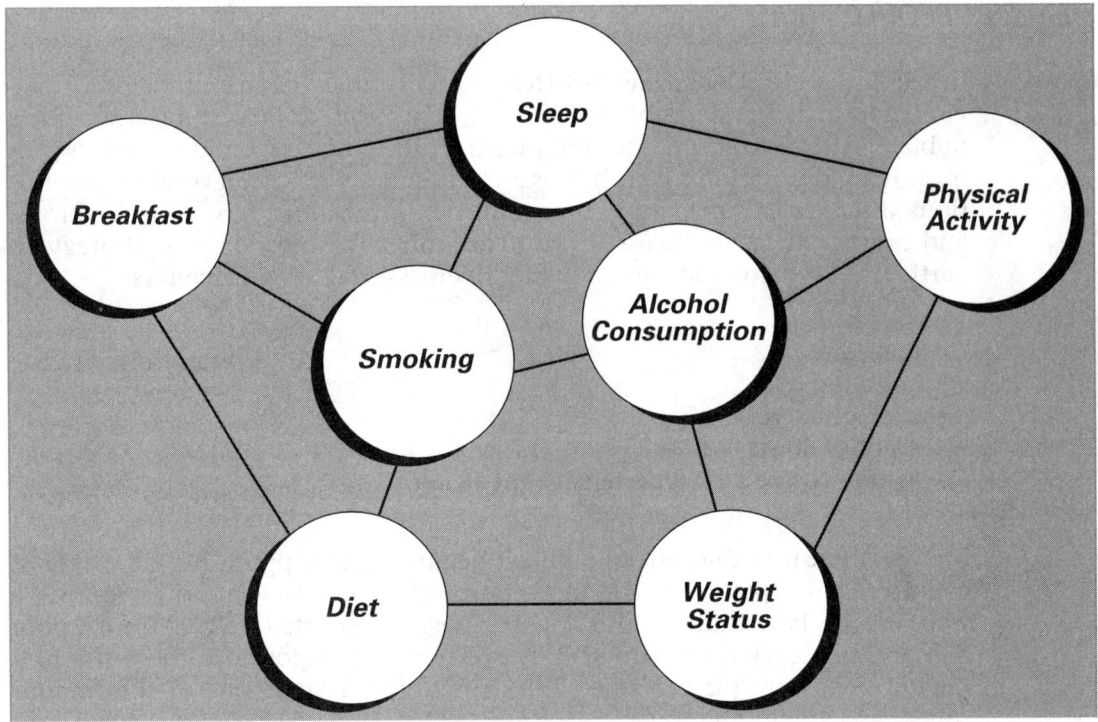

FIGURE 1.1 Seven Personal Health Practices

As Kanters and Montelpare (1994) indicate, humans have become a health care dependent rather than a health prevention society; therefore, people are reactive rather than proactive. If they become ill, they go to a doctor to get well. This notion stems from a belief that health services result in health improvements.

Ornstein and Ehrlich (1989), however, indicate that this is not the case. Medical intervention is responsible for only a three and a half percent decline in mortality since 1900. In addition, eighty percent of our health is affected by the environment, relationships, and the quality of education. For example, if all forms of cancer were cured, the average life expectancy would increase by only two years. Whereas, if good nutrition, adequate exercise, and appropriate health habits were adhered to, the average life expectancy would increase by as much as seven years.

In a real sense, modern society is characterized by the spectacle of humans fighting for perfection while knowing little about where they are headed. Efforts, all too often, fail to produce the peace of mind being sought. In an environment where speed, status, comfort, and economic success are high marks of achievement, it is not uncommon to find men and women who cannot adjust to increasing pressures. Too many become overfed and underactive. Others literally burn themselves out with insecurity, anxiety, worry, anger, and even hatred. Resulting tensions refuse to stay bottled up, thereby causing headaches, indigestion, sleeplessness, irritability, and fatigue.

A number of health statistics exist that relate as closely to the school-age population as to the adult population. Moreover, these statistics pertain in a number of dimensions to what is available in any community in terms of a quality physical education program. The community-wide business of advancing physical education skills and knowledge is no small undertaking. It calls for a real understanding of the intricate relationship of unhealthful practices and conditions with the positive and health-related consequences associated with experiences in the human movement domain. The following statistics emphasize the need for this relationship:

1. Heart disease and stroke deaths in the United States have dropped dramatically over the past fifteen years. In fact, the death rate for coronary heart disease has declined approximately fifty percent since 1970. Still, cardiovascular disease kills nearly as many Americans as all other diseases combined. It affects seven million Americans with more than 500,000 deaths annually. It is clear, however, that uncontrolled hypertension, obesity, and the sedentary life will slow this decline, particularly if health and physical education efforts are taken lightly and subsequent improvements are left to medical practice alone (*Healthy People 2000*, 1992).

2. Cancer is the second leading cause of death in the United States. The American Cancer Society (1990) indicates that cancer accounts for one out of every five deaths in the United States. More than a million new cancer cases will occur next year and one in three Americans now living will eventually have cancer. The National Cancer Institute (1986) provides evidence that everyday behavior, including diet, tobacco use, and occupational stress has much to do with this disease. Dietary modification, reduction of tobacco use, and an increase in physical activity to combat stress are, therefore, recommended strategies to reduce the incidence of cancer.

3. Unintentional injuries or accidents are the leading cause of death among school-age children, claiming more deaths than all other causes combined. There were nearly 94,000 accidental deaths in 1990. The Committee on Trauma Research (1988) indicates that up to age forty, accidents claim more lives than infectious or chronic diseases. Almost 100,000 people are killed each year in accidents; one accident nearly every five minutes, while millions are incapacitated with many suffering lifelong disabilities. Drownings are second only to motor vehicles as the major cause of accidental deaths (*Information Please Almanac*, 1994). The more than 7,000 drownings and 140,000 swimming-related injuries a year are primarily associated with recreational activities. This has occurred despite widespread opportunities for people to engage in swimming and water safety instruction. There is a considerable need for more safety instruction in all sports. For bicycling alone, more than eight hundred deaths and 300,000 hospital-treated injuries occur each year (National Safety Council, 1991). In addition, more than 320,000 football and 480,000 basketball injuries occur annually.

4. Approximately twenty-three million adults in this country have a mental illness. It is estimated that ten to twelve percent of children and adolescents suffer from mental disorders. Suicide is the most serious outcome from these mental disorders. More than 5,000 suicides a year are committed by individuals under the age of twenty-five. The contribution that stress makes to this occurrence is not completely understood. But, according to Goldberger and Breznitz (1982), good nutrition and regular exercise can produce short-term, if not long-term, relief.

5. The effects that drug abuse have on society are staggering, both on a personal and an economic basis. In a National Household Survey (1989), 65.7 million Americans indicated marijuana usage, with 21.2 million having tried cocaine. The use of these drugs by adolescents (ages twelve to seventeen) is steadily increasing. Approximately twelve billion dollars was spent by the federal government on drug control in the United States in 1992 (*Information Please Almanac,* 1994).

6. Estimates range from twenty-five to forty-five percent for obesity in American adults. More than twenty-five percent of all children are obese. Unfortunately, obesity acquired during childhood or adolescence may well persist into adulthood, increasing the risk for some chronic diseases (*Healthy People 2000,* 1992). Moreover, studies show that when these children are carefully observed, they are significantly less active than their non-obese peers. Many have little first-hand knowledge relating to what should be done about their condition. Too often, dieting is the solution to an obesity problem, even for children. Parents and children alike, need to be made aware that sound nutrition and physical activity are not alternatives, but rather complements. Both are crucial to good health now and for the future.

7. The fitness of both children and adults improved steadily from 1958 to the early 1980s. However, this trend is being reversed. Today's adolescents are in poorer health than their parents were at the same age. The findings of the 1985 National Children and Youth Fitness Study (Ross & Gilbert, 1985) indicates that one-third of American youth were not physically active enough for aerobic benefits. The findings of the 1987 study (Ross & Pate, 1987) and a ten year study (Updyke, 1994) show that children weighed more and had more percent body fat than their counterparts did twenty years earlier. It is clear that for many individuals the level of physical capacity for leading an active life is far below what it might be. The President's Council on Physical Fitness and Sports (1994) has demonstrated what can be done to improve fitness when adults, as well as children, are exposed to a quality physical education program that is carefully designed to meet individual weaknesses. Knowing there is a direct link between regular physical activity and improved health, more than four out of ten adults still indicate that they are not likely to increase physical activity in the near future.

Exercise is essential for the aging adult.

THE AGING AMERICAN

In 1950, eight percent of Americans were sixty-five years of age or older. By the year 2000, thirteen percent of the total population of the United States will be in that age group. In numbers, Americans sixty-five years of age and older will rise from twenty-eight million (one in ten) in 1990 to thirty-four million (one in five) by the year 2000. The implications of these statistics are far reaching. Older people will require more attention, will be more educated, will have more vitality than those who preceded them, and will affect many aspects of society from politics to health care.

A variety of human movement programs throughout the country for this aging group currently exist. In addition, exercise is quickly becoming an activity for people in long-term care facilities. Moreover the AAHPERD Committee on Aging has been working for years with grant money from the National Institute on the Aging to update knowledge pertaining to exercise limits for older adults.

Although biological implications from aging occur, including reduced flexibility, thinning hair, and increased clouding of the eye's lens, a residue of time-honored myths and social prejudices that propel older people into early senility and late-life depression do exist. The sad fact is that much of this could be prevented. When Americans clearly understand the role that fitness can play in the aging process, it is then that aging in this country can be redefined. As a person becomes physically fit, mental fitness is also improved. As a result, an individual ends up with greater human dignity in all aspects of life. Studies by the Life Extension Institute (Fisher, 1946) indicate that three primary factors determine a person's happiness following retirement (see Figure 1.2).

The Leisure-Time Pursuits factor is particularly meaningful when a person considers the nature of a lifetime education in preparation for two or more decades of retirement. The happiest retirees are those who stay in their home communities and remain active by carrying on regular physical, mental, and social involvement. Moreover, weight control, daily walking, and adequate sleep appear to be highly beneficial. The secret of a rewarding life during retirement is for an individual to remain interested in what is taking place. Boredom alone can be reason enough for fatigue.

Older people continue to need physical activity. Thousands do not begin meeting this need. Exercise is important to help strengthen the heart and lungs, lower blood pressure, prevent obesity, and protect against the start of adult-onset diabetes. Regular physical activity can help older adults maintain

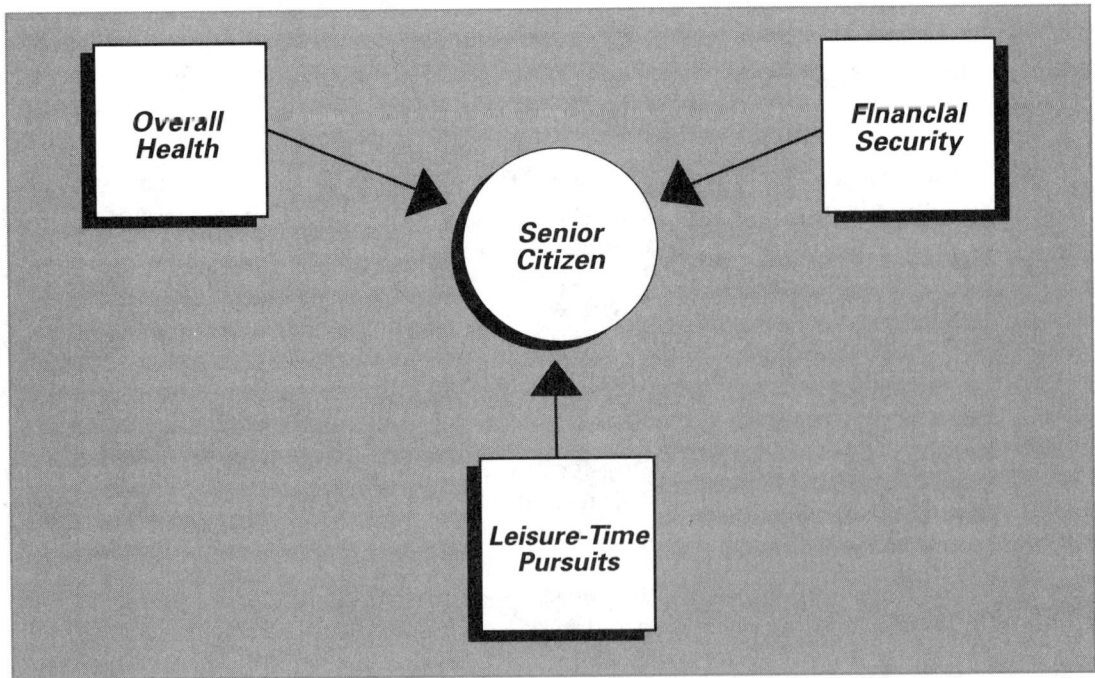

FIGURE 1.2 Factors Affecting Retirement Years

functional independence, and thereby enhance the quality of life (Katz, et al., 1983). It is significant in preventing the common degenerative disease of osteoporosis, which affects women particularly after menopause. Bone stress brought about by physical activity is necessary even in older adults. Interestingly, a large amount of exercise is not required. It is the general stress applied to all parts of the bone framework that contributes to regeneration. Robert Butler, former director of the National Institute on Aging (1986), states that if exercise could be packed into a pill, it would be the most widely prescribed and beneficial medicine in our nation.

Most people do not wear out; they rust out. In this respect, the playground movement champion, Joseph Lee, was accurate when he stated, "We don't cease to play because we grow old, we grow old because we cease to play" (Mero, 1909). Therefore, the way to keep lively is to be lively. The way to stay active is to be active. Physical fitness and its components—muscular strength, muscular endurance, flexibility, and aerobic endurance—cannot be attained in any other way. However, only recently have older people had the environmental accessibility in convalescent and retirement homes and in the expanding number of senior citizen centers to be exposed to this fitness message. The U.S. Department of Health and Human Services and the President's Council on Physical Fitness and Sports have promoted programs and implementation procedures for older citizens. These organizations have stressed that walking, jogging, and free exercise, as well as alternative and supplemental activities such as gardening, bicycling, and dancing be engaged in on a daily basis.

LEISURE PURSUITS

Recreational involvement in the United States and Canada during the last several decades has been so great that critics have referred to it as the *New Hedonism* of leisure pursuits. In addition, critics have suggested that this behavior maybe questioned as appropriate for responsible members of society. However, as Howe (1981) points out, the process of revitalizing the economy and getting well in the marketplace does not have to challenge or limit leisure services and activities. In examining the culture to see exactly where leisure fits in, Martin (1976) describes leisure as a continuing search for meaning. This search is specifically germane to physical education. Martin states:

> *It was at the 21st Olympics that a slight but splendidly controlled fourteen-year-old Romanian gymnast captivated the world by achieving perfection in her sport, her art. Nadia Comaneci personified an ideal that many are urged to strive for, but few are thoroughly convinced can be reached. In one week we were treated to a series of gymnastic exhibitions by this young woman that call to mind George Leonard's elegant portrayal of sport and excellence in* The Ultimate Athlete *and Richard Bach's urging in* Jonathan Livingston Seagull *that "There's reason to life! We can lift ourselves out of*

> *ignorance, we can find ourselves as creatures of excellence, intelligence and skill,"* and that *"there is such a thing as perfection . . . and that our purpose for living is to find that perfection and show it forth."*
>
> *Our culture is intensely caught up in a continuing search for meaning, purpose, and identity. What men, women, and children once derived from the church, work, and the family seems to have been dispersed and appears to be much sought for in what we now call leisure. The all important sense of well-being and its harmonic overtones—satisfaction, gratification, achievement, joy, etc.—are increasingly expected as outcomes of the leisure experience. The study and discussion of the leisure phenomenon and its relation to culture is considered important for many reasons. But it is through its relationship to our search for meaning that such efforts become increasingly significant.*

It should be remembered that society is composed of pluralistic viewpoints with various interest groups in need of the spontaneous and joyful experience of play. It is not something designed just for children. Kleiber and Fiscella (1982) indicate that if leisure is looked upon as an interlude, with a sense of psychological space or freedom, the word would take on a greater meaning.

The satisfaction derived from meeting leisure needs has become a key economic factor in the national well-being, as participants crowd into stadiums, theaters, museums, and music auditoriums. A constantly increasing number of individuals investing in these cultural activities is occurring, as well as in a variety of leisure hobbies.

Since the end of World War II, the number of sports and sport-related activities has been nothing less than phenomenal. Sports have become a way of life for the whole family in the United States, with readily available activities for grandparents and preschool children alike. Private and public facilities that were limited in number just a few decades ago are now commonplace and used year-round. Skiing—started in the United States with a single rope tow in Vermont in the 1930s—has grown from a shoestring operation, providing fun for a select few, to a multi-million dollar business, providing enjoyment for hundreds of thousands. An unprecedented number of people in the United States are taking part in sports that were once considered only for the wealthy. Millions of water skiers, golfers, and tennis players are active year-round. In addition to participation in the traditional team sports through local YMCA/YWCAs and park and recreation associations, Americans are playing racquetball, handball, and squash; are ice skating, roller skating, and bowling; and are fishing, camping, and backpacking. In addition, the increase in bicycling for all ages and the construction of both home and community swimming pools, indicates a clear picture that sporting activities are not only popular (an interest), but are also rewarding (a need).

In addition to increased attendance at professional and collegiate athletic events, increased participation in individual sports, and increased family recreation, is an increased amount of community-school recreation. In countless communities, the schools are opening doors to evening, weekend, and summer participation for citizens of all ages with programs encompassing a variety of physical, intellectual, and creative activities.

Since recreation has the potential of immediately involving the personal and social values of a participant, a significant task ahead for today's physical educators occurs. Related to this is the need to learn *how* to play and *how* to employ these recreational pursuits in a manner that will offset the anguish of mental and physical labor—an anguish often times associated with human virtue.

LEISURE, EDUCATION, AND FREEDOM

As indicated, the recreational movement is focusing on the true meaning of leisure. Thus, the full meaning of the word leisure needs to be understood. In the past, to different people it has meant different things, ranging from the philosophic to the ethical. According to Margaret Mead (1967), it became linked with recreation and revitalization, regards for duty done.

The word leisure comes from the Latin word *licere,* meaning "to be permitted freedom or opportunity to do something." In the medieval university, the first degree an individual earned was the *licentiate,* also derived from licere. Education, leisure, and freedom thus have a common root. In fact, education and leisure are so closely related that leisure may be considered a non-work activity, wherein one has the freedom to continue learning, a type of continuous schooling.

In its finest sense, leisure provides an opportunity for the individual to become refreshed, rejuvenated, and recreated. Leisure time activity without significance is not enough to satisfy; neither is insignificant work. Fullness results when recreation and work are blended together. Nash (1953) explains that the struggle for existence has not been our greatest enemy. Very often, it has been a stimulant to our lagging, puttering spirit. In the process of evolution, an unorganized nervous system became a brain and, later, when kicked into activity by a hostile environment, we found we could paint a picture, construct a bridge, write a novel, cure a disease, and create a civilization.

Today men and women are free, without any moral stigma, to use their time exactly as they choose. They have, indeed, been doing just that for many years. Perhaps the ultimate question a person must ask is whether the twenty-first century American is wise enough to plan the use of non-work time, so that civilization will flourish. The need for an education for leisure, therefore, must be given close study as the new age ripens and evolves. If this education is effective it may reap not only intellectual and physical satisfaction for the individual, but also creative, artistic, and spiritual satisfaction that is sufficient enough to contribute to an ultimate inner growth. As McCarville (1993) states, participation in meaningful, challenging leisure activities is necessary for a balanced and satisfying life.

If physical education, or any other kind of education for that matter, is to contribute to the concept of equilibrium (a balanced existence) and reach the untapped resources of all human beings, it will have to bridge the gap between the working-stress world of the individual and the utopian state of meaningful recreational activity. In so doing, it will fortify the individual for both the world of work and the world of play.

SPORT AS AN ART FORM

If mass recreation is to continue being a blessing and to enrich life, opportunities for active engagement must be made available as well as occasions for sitting and viewing the sporting event. A significant reason for the widespread acceptance of sports by both spectators and participants, is the intrinsic feelings developed for and the satisfaction received from the display of high-quality skill. This display is an artistic accomplishment that rivals the finest performance in any theater.

In the American past, sports served several functions. The least of these functions was artistic due to the fact that art was equated with the stage, gallery, or studio. Not surprisingly, then, is when music is added to the performance of a figure skater, gymnast, or synchronized swimmers, the athlete comes alive, gains color, and takes on a form that elicits a genuine, emotional response from the spectator. Superficially, the music makes the difference, but these activities can stand alone as aesthetically pleasing.

In recent years, the qualities of the aesthetic—the cultivation of beauty—have gone beyond the art-by-association activities to both individual and teams sports. Thus, the balance, rhythm, and direction of the performance on the floor mat, trampoline, or diving board depicts the beauty of the human in specialized movements. The stick handling in ice hockey, the catch and pass in lacrosse, and the diving reception by a flanker back in football are equally beautiful. Kovich (1971) accurately expresses this viewpoint when he says:

> *The spectator cannot divorce man from his movements. Sport is a truly human form of art, for it is not just the product of man's abilities which is on display; it is man. Research in electromyography has shown that observers mimic in a minute way the movement patterns of the performer, thus including a form of restrained participation. As the performer feels the art being created, so can a perceptive spectator feel the same quality, although not to the same extent. Whether intended or not, there is a silent communication between the performer and the spectator. Empathy with the elements of time, force, and space, in the world of the performer and his/her movements can account, in part at least, for the spectator interpreting these movements as both meaningful and beautiful.*

Sports participation as an art form, directly or indirectly, will continue to grow throughout the world because of its cultural significance. Some people argue that sports and physical education activities belong with the arts of humanity. Such activities have formed a basic part of all cultures, including all racial groups and all historical ages, because they are a fundamental form of human expression just as music, poetry, and painting are.

Realistically, sport is more than an art form or an escape mechanism for a stress-ridden civilization. Sport is a social institution. It permeates most levels of contemporary society. It deeply influences everything from personal status and race relations to language and ethical values. Undoubtedly, sport will continue to hold a place of prominence, especially if society continues to (a) cherish extraordinary physical ability and (b) look at sport as a means of reinforcing the values regulating behavior.

DANCE IN AMERICA

As a primary form of artistic and social expression, dance has no equal. From the days of primitive people to the present, dance has met the fundamental human need to express oneself. Dance is a representation of a people and their cultural relationship with their environment. Furthermore, it presents a correlation between the purpose and the roots of human existence (Berryman-Miller, 1991). Since the medium of expression is through the movements of the total body, it has been natural to link dance with both physical education and the arts. Through body movement dance becomes a topic that overlaps the broad fields of aesthetics, religion, and education. Kraus (1977) explains that dance fulfills the aspirations to worship, to engage in courtship, to express tribal or national loyalties, to express both artistic and creative urges, to assist in the therapeutic process, and to provide a means for social or recreational group activity.

Dance in its many forms is flourishing in western society today. The creative and concert forms, including ballet, modern, and ethnic are appearing not only in metropolitan areas but also in small communities throughout the United States that heretofore had no such programs. There is a renewed interest in social dancing, including rock and roll, ballroom, and country and western. Dance clubs and community dance programs sponsored by recreational centers are increasing. Although less than a quarter century old, regional ballet is increasing and several amateur companies have climbed to a professional level. Observers of dance in the American scene will see and feel much that ultimately relates to their recreational and educational interests. What has occurred to make dance a vital part of the cultural and educational scene is an awakening of the general population to the significance of dance in their lives. This awakening has brought classical ballet, avant-garde modern dance, and other forms of dance into the local communities. In addition, its place in an educational setting has shown a renewed emphasis. From the anticipatory preschool child, through the ever-changing middle school adolescent, to the emerging senior high school adult, dance education is accepted as a teaching/learning medium that stimulates individuals to become inquiring, interactive, attentive, and considerate. These are qualities that Shuker (1993) assures can be readily transferred to life outside the school.

THE EXERCISE MOVEMENT

Appearing in and about the community wearing gymnastic attire, tennis shoes, or a jogging suit no longer causes undue attention from onlookers. Laughing children and barking dogs have given way to a sense of wonderment, and even envy, as both men and women work to trim waistlines, bolster heart muscles, and enjoy the fruits of regular exercise. The nearly ten million joggers, of course, are only a part of this fast-changing exercise scene. Stone (1990) states that a national obsession with personal fitness and the concept of wellness, living a health-conscious life-style now exists. Therefore, rather than relying on modern medicine to cure the ills of everyday living, the wellness approach calls on individuals to live a life so as to never, in theory, need modern medicine. Siedentop (1994) indicates that the wellness approach takes a holistic view, suggesting that a person's physical, mental, and psychological problems are all interrelated. Siedentop adds that for an individual to achieve wellness, that person must work, play, and socialize in a positive, balanced manner.

From what we eat to what we wear, the promotion of sport and fitness permeates our society. More money has been distributed in the sport and fitness industry than the gross national products of most third world countries (Stone, 1990). A few years ago the Opinion Research Corporation conducted a national adult physical fitness survey consisting of detailed personal interviews with nearly 4,000 men and women, twenty-two years of age or older, living in private households in the United States. The greatest participation in physical fitness activities was found in men and women living in single family situations in relatively new suburban areas. The lowest participation was recorded by women in city apartments. Walking was the most prevalent activity.

In 1990, a physical activity survey was conducted by Aldana and Stone (1991). Subjects included more than 30,000 adults and their dependents, ranging in ages from 16–88. Results showed that more adults are getting regular, vigorous physical activity than at any other time in the past twenty years (Perrier, 1979; President's Council on Physical Fitness and Sports, 1973; National Center for Health Statistics, 1975). Of those surveyed, sixty-one percent indicated regular exercise. Seventy-two percent of males over the age of sixty-five and seventy-five percent under the age of twenty-five exercised regularly. Nearly forty-five percent indicated walking at least once a week, with this percentage increasing with age. Only eleven percent indicated some type of running or jogging activity once a week. As expected, this percentage fell quickly as age increased. Other types of involved physical activity included aerobics, bicycling, swimming, weight lifting, dance, basketball, and calisthenics. Three times as many females did aerobics. The number of adults bicycling and swimming remained basically the same through all categories, whereas weight lifting participation decreased with age.

In 1994, the National Sporting Goods Association (NSGA) found exercise walking to be the most popular participatory sport or fitness activity. In sampling 10,000 United States households, NSGA found a ten percent increase from 1993 in the number of individuals who walked for exercise. Swimming was second on the list and bicycling was third. More than twenty-five percent increase occurred in the number of Americans who exercise with equipment. In-line skating and roller hockey showed the highest growth at fifty-seven percent and fifty percent, respectively, while hiking showed a thirty percent increase in the number of participants.

Based on current research, the physical dimension is no longer neglected, as ninety million men and women engage regularly in some form of physical activity and contribute somewhat to the prediction of futurists that there will be even more emphasis on physical activity as new ways to keep healthy and fit are developed. In this respect, it is important to note that one of the new ways should be concerned with the depth of exercise activity. Research clearly indicates that a minimum exercise frequency of three times per week is necessary for significant aerobic and related physiological improvements to be realized. It is predicted that as we move into the twenty-first century, the majority of American industries will employ health and fitness personnel to implement wellness programs. The corporate fitness boom sparked the founding of the American Association of Fitness Directors in Business and Industry in 1974. By the 1980s, it was clear that sport and other physical activities are interconnected with the economy as they contribute to improved job performance, positive work attitudes, increased stamina, sounder sleep, and potential, improved employee longevity.

The need for quality elementary, middle, junior high, and high school programs of physical education for continuing education in the lifetime or carry-over activities and the need to address weaknesses in adult physical fitness practices both exist. A major necessity is to make easily accessible paths for bicycling, jogging, and walking; greater opportunity for swimming; and a stronger effort to disseminate information to the public on the value of exercise for the total effectiveness of the individual. Supportive research is available, and such organizations as the President's Council on Physical Fitness and Sports exists to help even on the local level.

It is apparent that an unprecedented obsession with physical fitness due to an overdose of television sports, the fear of coronary occlusion, and/or the desire to look and feel young exists. Whatever the reason, these valid arguments in support of both existing and expanding exercise programs suggests a swing away from the materialism or the comfort values of the *homo sedentarius* toward what has been called a *new feeling state*. Leonard (1975) expressed it well when he said, "We are discovering that every human being has a God-given right to move efficiently, gracefully, and joyfully."

INTERNATIONAL PHYSICAL EDUCATION AND SPORT

For several decades, a growing belief has existed that physical education and sport can and should make a more effective contribution to the inculcation of fundamental human values underlying the full development of people everywhere in the world. In our vastly shrinking world both the increasing multicultural knowledge and understanding of the nations are essential. Through sport and physical education involvement, countries can build better international friendships and understanding that could have a positive effect on international peace. Such a belief has the full support of the United Nations Educational, Scientific and Cultural Organization (UNESCO). In fact, the practice of physical education is considered a fundamental right for all and an essential element of lifelong education in the overall education system. Moreover, the UNESCO Articles (1947) call specifically for programs designed to meet individual and social needs, with certain priorities given to disadvantaged groups in society. UNESCO has triggered worldwide efforts toward the expansion of opportunities in physical education. This is exemplified by its ratification of an International Charter of Physical Education and Sport. The charter indicates that the practice of physical education and sport is a fundamental right for everyone. More specifically, the freedom to develop physically, mentally, and morally through physical education and sport must be guaranteed within both the educational system and the various aspects of one's social life.

In addition to UNESCO, the following three international organizations warrant discussion:

- AIESEP
- FIEP
- ICHPERSD

AIESEP (Association Internationale des Ecoles Superieures d' Education) or the International Association for Physical Education in Higher Education, began in 1962, is currently organized in forty countries. The association's primary objectives are to (a) promote physical education and sport in higher education, (b) encourage the on-going exchange of information among members, and (c) conduct research on new teaching methodology and evaluation techniques.

FIEP (Federation Internationale d'Education Physique) or the International Federation for Physical Education, was founded in 1923. The federation works to (a) develop physical education programs and activities in all countries and (b) promote international exchange and cooperation.

ICHPERSD (International Council for Health, Physical Education, Recreation, Sport, and Dance), first organized in 1958, is concerned with programs, policies, and educational aspects of the various allied fields. In addition, the council serves as a clearinghouse for information and ideas relative to these areas.

THE ULTIMATE ENDEAVOR

The primary emphasis in this chapter has been to point out that the study of human function and well-being requires consideration of information from a broad spectrum of both medical and nonmedical fields. It is a multidisciplinary approach in which the physical education specialist has a substantial role to play. Ultimately, any proposed program of physical education should reflect this view. Moreover, such a program should make provisions for a coordinated effort in which the various medical and nonmedical parties work together to maintain and advance human welfare and thus give the *celebration of life* concept unquestioned support.

If anything is to be learned about the present condition of adult mankind, it should be that the problems, diseases, and inadequacies of the moment did not suddenly appear. Rather, they emerged gradually, having been established during the elementary school years. Backaches, ulcers, hypertension, obesity, chronic fatigue, and the neurotic and psychotic behaviors related to such feelings as anxiety, worry, and jealousy are all tied directly to a pattern of living. An understanding of and an appreciation for the value of movement formed early in life, coupled with the proper skills and knowledge, set the stage for good health. The part that physical education can play in these formative years is immeasurable.

In the years ahead, the challenge to physical education as a vital, essential part of the total education effort is of considerable consequence. The widespread and general understanding of the true nature and potentialities of physical education has never been achieved. Some progress is being made as human movement is studied in its fullness. With the determination to begin now and the desire to work for quality programs, a golden era of physical education may arise as the year 2000 approaches.

SUMMARY

1. Our hope is to live a celebrated life as an awakened, enlightened individual with the desire to make a contribution to the advancement of mankind.
2. The true worth of physical education is best determined by how it affects the values of the individual members of the society within which it is taught.
3. Noted physical education philosophers, including Clarke, McCloy, McKenzie, Nash, Rogers, and Williams stressed the importance of educating our youth to be active.
4. Technology has had a profound effect on the total well-being of the worker, causing a need for health promotion and work-site fitness programs.
5. Cultural diversity has resulted in a need for multicultural education. This diversity poses a challenge for all of education as it strives to develop students who care about people and are moved to improve society.

6. Physical education can play a part in lessening the problems brought on by both an increase in population and population density.
7. The U.S. Department of Health and Human Services report, *Healthy People 2000,* provides (a) data on our current health practices and (b) a strategy for improving our health.
8. Physical education can play a vital part in increasing a person's longevity and happiness throughout the retirement years.
9. Physical education has a lot to offer a society with a heightened need for leisure.
10. Sport has an aesthetically pleasing quality and can thereby be viewed as an art form.
11. Dance, in its many forms, has had a resurgence in recent years, resulting in an interest in virtually all forms of dance.
12. The fitness/wellness boom is apparent as increasing numbers of adults regularly engage in some form of physical activity.
13. Physical education provides a medium to enhance international friendship and understanding among the nations of the world.

QUESTIONS AND LEARNING ACTIVITIES

1. Does education have any responsibility for consciously changing our culture or do educators simply exist to keep existing truths alive?
2. One of the liabilities of modern education, according to Norman Cousins, is that it has contributed to a compartmentalization of knowledge and that what is needed today is an understanding of the interrelationships within the entire province of knowledge. Do you agree or disagree with this view? How do you see it relating to physical education?
3. Interview one or more eighty-year-old men or women. Ask:
   a. How many hours a day they worked at making a living
   b. What new products or inventions impressed them the most during their teen years
   c. Who their heroes were as they grew up
   d. What games they played as youth
   e. How they used their leisure time as youth
4. In his utopian book, *The Shape of Things to Come,* H. G. Wells assumed that scientific thinking, modern engineering, and public education, by their intrinsic worth, would prepare the kind of future of which an educated, middle-class citizen would approve. Later, when he wrote *Mind at the End of Its Tether,* he had become disillusioned as he noted that Nazi Germany scored higher on scientific rationalism, engineering, and public education than did any other European nation. Take a moment to examine this observation. Are there implications here of any particular significance? Do educational goals and programs need careful definition as they relate to a civilization? List some specific implications for educators and others who build a society close to the heart's desire.

5. Examine the effects of sports on the American culture. Give particular attention to sports as an art form.

6. Provide a clear definition for value illness. What can physical education do to curtail the spread of this disease?

7. What can physical education do to help develop a culturally awakened individual?

8. In one sentence, provide your philosophy of physical education.

9. What can physical education do to combat the problems brought on by inner-city life?

REFERENCES

Aldana, S. G., & Stone, W. J. (1991). Changing physical activity preferences of American adults. *Journal of Physical Education, Recreation, and Dance, 62*(4), 67–71, 73.

Alighieri, D. (1948). *The divine comedy, the inferno, purgatorio, and paradiso.* New York: Pantheon Books.

American Cancer Society. (1990). *Cancer facts and figures—1989.* New York: The Society.

American College of Sports Medicine. (1993). *Resource manual for guidelines for exercise testing and prescription.* Philadelphia: Lea & Febiger.

Baldwin, J. (1989). A talk to teachers. In R. Simonson, & S. Walker (Eds.), *The graywolf annual five: Multicultural literacy.* St. Paul, MN: Graywolf Press.

Banks, J. A. (1992). Creating multicultural learner-centered schools. In A. Lieberman, *Building learner-centered schools: Three perspectives.* New York: National Center for Restructuring Education, Schools, and Teaching.

Bennett, C. I. (1990). *Comprehensive multicultural education: Theory and practice.* Boston: Allyn & Bacon.

Berryman-Miller, S. (1991). Multicultural dance: The spirit of cultural tradition. *Journal of Physical Education, Recreation, and Dance, 62*(2), 33.

Butt, K. L., & Pahnos, M. L. (1995). Why we need a multicultural focus in our schools. *Journal of Physical Education, Recreation, and Dance, 66*(1), 48–53.

Cawelti, G. (1990). How will students be different in the 21st century? *Interchange: Alliance for arts education.* Washington, DC: The John F. Kennedy Center for the Performing Arts.

Centers for Disease Control. (1987). Bicycle-related injuries: Data from the national electronic injury surveillance system. *Mortality and Morbidity Weekly Reports, 36,* 269–271.

Chepyator-Thomson, J. R. (1994). Multicultural education: Culturally responsive teaching. *Journal of Physical Education, Recreation, and Dance, 65*(9), 31.

Committee on Trauma Research, Commission on Life Sciences, National Research Council, and Institute of Medicine. (1988). *Injury in America: A continuing public health problem.* Washington, DC: National Academy Press.

Conant, J. F. (1961). *Slums and suburbs.* New York: McGraw-Hill.

Dubos, R. (1981). *Celebrations of life.* New York: McGraw-Hill.

Eddy, J. M., & Beltz, S. M. (1989). Health-related outcomes of participation in CIGNA's preventive medical program. *Fitness in Business,* April, 164–170.

Ehrlich, P. R., & Ehrlich, A. H. (1972). *Population resources, environment: Issues in human ecology.* San Francisco: W. H. Freeman & Company Publishers.

Fisher, I. (1946). *How to live: Rules for healthful living based on modern science.* New York: Funk & Wagnalls Company.

Goldberger, L., & Breznitz, S. (Eds.). (1982). *Handbook of stress: Theoretical and clinical aspects.* New York: The Free Press.

Health Education and Public Law 93.641. (1977). *Focal points.* Atlanta, GA: Bureau of Health Education, July, 2–4.

Howe, C. Z. (1981). From leisure ethic to reindustrialization. *Journal of Physical Education, Recreation, and Dance, 52*(9), 38–39.

Information Please Almanac. (1994). New York: Houghton Mifflin Company.

Kanters, M. A., & Montelpare, W. J. (1994). Enabling healthy lives through leisure. *Journal of Physical Education, Recreation, and Dance, 65*(4), 27.

Katz, A., Branch, L., Branson, M., Papsidero, J., Beck, J., & Greer, D. (1983). Active life expectancy. *New England Journal of Medicine, 309,* 1218–1224.

Kennedy, J. F. (1960). The soft American. *Sports Illustrated,* December 26, 15–17.

King, C. S. (Ed.). (1987). *The words of Martin Luther King, Jr.* New York: Newmarket Press.

Kleiber, D. A., & Fiscella, J. (1982). Leisure as interlude. *Journal of Physical Education, Recreation, and Dance, 54*(9), 46.

Knott, E. S. (1991). Working with culturally diverse learners. *Journal of Developmental Education, 13*(2), 14–18.

Kovich, M. (1971). Sports as an art form. *Journal of Physical Education and Recreation, 42*(8), 42.

Kraus, R. G. (1977). *Recreation today: Program planning and leadership.* Santa Monica, CA: Goodyear.

Leonard, G. B. (1975). *The ultimate athlete: Revisioning sports, physical education, and the body.* New York: Viking Press.

Martin, F. W. (1976). Leisure, culture, and the continuing search for meaning. *Journal of Physical Education, Recreation, and Dance, 54*(8), 46.

Maslow, A. (1962). *Toward a psychology of being.* New York: Van Nostrand.

May, R. (1953). *Man's search for himself.* New York: Dell Publishing Company.

McCarville, R. E. (1993). Keys to quality leisure programming. *Journal of Physical Education, Recreation, and Dance, 64*(8), 34–36, 46–47.

McGinnis, J. M. (1987). The national children and youth fitness study II: Introduction. *Journal of Physical Education, Recreation, and Dance, 58*(10), 46.

Mead, M. (1967). *The changing patterns of work and leisure.* Washington, DC: U.S. Department of Labor.

Mero, E. B. (1909). *American playgrounds: Their construction, equipment, maintenance, and utility.* Boston: The Dale Association.

Nash, J. B. (1953). *Recreation: Pertinent readings.* St. Louis, MO: Mosby.

Nash, J. B. (1965). *Philosophy of recreation and leisure.* Dubuque, IA: Wm. C. Brown Company Publishers.

National Cancer Institute. (1986). *National Cancer Institute monographs 2.* Bethesda, MD: U.S. Department of Health and Human Services.

National Center for Health Statistics. (1975). *Vital and health statistics: Exercise and participation in sports among persons 20 years of age and over.* Washington, DC: U.S. Government Printing Office.

National Institute on Aging. (1986). *Age pages.* Washington, DC: U.S. Department of Health and Human Services.

National Institute on Drug Abuse. (1989). *National household survey on drug abuse: Population estimates 1988.* Washington, DC: U.S. Department of Health and Human Services.

National Safety Council. (1991). *Accident facts.* Chicago: National Safety Council.

National Sporting Goods Association. (1994). *Sports participation in 1994.* Mount Prospect, IL: National Sporting Goods Association.

Office of Disease Prevention and Health Promotion. (1987). *National survey of worksite health promotion activities: A summary.* Washington, DC: U.S. Department of Health and Human Services.

Ornstein, R., & Ehrlich, P. (1989). *New world—new mind: Moving toward conscious evolution.* New York: Doubleday.

Perrier. (1979). *The Perrier study: Fitness in America.* New York: Perrier.

President's Council on Physical Fitness and Sports. (1973). National adult physical fitness survey. *Newsletter,* 1–27.

President's Council on Physical Fitness and Sports. (1994). American attitudes toward physical activity and fitness. *Journal of Health, Physical Education, Recreation, and Dance, 65*(1), 15.

Ross, J. G., & Gilbert, G. G. (1985). The national children and youth fitness study: A summary of findings. *Journal of Physical Education, Recreation, and Dance, 56*(1), 45–50.

Ross, J. G., & Pate, R. R. (1987). The national children and youth fitness study II. *Journal of Physical Education, Recreation, and Dance, 58*(9), 51–56.

Shuker, V. B. (1993). Dance education K–12: Theory into practice (part II). *Journal of Physical Education, Recreation, and Dance, 64*(5), 41.

Siedentop, D. (1994). *Introduction to physical education, fitness, and sport.* Mountain View, CA: Mayfield.

Stone, W. J. (1990). *Fitness for you: A guide to wellness.* St. Paul, MN: West Publishing Company.

Tiedt, A. L., & Tiedt, I. M. (1990). *Multicultural teaching: A handbook of activities, information, and resources.* Boston: Allyn & Bacon.

United Nations Preparatory Educational, Scientific, and Cultural Commission. (1947). *Fundamental education, common ground for all peoples.* A report to the United Nations Educational, Scientific, and Cultural Organization. New York: Macmillan Publishing Company.

U.S. Department of Health and Human Services. (1992). *Healthy people 2000: National health promotion and disease prevention objectives.* Washington, DC: U.S. Department of Health and Human Services.

Updyke, W. F. (1994). Fitness trends in a large population of 6–10-year-old children. *Summary Report of the Chrysler-AAU Physical Fitness Testing Program.* Poplars Building, Bloomington, IN: Amateur Athletic Union.

2
EDUCATIONAL FOUNDATIONS

Outline

Defining the Ends
Lifestyles and Educational Objectives
Physical Education Objectives
Health-Related Fitness
Recreational Competency
Social Efficiency
Intellectual Competency
Culture
America 2000

Outcomes

After reading and studying this chapter, you should be able to:
- Define
  Aerobic endurance
  Body composition
  A cultured person
  Education
  Flexibility
  Health-related fitness
  Intellectual competency
  Muscular endurance
  Recreational competency
  Social efficiency
  Strength
- Explain what it means to be a physically educated person.
- Identify the essential purposes/goals of physical education.
- Identify the five general objectives of physical education.
- Discuss both the physical and mental benefits of activity.
- Discuss the impact the *America 2000* goals have for physical education.
- Formulate a personal definition for physical education.

When asked, *"Why do you run?"* Beach (1982) answered:

I run to celebrate the joy of my being . . . the ecstasy that I am! I run that I may be alone with myself and together with my universe. I run to find the rhythm of the pounding rush of my own heart which sets its beat to the pulsing of time. I run in time ever present as it passes through my world garbed in the white robes of winter, the patchwork of fall, stripped to the simplicity of summer or garlanded with the new growing things of spring. . . . I run seeking the feeling of harmony that is mine if I will but open to it. I run to feel the earth chains break and drop along my path. I run until I am numb to the everyday cares and woes and I flow forward; a part of the air which I suck into thirsty lungs the earth which softens the placement of my feet. The sounds of this space through which I pass are music to my soaring spirit. The sights lure me ever onward. The process carries me ever upward—higher and higher.

I turned and I asked them, *"How can you not run?"*

A question arising from this thoughtful response is what special combination of educational knowledge, skills, and values should be developed in order to build the kind of educational foundation that substantiates and gives meaning to the Beach question, "How can you not run?" To answer this question it is necessary to examine educational fundamentals and determine to what extent they make available in the life of coming generations the funded and growing wisdom, knowledge, and aspirations of the race. More specifically, how is knowledge disseminated, how are minds liberated, how are skills developed, and how is the creative spirit encouraged to such an extent that the joy in movement has real meaning?

Currently the physical education profession is making progress in a back to basic movement in middle and secondary schools by insisting that physical education is indeed a basic, an essential educational concern no less important than the fundamental processes of calculating and communicating. What it means to be physically educated is shown in Table 2.1 (NASPE, 1992). This is especially encouraging since Gallup and other poll-taking organizations have shown many times that a high percentage of parents know little about the public schools their children attend, and they know even less about the purposes of physical education in these schools.

DEFINING THE ENDS

Educational objectives have meaning when there is a personal striving to make progress in a definite direction. To make progress, it is necessary to possess what Dewey (1970) referred to as a means of execution—that is, something has to happen if an aim or objective is to be realized. The word education signifies this idea since it comes from the Latin word *educare,* which

TABLE 2.1 The Physically Educated Person

HAS Learned Skills Necessary to Perform a Variety of Physical Activities

- Moves using concepts of body awareness, space awareness, effort, and relationships
- Demonstrates competence in a variety of manipulative, locomotor, and nonlocomotor skills
- Demonstrates competence in combinations of manipulative, locomotor, and nonlocomotor skills performed individually and with others
- Demonstrates competence in many different forms of physical activity
- Demonstrates proficiency in a few forms of physical activity
- Has learned how to learn new skills

IS Physically Fit

- Assesses, achieves, and maintains physical fitness
- Designs, safe, personal fitness programs in accordance with principles of training and conditioning

DOES Participate Regularly in Physical Activity

- Participates in health-enhancing physical activity at least three times a week
- Selects and regularly participates in lifetime physical activities

KNOWS the Implications of and the Benefits from Involvement in Physical Activities

- Identifies the benefits, costs, and obligations associated with regular participation in physical activity
- Recognizes the risk and safety factors associated with regular participation in physical activity
- Applies concepts and principles to the development of motor skills
- Understands that wellness involves more than being physically fit
- Knows the rules, strategies, and appropriate behaviors for selected physical activities
- Recognizes that participation in physical activity can lead to multicultural and international understanding
- Understands that physical activity provides the opportunity for enjoyment, self-expression, and communication

VALUES Physical Activity and its Contributions to a Healthful Lifestyle

- Appreciates the relationships with others that result from participation in physical activity
- Respects the role that regular physical activity plays in the pursuit of life-long health and well-being
- Cherishes the feelings that result from regular participation in physical activity

From *Outcomes of quality physical education* by the Outcomes Committee of NASPE, 1900 Association Drive, Reston, VA 22091. Reprinted with permission.

means to "lead forth" or "draw out" the latent or potential qualities of a person. Education, therefore, is a process of changing behavior toward certain preconceived goals. The emphasis is on the process because it is not haphazard; it is orderly and planned.

The essential purposes of education have changed somewhat in the last century. What Spencer (1860) wrote in the nineteenth century regarding the question "What knowledge is of most worth?" differs from modern ideas. According to Spencer, education was concerned with:

- Life and health
- Earning a living
- Family rearing
- Citizenship
- Leisure

This list differs from the 1918 *Cardinal Principles of Secondary Education*. These principles include:

- Health
- Command of fundamental processes
- Worthy home membership
- Vocation
- Citizenship
- Worthy use of leisure time
- Ethical character

As far as health and physical education are concerned, both sets of purposes stress health as a primary aim and point to the need of education for leisure pursuits.

It is apparent that some of the first writers on education, including Socrates, Locke, and Rousseau, were just as enthusiastic about healthful living and its relationship to other educational objectives as were the more recent educators, including James, Dewey, and Piaget. Moreover, the goals these great educators envisioned do not differ significantly from the Educational Policies Commission's (1961) purposes of (a) self realization, (b) human relationship, (c) economic efficiency, and (d) civic responsibility. Up to this time any differences in stated objectives had been mostly a matter of emphasis.

No matter how times change, there is an importance for individuals who are dynamically healthy, able to satisfy personal needs, and able to contribute to the welfare of society. The long-range goal of the physical educator, therefore, is to prepare individuals with the ability to struggle toward the following objectives:

- Optimum organic health and the vitality of meeting emergencies
- Mental well-being for meeting the stresses of modern life
- Adaptability to and social awareness of the requirements of group living

- Attitudes and values leading to optimum health behavior
- Moral and ethical qualities contributing to life in a democratic society

LIFESTYLES AND EDUCATIONAL OBJECTIVES

In any era, the effort of realizing educational objectives must relate to the current and predicted future lifestyles of the population. In the last several years some progress occurred in effecting healthful behavioral changes and in modifying lifestyles. As Dobos (1981) pointed out, humans can never adapt biologically to the diseases of civilization, but through creative adaptation their lives can be shaped through their responses to disease.

A person's success in adapting to environmental challenges, though remarkable, does have limits. Social, technological, and economic changes present novel challenges that sometimes exceed the adaptive capacities of most people. However, constant attention to the aspects of one's daily lifestyle, individually and in combination with others, reveals that a significant educational impact can be made on a person's overall physical and mental capacity. Certain components of lifestyle, such as sedentary living and obesity, are now viewed as major risk factors. Moreover, mortality research indicates that nearly half of the ten leading causes of death in the United States can be traced to lifestyle. Fortunately, behavioral research has made it possible to understand behavior more in keeping with an individual's day-to-day activities. For example, getting a sedentary person to exercise is more a matter of behavioral modification than that of a traditional practice of medicine.

Although physicians are being encouraged by both medical schools and associations to look more carefully into individual lifestyles, their limited and somewhat sporadic contact with people can have little effect. Increasingly, the guidance of individuals into more healthful living patterns will fall to health and physical educators in the school and communities.

To modify or change behavior, the student must be viewed as a unity and not a conglomeration of parts. The whole person must be considered in order to affect a positive change in lifestyle and well-being. Decades ago in their writings, both Jesse Feiring Williams and John Dewey championed this view. Oberteuffer (1965) said this is the crucial issue for physical education. He asked more than thirty years ago:

> What meaning does it have? What experience does it offer in the direction of that meaning? Does it make a contribution to man's entirety? . . . To survive, the physical education programs of the day must recognize the totality of man and be constantly mindful that man lives in a social setting, not in isolation.

Glasser (1976) refers to a poor-quality lifestyle as a condition that occurs when people lack the vitality and strength of finding the happiness enjoyed by others. Missing is the perception and dynamism of overcoming difficulties associated with fulfillment, pleasure, recognition, and a sense of personal value. Glasser's positive addiction theory states that people have positive lifestyles. This theory shows that runners are in a very favorable category since they only have to think about putting on running shoes to feel the kinesthetic pleasure of movement. It is the platonic idea of knowing thyself that Beach alluded to earlier.

PHYSICAL EDUCATION OBJECTIVES

Physical education concentrates on both the art and science of human movement. However, the ultimate objective is to employ movement as a means of contributing to the physical, mental, and social goals of education. Thus, physical education may properly be defined as education through physical means, primarily through large-muscle activity. It is learning to move by moving.

The five main objectives of physical education are the development and maintenance of:

- Health-related fitness
- Recreational competency
- Social efficiency
- Intellectual competency
- Culture

From time to time, teachers of physical education must be willing to scrutinize and carefully reappraise both the existing physical education goals and the emphasis that is given to these goals. Perhaps the matter of emphasis needs more attention. When reviewing the history of physical education, it is clear that some objectives were neglected in the past while others were overemphasized. Periods of great attention were given to (a) posture and mental health, (b) character development through sports participation, (c) body awareness through movement exploration; and (d) physical fitness.

Various professionals have sometimes asked if physical education should have a hierarchy of objectives. Should these objectives be prioritized? Such a hierarchy could bring additional attention to certain objectives that appear to be of major importance in a specific year. However, this could backfire since some objectives may receive less emphasis than others.

There was a spirit in ancient Greece, with its cultural emphasis on sport, that has no comparable counterpart. Not only was sport more prominent in Greek life than in any other culture before or since, but even more significantly, as Siedentop (1971) indicated, competitive athletics were the central focus of the culture and a primary criterion by which civilization was distinguished from barbarism. Moreover, a large part of Greek life centered in the palaestra and the gymnasium. Greek youth received sports skills instruction from dawn to midday. This experience formed the core of Greek education, an education to fulfill all human needs. The values derived from competition were intrinsic, not extrinsic and material. The goal was embodied in the concept of aerate, that is, excellence in performance and noble behavior. Homer (White, 1989) described this concept as he wrote about the lives, personalities, and deeds of the early heroes who sought a conduct of just and righteous living.

HEALTH-RELATED FITNESS

Defined briefly, physical fitness is the capacity for activity. It is a very important aspect in contemporary life, worthy of serious attention (Siedentop, 1994). It is a positive and dynamic quality closely related to two variables—diet and exercise. It is often referred to as organic vigor or vitality, the physical element of behavior that permits a person to be active. It is demonstrated through physical performance.

Although related to health in general, physical fitness is more specific when carefully evaluated. For example, several people may be thoroughly checked by a physician and found to be free from disease and defects. Yet these people may vary in the degree to which they can perform physically. Some may tire in walking a short distance. Others may run the same distance without being winded. The greater the physical fitness, the greater the physical endurance and precision of movement. The greater the physical fitness, the longer people will be able to keep going or endure. The greater the physical fitness, the more efficiently people will be able to both perform and recuperate from fatigue. Undergirding physical fitness is an organic soundness consisting of five components (see Figure 2.1)

Strength is the ability of a muscle to develop tension resulting in the force necessary to move an object through space. Strength is typically exhibited in the human body as (a) postural strength, the ability to stand upright against the force of gravity; (b) dynamic strength, the ability to manipulate the body while performing locomotor skills, including walking, running, and jumping; (c) ballistic strength, the ability to move the limbs through various ranges of movement while performing basic game skills, including throwing, kicking, and striking; and (d) isometric strength, the ability to stabilize the body, parts of the body, or objects against the pull of external forces. *Muscular endurance* is the ability of a muscle to sustain the force necessary to move an object through space repeatedly. Strength is necessary to perform the push-up movement, while muscular endurance is necessary to perform the push-up movement continuously. *Flexibility* is the ability to move a limb or body segment through its full range of movement. *Aerobic endurance* is the ability of the heart, lungs, and vascular system to provide sufficient amounts of oxygen and nutrients to the working muscle and carry the by-products of muscular work away from the working muscle. *Body composition* is the percentage of muscle, fat, bone, and other tissue in the body. The effectiveness of all body movements, whether large muscle or small muscle, depends on the status of these five, interrelated components.

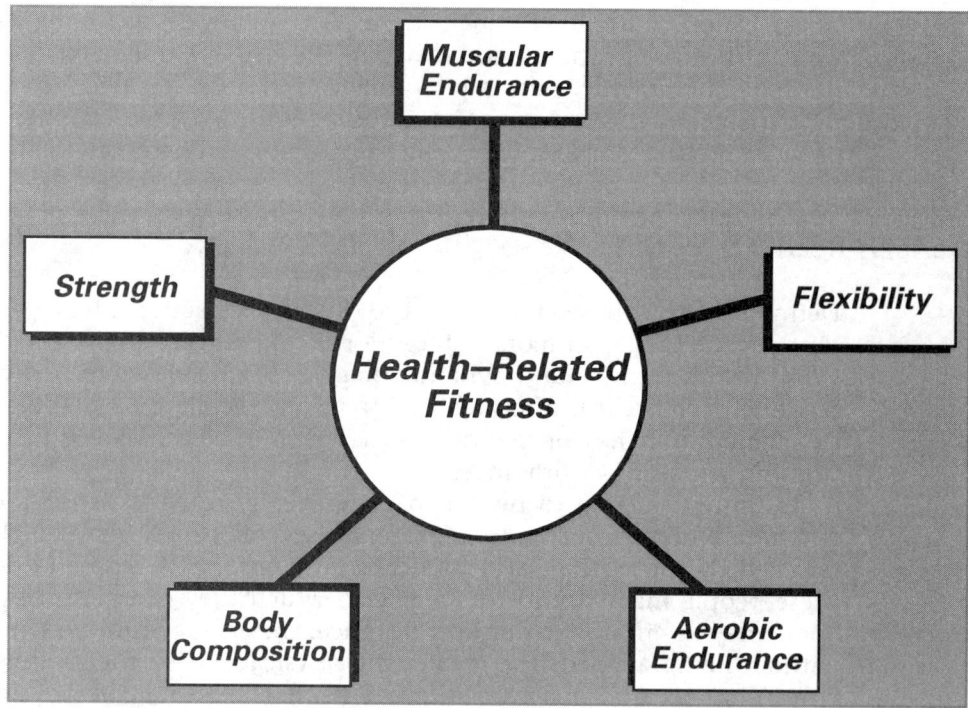

FIGURE 2.1 Components of Health-Related Fitness

In 1938 Conrad and Meister wrote that "Man is born; he struggles; he dies." This concept signifies a pretty short life history. The key word in this remark is *struggles*. Life is a struggle. Therefore, the capacity to perform becomes key to the individual. With it, a person is able to strive and achieve a degree of happiness. This is accomplished not by acquiescing with what is but by struggling for what should be; not by accepting but by questioning; not by receiving but by giving; and not by resting but by moving (Lawton & Rogers, 1937).

Physical activity is one way that our species makes itself known as a human animal. The ability to move is the foundation for physical education. Corbin and Lindsey (1994) emphasized the importance of physical activity when they presented its physical and mental benefits. Among these benefits include:

- A stronger heart
- A lower resting heart rate
- A lessened chance of heart attack
- A heightened chance of surviving a heart attack
- Enhanced sports performance
- Decreased susceptibility to disease
- Quicker recovery from disease/injury

Maintaining health-related fitness

- Ability to cope better with daily stressors
- Increased work efficiency
- Better quality of life

Physical inactivity as well as excessive food intake are both etiological factors that lead to human obesity. Desirable weight is a matter of correct balance between energy intake and energy expenditure. Obesity is consistently encountered as a cause of physical unfitness among students and adults, but the results of controlled physical activity like simple walking, jogging, and running in reducing percent body fat are measurable.

Working with the health teacher and others in school, the physical educator can do much to reduce the weight of an obese adolescent. Improper dietary habits combined with inactivity contribute to a rise in the incidence of cardiovascular disease. Evidence supporting this condition is convincing, from the historical Framingham Heart Study (U.S. National Heart Institute, 1968), to the research of Cooper (1978), and others. Seneca's (1908) remark that "Man does not die, he kills himself" is more accurate today than when those words were spoken.

Physical activity aids the body's attempt in adapting to apprehension, worry, and anxiety by improving the sensitivity of the adrenal glands so they provide more steroids for counteracting stress. Physical activity improves functional efficiency at any age because the human biological design has not changed. Humans are meant to be active, not sedentary. As people grow older, fatigue is an obstacle to a happy life. Perhaps the best prescription for fatigue in older citizens, if not all citizens, is physical activity. Acknowledging the need for maintaining functional efficiency at every age, a number of well-known corporations have introduced physical fitness programs and built facilities for their employees (see Chapter 1).

An abundance of evidence shows a significant difference between the longevity of individuals who are physically active and those who are not. Functional ability and physiological age can be extended for older people through controlled programs of walking, jogging, swimming, and relaxing. As fitness improves, self-esteem rises, and an inner sense of worth occurs, and a stronger will to live is present. This, in turn, reduces the mortality rate for a number of cardiovascular diseases and becomes an obvious contributor to longevity.

RECREATIONAL COMPETENCY

People are born for great joy. In order to find life worth living people must have either joy in their lives or some hope of joy. It is joy that refreshes and recreates humans. The whole organism is involved. Recreation, therefore, is more than a game just for fun. It is an act of restoration for the individuals normal self. This restoration occurs by a renewal of the physical, mental, and spiritual state and it is more than a simple motor act. It involves deeper parts of the brain where the desire for divergence and refreshment is felt. Recreation can be viewed as an attitude of mind. It is as much akin to mental health as it is to physical well-being.

The recreation function is much more important than it may appear. In a world of increasing tension, both physical and psychological, an antidote must exist. Glands adjust to the constant demands of stress by releasing excess hormones for keeping the body in balance and striving for homeostasis. Without appropriate relief the body will suffer. Selye (1978) explains that the glands succeed for a while but in the end the defense mechanism breaks down, arteries harden, blood pressure rises, and heart disease develops. Happiness is related to freedom from stress. An individual must have hope, faith, and self-respect if not in work, then in recreation.

A variety of recreational skills, and specifically those that are physical, need to be mastered early in an individual's life so participation and enjoyment can be carried on throughout a lifetime. The paramount need, therefore, is to develop competency in a variety of skills. Poorly taught, poorly learned, and seldom practiced skills will rarely carry into adult life. A rewarding experience is one that leaves the participant in a state of mental and physical exhilaration, sufficient to promote peaceful relaxation and appreciation.

SOCIAL EFFICIENCY

Social efficiency is the ability to get along with others and exhibit desirable standards of conduct. It is a kind of social well-being related to mental and emotional health. School physical education can contribute measurably to the development of social efficiency by providing learning situations in which students can express themselves. This expression may occur through initiative, cooperation, leadership, followership, self-restraint, and loyalty to the group. A limited physical capacity sometimes handicaps an individual in pursuing social goals.

More than any other subject in the curriculum, physical education is organized to deal specifically with the elements of appropriate social behavior. Through carefully selected games, activities, and dances, students must assume a variety of responsibilities when working with others. Cooperation stems from a feeling for others or group consciousness. Initially experimental, this awareness of others develops a degree of participation through both leadership and followership. Significantly, it is the freedom within the rules of the play situation that gives meaning to sportsmanship. This may be one of the most important concepts in education because without rules, freedom is meaningless; and without freedom, there is no long-term survival. This area in the sports movement has much to offer. It encourages a degree of freedom to which proper restraint and the rules of the game must be adhered. Moreover, the power of the word sportsmanship is universal. It is probably the clearest and most popular expression of morals today.

Sport and play have deep roots in culture and humanities simply because both provide life enrichment and fulfillment opportunities. Sport has had a profound impact on civilization for years. Sport has proven to be a means of allowing us to better understand not only how people live and work but also how they think. People learn how to live with others through the sport experience. Sports are an education in themselves. Sports relate directly to play and so they become a means of escape from the stresses of work and routine.

Widely considered a social institution of considerable magnitude, sport functions as something more than mere entertainment. It is now necessary to educate groups involving those who participate and those who spectate because the number of people who do both is increasing. Participation in organized sport through community Park and Recreation programs, YMCA/YWCA programs, and sports clubs, and watching a variety of sports at all levels is popular today. Education will help promote a lifestyle that includes a suitable sport experience. Importance has been placed on sport in society. The term *sport sociology* has evolved because of this societal impact. A strong case has been made by several sociologists and historians for this sociology of sport in the tradition of the social sciences. Loy and Kenyon (1981) especially supported this idea. They define sports sociology as the study of sport in society as it affects human development, forms of expression, value systems, and the interrelationships of sport with other elements of the culture. Based on this definition, how can sports education be anything but a prime concern to all educators?

Aside from the health and social experience, Loy and Kenyon view the sports experience in terms of the independent dimensions of pursuit of vertigo, aesthetic experience, catharsis, and/or ascetic experience. These underlying ways contribute to the sports experience of an individual's personal growth. Somewhat risky to the participant, the vertigo event is provided through the thrill of speed, acceleration, sudden change of direction, or exposure to dangerous situations. The aesthetic experience is captured through several senses. Catharsis is achieved through the release of tension that builds with frustration. The ascetic experience is seen as the punishment a person endures in both competitive situations and extended training periods as the gratification received from achievement is delayed.

A positive relationship exists between an individual's personality traits and social adjustment and the high levels of skill in sporting activities. Individuals with high general motor ability were inclined to be more sociable, dependable, tolerant, competitive, and popular among peers. Boys with low general motor ability tended to have feelings of insecurity, difficulty in social relationships, emotional instability, and negative self-concept. However, it is the opportunity to display one's general motor ability—so highly correlated with game skills—in a group sport situation that fosters efficient social actions.

Individuals simply have to make adjustments in order to function in a social group. This group, as defined by Cratty (1967), is a collection of people mutually interacting to solve a common problem. Variables that influence group performance include the size of the group, its leadership, the nature of the task, the influence of affiliation needs versus achievement needs on the part of the members, and the cohesiveness of the group. Basically, this is the way participants find themselves as they struggle for higher levels of performance. The spirit of the Athenians is reborn each time players come to grips with themselves while struggling for perfection. Thus the athlete does not retreat from life but rather immerses in it completely and experiences a joy of mind, body, and spirit. This spirit, possessed by the adventurers who climbed Delphi mountain, demands that athletes do their best. This is the way a peak experience in sport is attained—an experience in which the individual has an involuntary, transient experience of being totally integrated, functioning fully, and in complete control of the situation.

The social efficiency objective takes on greater magnitude when the inner purposes of play are considered. Cowell and France (1963) summarized the values of play education. When asked why play is important to children, they responded that play:

- Is a wholesome safety valve of prehuman origin for aggressions and other drives.
- Allows the organism to test not only its ordinary powers, but its originalities, before responsibilities are too critical.
- Bears some relation to the business of life, being in some measure the young form of work.
- Provides wholesome compensations for frustration and failure experienced in other areas.
- Provides opportunities for creativity.
- Satisfies psychic hunger for activity, achievement, belonging and recognition, and similar needs.
- Affords the normal mechanism for release of the imagination and a legitimate means for needed occasional escape from reality.
- Provides opportunities for experiencing thrills and successes, as well as proper dosages of risks and failures that contribute to character-building.
- Develops an individual's resources for effective adjustment to solitude.
- Develops a give and take, a subordination of the self and a loyalty to the team which are of great social value.
- Has moral significance, providing for improvement of values concerning fair play, cooperation, and other social virtues.
- Encourages attention and therefore personality integration since interest is inherent in the activity itself without extraneous or interest-distorting motivations.

INTELLECTUAL COMPETENCY

One of the primary responsibilities of the physical educator is to find ways and means of insuring a continued participation in physical activities, long after the students have left school. One approach is to provide an adequate knowledge and understanding of the important values in physical activity. Inherent in this provision is having an appropriate answer to the common question by students, "why?" More specifically:

- Why do we need to exercise?
- Why must we warm-up before playing?
- Why must we do drills?

As physical educators, it is imperative that answers exist to these and other *whys*. Individuals defend things thoroughly understood. Moreover, people tend to act in support of their convictions. Today's students need to (a) understand why exercise is necessary and why physical skills are beneficial and (b) appreciate the unique role of recreational activity in providing for a rich and full life. This is one way to meet the intellectual competency objective. A second method is to teach cognitive content as well as the psychomotor. An understanding of cognitive content including game rules, terminology, and strategy is essential if students are to fully appreciate the activities and sports in the curriculum. Generally, this can be accomplished using a variety of techniques including lectures, videotapes, and independent study.

Vigor and intellectual growth are natural allies. Together they account for more than being separate entities and even more than the sum of the individual parts. If students understand not only the *what* and *how* but the all-important *why* of physical education they, as future parents, will be more apt to lend enlightened support to our programs in years to come.

CULTURE

The objective of physical education lacking the most consideration, perhaps because it is the least understood, is the development of the cultured person. Culture is not something ethereal, but rather a concept that can be grasped. It is practical, involving a deep appreciation for life's activities, and is closely associated to the rich and full life.

Teachers of physical education who develop appreciation for rhythm and music through specific sport skills and dances and who employ form and color in creative activities are helping to develop the cultured person. Moreover, every teacher of physical education who successfully teaches a student a useful motor skill is contributing to the cultural objective. The meaning of culture substantiates this process because culture implies enlightenment, a refinement of thought. The mark of a cultured person is the refinement in both mental and moral powers, as a result of particular training and its subsequent enlightenment. The cultured person feels a concern for many things. Careful cultivation, along with the product of learning that enriches and fills one with an appreciation of the arts and an appreciative attitude toward the arts both signify a cultured person. Art in its many forms—a graceful ballet, an emotional opera, a thought-provoking painting—enrich the human experience both from a participant and a spectator perspective. Sports and games are capable of enhancing the human spirit. The French philosopher, Maheu (1963) developed the viewpoint that spectator sports are the true theater of our day when he said:

> *Think of the tens of thousands who fall silent as the athlete prepares to jump and then shout with relief as he/she soars upward. This participation by the spectator as well as the performer, this close link generating a current of sympathy, understanding, and support from the nameless crowd of watchers or listeners to the individual taking the stage and expending himself . . . takes us back to the theater of Greece. That is why sport . . . is able to release and, in the Aristotelian sense, to purge the emotions of the spectator, just as effectively as any work of art.*

Physical education can also enhance the development of culture through the creation of the kinesthetic sense, the consciousness within the body for specific skilled movements. The appreciation developed through the kinesthetic sense is an artistic experience and is comparable to other artistic qualities. Accomplishing a difficult skill and gradually learning a new skill involves the same neural pathways and ends in a neural pattern no less important to artistic appreciation than stimuli received through other senses. Listening to a symphony may unconsciously cause a person to close their eyes and relax their body in the fullest appreciation. Art lovers may be completely lost in space as they view a favorite gallery masterpiece. Likewise, an athlete may hit a golf ball so perfectly or serve the tennis ball so accurately that a feeling of supreme satisfaction is experienced. The reactions of both art and music lovers are not unlike those of the movement lovers. These reactions are outward manifestations of the cultured person. All three—art, music, and movement—have the capability of developing a fine artistic sense.

The inner feeling is what counts in a discussion regarding culture. Music expresses the inexpressible. The same is true when describing the feeling one gets from viewing a highly skilled movement. The pure beauty of a thoroughbred turning at the post, the gymnast balancing motionless on the beam, a wide receiver coming down with the ball as both feet touch the ground just inside the white line, all bring culture to the heart of the spectator. Just as it is easier to describe the symphony performance than the actual music, it is likewise easier to describe the spectators at a football game or tennis match than the rousing impact of the physical activity itself. Both participants and spectators departing with similar feelings is what signifies cultural overtones.

AMERICA 2000

The U.S. Department of Education published *America 2000: An Educational Strategy* in 1991. Sadler, Tentinger, and Wiedon (1993) indicate that by presenting this document to the American public, the federal government has taken a bold step toward increasing its participation in educating America's children. Furthermore, this participation will go beyond the traditional role of just providing financial support.

In this document, the government outlined six national goals (see Table 2.2). Although physical education is not listed as a priority, direct implications exist for its inclusion. As Sadler, Tentinger, and Wiedon (1993) state, physical educators need to recognize the opportunity for enhancing each child's total learning experience and to do so by keeping physical education in the mainstream of formal, academic education. To accomplish this objective, selected changes must occur that include:

- Recognition of physical education, particularly motor skill development, as a viable component in national education policies.
- Institutional endorsement of multidisciplinary activities borrowing from the expertise of all teachers and available resources.
- Development of teacher preparation programs that focus on holistic health and lead to acquisition of higher order fitness objectives for all students.

TABLE 2.2 America 2000 Goals

Goal 1	By the year 2000, all children in America will start school ready to learn.
Goal 2	By the year 2000, the high school graduation rate will increase to at least ninety percent.
Goal 3	By the year 2000, American students will leave grades four, eight, and twelve having demonstrated competency over challenging subject matters including English, mathematics, science, history, and geography; and every school in America will ensure that all students learn to use their minds well so they may be prepared for responsible citizenship, further learning, and productive employment in the modern economy.
Goal 4	By the year 2000, U.S. students will be first in the world in mathematics and science achievement.
Goal 5	By the year 2000, every American adult will be literate and will possess the knowledge and skills necessary to compete in a global economy and to exercise the rights and responsibilities of citizenship.
Goal 6	By the year 2000, every school in America will be free of drugs and violence and will offer a disciplined environment conducive to learning.

- Public relations efforts to *sell* the benefits of wellness to the entire community.
- Integration of wellness concepts into a broad range of subjects in the curriculum.
- Refocusing of upper secondary physical education away from sport performance but toward lifetime fitness.
- Adoption by school boards of NASPE's outcomes and benchmarks (1992) for a comprehensive physical education program. These are discussed in Chapter 3.

SUMMARY

1. Education is a process of changing behavior toward preconceived goals. It is essential in an educational setting that this process be orderly and well planned.
2. Physical education has been defined as learning to move by moving. It is a medium that employs movement to enhance a student's total development, that is physically, mentally, and socially.
3. The National Association for Sport and Physical Education has provided a thorough and explicit definition of a physically educated person.
4. The instruction of physical education should be guided by five major objectives/goals that include the development and maintenance of health-related fitness, recreational competency, social efficiency, intellectual competency, and culture.

5. Fitness is a capacity for activity that has become an important aspect in today's society. One's ability to function through both work and play is dependent on the status of the five interrelated components of health-related fitness.
6. Recreational competency is achieved through the development of motor skills. The development of both the fundamental movement skills and the sport-specific skills allows the student to participate in and thereby enjoy a variety of physical activities.
7. The ability to get along with others and exhibit desirable standards of conduct leads to social efficiency. Physical education is an ideal medium for dealing with the elements of appropriate social behavior, among those being cooperation, self-restraint, and sportsmanship.
8. Providing knowledge about and an understanding of physical education is a way of developing intellectual competency.
9. Culture implies enlightenment, a refinement of thought. In physical education and sport activities, the student can develop an appreciation for movement. Furthermore, through structured activities, students can develop an appreciation for shape, form, expression, and creativity, thereby leading to the cultured person.
10. *America 2000,* created under the Bush administration, recognized the need for increased quality in all educational programs including the physical education curriculum at the elementary and secondary school levels.

QUESTIONS AND LEARNING ACTIVITIES

1. As civilization becomes more complex, is there a tendency for education to become somewhat divorced from life? Is this true of physical education?
2. Formulate a list of contributions that physical education can make to a student's physiological, psychological, and sociological development. Be prepared to share this with others.
3. "Play is an attitude," said Luther Gulick, founder of the Camp Fire Girls. This was the basis of his philosophy. Collect a number of definitions of play as expressed by philosophers, educators, therapists, and others. How do these definitions relate to play as an attitude? How do they relate to play as a means of education?
4. Human needs are not always realized by educational goals unless the planners of these goals are aware of both the aspirations and problems of mankind. Formulate a list of obstacles that stand in the way of achieving educational goals. Consider negative items not only within the culture but at the local school and community level.
5. Interview a number of physical educators in different schools and at different levels in order to determine what they believe to be physical education's general objectives.
6. Prioritize the chapter's five general objectives for physical education. Provide published support for your rankings.

7. What do you think are the three main purposes of today's school? Attempt to provide published support for your listings.

8. What does it mean to be recreationally competent?

9. List specific ways that physical education can develop and maintain culture.

REFERENCES

Beach, B. (1982). Why do you run? *Journal of Physical Education, Recreation, and Dance,* 53(3), 25.

Commission of the Reorganization of Secondary Education. (1918). *Cardinal principles of secondary education.* Washington, DC: Bureau of Education, Bulletin 35.

Conrad, H. L., & Meister, J. F. (1938). *Teaching procedures in health education.* Philadelphia: Saunders.

Cooper, K. (1978). *The aerobics way.* New York: Bantam Books.

Corbin, C., & Lindsey, R. (1994). *Concepts of physical fitness with laboratories.* Dubuque, IA: Brown & Benchmark.

Cowell, C. C., & France, W. L. (1963). *Philosophy and principles of physical education.* Englewood Cliffs, NJ: Prentice-Hall.

Cratty, B. J. (1967). *Social dimensions of physical activity.* Englewood Cliffs, NJ: Prentice-Hall.

Dewey, J. (1970). *The way out of educational confusion.* Westport, CT: Greenwood Press.

Dobos, R. (1981). *Health and creative adaptation in the nation's health.* San Francisco: Boyd & Fraser.

Educational Policies Commission, (1961). *Policies for education in American democracy: The central purpose of American education.* Washington, DC: National Education Association.

Glasser, W. (1976). *Positive addiction.* New York: Harper & Row.

Lawton, S. U., & Rogers, F. R. (1937). *Educational paths to virtue, I.* Newton, MA: Pleides Company.

Loy, J. W., & Kenyon, G. S. (1981). *Sport, culture, and society: A reader on the sociology of sport.* Philadelphia: Lea & Febiger.

Maheu, R. (1963). Sport and culture. *Journal of Health, Physical Education, and Recreation,* 39(8), 18–21.

National Association for Sport and Physical Education. (1992). *Outcomes of quality physical education programs.* Reston, VA: AAHPERD.

Oberteuffer, D. (1965). *Background readings for physical education.* New York: Holt, Rinehart & Winston.

Sadler, W. C., Tentinger, L. G., & Wiedon, G. A. (1993). America 2000: Implications for physical education. *The Physical Educator,* 50(2), 77–86.

Selye, H. (1978). *The stress of life.* New York: McGraw-Hill.

Seneca, L. A. (1908). *Selected essays of Seneca and the satire on the deification of Claudius.* New York: Macmillan Publishing Company.

Siedentop, D. (1971). Differences between Greek and Hebrew views of man. *Canadian Journal of History of Sport and Physical Education,* 30–49.

Siedentop, D. (1994). *Introduction to physical education, fitness, and sport.* Mountain View, CA: Mayfield.

Spencer, H. (1860). *Education: Intellectual, moral and physical.* New York: Appleton-Century-Crofts.

U.S. Department of Education. (1991). *America 2000: An educational strategy.* (ED/0s91-13). Washington, DC.

U.S. National Heart Institute. (1968). *The Framingham study: An epidemiological investigation of cardiovascular disease.* Bethesda, MD.

White, F. A. (1989). *The complete life of Homer.* London: Bell & Sons.

3

THE STUDENT AND CURRICULUM OBJECTIVES

Outline

The Student and the Times
The Physical Education Potential
From Philosophy to Objectives
Specific Objectives in Physical Education
Behavioral Objectives in Physical Education
Outcomes-Based Physical Education
The Nature of Curriculum
Curriculum Models
Physical Education Curriculum Models
The Hidden Curriculum
The Teaching Dimension

Outcomes

After reading and studying this chapter, you should be able to:
- Define

    At risk

    Behavioral objective

    Curriculum

    General objective

    Hidden curriculum

    Outcomes-based physical education

    Specific objective

- Explain what is meant by the physical education potential.
- Understand and apply the taxonomies of educational objectives proposed by Krathwohl, Bloom, and Masia.
- Distinguish the differences between general, specific, and behavioral objectives.
- Identify the basic components of a well stated behavioral objective.
- Explain the basic school-level curriculum models.
- Describe each of the ten physical education curriculum models presented.
- Explain what the hidden curriculum is and how it can impact students.

In hundreds of school systems a substantial amount of change and innovation has existed, resulting in an admirable effort to make the whole process of schooling more pertinent to the needs of society and more vital in the eyes of young people. Many of these changes have been accomplished precisely because of influential views from individuals like Thomas Hopkins (1941) and Jerome Bruner (1974). Their views stress the need for a sound philosophical base and clearly stated objectives for any and all educational programs. In physical education this practice has been productive and demonstrated in numerous ways:

- assigning more time to curriculum development
- surveying student interests
- bolstering girls' and womens' programs
- increasing the number of activity offerings
- permitting individual student concentration in an activity
- arranging personal conditioning programs
- providing a variety of adventure activity classes
- instituting wider school-community programming of sports, dance, and recreational opportunities for people of all ages.

Such an expression of concern for youth comes from a growing awareness of the intricate relationship between the feelings and aspirations of students and the program itself. In short, how do students view themselves? How do they view their lives? How do they view their school? How do they view their physical education curriculum?

THE STUDENT AND THE TIMES

The demand for accountability, a return to more traditional teaching subjects, and an increasing rise in enrollment teamed up with decreasing financial support at the federal and the state levels challenge both school personnel and students to respond appropriately. Equally involved is the lack of respect the teaching profession faces. What was an admirable vocation fifty years ago is now viewed by many as what you do when you can not do anything else. Whether the reason involves (a) attempts to increase taxes to support education, (b) an increase in one-parent families, or (c) society equating an individual's importance to the size of the income, being a teacher is not an easy task. In addition, experience indicates that students have their own unique reactions to most educational pronouncements, programs, and processes based on their perceptions. To compound this, these perceptions may not always be correct or rational. Yet these ideas are a major factor in determining how well students function in school.

Hellison and Templin (1991) indicate that today's students are not the same because the world in which they live is not the same. Too many of today's children receive insufficient guidance. This is partly due to one-parent families, working parents, parents whose lifestyles focus less on their children, and the diminishing number of family-oriented neighborhoods that were once instrumental in raising everyone's children. Whatever the reason, the Children's Defense Fund (1992) presents some troubling data:

- Every twelve seconds of the school day, an American child drops out of school (380,000 a year).
- Every thirteen seconds, an American child is reported abused or neglected (2.7 million a year).
- Every twenty-six seconds, an American child runs away from home (1.2 million a year).
- Every sixty-seven seconds, an American teenager has a baby (472,000 a year).
- Every nine minutes, an American child is arrested for a drug offense (58,400 a year).
- Every forty minutes, an American child is arrested for drunk driving (13,140 a year).
- Every fifty-three minutes, an American child dies from poverty (9,917 a year).
- Every three hours, an American child is murdered (2920 a year).

Students have always been influenced, to some degree, by the social and economic climate of the times. Students' lifestyles relate to a slice of pizza, the expense of gasoline, or the guilt associated with asking parents for money. Students' lifestyles relate to the nature of their peer groups, the nearness of recreational facilities, and the influence of church and other community groups. Their lifestyles relate to an all-too-often conflict between parental controls and an awareness of individual rights.

Swanson (1991) explains that many students develop attitudes and learn the types of skills that will prevent them from supporting social institutions as adults. The resulting behavior too often produces students who avoid responsibility, show disrespect for authority, and/or engage in what borders on criminal behavior. Csikszentmihalyi and McCormack (1986) argue that today's young people lack meaningful goals which most likely accounts for the unprecedented surge of social pathology in the United States today. The tragedy is that this situation is often preventable. These students have been called *at risk*. Although this meaning is unclear, an at-risk student has unsatisfactory academic achievement and poses the potential of not completing high school, being unemployed, and having a negative effect on society.

Peterson (1987) further defines this population by including students who are environmentally at risk. In other words, biologically and genetically normal students whose life experience and/or environment impose a threat to their developmental well-being resulting in low academic achievement, juvenile delinquency, drug abuse, and/or teenage pregnancy (Hellison & Templin, 1991).

Austin and Meister (1990) indicated that the proportion of students who are at-risk is increasing. Responding to their needs must become a national priority. All educators, physical educators included, need to be aware of this at risk population and both develop and implement programs that are proven to be effective learning experiences.

Young people identify with programs that permit them to explore and feel the forces around them. From an early age they are ready to identify with people, situations, and the skills of cognition, sociability, and physical movement. Therefore, it becomes extremely important for the physical educator to meet this need for self-actualization by providing a curriculum whereby students can identify who they are. A child's self-concept (the value-free view of oneself), a child's self-esteem (the value one places on this view), and a child's self-confidence (one's belief in the ability to perform) all play a part in determining how that child will act and subsequently react. If children feel physically inept they probably will display a reluctance to move. If children feel clumsy they probably will not move gracefully. If children feel stupid they surely will present a non-comprehending face to the world.

Frequently camouflaged behind protestations and frustrations are the real concerns about where youth are headed. To fully understand young people, one must realize that they live in an intense present, a *here now* environment. Much of what seems important lies either in the immediate life situation or in the near future. Youth rarely look into the distant future. To be effective, therefore, the physical educator must get close to the student's personal value system of *the moment*.

THE PHYSICAL EDUCATION POTENTIAL

Physical education (movement) was made for youth. It is the one subject in the curriculum that appeals frequently to large numbers of children chiefly because of the chance to run, jump, skip, throw a ball, kick a ball, and express themselves through movement. It provides a means to challenge all students. Moreover, if physical education is properly presented it will bring people of many persuasions together. Therefore, youth are more apt to buy it and subsequently drop some of their hostility to the system.

Today's schools need organized, cooperative activities in which students can interact with peers. A curriculum properly conceived and content properly taught can promote group interactions and appropriate social behavior. In the school environment, the physical education program—perhaps more than any other program in the school—is where this process can readily occur. But for programming to be effective, it is important to remember that meeting students' needs is clearly an important factor.

FROM PHILOSOPHY TO OBJECTIVES

Fundamentally, it is the responsibility of every upcoming and present-day teacher to think about both the ultimate purposes of and the existing practices in education. Philosophizing is an earmark of a professional.

Physical educators ranging from the department supervisor to the gymnasium instructor must rationalize the program by thinking and struggling with diverse viewpoints. This rationalization is as germane to the development of the curriculum as is the availability of facilities and equipment. In fact, to rely solely on others for planning and preparing a list of desired student objectives, competencies, outcomes, and curriculum content for meeting these outcomes is to miss experiencing some of the challenging activities endearing the profession of teaching. In addition, every teacher needs to be able to establish goals for which to strive. Through the process of resolving doubts and convictions, teachers can achieve the personal fulfillment that is the ultimate hope of free people everywhere. Ideally then, the supervisor and curriculum coordinators are only facilitators in the process of program change. As Gibran (1923) expressed, they lead teachers to the threshold of their own minds. What happens beyond that point is up to the teacher.

A number of authors and philosophers in the physical education field have contributed to the discussion of objectives. They strongly support the rationale that objectives must ultimately relate to the potential meaning they have for the student. Nixon and Jewett (1980) express their objectives in terms of three clusters—fitness, performance, and transcendence. These refer, respectively, to physical condition, skill level, and psychological characteristics including self-awareness, heightened perception, kinesthetic discovery, self-mastery, creative expression, and joy of movement. More specific, Jewett and Miller (1977) present their objectives as purposes in a framework that ties in with the curriculum experiences. This Purpose Process Curriculum Framework (PPCF) contains twenty-two purpose elements spread through three major conceptual topics—individual development, environmental coping, and social interaction.

After examining the fundamental movements and other content associated with physical education, Annarino, Cowell, and Hazelton (1986) divide objectives into five traditional categories of emotional responsiveness, interpretive and intellectual development, neuromuscular development, organic power, and personal-social attitudes and adjustment. These more traditional objectives are illustrated in an informational manner in Table 3.1. However, because of the present-day emphasis placed on developmental physical education and the need for defining exactly what it is that physical education wants to accomplish, the authors have placed their objectives into one of six developmental categories (see Table 3.2).

After discussing objectives and recognizing such underlying concepts as how one perceives, patterns, varies, adapts, improvises, and refines, Cheffers and Evaul (1978) described human movement. They categorized the scope of human movement as that endeavor which pertains to how an individual adapts personal movement to *fit in* with the environment or *to change* the environment to suit personal needs and interests. Further effort to examine the score of human development was done when Harrow (1972) set forth the psychomotor domain somewhat similar to the parameters employed by Krathwohl, Bloom, and Masia (1964) in their monumental treatment of

TABLE 3.1 Traditional Physical Education Objectives

Emotional responsiveness—an attempt to have students express job at participation in games and sports; accept challenges that mean overcoming difficulties; derive enjoyment from a cooperative experience; and develop an increased appreciation of the aesthetic experiences inherent in all activity including games, sports, and dance.

Interpretive and intellectual development—an attempt to encourage students to approach whatever they do with both imagination and originality.

Neuromuscular development—an attempt to develop skills, grade, and a sense of rhythm.

Organic power—an attempt to strengthen muscles, develop resistance to fatigue, and increase aerobic efficiency; the ability to maintain adaptive effort.

Personal-social attitudes and adjustment—an attempt to place students in situations that encourage self-confidence, sociability, initiative, self-direction, and a feeling of belonging.

Reprinted by permission of Waveland Press, Inc. from Annarino, et al. Curriculum Theory and Design in Physical Education, 2nd ed. (Prospect Heights, Il; Waveland Press, Inc. 1980 [reissued 1986]) All rights reserved.

cognitive and affective domains. Seven years later Bloom, Hastings, and Madaus (1971) emphasized that all fields of education should inspect and subscribe to the cognitive objectives. Briefly, the six objectives can be applied to physical education as follows:

1. Knowledge: The student is able to recall specifics—methods, processes, theories, structures, or settings. (*Example:* Understands sport-specific terminology, history, and rules.)
2. Comprehension: The student is able to make use of something without necessarily relating it to other things; can demonstrate the ability to translate or paraphrase communication; the lowest level of undertaking. (*Example:* Explains the meaning of such items as cardiovascular endurance, aerobic activity, and sportsmanship.)
3. Application: The student is able to employ technical principles or abstractions, ideas, and theories in some way; can use information in a concrete situation. (*Example:* Observes a sporting situation or motor skill and clearly indicates how it may or may not be representative of what is expected.)
4. Analysis: The student is able to examine an idea, concept, or structure by breaking it down into its component parts so that the relationship between the parts is clear. (*Example:* Responds to a certain game situation by breaking down the intricate structure and patterns leading to successful participation.)
5. Synthesis: The student is able to bring together all parts and elements to form a whole; can work with pieces and make arrangements in a manner to create a structure or pattern not there before. (*Example:* Creates a dance or gymnastics routine from a number of individual skills.)

TABLE 3.2 Developmental Objectives of Physical Education

Organic

Proper functioning of body systems so the individual may adequately meet the demands placed on him/her by the environment; a foundation for skill development

- Muscle strength
  Ability of a muscle or muscle group to sustain effort for a prolonged period of time
- Cardiovascular endurance
  Capacity of an individual to persist in strenuous activity for periods of some duration; this depends on the combined efficiency of the blood vessels, heart, and lungs
- Flexibility
  Range of motion to joints needed to produce efficient movement and to minimize injury

Neuromuscular

Harmonious functioning of the nervous and muscular systems to produce desired movements

- Locomotor skills
  Walking, skipping, sliding, leaping, pushing, running, galloping, hopping, rolling, pulling, jumping
- Nonlocomotor skills
  Swaying, twisting, shaking, stretching, bending, hanging, stooping
- Game-type fundamental skills
  Striking, catching, kicking, stopping, throwing, batting, starting, changing direction, bouncing, rolling, trapping, volleying
- Motor factors
  Accuracy, rhythm, kinesthetic awareness, power, balanced reaction time, agility
- Sport and dance skills
  Soccer, softball, volleyball, wrestling, track and field, football, baseball, basketball, archery, speedball, hockey, fencing, golf, bowling, tennis, dance
- Recreation skills
  Shuffleboard, croquet, deck tennis, hiking, table tennis, swimming, horseshoes, boating

Perceptual

Ability to receive and distinguish among available cues in a given situation in order to perform more skillfully

- Spatial relationships
  Ability to recognize objects as being in front of, below, or to the right or left of one's self
- Visual-motor coordination
  Ability to coordinate vision with gross motor skills involving hands, body, and/or feet
- Figure-ground relationships
  Ability to select a stimuli from a mass of sensory intake or to select a limited number of stimuli on which to focus attention

Source: From Annarino, A. A. *Fundamental movement and sport skill development.* Columbus, OH: Charles T. Merrill Co., 1973, pp. 4–5. Reprinted with permission.

TABLE 3.2 *Continued*

Perceptual *(Continued)*

- Body balance (static, dynamic)
  Ability to maintain static or dynamic equilibrium
- Dominancy
  Consistency in the use of the left or right hand or foot in throwing and striking
- Laterality
  Ability to distinguish the difference between left and right sides of the body and between left and right within one's own body
- Body image
  Awareness of the parts of the body or the whole body and the relationship to space

Cognitive

Ability to explore, to discover, to understand, to acquire knowledge, and to make value judgments

- Knowledge of game rules, safety measures, and etiquette
- Use of strategies and techniques involved in organized activities
- Knowledge of how the body functions and its relationship to physical activity
- Appreciation for personal performance; the use of judgment related to distance, time, space, form, speed, and direction in the use of activity implements, balls, and self
- Understanding of growth and developmental factors affected by movement
- Ability to solve developmental problems through movements

Social

Adjustment to both self and others by integration of the individual to society and the environment

- Ability to make judgments in a group situation
- Learning to communicate with others
- Ability to exchange and evaluate ideas within a group
- Development of the social phases of personality, attitudes and values in order to become functioning members of society
- Development of a sense of belonging and acceptance by society
- Learning for the constructive use of leisure time
- Development of attitude that reflects good moral character

Emotional

Healthy response to physical activity through a fulfillment of basic needs

- Development of positive reactions in spectatorship and participation through either success or failure
- Release of tension through suitable physical activities
- Outlet for self-expression and creativity
- Appreciation of the aesthetic experiences derived from correlated activities

6. Evaluation: The student is able to make judgments pertaining to the worth of ideas, techniques, and materials. (*Example:* Demonstrates the ability to differentiate between an effective and ineffective volleyball serve, particularly as it contributes to the overall game objective.)

The literature in the physical education field contains listings of objectives that would be suitable for giving direction to teachers and students alike. Frequently, these lists serve as indications for the function of physical education and therefore have some merit for school use.

SPECIFIC OBJECTIVES IN PHYSICAL EDUCATION

In discussing objectives, it is customary to proceed from (a) the program's major aims or goals—called general objectives (see Table 2.1) to (b) its specific objectives to (c) the behavioral objectives for the students. In curriculum development the specific objectives further define the general objectives and often times are related to a specific activity or content area. Table 3.3 provides the five general objectives discussed in Chapter 2 with examples of two specific objectives for each.

BEHAVIORAL OBJECTIVES IN PHYSICAL EDUCATION

Moving closer to the student should prompt stated objectives to become more precise. The objectives closest to the student are called behavioral objectives. Other published terms include performance objectives, terminal competencies, and summative expectations. In recent years, due to teacher accountability,

TABLE 3.3 Specific Objectives within Each General Objective

The Development and Maintenance of:

- Health-related fitness
  The student will improve aerobic endurance.
  The student will improve abdominal muscular strength and endurance.
- Recreational competency
  The student will be able to drive a golf ball.
  The student will be able to kick a soccer ball.
- Social efficiency
  The student will display sportsmanship.
  The student will demonstrate self-direction.
- Intellectual competency
  The student will understand the basic rules of basketball.
  The student will describe the task sequence for a tennis forehand.
- Culture
  The student will develop an appreciation for square dance.
  The student will develop an understanding of the place and importance of basketball in our society.

TABLE 3.4 Key Words Describing Behavior

analyzes	determines	hits	portrays
applies	develops	interprets	relates
appreciates	differentiates	investigates	runs
catches	discriminates	jumps	selects
chooses	distinguishes	leaps	swing
dances	evaluates	passes	throws
demonstrates	explains	plays	values
describes	feels	pleases	walks

considerable attention has been given to the writing of these behavioral objectives because they focus attention on explicit behaviors. Anything observable can be stated in a behavioral objective form and can be set forth in terms of action words. These observable acts include all behaviors, whether psychomotor, cognitive, or affective. Examples of key words that can be used to describe a selected behavior are shown in Table 3.4.

The main advantage of establishing student behavioral objectives is that from the beginning, the attention of the physical educator can be specifically directed toward attaining the prescribed outcomes. A second advantage to writing clearly defined behavioral objectives is to allow the physical educator to be more selective of the course content, methodology, and resources necessary for meeting these outcomes.

Mager (1984) presents a method for writing behavioral objectives. A well written behavioral objective contains three basic components that include (a) the observable, terminal behavior or task, (b) the condition(s) or situation under which this behavior is to be performed, and (c) the criterion or performance level which indicates that the behavior has been completed. The task component of a behavioral objective is written as a verb describing *what* the student is to do. Examples of tasks include dribble, catch, and define. The criterion component of a behavioral objective indicates the degree of acceptable behavior by describing *how well* the learner must perform the selected behavior. The criterion can be stated (a) quantitatively, relative to such measures as time, distance, and percentages; or (b) qualitatively, relative to form or technique. The condition component of a behavioral objective describes under what situation(s) the behavior is to be performed. It further defines *when* the behavior is to be completed. Examples of conditions are shown in Table 3.5.

TABLE 3.5 Condition Component of a Behavioral Objective

Behavior	Condition
Tennis forehand	When tossed from a pitching machine
Basketball free throw	In a game situation
Softball swing	From a batting tee
Soccer dribble	Around cones
Volleyball forearm pass	From a served ball

TABLE 3.6 Physical Education Behavioral Objectives

Psychomotor

- The student will dribble the soccer cone maze in less than fifteen seconds on the eighteenth day of the unit.
- The student will score a minimum of twenty on the AAHPERD volleyball serving skill tests on the last day of the unit.
- The student will average 125 pins over the final three games bowled.
- The student will display correct form during the approach, hurdle, takeoff, flight, and entry phases of the forward dive.

Cognitive

- The student will score seventy-five percent on the tennis knowledge test on the final day of the unit.
- While viewing a videotape of an unskilled batter, the student will identify the three major errors of execution.
- The student will list all tennis court line markings when asked to do so.
- The student will describe the task sequence of performing an overhead volleyball serve.

Affective

- The student will exhibit sportsmanship in the basketball unit by indicating when a foul was committed.
- The student will choose a level of practice that is both appropriate and challenging for his/her ability level.
- The student will demonstrate self-direction by using pre-class time wisely.
- The student will assist a partner in developing proper technique, using Mosston's reciprocal teaching.

Examples of complete physical education behavioral objectives in each of the three learning domains are shown in Table 3.6.

OUTCOMES-BASED PHYSICAL EDUCATION

The determination of whether students have learned, gained knowledge, and/or changed behavior as a result of exposure to a year of physical education is a measure of educational value. The need and/or desire for this determination has resulted in some kind of satisfaction for educational accountability by parents and the public at large. The desired change in student behavior has been approached recently from an outcomes-based approach. As Siedentop (1994) states:

> At the end of a term in algebra, students can do many things they could not do at the start of the term. At the end of an American history course, students know things they did not know when the course began. The same sense of outcomes must pervade physical education if it is to achieve greater credibility among the lay public and the education profession.

To achieve these goals two things must happen. Today's physical educator must:

- Carefully select the desired outcomes.
- Teach to achieve these outcomes.

To guide the selection process of what outcomes are desired, the National Association for Sport and Physical Education (NASPE) formed an outcomes committee in 1986 to (a) identify outcomes that define the physically educated student (see Table 2.1) and (b) identify grade-specific competencies that serve as stepping stones, called *benchmarks,* for the physically educated student to achieve. NASPE (1992) published a list of suggested benchmarks for kindergarten and grades two, four, six, eight, ten, and twelve. Benchmarks for grades two, six, and ten are shown in Tables 3.7, 3.8, and 3.9, respectively.

Following this publication, a Standards and Assessment Task Force was appointed to establish (a) content standards for the physical education school program that clearly identify what a student should know and be able to do as a result of being exposed to a quality physical education program and (b) teacher-friendly guidelines for assessment of these content standards. The task force's work resulted in NASPE's 1994 publication, *National Standards for Physical Education: A Guide to Content and Assessment.* In addition, work has begun at the state department level (Stillwell & Reneau, 1992). Of the twenty-nine state agencies providing curriculum guide materials, Stillwell and Reneau found that all provided outcomes for students. The stating and achievement of these outcomes is a means for physical education to gain credibility with the lay public, colleagues, administrators, and legislators.

THE NATURE OF CURRICULUM

Although the word curriculum has already been used several times in this chapter, little attempt has been made to examine its meaning. This is because a detailed discussion of curriculum is ideally preceded by a study of educational philosophy and objectives. The word curriculum is derived from the Latin word *currere,* meaning to run. It was associated with the running of races and with race courses. Therefore, curriculum may have had a physical education beginning.

More common definitions of a curriculum include "a specified course of study," "all planned school activities," and "the body of courses offered by an educational institution." The derived word, as well as the definitions, seems to suggest both an orderly plan and progression. An individual does not arrive at a schedule or course of study without engaging in some degree of organizing and planning.

In American public schools, the word curriculum is an all-inclusive term referring to the total program. All of the academic programs and the extra-class activities like band, student council, yearbook committee, intramurals, and interscholastic athletics are included in the curriculum and thereby are

TABLE 3.7   Examples of Benchmarks—Second Grade

As a result of participating in a quality physical education program it is reasonable to expect that the student will be able to:

1. Travel in a backward direction and change direction quickly and safely without falling.
2. Travel, changing speeds and directions, in response to a variety of rhythms.
3. Combine various traveling patterns in time to the music.
4. Jump and land using a combination of one- and two-foot take-offs and landings.
5. Demonstrate skills of chasing, fleeing, and dodging to avoid or catch others.
6. Roll smoothly in a forward direction without stopping or hesitating.
7. Balance, demonstrating momentary stillness, in symmetrical and asymmetrical shapes on a variety of body parts.
8. Move feet into a high level by placing weight on the hands and landing with control.
9. Use the inside or instep of the foot to kick a slowly rolling ball into the air or along the ground.
10. Throw a ball hard demonstrating an overhand technique, a side orientation, and opposition.
11. Catch, using properly positioned hands, a gently thrown ball.
12. Continuously dribble a ball, using the hands or feet, without losing control.
13. Use at least three different body parts to strike a ball toward a target.
14. Strike a ball repeatedly with a paddle.
15. Consistently strike a ball with a bat from a tee or cone, using a correct grip and side orientation.
16. Repeatedly jump a self-turned rope.
17. Combine shapes, levels, and pathways into simple sequences.
18. Skip, hop, gallop, and slide using mature motor patterns.
19. Move each joint through a full range of motion.
20. Manage own body weight while hanging and climbing.
21. Demonstrate safely while participating in physical activity.
22. Participate in a wide variety of activities that involve locomotion, nonlocomotion, and the manipulation of various objects.
23. Recognize similar movement concepts in a variety of skills.
24. Identify appropriate behaviors for participating with others in physical activity.
25. Identify changes in the body during physical activity.
26. State reasons for safe and controlled movements.
27. Appreciate the benefits that accompany cooperation and sharing.
28. Accept the feelings resulting from challenges, successes, and failures in physical activity.
29. Be considerate of others in physical activity settings.

From *Outcomes of Quality PE Programs* by the Outcomes Committee of NASPE. Reprinted with permission.

considered important. These activities, once called extra-curricular (outside the curriculum) are now classified as co-curricular. The curriculum is a body of experiences that lies between the objectives and the teaching methodology employed for meeting these objectives (see Figure 3.1).

A full program of activities will signify the original aims and objectives. But it is not foolproof because its success with individuals will always depend

TABLE 3.8   Examples of Benchmarks—Sixth Grade

As a result of participating in a quality physical education program it is reasonable to expect that the student will be able to:

1. Throw a variety of objects demonstrating both accuracy and distance (e.g., Frisbees, deck tennis rings, footballs).
2. Continuously strike a ball to a wall, or a partner, with a paddle using forehand and backhand strokes.
3. Consistently strike a ball using a golf club or a hockey stick so that it travels in an intended direction and height.
4. Design and perform gymnastics and dance sequences that combine traveling, rolling, balancing, and weight transfer into smooth, flowing sequences with intentional changes in direction, speed, and flow.
5. Hand dribble and foot dribble while preventing an opponent from stealing the ball.
6. Keep an object continuously in the air without catching it while in a small group (e.g., ball, footbag).
7. Consistently throw and catch a ball while guarded by opponents.
8. Design and play small group games that involve cooperating with others to keep an object away from opponents (basic offensive and defensive strategy) (e.g., by throwing, kicking, and/or dribbling a ball).
9. Design and refine a routine combining various jump rope movements to music so that it can be repeated without error.
10. Leap, roll, balance, transfer weight, bat, volley, hand and foot dribble, and strike a ball with a paddle using mature motor patterns.
11. Demonstrate proficiency in front, back, and side swimming strokes.
12. Participate in vigorous activity for a sustained period of time while maintaining a target heart rate.
13. Recover from vigorous physical activity in an appropriate length of time.
14. Monitor heart rate before, during, and after activity.
15. Correctly demonstrate activities designed to improve and maintain muscular strength and endurance, flexibility, and cardiorespiratory functioning.
16. Participate in games, sports, dance, and outdoor pursuits, both in and outside of school, based on individual interests and capabilities.
17. Recognize that idealized images of the human body and performance, as presented by the media, may not be appropriate to imitate.
18. Recognize that time and effort are prerequisites for skill improvement and fitness benefits.
19. Recognize the role of games, sports, and dance in getting to know and understand others of like and different cultures.
20. Identify opportunities in the school and community for regular participation in physical activity.
21. Identify principles of training and conditioning for physical activity.
22. Identify proper warm-up, conditioning, and cool-down techniques and the reasons for using them.
23. Identify benefits resulting from participation in different forms of physical activities.
24. Detect, analyze, and correct errors in personal movement patterns.
25. Describe ways to use the body and movement activities to communicate ideas and feelings.
26. Accept and respect the decisions made by game officials, whether they are students, teachers, or officials outside of school.
27. Seek out, participate with, and show respect for persons of like and different skill levels.
28. Choose to exercise at home for personal enjoyment and benefit.

From *Outcomes of Quality PE Programs* by the Outcomes Committee of NASPE. Reprinted with permission.

TABLE 3.9 Examples of Benchmarks—Tenth Grade

As a result of participating in a quality physical education program it is reasonable to expect that the student will be able to:
1. Demonstrate basic competence in physical activities selected from each of the following categories: aquatics; self-defense; dance; individual, dual, and team activities and sports; and outdoor pursuits.
2. Perform a variety of dance (folk, country, social, and creative) with fluency and in time to accompaniment.
3. Assess personal fitness status in terms of cardiovascular endurance, muscular strength and endurance, flexibility, and body composition.
4. Design and implement a personal fitness program that relates to total wellness.
5. Participate in a variety of game, sport, and dance activities representing different cultural backgrounds.
6. Participate cooperatively and ethically when in competitive physical activities.
7. Participate in several outdoor pursuits indigenous to the geographic area.
8. Identify participation factors that contribute to enjoyment and self-expression.
9. Compare and contrast offensive and defensive patterns in sports.
10. Discuss the historical roles of games, sports, and dance in the cultural life of a population.
11. Categorize, according to their benefits and participation requirements, activities that can be pursued in the local community.
12. Analyze and compare health and fitness benefits derived from various physical activities.
13. Analyze and evaluate a personal fitness profile.
14. Use biomechanical concepts and principles to analyze and improve performance of self and others.
15. Appreciate and respect the natural environment while participating in physical activity.
16. Enjoy the satisfaction of meeting and cooperating with others during physical activity.
17. Desire the enjoyment, satisfaction, and benefits of regular physical activity.

From *Outcomes of Quality PE Programs* by the Outcomes Committee of NASPE. Reprinted with permission.

on sound teaching methods, effective teaching, resources, and proper evaluation techniques. In short, the human factor—the teacher—has a lot to do with the achievement of curriculum objectives. It is possible to plan and develop a fine course of study only to find that it partially does the job for which it was intended because some teacher(s) either failed to grasp its significance or were indifferent to its content.

An elementary school curriculum guide, for example, may give a detailed breakdown of student activities associated with the learning of specific game skills such as throwing, catching, and kicking. However, the teacher may resort to a specific way of teaching the skills which may not involve the same experiences set forth in the curriculum guide. When the students are evaluated, if it is clearly evident that the students did not learn the skills, the teacher may be responsible because of the decision to ignore the guide.

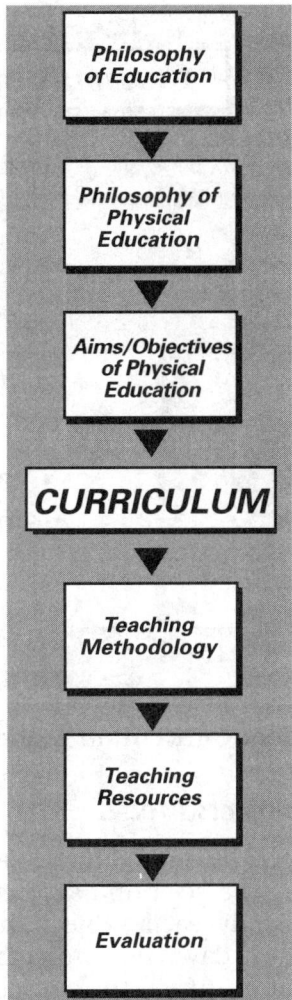

FIGURE 3.1 Central Position of Curriculum

Obviously, some room for flexibility exists when following a prescribed course of study. However, the physical educator who tries teaching within the framework of a well designed course of study and periodically checks student progress will generally contribute to the attainment of the program's objectives.

CURRICULUM MODELS

At the school level there are three basic curriculum models (see Figure 3.2).

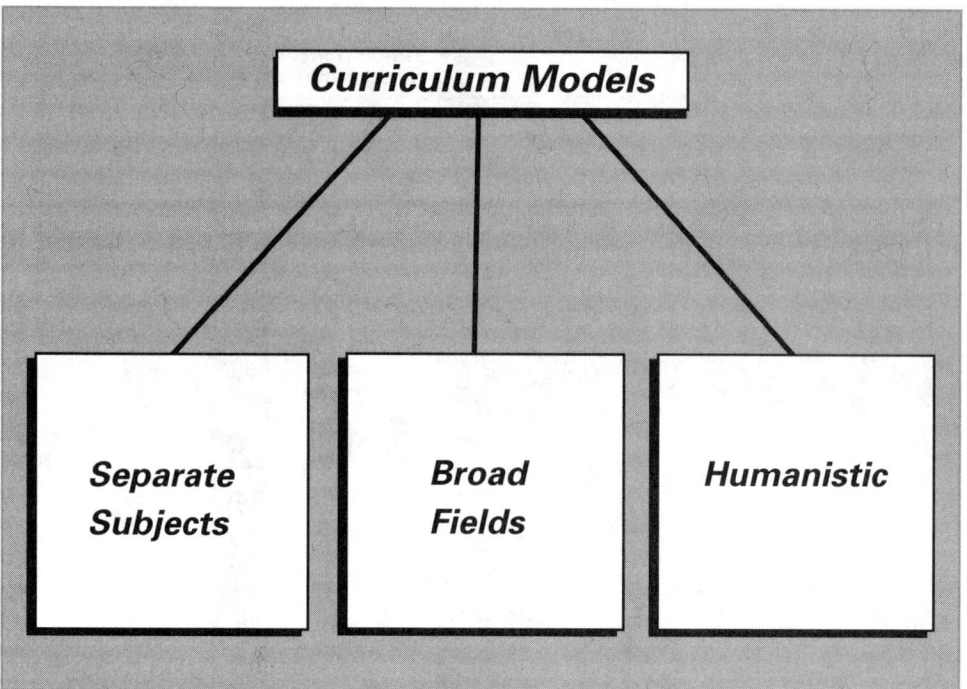

FIGURE 3.2 School Curriculum Models

The Separate Subjects Model

The separate subjects model is often called by other names, including the subject-matter model, the scientific subjects model, or the discipline-centered model. Students study each subject the school has to offer for a certain amount of time each day. The emphasis is placed almost exclusively on the subject as a separate entity in the curriculum, not on science as a subject but on chemistry, physics, and biology; not on language arts as a subject, but on grammar, literature, and writing; not on social studies as a subject, but on history, geography, and sociology. Little, if any, attempt is made to relate one school subject to another. For example, physical education would be taught without any reference to health, wellness, or safe living. Within this model, there is a tendency for students to learn isolated facts and skills without seeing each content area as a part of the whole.

The separate subjects model creates few immediately visible problems for the secondary school physical education program in which teachers have been prepared as specialists in a major field. It can, however, present implications for the elementary school physical education program. In all but a few states elementary teachers are prepared as generalists rather than subject-matter specialists. If physical education is not taught by a specialist then this responsibility falls on the classroom teacher. Too often, generalists have a limited physical education background. In addition, within the time allotment for a day, they decide what and how much time to devote to each separate subject. Therefore, it is not uncommon for physical education to be either limited or ignored in both time and content.

The Broad Fields Model

The broad fields model emerges from the awareness that students need balance between the many competencies and the kinds of understanding in order to survive in a world of varied influences. In a limited sense, this is a curriculum approach in which subject-matter areas are grouped together under a common umbrella. For example, a course entitled language arts may include content dealing with spelling, reading, writing, literature, and oral communication; a course entitled general science may include content dealing with biology, geology, chemistry, physics, and astronomy; and a course entitled social science may include content dealing with American history, world history, political science, sociology, and geography.

In physical education the course may include content dealing with personal health, wellness, and fitness. Such a course, implemented in Florida (Williams, et al., 1983), is currently required of all ninth-grade students in the state. The one-semester course is entitled personal fitness. Its purpose is to provide opportunities for students to develop an optimal level of fitness, to acquire knowledge of fitness concepts, and to understand the significance that lifestyle has on a person's health and fitness. Curriculum content includes:

- Knowledge of the importance of being fit.
- Assessment of the health-related components of fitness.
- Knowledge of health problems associated with inadequate fitness.
- Knowledge and application of biomechanical and physiological principles to improve and maintain fitness.
- Knowledge of safety practices associated with fitness.
- Knowledge of psychological values of fitness including stress management.
- Knowledge of sound nutritional practices related to fitness.
- Knowledge of consumer issues related to fitness.

Regardless of the subject area, this *total* approach more thoroughly allows the student to see, understand, and appreciate the relationships among several separate subjects learned under one general area. As the number of separate subjects is reduced the number of teaching periods is also reduced, making it possible to lengthen the time of each period or to provide an opportunity for flexible scheduling. This allows the teacher, including the physical educator, to work without interruption to more fully develop the student's knowledge, skill, and appreciation.

The Humanistic Model

Humanists share the view that education should contribute to the total well-being of the individual. Their philosophy is founded on the basis that humanism is a way of life centered on human interests and/or values. As a result, the humanistic model may emphasize an application for methodology more fully than for curriculum since it is grounded in the principle of respect for the individual and his/her personality. This model is supported because it focuses on what the students should be rather than on what they should know.

The humanistic or existential curriculum reduces importance on the mastery of subject matter. It places emphasis on programs based on student needs. From time to time other curriculum patterns have existed that employ a similar approach. Some varieties include the *activity curriculum* and the *emerging curriculum,* both of which call for a good amount of creativity on the part of the teacher.

Within the humanistic curriculum students will not be grouped for instruction chronologically but rather on ability. This non-graded system is designed to meet the student's needs by providing an opportunity for each child to advance at his/her own rate. Two implications arising from this approach are (a) determining how to insure that the students are grouped accordingly and (b) planning to meet individual needs. If planning for the successful development of skills and knowledge is difficult, consider how much more difficult it will be to plan for human interests and values. In any case, the humanistic curriculum illustrates the extremely close relationship between the curriculum and the caring, personal methodology employed by the teacher. It is in this model that the true *art* of teaching is best realized.

Caldwell (1972) indicates that the emergence of a physical education in accordance with the direction of the humanistic design would be characterized by a trust toward Maslow's self actualization, and movement exploration activities seem to be a means of achieving this end. Siedentop (1974) believes that humanistic efforts in physical education will eventually be demonstrated by teachers who are selected more for therapeutic and social qualities than for knowledge. He states:

> *The development of skill in sport and dance will remain an objective, but less and less attention will be paid to it as physical educators shift their focus to the affective aspects of activity. Less time will be spent in actually practicing the skills and more time will be spent in introspection, discussion, and other group-oriented techniques associated with humanistic educational methodology.*

Felshin (1974) supports Siedentop's modification on the mastery of skills but does not rule out the attention required for obtaining quality motor skill. In short, the affective domain is not to be overlooked. The humanistic emphasis, contributing to a shift from programs based on the competitive models for human striving and behavior to programs based on a more humane approach in which meaning, relevance, and ability are the primary values.

It is apparent today that the rights of the student determine, in part, the nature of the curriculum in all areas of education. Therefore, curriculum planning in physical education must consider the student's right to choose, right to safety, right to be informed, and right to be heard. Humanism applies as much to sports and exercise, which are major aspects of the physical education curriculum, as to other scholastic subjects.

PHYSICAL EDUCATION CURRICULUM MODELS

At the departmental level there are a number of models or conceptual frameworks (Jewett, Bain, & Ennis, 1995) or theoretical constructs (Thomas, Lee, & Thomas, 1988) that can be used to meet the objectives discussed in Chapter 2. Ten models are discussed next. These physical education curriculum models are designed to provide an effective means of selecting activities, developing teaching strategies, and providing movement experiences to meet the program's objectives (Kirchner & Fishburne, 1995).

The Developmental Model

Siedentop (1994) explains that this curriculum model is, perhaps, the most important for physical education this century. This model is based on the belief that movement can be a medium used to attain developmental objectives. Wuest and Bucher (1995) presented the objectives for this model (see Table 3.10). In using this model, the physical educators select developmentally appropriate content (activities) to enhance both the rate and the quality of the student's development in these four areas. Developmental physical education pertains to the uniqueness of the individual, and thereby is based on the belief that motor development is age-related and not age-dependent. The decisions on (a) what activities to include in the curriculum, (b) when to teach these activities, and (c) how these activities should be taught are based primarily on the activity's appropriateness for the individual student and secondarily on its appropriateness for a specific age group (Gallahue, 1996).

The National Association for the Education of Young Children (NAEYC) defines a developmental curriculum model as one based upon knowledge of what is age-appropriate for students. The implication for one either planning or teaching within a developmentally appropriate model is to be familiar with the knowledge base regarding child development (Bredikamp, 1992). For example, selecting and implementing a physical education program appropriate for a kindergarten class requires an understanding of the total (physical, motor, mental, and social) development of children at this age level.

TABLE 3.10 Physical Education Developmental Objectives

Physical development objective—the physical development objective is concerned with the program of activities that builds physical power in an individual through the development of the various organic systems of the body.

Motor development objective—the motor development objective is concerned with making physical movement useful and with as little expenditure of energy as possible, and being proficient, graceful, and aesthetic in this movement.

Mental development objective—the mental development objective is concerned with the accumulation of a body of knowledge and the ability to think and interpret this knowledge.

Social development objective—the social development objective is concerned with helping an individual in making personal adjustments, group adjustments, and adjustments as a member of society.

Wuest, D. A., & Bucher, C. A. (1995). *Foundations of physical education and sport.* St. Louis, MO: Mosby. Reprinted by permission of Mosby.

The Movement Education Model

The movement education model is a basic alternative to the developmental model. It uses Laban and Ullmann's (1960) analysis of movement classification, whereby movement themes are focused around such elements as body awareness, spatial awareness, and temporal awareness. The emphasis is placed on helping students learn how they move using a variety of educational gymnastics, educational dance, and educational games.

Movement education, termed the new physical education by Kruger and Kruger (1982), uses traditional content but a different process to achieve predetermined objectives. Wuest and Bucher (1995) provide the following key concepts of movement education by saying that movement education:

- Is individual exploration.
- Is student centered.
- Is less formal than traditional physical education.
- Involves problem solving.
- Facilitates the learning of motor skills.
- Seeks to produce a feeling of satisfaction in movement.

Logsdon, et al., (1984) indicate that the purposes of movement education are to teach students to:

- Move skillfully, demonstrating versatile, effective, and efficient movement in situations requiring either planned or unplanned responses.
- Become aware of the meaning, significance, feeling, and joy of movement both as a performer and an observer.
- Gain and apply the knowledge that governs human movement.

To this end the authors provide direction in using this model by stressing the importance that physical education should be versatile and unplanned. Children need to learn to move with ease but in doing so also need education for coping with the unexpected in situations requiring movement, rather than being educated to rely on predetermined, prescribed motor responses.

Kirchner and Fishburne (1995) indicate that movement education as an all-inclusive approach has proven to be most successful at the primary grade level. At the intermediate grade and secondary school levels, however, Laban and Ullmann's (1960) themes work best when integrated with other physical education curriculum models.

The Fitness Model

The five components of health-related fitness (muscular strength, muscular endurance, aerobic endurance, flexibility, and body composition) in the fitness model provide the content for the curriculum. The primary objective is twofold: to not only produce students who are fit, but also produce students who learn how to maintain that fitness. Smith (1993) states that physical educators utilizing this model should provide students with a lecture-laboratory approach. Classroom lectures on a variety of health-related topics including drug abuse, cardiovascular disease, and the physiological basis of fitness are combined with practical lessons in which fitness activities such as jogging, aerobics, and weight training are taught.

The Academic Discipline Model

The academic discipline model's primary focus is to foster the student's cognitive development. Content involves knowledge about the numerous subdisciplines of physical education including physiology, biomechanics, motor learning, sport sociology, sport psychology, and sport history. This model was developed due to the education reform in the late 1980s, as physical education became more academic (Taylor & Chiogioji, 1987).

Other model names include concept curriculum (Siedentop, Mand, & Taggart, 1986) and kinesiological studies (Jewett, Bain, & Ennis, 1995). Advocates of this model include Carroll (1981), Jagger (1977), and Lawson and Placek (1981). AAHPERD has demonstrated its support for this curricular approach with the initial publication of the *Basic Stuff* series in 1981 and again in 1987.

The Personal-Social Developmental Model

The personal-social developmental model stems from the humanistic education movement. The strongest advocate in physical education has been Hellison (1973, 1978, 1982, 1983, 1985, 1991). The ultimate goal of this model is to enhance the student's personal-social development through the teaching of both self and social responsibility. More precisely, the purposes are to help students:

- Cope within a highly complex world.
- Achieve a higher degree of self-control.
- Contribute more positively to the society in which they live (Siedentop, 1994).

This model was originally intended for at-risk students. But Smith (1990) has used the model successfully with students not considered to be at risk.

Perhaps the best framework to follow is Hellison and Templin's (1991). Their approach is (a) to empower students to assume more responsibility for their lives in a world presenting a variety of challenges; and (b) to teach students that they have a social responsibility to be sensitive to the rights, needs, and emotions of others. In so doing, students should:

- Feel empowered and purposeful.
- Experience making responsible commitments to themselves and others.
- Strive to develop themselves despite external forces.
- Be willing to risk popularity in order to live by a set of principles.
- Understand their essentials related to others.
- Distinguish between their own personal preferences and activities that infringe on the rights and welfare of others.

Specific goals that provide the framework for this model are to:

- Develop sufficient self-control for respecting the rights of others.
- Participate with effort.
- Develop self-esteem.
- Care about and help others.

To achieve these goals, Hellison (1985) developed a six-level progression of socialization (see Figure 3.3). Selected strategies are employed to help students interact as they hopefully work their way from one level to the next in becoming caring individuals who ultimately possess and exhibit leadership qualities. These strategies include providing opportunities to:

- Learn the goals and the rationale for them.
- Experience the goals.
- Make personal decisions.
- Solve group problems.
- Self reflect.

The Sport Education Model

The sport education model has sport as the only content. According to Siedentop, et al. (1986), its intention is to help students become skillful sports participants and sports persons. To achieve this process, as many aspects of

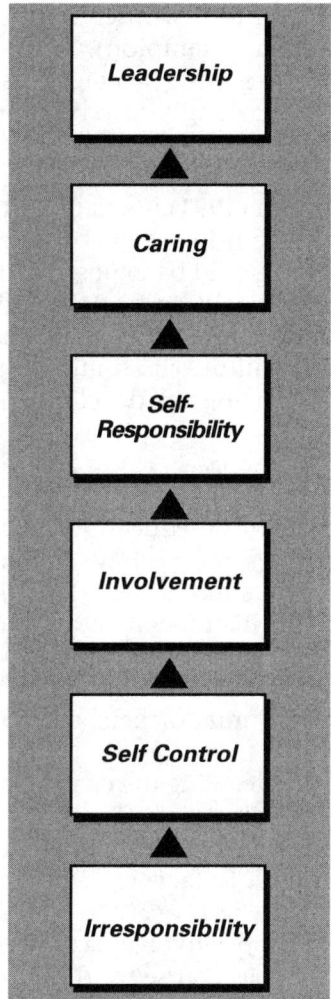

FIGURE 3.3 Hellison's Levels of Responsibility

sport as possible are incorporated into the physical education program. The true sport education model has five key characteristics:

- Sport seasonality—the yearly curriculum is organized by sport seasons rather than units.
- Team affiliation—students are members of a team and retain that membership throughout the sport season.
- Formal competition—competition is arranged in the beginning and utilized throughout the season (e.g., a round robin tournament).

- Culminating event—a winner is determined each sport season (e.g., a conference or state champion).
- Record keeping—scoring averages, assists, rebounds, etc., are kept and published to enhance interest and build tradition within this curriculum model (Siedentop, 1994).

Hellison and Templin (1991) indicate that this curriculum model is criticized. With the abuses evident in organized sports at virtually all levels, these critics argue that students should be exposed to fewer activities based on the professional sports model. Hellison and Templin continue by stating that proponents of this model argue that since sport has gained such a position of prominence in our culture, it should be included in the physical education curriculum for enhancing the development of appropriate sport behavior.

The Adventure Education Model

The interest in adventure education has increased as a result of two recent trends: (a) adventure activities have potential for education and (b) the interest in outdoor pursuits has increased markedly in the past few decades.

The purposes of this model are for students to:

- Learn outdoor sports skills and enjoy the satisfaction of competence.
- Live within the limits of personal ability related to an activity and the environment.
- Find pleasure in accepting the challenge and risk of stressful physical activity.
- Learn mutual dependency of self and the natural world.
- Share this experience and learning with classmates and authority figures (Siedentop, Mand, & Taggert, 1986).

Adventure education involves activities where either (a) an environment is created, such as a ropes course; or (b) an environment is contrived, such as a wall, and the students are challenged to complete the task presented by each. In doing so the students are required to function through anxiety and/or under stress. The focus is not on developing the skills necessary to complete the task or even on the completion of the task itself, but rather on the group involvement and specifically on cooperation, problem solving, and self-awareness.

The Multi-Activity Model

The multi-activity model is defined by the various activities offered within it (see Table 3.11). The model has skill acquisition as its primary objective. To ensure that this objective is met, the students are exposed to a variety of activities including team sports, individual-dual sports, adventure activities, fitness activities, and dance. Advocates think this diversity is necessary for meeting the needs of each student. Other critics argue that exposure to a

Challenging students through adventure education

TABLE 3.11 Multi-Activity Program Options

Team Sports	Individual Activities	Recreational Activities
Basketball	Aquatics	Angling
Football	Diving	Backpacking/hiking
Flag	Swimming	Bowling
Touch	Water polo	Camping
Hockey	Water safety	Canoeing
Field	Archery	Cycling
Floor	Badminton	Dance
Lacrosse	Conditioning	Folk
Rugby	Aerobic dance	Modern
Soccer	Aqua aerobics	Social
Softball	Circuit training	Square
Speedball	Jogging	Horseshoes
Team handball	Slimnastics	Orienteering
Volleyball	Golf	Rappelling
	Gymnastics	Sailing
	Rhythmic	Shuffleboard
	Traditional	Skating
	Handball	Ice
	Martial arts	Roller
	Akido	
	Judo	
	Karate	
	Paddleball	
	Pickleball	
	Racquetball	
	Self-defense	
	Skiing	
	Snow	
	Water	
	Squash	
	Table tennis	
	Tennis	
	Track and field	
	Weight training	
	Wrestling	
	Yoga	

wide variety of activities rather than extended exposure to a few activities will lead to a minimum level of skill competency at best. The selection of specific activities within this model is somewhat determined, in part, by student interest, the popularity of activities in a local community, and available resources.

The Games for Understanding Model

The games for understanding model evolved from the early work of Almond (1983) and the studies of Bunker and Thorpe (1982). According to Smith

(1992), this model consists of various categories of games and sports that should be selected from a games framework (Werner & Almond, 1990) and taught through a cognitive approach, utilizing guided discovery and divergent thinking (Mosston & Ashworth, 1994). This model allows the physical educator to provide students with the opportunity of solving strategic problems within game play. This is a move away from the traditional approach of using the more direct styles of teaching for developing sports skills.

To effectively use this model, the physical educator must first select games from a classification. This classification system was proposed by Ellis (1983) and is outlined in Table 3.12. Court games involve a projectile being struck either in a shared court (handball and racquetball) or in a separated or divided, court (badminton and tennis). Field games involve opposing teams taking turns offensively and defensively on either a fan-shaped field (softball) or an oval-shaped field (cricket). Target games involve a projectile directed toward a target that is either opposed (shuffleboard) or unopposed (archery and golf). Territory games involve invasion by the opponent. They are divided into games in which either a goal is attacked (basketball, soccer, and hockey) or a line is attacked (football and rugby).

Secondly, the game is played in a lead-up (conditioned) format. Students are guided to use correct strategies in each classified game by being asked specific questions. As the students become more strategic, the imposed game condition(s) are removed. Once the students are proficient game performers they are encouraged to suggest game modifications and provide rationale for these modifications.

Lastly, students are grouped and encouraged to invent new games. This is accomplished as the teacher moves from being a facilitator, to an advisor, to a passive observer. Smith (1992) cautions that moving too quickly through

TABLE 3.12 Game Classification

Court

- Shared
- Divided

Field

- Fan shaped
- Oval shaped

Target

- Opposed
- Unopposed

Territory

- Goal
- Line

these three stages may be disastrous. Sensitivity to individual differences and student interactions is essential when grouping during the final stage. In addition, the physical educator not only needs to be cognizant of the discovery styles of teaching but also needs to be prepared to teach in an environment where students are given the freedom to make decisions relative to learning.

The Eclectic Model

The eclectic model, though probably not a *true* model, is included because it involves the framework adopted by most schools. This model is comprised of two or more of the models previously discussed. Siedentop (1994) indicates that this model works well in a program involving both required and elective content. For example, all students could be required to take a course developed within a health-related fitness model. But then students also have the freedom to choose elective courses developed within an academic discipline, sport education, and/or an adventure education model.

THE HIDDEN CURRICULUM

As stated earlier it is essential to objectively present those behaviors that physical educators want students to exhibit. In doing so it allows the physical educator the opportunity to better select the content and methodology for achieving these objectives. But a number of unplanned and unrecognized values exist that are taught and subsequently learned in a physical education environment. This has been called the *implicit curriculum* (Dodds, 1983) or the *hidden curriculum,* (Bain, 1975, 1976). Bain explains that students are repeatedly exposed to unconscious acts that are consistent in meaning. Examples of such acts include sex-role modeling by teachers, competition, and aestheticism (emphasis on physical beauty). Additional neglected values adapted from Melograno (1979) are shown in Table 3.13.

Jewett and Bain (1985) indicate that the primary concern—from an educational perspective—is that these acts, which communicate implicit values

TABLE 3.13 Neglected Values in an Implicit Curriculum

Asceticism—the amount of pain or suffering in the activity
Chance—the degree to which activity outcome(s) are affected by luck
Contact—the amount of physical contact
Cooperation—the degree of joint effort
Orderliness—the amount of routine in the activity
Restraint—the amount of control imposed by rules and/or boundaries
Social structure—the degree of interaction
Vertigo—the amount of risk taking

From *Designing Curriculum and Learning A Physical Coeducational Approach* by Vincent Melograno. Copyright 1979 by Kendall/Hunt Publishing Company.

to the student, may not be consistent with the explicit philosophy of the teacher and/or the school. Jewett and Bain provide the following example:

The physical educator believes explicitly that the treatment of students on the basis of individual differences (ability, race, sex, or social class) is inappropriate. During the early lessons of the basketball unit no problems exist. The individual and combined drills result in no differential treatment. However, during the unit-ending tournament no adjustment is made to consider individual differences. As a result, a more skilled student tends to dominate play. When such a distinction is allowed to continue and is unconsciously promoted, the less skilled students may question the implicit value of basketball, and physical education in general.

When developing the curriculum and teaching the content within the curriculum, it is important for the physical educator to be cognizant of the fact that this hidden curriculum exists and work to lessen its effect.

THE TEACHING DIMENSION

The value of any curriculum, regardless of the model(s) selected, depends on teacher effectiveness. It is beyond the scope of this text to delve into the procedures of how teachers should teach. This is more the charge of a methodology text. It is unrealistic, however, not to comment on this topic since curriculum and methodology are so closely linked.

Carefully developed program content and quality instruction in physical education present a tightly interwoven situation in which physical activity points toward motor development and the advancement of social skills and self concept. But this situation depends on the variety and duration of many in-class behaviors. Psychologist Carl Rogers (1969) clearly stated that students will learn only what they want to learn and that teachers are first and foremost provocateurs who set the stage for student learning. Siedentop, Mand, and Taggert (1986), assure that teachers are the backbone of education and effectiveness lies in their day-to-day teachings. The level of effectiveness is judged by student performance. This basic assumption exemplifies the need for a meaningful curriculum, clearly defined objectives, and carefully selected teaching strategies.

SUMMARY

1. Today's curriculum reformers face the challenge of providing a program that will meet both the needs and interests of all students. This challenge is compounded since today's students are vastly different from those of a generation ago.
2. Physical educators need to be aware of the at-risk students and implement effective programs for meeting their special needs since physical education has this potential.

3. Objectives move from general to specific to behavioral. The objectives closest to the student are behavioral and, when stated, should contain the task, the condition, and the criterion.
4. The National Association for Sport and Physical Education has published a list of benchmarks (competencies) by grade level to clarify what it means to be physically educated.
5. The physical education curriculum includes the experiences that fall between the objectives and the teaching methodology.
6. At the school level the curriculum can be organized using the separate subjects model, the broad fields model, or the humanistic model.
7. The developmental model is based on the premise that movement is a means of attaining developmental goals. The movement experiences included in this curriculum are selected relative to their ability to enhance the rate and quality of the student's total development.
8. The movement education model has become the basic alternative to the developmental model, utilizing a different teaching process.
9. The fitness model has shown renewed interest and is designed to produce students who are fit and know how to stay fit.
10. The academic discipline model, an answer to education reform, is designed to enhance cognitive development.
11. The personal-social developmental model, which is humanistic in foundation, has the sole objective of enhancing the student's social development.
12. The sport education model is designed to develop skillful sports participants.
13. The adventure education model provides challenges to the student in either a natural or teacher-designed environment.
14. The multi-activity model has skill acquisition as its primary objective since students are exposed to diverse activities.
15. The games for understanding model is based on the premise that games should be taught through a cognitive approach.
16. The eclectic model is composed of two or more of the physical education models.
17. The hidden curriculum is composed of unplanned and/or unrecognized values that are taught in the physical education curriculum.
18. Just as the teacher is the key to curriculum development, effective teaching is the key to learning.

QUESTIONS AND LEARNING ACTIVITIES

1. *Curriculum: Quest for Relevance* by William Van Til states his viewpoint that tomorrow's educated citizen will need more liberal education in the Greek sense of the word than ever before. Van Til thinks people will soon have the leisure to cultivate grace and beauty. Therefore, physical education should regain the place it had with the Greeks. How do you feel about this viewpoint?
2. Many professionals think a real need exists for improved accountability procedures in physical education. Some believe this can be accomplished by spelling

out, in precise terms, exactly what behaviors are expected of the student. Do you agree? Are there any problems inherent in this approach?

3. Write three specific objectives for each of the five general objectives for physical education.

4. Select a physical education activity and write a complete behavioral objective within the psychomotor, cognitive, and affective domains at the fifth-grade level. Select a different physical education activity and write a complete behavioral objective within the same three domains at the ninth-grade level.

5. Curriculum has been defined as being central to a student's education. Explain what is meant by this.

6. Interview a number of high school students. Find out what they like and dislike about their physical education programs.

7. Secure several recent state and/or local curriculum guides to see how their objectives are presented. Does each include general, specific, and behavioral objectives? Are concepts/outcomes/benchmarks more popular than objectives as a means of objectifying the program? Are there statements in the guide that attempt to alert teachers as how objectives are linked to evaluation practices?

8. If you were a K–6 physical educator, which physical education curriculum model would you use? Why?

9. If you were a grade 7–12 physical educator, which physical education curriculum model would you use? Why?

REFERENCES

Almond, L. (1983). Games making. *Bulletin of Physical Education, 19*(1), 25–32.

American Alliance for Health, Physical Education, and Recreation. (1981). *Basic stuff series I.* Washington, DC: AAHPERD.

American Alliance for Health, Physical Education, and Recreation. (1981). *Basic stuff series II.* Washington, DC: AAHPERD.

American Alliance for Health, Physical Education, and Recreation. (1987). *Basic stuff series I.* Washington, DC: AAHPERD.

American Alliance for Health, Physical Education, and Recreation. (1987). *Basic stuff series II.* Washington, DC: AAHPERD.

Annarino, A. A., Cowell, C. C., & Hazelton, H. W. (1986). *Curriculum theory and design in physical education.* Prospect Heights, IL: Waveland Press.

Austin, S., & Meister, G. (1990). *Responding to children at risk: A guide to recent reports.* Philadelphia: Research for Better Schools.

Bain, L. L. (1975). The hidden curriculum in physical education. *Quest, 24,* 92–101.

Bain, L. L. (1976). Description of the hidden curriculum in secondary physical education. *Research Quarterly, 47,* 154–160.

Bloom, B. S., Hastings, J. T., & Madaus, G. F. (1971). *Handbook on formative and summative evaluation of student learning.* New York: McGraw-Hill.

Bredikamp, S. (1992). What is developmentally appropriate and why is it important? *Journal of Health, Physical Education, Recreation, and Dance, 63*(6), 31–32.

Bruner, J. (1974). *The process of education.* New York: Vintage Books.

Bunker, D., & Thorpe, R. (1982). A model for the teaching of games in secondary schools. *Bulletin of Physical Education, 18,* 5–8.

Caldwell, S. F. (1972). Toward a humanistic physical education. *Journal of Health, Physical Education, and Recreation, 43*(3), 31–32.

Carroll, R. (1981). CSE in physical education: An evaluation. *Bulletin of Physical Education, 17,* 5–15.

Cheffers, J., & Evaul, T. (1978). *Introduction to physical education: Concepts of human movement.* Englewood Cliffs, NJ: Prentice-Hall.

Children's Defense Fund. (1992). *The state of America's children.* Washington, DC.

Csikszentmihalyi, M., & McCormack, J. (1986). The influence of teachers. *Phi Delta Kappan, 67,* 415–419.

Dodds, P. (1983). *Consciousness raising in curriculum: A teachers' model for analysis.* Paper presented at the Third Physical Education Curriculum Theory Conference, Athens, GA, February 10–12.

Ellis, M. (1983). *Similarities and differences in games: A system for classification.* Paper presented at the International AIESEP Congress.

Felshin, J. (1974). Cultural considerations for physical education. In G. H. McGlynn (ed.), *Issues in physical education and sports.* Palo Alto, CA: National Press Books.

Gallahue, D. L. (1996). *Developmental physical education for today's children.* Dubuque, IA: Brown & Benchmark.

Gibran, K. (1923). *The prophet.* New York: Alfred A. Knopf.

Harrow, A. J. (1972). *A taxonomy of the psychomotor domain.* New York: David McKay.

Hellison, D. R. (1973). *Humanistic physical education.* Englewood Cliffs, NJ: Prentice-Hall.

Hellison, D. R. (1978). *Beyond balls and bats.* Washington, DC: AAHPERD.

Hellison, D. R. (1982). Attitude and behavior change in the gym: The Oregon story. *The Physical Educator, 34*(2), 67–70.

Hellison, D. R. (1983). Teaching self-responsibility (and more). *Journal of Physical Education, Recreation, and Dance, 54*(8), 23.

Hellison, D. R. (1985). *Goals and strategies for teaching physical education.* Champaign, IL: Human Kinetics.

Hellison, D. R. & Templin, T. J. (1991). *A reflective approach to teaching physical education.* Champaign, IL: Human Kinetics.

Hopkins, C. T. (1941). *Interaction: The democratic process.* Lexington, MA: Heath.

Jagger, B. (1977). A characterization of physical education and human movement. In J. E. Kane (Ed.), *Movement studies and physical education.* London: Routledge & Kegan Paul.

Jewett, A. E., Bain, L. L., & Ennis, C. D. (1995). *The curriculum process in physical education.* Dubuque, IA: Brown & Benchmark.

Jewett, A. E., & Miller, M. E. (1977). *Curriculum design: Purposes and processes in physical education teaching-learning.* Washington, DC: AAHPERD.

Kirchner, G., & Fishburne, G. (1995). *Physical education for elementary school children.* Dubuque, IA: Brown & Benchmark.

Krathwohl, D. R., Bloom, B. S., & Masia, B. B. (1964). *Taxonomy of educational objectives: Handbook II affective domain.* New York: David McKay.

Kruger, H., & Kruger, J. (1982). *Movement education in physical education.* Dubuque, IA: Wm. C. Brown Company Publishers.

Laban, R., & Ullmann, L. (1960). *The mastery of movement.* London: McDonald & Evans.

Lawson, H. A., & Placek, J. H. (1981). *Physical education in the secondary schools.* Boston: Allyn & Bacon.

Levine, D. U. (1988). Teaching thinking to at-risk students: Generalizations and speculation. In B. A. Presseisen, (Ed.), *At-risk students and thinking: Perspectives from research.* Washington, DC: NEA/RBS.

Logsdon, B., Barrett, K., Ammons, M., Broer, M., Helverson, L., McKee, R., & Robertson, M. (1984). *Physical education for children: A focus on the teaching process.* Philadelphia: Lea & Febiger.

Mager, R. F. (1984). *Preparing instructional objectives.* Belmont, CA: Lake Publishing Company.

Masser, L. (1990). Teaching for affective learning in elementary physical education. *Journal of Physical Education, Recreation, and Dance, 62*(8), 18–19.

Melograno, V. J. (1996). *Designing the physical education curriculum.* Champaign, IL: Human Kinetics.

Mosston, M., & Ashworth, S. (1994). *Teaching physical education.* New York: Macmillan College Publishing Company.

National Association for Sport and Physical Education. (1992). *Outcomes of quality physical education programs.* Reston, VA: AAHPERD.

National Association for Sport and Physical Education. (1994). *National standards for physical education: A guide to content and assessment.* St. Louis, MO: Mosby.

Nixon, J. E., & Jewett, A. E. (1980). *An introduction to physical education.* Philadelphia: Saunders.

Peterson, N. L. (1987). *Early intervention for handicapped and at-risk children.* Denver, CO: Love Publishing Company.

Rogers, C. (1969). *Freedom to learn: A view of what education might become.* Columbus, OH: Merrill Publishing Company.

Siedentop, D. (1974). *The humanistic education movement: Some questions and issues in physical education and sports.* Mountain View, CA: National Press Books.

Siedentop, D. (1994). *Introduction to physical education, fitness, and sport.* Mountain View, CA: Mayfield.

Siedentop, D., Mand, C., & Taggart, A. (1986). *Physical education: Teaching and curriculum strategies for grades 5–12.* Mountain View, CA: Mayfield.

Smith, M. D. (1990). Enhancing self-responsibility through a humanistic approach to physical education. *Bulletin of Physical Education, 26*(3), 27–31.

Smith, M. D. (1992). Utilizing the games for understanding curriculum model at the elementary school level. *The Physical Educator, 48*(4), 184–187.

Smith, M. D. (1993). Utilizing different curriculum models to achieve the objectives of physical education. *Bulletin of Physical Education, 29*(1), 15–22.

Stillwell, J. L., & Reneau, P. (1992). A survey of state agency physical education curriculum material. *The Physical Educator, 49*(4), 170–173.

Swanson, M. S. (1991). *At-risk students in elementary education.* Springfield, IL: Charles C. Thomas.

Taylor, J., & Chiogioji, E. (1987). Implications of educational reform on high school programs. *Journal of Physical Education, Recreation, and Dance, 58*(2), 22–23.

Thomas, J. R., Lee, A. M., & Thomas, K. T. (1988). *Physical education for children: Concepts into practice.* Champaign, IL: Human Kinetics.

Werner, P., & Almond, L. (1990). Models of games education. *Journal of Physical Education, Recreation, and Dance, 61*(7), 23–27.

Williams, C., Varnes, J., Smith, C., Mack, C., Harageones, M., Holton, T., & Holyoak, O. (1983). Physical education requirement: FAHPERD recommendations for content specificity. *Florida Journal, 21*(3), 10–11, 20.

Wuest, D. A., & Bucher, C. A. (1995). *Foundations of physical education and sport.* St. Louis, MO: Mosby.

4

CURRICULUM PLANNING IN PHYSICAL EDUCATION

Outline

Curriculum Development
Factors Affecting Program Planning
Personal Factors
School Factors
Non-School Factors
State Requirements for Physical Education
Title IX
Public Law 94.142
Liability
Concept Approach to Curriculum Development
Selection and Balance in Program Planning
The Broad and Varied Program
Structuring for Quality

Outcomes

After reading and studying this chapter, you should be able to:
- Define
    Breach of duty
    Concept
    Damage
    Established duty
    Legal cause
    Legal liability
    Malfeasance
    Misfeasance
    Negligence
    Nonfeasance
    Public Law 94.142
    Student diversity
    Title IX
- Justify the need for a quality physical education curriculum.

- Identify the three categories of factors affecting curriculum development.
- Discuss the impact that Title IX has had on the physical education curriculum.
- Discuss the impact that Public Law 94.142 has had on the physical education curriculum.
- Discuss the impact that liability has had on the physical education curriculum.
- Discuss the three forms of negligence.
- Identify the four central questions to answer at the beginning of the curriculum development process.

Ted Williams (1969) said:

> I wanted to be the greatest hitter who ever lived. A man has to have goals, and that was mine, to have people say, "There goes Ted Williams, the greatest hitter who ever lived."

Ted Williams, at work, was an art form—his stance with the bat in his hand, the concentration, the swing, the follow-through—all were carefully engineered for the primary purpose of hitting a baseball out of the ballpark. For nineteen major league seasons, Williams planned ahead by studying pitchers, arranged special practice sessions, and casted an eye for anything that may give him an edge. He was a superb example of how planning can help achieve a goal. It is through planning that a person's objectives are best attained. It is through planning that a teacher of physical education appropriately selects and harmoniously arranges the goal-reaching movement experiences. The physical education content is very important for fully developing students. "For harmony," said the Greeks, "is the music of the Gods."

Although the term is used to identify a field of study, *curriculum* is more appropriately used to illustrate a plan for the education of learners. Such a plan is founded on theory, research, and past professional practice. It is designed for the purpose of achieving predetermined objectives. Otherwise, a limited, short-sighted approach to planning may occur. As a preventative, an orderly process of gathering, sorting, selecting, balancing, and synthesizing the relevant information from numerous sources is required.

The finest curriculum is always subject to change. Publius Syrus said in 42 B.C. that "It is a bad plan that admits of no modification." Admirable accomplishments in education often occur as the result of careful planning. In the long run, things left to chance seldom succeed. The Chinese philosopher Lao Tzu said in the affairs of men, there is a system. A reasonable plan for each community should be the near-at-hand objective. Begin gradually, run pilot programs, solicit comments, evaluate results, and then with this background of experience the physical education effort can safely be extended.

CURRICULUM DEVELOPMENT

Curriculum has been a consideration of educators for centuries, but the specialized and systematic study of curriculum did not truly occur until the twentieth century (Kliebaard, 1968). The roots of curriculum development date back to the days of Johan Friedrich Herbert (1776–1841), a German educator whose ideas were widely accepted in America. Herbert taught that learning required an orderly attention to the selection and organization of subject matter. Moreover, he applied his views to what is now called physical education, as well as to other educational fields. In fact, he was one of the early philosophers to recognize the essential nature of a properly conceived and structured program of physical activity.

Annarino, Cowell, and Hazelton (1986) indicate that a curriculum of public education is a product of socioeconomic forces. As a result it will find its fundamental philosophical purposes in the social and cultural sector in which it exists. The curriculum considerations of Hass (1987) includes a concern for social forces as reflected in social goals, cultural uniformity and diversity, social pressures, social change, future planning, and concepts of culture. It is apparent that, as a society, people could be improved through education. Perhaps the curriculum is the best medium to bring about this improvement.

Education, and specifically physical education, has reached a level of sophistication where serious thought must be given to a carefully reasoned and well designed curriculum for the learner—one that can replace the disjointed divisions of the past. In fact, Birch (1992) explains that curriculum development can be critical to any school program. A well planned, skillfully designed curriculum development process can produce not only meaningful content but also program support from administrators, colleagues, and parents.

A proper physical education curriculum accounts for the following things:

- It is conceived as an essential part of the total school effort.
- It reflects the nature and needs of a democratic society in which a respect for the interests and capacities of all individuals exists.
- It is organized into an unbroken flow of experiences, beginning with early childhood and extending through post-secondary education and later-life education.
- It is well balanced and affords varied experiences that will contribute to desirable outcomes for all age groups.
- It adheres to the philosophies, insights, major trends, methods, and materials of physical education in general.
- It is based on rigorous criteria for content selection.
- It is more than loosely related to the health and guidance programs of the school.
- It promotes and encourages professional growth to the instructional staff.
- It is associated in a number of significant ways with the community it serves.

Building a course of study for students from kindergarten to grade twelve should be a challenging undertaking. It should be an ideal occasion and an air of excitement and great expectation should prevail. On the other hand, if it is viewed as a red-tape procedure that is untimely, unwarranted and painfully uninteresting then the project is doomed to fail from the beginning. Moreover, the people involved in its preparation will probably show little enthusiasm for its implementation.

The procedures used in planning a physical education curriculum will vary from one setting to another but certain common concerns exist that need to be addressed. Tyler (1949) suggests that four central questions need to be addressed as the process of curriculum development begins.

- What educational purposes should the school seek to attain?
- What educational experiences can be provided that are likely to help attain their purposes?
- How can these educational experiences be effectively organized?
- How can people determine whether these purposes are being attained?

These questions provide a solid base in which the curriculum development process may begin and then proceed into this four step process for curricular development (see Figure 4.1).

Curriculum development is, fundamentally, a local responsibility that provides for definite advantages (Tyler, 1981). Some of these advantages include:

- Programs developed locally are more likely to meet the needs of the community.
- Program modifications and adjustments can be made more quickly on a local level.
- Program planning involvement will increase the educator's commitment to the program and its implementation.

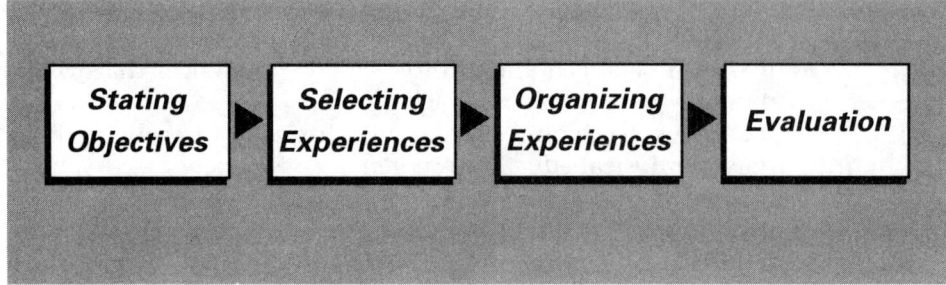

FIGURE 4.1 Four-Step Process for Curriculum Development

FACTORS AFFECTING PROGRAM PLANNING

Thomas, Lee, and Thomas (1988) state that although the selection of a rational, theoretical model—that is, developmental, movement education, or fitness—is necessary for a foundation, other conditions exist that must be considered. These conditions have been categorized and discussed by others.

Kruger and Kruger (1982) present an overview of the factors influencing curriculum planning in a question framework (see Figure 4.2). These factors can also be grouped into three categories as shown in Figure 4.3.

PERSONAL FACTORS

Personal factors deal with the learner. Since the program is ultimately designed for students, an understanding of their makeup is essential.

The topic on pupil growth and developmental characteristics is especially germane in the curriculum-construction process. Activities need to be selected that coincide with the physical/physiological, intellectual, social, and emotional behavior of children at specific age levels.

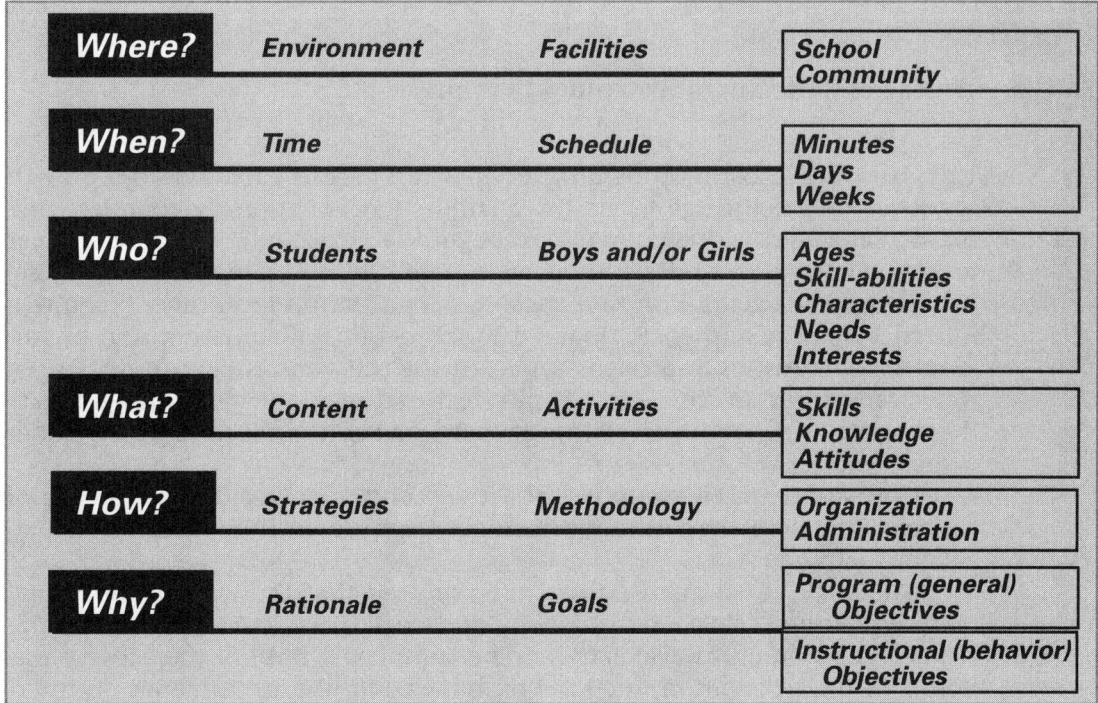

FIGURE 4.2 Factors Influencing Curriculum Planning

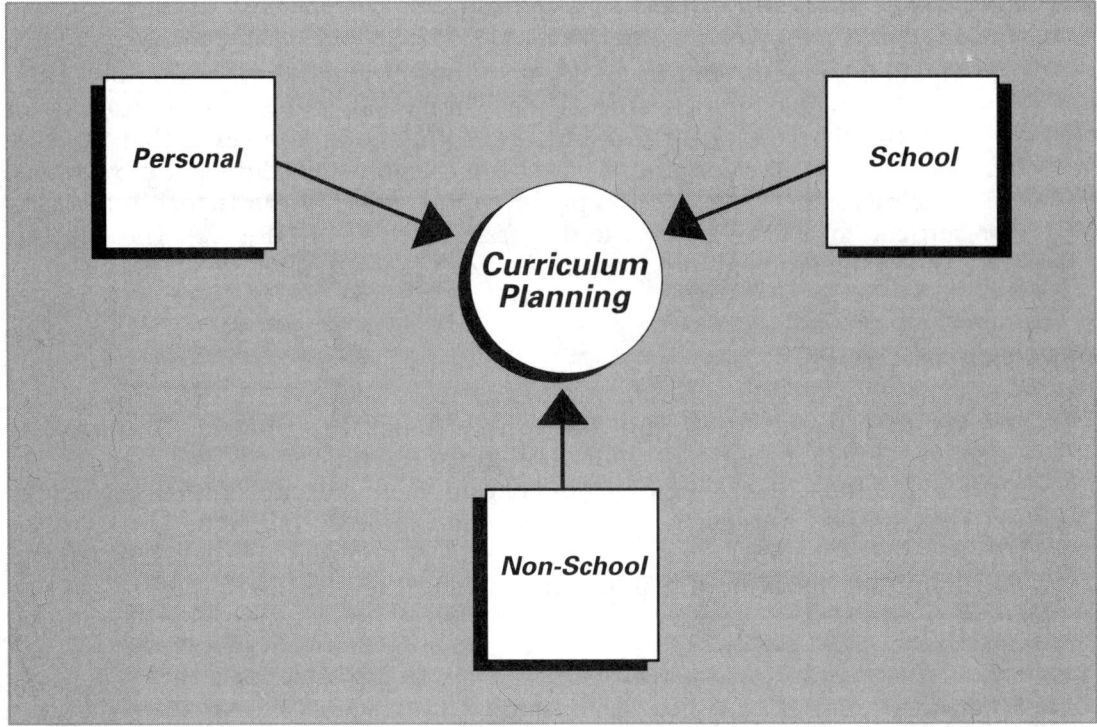

FIGURE 4.3 Factors Affecting Curriculum Planning

Growth is a continuous process. It is difficult to subdivide the growth period into specific age levels since children never abruptly complete one particular stage of development and begin the next. Moreover, a time never exists when all children in a class are at the same growth stage. Chronological age and physiological age (maturation level) may be quite a distance apart. Chapters 8, 9, and 10 provide a detailed description of student characteristics and needs set forth for the various age categories. In physical education, the level of physical maturity and development may have more to do with determining what to teach than it does in any other subject matter.

How students perceive physical activity and understanding the depth of interest can help shape the curriculum at any stage from kindergarten to senior high school.

Bain's (1979) study of perceptions, showed that the way an individual perceives fitness, aesthetic qualities, and social dynamics determines the value placed on a physical activity. The complexity level of the activity was also a factor. In addition, the level of maturation had an influence on interest. Therefore, a teacher can frequently gain first-hand information from watching students at play, listening as they talk with each other, and discussing student interests with parents and other teachers.

Students' interest can be used as a basis for establishing program content. Interest inventories are self report instruments in that students can express likes and dislikes for certain activities. An inventory instrument designed to measure the level of activity interest of secondary school students is shown in Figure 4.4. Surveying students' interests in this *personal factors approach* may lead to a more meaningful curriculum for students. Additional invaluable information may be gained from the addition of open-ended questions. By asking students to indicate what they like and dislike about physical education, the strengths and weaknesses of the program can be ascertained.

In addition to interests, students' motivations are important. Although motivations change, Cowell and France (1963) indicate that a number of motives remain consistent throughout elementary and secondary schools. These motives are shown in Tables 4.1 and 4.2.

One more source of information that can be used to guide program planning is the student data collected on selected measures in the physical domain (see Chapter 12). This data may include the student's medical status and such measures as posture and fitness assessment.

A significant change in recent years has been in student diversity—a range of differences among students. Before physical educators approach curriculum change, they need to accept that differences *do* exist. More importantly, educators need to understand these differences and the implications these differences present for the curriculum. Jewett, Bain, and Ennis (1995) indicate that categories of student diversity include race, gender, social class, and style of learning. These authors provide both a complete discussion of each category and the effect on the learning of motor skills in their text.

McCarthy (1990) warns that issues of diversity are generally looked at independently. Often times a combination of two or more of these categories may not only hinder a student's learning but also adversely affect the opportunity to learn. The following example provides a clear situation. Diane was a ninth grade student with a strong desire to participate in high school football. While making this desire known, because of gender, she had to endure ridicule not only from her peers but also from the coach who expressed an unwillingness to work with her. In addition, she could not afford the participation fee. As a result, Diane experienced a *double oppression* due to both gender and social class.

Too often, physical educators do not view students as an important factor in curriculum planning. The previous discussion makes it apparent that information about and from students is invaluable for this purpose.

SCHOOL FACTORS

The school, as a social institution, is the primary agency responsible for the education of today's children. As a result, its influence on curriculum planning is extremely important. Therefore, a complete understanding of its organizational characteristics is essential if both the planning and the implementation

Name: _____ Age: _____

Sex: _____ Grade: _____

Instructions: After each activity listed, place an "X" in the column that best indicates your interest in the activity. If you enjoy the activity, place an "X" in the *Strong Interest* column. If you do not enjoy the activity, place an "X" in the *No Interest* column. An "X" in the middle column indicates uncertainty about whether you enjoy the activity or not.

Activity	Strong Interest	Unsure	No Interest
Archery			
Badminton			
Basketball			
Bicycling			
Bowling			
Dance—Folk			
Dance—Modern			
Dance—Square			
Fencing			
Field hockey			
Flag football			
Floor hockey			
Golf			
Gymnastics			

FIGURE 4.4 Physical Education Activity Interest Inventory

Adapted from Straub, W. (1976). *The lifetime sports oriented physical education program.* Figure 2.1. Reprinted by permission of Prentice-Hall, Englewood Cliffs, NJ.

Activity	Strong Interest	Unsure	No Interest
Handball			
Hiking			
Horseshoes			
Judo			
Karate			
Lacrosse			
Orienteering			
Shuffleboard			
Skating—Ice			
Skating—Roller			
Soccer			
Softball			
Swimming			
Table tennis			
Tennis			
Track and field			
Volleyball			
Weight training			
Wrestling			
Other			

FIGURE 4.4 *Continued*

TABLE 4.1 Possible Physical Education Motives, Ages 6–12 Years

- Love of activity, motion, hunting, climbing, chasing, fighting.
- Idealizes others; wishes to emulate and be like those he/she loves.
- Highly imaginative and curious; will try many things.
- Function pleasure; pleasurable sensory feeling and sheer joy by using muscles and in testing budding capabilities.
- Expression of independence and self-assertion; is daring and adventurous.
- Pride in performance; pride in growth and development.
- Pleasurable feeling from sense of mastery and achievement.
- Group status and social recognition due to values placed on health, physical development, and game skills in a given culture.
- Rational understanding of the relationship between health and physical education practices; satisfies many of the motives implied above. (This is a gradual progressive process starting with nursery school.)

of the curriculum is to be successful. Jewett and Bain (1985) provide a list for guiding the analysis of the educational agency (see Figure 4.5).

The selection of activities to include in a physical education curriculum is affected by a variety of school factors. These factors include the following:

- Facilities
    - Indoor
    - Outdoor
- Equipment
    - Commercial
    - Homemade
- Budget allocation
- Time allotment
    - Days per week
    - Minutes per day

TABLE 4.2 Possible Physical Education Motives, Ages 13–18 Years

- Desire to understand the scientific bases (the *why*) behind health and physical education activities.
- Interest in growth, development, and the physiological changes of puberty.
- Interest in the opposite sex.
- Desire to be liked by classmates; sense of belonging.
- Desire for group status and acceptance of prescribed values of the group or gang.
- Seek for self-discovery, self-testing, self-realization, and self-assertion.
- Satisfaction of desire for mastery and achievement.
- Affection for those whom one admires and respects.
- Excitement, adventure, and new experiences.
- The sheer joy of the game itself; the wholesome pleasure, richer personal contacts, and friendships it makes possible.

Power and Authority
- Who are the people that have power?
- To what extent is that power seen as legitimate by others?
- Is the authority of teachers sole-determined (based on position), professional (based on expertise), or personal (based on *charm*)?

Structure
- What are the characteristics of the members of the organization (age, gender, socioeconomic background, etc.)?
- What are the formal and informal sub-groups in the organization (classes, clubs, teams, teachers' organizations, etc.)?
- How tightly controlled are the sub-groups?
- How much autonomy do the members have?

Control and Sanctions
- What student behaviors do teachers consider acceptable and unacceptable?
- What behaviors do students consider acceptable and unacceptable?
- What rewards are given for acceptable behavior?
- How is unacceptable behavior treated?

Cohesiveness
- What is the attitude of teachers and students toward the institution? Toward the sub-groups?
    Committed—strong loyalty and support
    Calculative—plays the game in order to get along
    Alienated—negative and hostile
- What are the rituals and symbols used to increase cohesiveness?

FIGURE 4.5 Agency Analysis

From Jewett A. E., and Bain, L. I. *The curriculum process in physical education.* Copyright © 1985 Wm. C. Brown Communications, Dubuque, IA. All Rights Reserved. Reprinted by permission.

- Faculty
    Gender
    Expertise
- Class size
- Class composition
    Coeducational
    Noncoeducational
- Administrative policy
    School board
    Departmental

NON-SCHOOL FACTORS

Non-school factors include items such as state and federal policy, evidence of contemporary curricular trends, and perhaps the most important—the community. A careful analysis (see Figure 4.6) of the values, beliefs, and behaviors of the community in which the program will be implemented can prove

What Are the Physical Characteristics of the Community?
- Find a map of the community and mark the boundaries of the area from which clients are drawn. Identify areas that are primarily residential or commercial.
- Are the residential areas single-family homes or multiple-family dwellings?
- Do residents rent or own?
- Mark the location on the map of schools, parks, recreation facilities, libraries, and shopping.
- How readily can residents get to and from these facilities?
- Is public transportation available?

Who Lives in the Community?
- What is the age distribution of the residents?
- What is the ethnic and racial heritage of the residents?
- What languages are spoken?
- Describe the educational background and religious affiliations of the residents.
- How transient is the population?

What Is the Economic Base of the Community?
- Where do community residents work?
- Who are the major employers?
- What kinds of jobs do the residents have?
- What is the average income?
- Do most households have one or more than one person employed?
- What is the rate of unemployment?
- What kind of financial support is provided for public schools?
    Private schools?
    Other educational agencies?
    Recreational agencies?
    Health services?

What Is the Political System in the Community?
- What is the form of local government?
- Who holds the power?
- Describe the political voting patterns of the areas.
- Do residents belong to community action groups?
    Unions?
    Other organizations with political goals?

What Is the Culture in the Community?
- What are the popular recreational activities of residents?
- Where do residents *hang out*?
- Who are the neighborhood heroes?
- What things are the residents proud of?
- What do the residents apologize for?
- What do the residents disapprove of?
- What do the residents hope for?
- How much crime occurs?
- Are people fearful of crime?
- How are outsiders viewed by residents?

FIGURE 4.6 Community Analysis

From Jewett A. E. and Bain, L. I. (1985). *The curriculum process in physical edcuation.* Copyright © 1985 Wm. C. Brown Communications, Dubuque, IA. All Rights Reserved. Reprinted by permision.

beneficial since these aspects have implications for planning (Jewett & Bain, 1985). What a community considers as school objectives and the attitude of parents toward the particular physical education objectives have a bearing on the development of any worthwhile program. Moreover, the concerns of both parents and community leaders cannot be underestimated as one attempts to determine what to plan for and what to teach.

The availability of community resources may affect the curriculum and thereby should be considered when planning a curriculum in physical education. Possible resources include the following:

- *Facilities* such as bowling lanes, swimming pools, and golf courses are often times available at little or no expense. To better plan, a survey of community resources is recommended. Figure 4.7 is a modification of an inventory form developed by Straub (1976).
- *Personnel* refers to individuals available to complement the program by serving as guest speakers, paraprofessionals, or part-time instructors.

STATE REQUIREMENTS FOR PHYSICAL EDUCATION

Laws made at the state level govern how much subject matter is required in American schools. As a result, the yearly and daily requirements for physical education differ markedly. For example, the National Association for Sport and Physical Education (1993) reported that three years after the federal government established daily physical education for all students K–12 as a physical activity and fitness goal, Illinois remains the only state requiring daily physical education. Six years after Congress passed *Resolution 97* encouraging state and local governing bodies to provide *quality* physical education programs, only thirteen states require elementary physical education specialists to teach elementary school physical education. More than half of the states either have no requirements for physical education or require only one year in grades 9–12.

TITLE IX

The *Title IX of the Education Amendments* was passed by Congress in June, 1972. The provision indicated that no person, on the basis of sex, be excluded from participation in, be denied the benefits of, or be subjected to discrimination under any program or activity receiving federal funding. Title IX has had a profound national impact because nearly every school in the United States receives some form of federal financial assistance. By law all U.S. schools were required to complete a self-study during 1975–1976 to (a) identify areas of noncompliance and (b) develop strategies for full compliance by 1978. Durrant (1992) indicates that the result of this mandated self-study has been the identification and correction of various inequities. Title IX had no

Part I: Facilities

Evaluator: _____ Date: _____

Community: _____

Instructions: Place an "X" if the facility may be available in your community or in near-by-communities.

	Indoor	Outdoor
Archery range	_____	_____
Badminton courts	_____	_____
Bicycle paths	_____	_____
Boating marina	_____	_____
Boccie courts	_____	_____
Bowling lanes	_____	_____
Camping area	_____	_____
Curling area	_____	_____
Dance studio	_____	_____
Deck tennis courts	_____	_____
Fencing area	_____	_____
Golf course	_____	_____
Golf driving range	_____	_____
Handball/racquetball courts	_____	_____
Hiking trails	_____	_____
Horseback riding stable	_____	_____
Lake area	_____	_____
Miniature golf course	_____	_____
Orienteering course	_____	_____
Rifle range	_____	_____
Sailing marina	_____	_____
Shuffleboard courts	_____	_____
Skating—Ice rink	_____	_____
Skating—Roller rink	_____	_____
Squash courts	_____	_____
Ski—Cross country paths	_____	_____
Ski—Downhill slopes	_____	_____
Swimming pool	_____	_____
Tennis courts	_____	_____
Weight-training facility	_____	_____
Others	_____	_____

FIGURE 4.7 Community Resource Inventory

Part II: Detailed Facilities Analysis

Instructions: Carefully complete each of the following statements.

Name of facility: _____

Address: _____

1. What type(s) of activities can be taught in this facility? _____
2. What is the distance between the facility and the school? _____ miles
3. Owner of facility: _____
   Telephone number: _____
4. Manager of facility: _____
   Telephone number: _____
5. Cost for use of the facility: $_____
6. Number of people facility may accommodate: _____
7. Equipment or supplies available: _____
8. Days and times in which facility may be utilized: _____
9. Safety factors:
   a. Are there any hazards that may result in injuries to students?   yes   no
      Comment(s): _____
   b. Are the exits properly marked and readily accessible to building occupants?
      yes   no
      Comment(s): _____
10. Are alcoholic beverages sold on the premises?   yes   no
    Comment(s): _____
11. Does the owner(s) have insurance coverage?   yes   no
    Comment(s): _____

Summary: What is the desirability of utilizing this facility for class instructional and/or intramural purposes?

_____
_____
_____
_____

FIGURE 4.7 *Continued*

Straub, W.B. (1996). *The lifetime sports-oriented physical education program,* Figure. 2.3. Reprinted by permission of Prentice-Hall, Englewood Cliffs, NJ.

Play was made for all children.

mandate for specific curriculum content, but it does state that equal access for boys and girls to the physical education curriculum be maintained.

In addition to these legal implications, Siedentop (1994) indicates that moral implications exist and these are more profound. To act merely to comply with the mandate is one thing, but to do it because it is the right thing to do is another.

PUBLIC LAW 94.142

In 1975 Congress passed the *Education for All Handicapped Children Act* (a more complete discussion of this topic appears in Chapter 10). Its passage ensures a free, appropriate public education including physical education for all exceptional children. If at all possible, it is recommended that students be educated in the regular physical education program. However, specialized programming must be provided if necessary.

LIABILITY

Teachers act *in loco parentis,* that is, in place of the parent. In doing so a legal responsibility called *liability* is assumed for students. Legal liability is incurred through negligence, a failure to act as a reasonably careful and prudent person would act. The three types of negligence are shown in Figure 4.8.

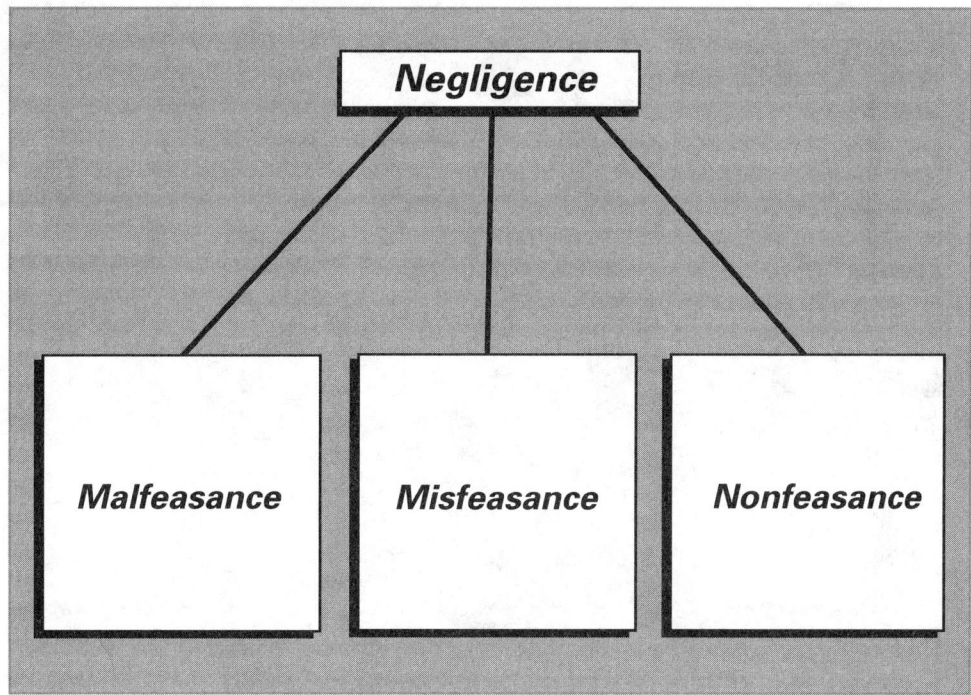

FIGURE 4.8 Types of Negligence

Malfeasance refers to committing an unlawful act. Examples include failing to comply with Public Law 94.142, using unauthorized corporal punishment, or discriminating against a student because of sex, length of hair, or religious beliefs.

Misfeasance refers to improperly performing a lawful act. In other words, the teacher acts lawfully, but not up to reasonable standards of behavior as described by law. Examples include not following school policy when providing for an injured student, using incorrect first aid procedures, or using improper spotting techniques.

Nonfeasance is failing to perform a required act. It is called an act of omission, that is, failing to do what is deemed legally necessary. Examples include failing to provide a spotter in a gymnastic activity, failing to provide first aid following an injury, or failing to allow students to wear protective equipment in a softball lesson.

Four elements of negligence (see Figure 4.9) must be proven for a teacher and/or school district to be liable. Established duty is an obligation that the teacher has to each student. It requires the teacher to (a) anticipate the foreseeable risks in an activity, (b) provide a warning relative to these risks, (c) take reasonable steps to prevent injury, (d) provide comfort and aid to an injured student, and (e) prevent an increase in the severity of the injury (Kirchner & Fishburne, 1995).

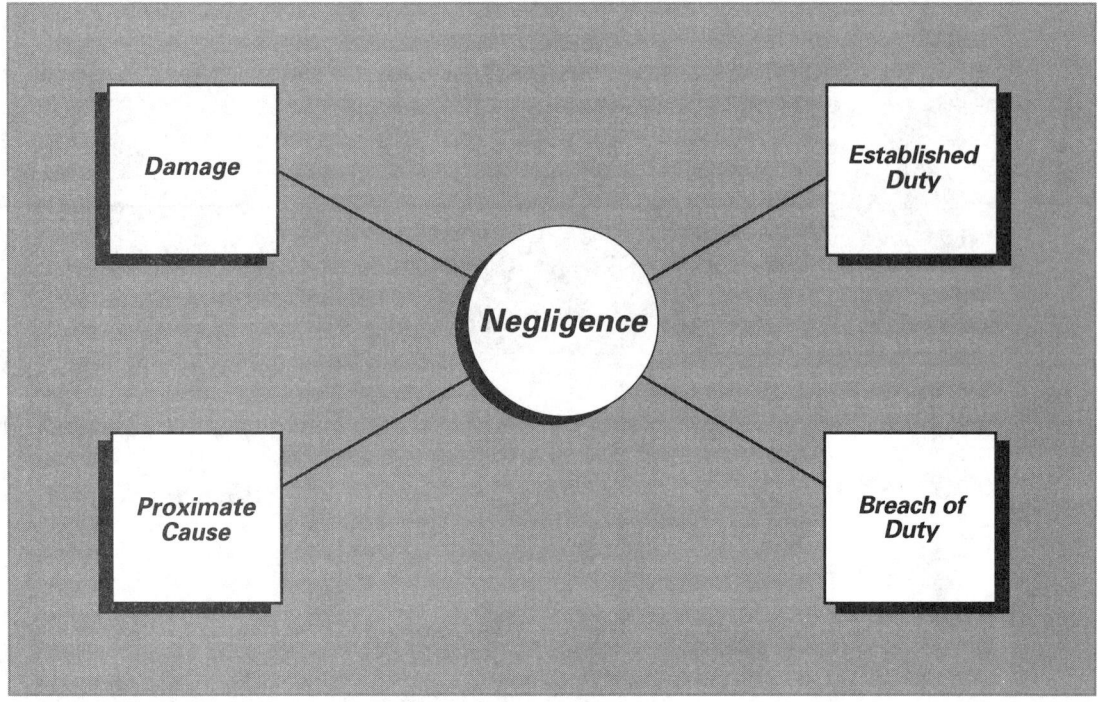

FIGURE 4.9 Elements of Negligence

Breach of duty is explained as the teacher failing to conform to the standards of behavior. This breach can occur in one of two ways:

- A wrongful act—doing something one should not have done.
- A failure to act—not doing something one should have done.

Proximate cause must be determined if a breach of duty has been proven. A relationship must exist between the teacher's behavior and the injury incurred.

Damage refers directly to the injury. The question that needs to be answered in proving damage is did the injury occur while the student was under the supervision of a teacher?

This avoidance of negligence or the fear of legal action can, and often times does, have an impact on curriculum planning. The selection of activities is, in part, made relative to safety. In fact, activities are occasionally excluded from a physical education program because of perceived liability risks (Siedentop, 1994).

CONCEPT APPROACH TO CURRICULUM DEVELOPMENT

A concept is a generalization about something. It is usually built from a number of related sensations, precepts, and images. Engelman (1969) explains that concepts are both interesting and elusive because they are present in the educational setting yet difficult to measure, quantify, and discuss.

Concepts range from ideas about very simple things to high-level abstractions. A definition phrased for curriculum planning states that a concept is a relatively complete and meaningful idea in the mind of a person. In other words, a concept is a meaning attached to something and an understanding of something. To the student a concept is a personal organization of numerous interpretations of things to which he/she has been exposed. The concepts approach provides a means of enriching the students' lives physically, cognitively, and effectively with the focus on improving fundamental movement skills and not just on the playing of games (Stevens, 1994).

When attempting to teach a concept the dilemma signifying the inability to give the student the concept directly exists. At best, the teacher can only verbally describe the concept. So rather than teaching a concept, the teaching should be directed toward the concept. Therefore the instructor is working with students in terms of whole ideas even through bits of knowledge and skills are being employed along the way. Specifically, the concept approach to learning is one in which all facts, rules, and skills are centrally related.

For too many years, teachers of physical education have taught isolated facts, rules, and skills in nearly the same fashion that history teachers have taught people, places, and dates. The student learned facts by rote memorization or repetition without seeing them as part of a whole—a part of his/her life. Certainly, the facts did not become a part of the student's value system. The historical dates and places were soon forgotten and the physical education facts, rules, and skills were relegated to the formative years and not carried into adult life.

The concept approach offers the program planner a realistic pattern for the development of physical education curriculum content. Jewett, Bain, and Ennis (1995) state that a concept-based curriculum has the following four characteristics:

- The content to be taught is directly related to the physical education body of knowledge.
- Students learn content from this body of knowledge.
- Students are encouraged to ask *why*, to ask movement questions, and to develop unique solutions to movement problems.
- Students are taught how to accept personal responsibility for learning.

If the activities planned for the physical education curriculum are to carry over from one grade level to another and eventually into adult life, then they need to relate to the individual as a whole person and to our expanding society. The exercises, games, sports, and dances must be related not only to the individual student but to the family and the community at large. In addition, the student needs to develop an understanding of (a) why movement is important in maintaining a healthy lifestyle and (b) how to move skillfully.

The concepts approach is a means of helping curriculum builders put together a program that will provide students with a more complete understanding of what it is they are to learn. For example, when square dancing is planned for a seventh grade physical education class it should consist of more than just the music and dance figures. Just as important is planning a discussion relative to the following questions:

- Is the dance appropriate or of interest to seventh graders?
- Is the dance of cultural importance?
- Is the dance done in the community?
- Can the dance be done by a family?

SELECTION AND BALANCE IN PROGRAM PLANNING

Contributing to the lack of agreement on what to include in the physical education program is the obvious fact so many possible activities choices exist than can ever be implemented. As a person scans the extensive list of activities (see Figure 4.4), from archery to wrestling, it becomes obvious that only those activities most appropriate for a given situation can be considered. The problem is further complicated by noting that an increasing number of activities to choose from exists today. Thirty years ago coeducational instruction was rare. Bowling and golf were completely outside the realm of a physical education program, as were such nontraditional activities as bicycling and roller skating.

What to select and how long to teach each selection are real questions. "Six weeks for volleyball," is how one course of study is stated. "Eight weeks of gymnastics," is how another reads. How was this determined? In relation to this are the following issues:

- The sequence of physical education activities in a school year.
- The sequence of physical education activities over a span of several years.
- The problem of the comprehensive curriculum, which attempts to do a little bit of everything all in one year.
- The question of the repetitious curriculum that continues from year to year without change or innovation.
- The relationship of the curriculum parts to the whole; for example, how much teaching of game skills should be conducted as physical education class work and how much should be covered in the intramural program?
- The requirements for a broad and varied curriculum.

THE BROAD AND VARIED PROGRAM

The development of a broad and varied program of physical education activities, although theoretically sound, is not an easy task. When discussed, certain questions come up:

- How can the school provide a balanced program of physical activity amid various pressures for specialization?
- How comprehensive can a program of physical education be when many teachers have one or two favorite activities they like to stress, frequently at the expense of other meaningful, high interest activities?
- How often have students said:
  — All we do is play basketball. Can't we be taught something else?
  — All we do is exercise. Why can't we do more activity?
  — All our physical educator does is teach soccer all fall. I wish we could learn something new.

In extolling the value of physical education many professionals have carefully indicated that only a broad and varied program will appeal to all students. Programs are adequate when the variety of interests, needs, and abilities of both boys and girls is considered. This suggests a necessity for variety, including individual and self-testing activities, dual activities, rhythmics, and team sports that provide both vigorous and challenging experiences.

The issue of balance is as old as the species. To make full use of human resources is always a basic consideration. Achieving harmony in physical education is not easy especially at a time when there are powerful forces crying for more attention to items such as movement exploration and physical fitness. These activities must be properly focused on so that an orchestration of many powers may be achieved.

Although not all worthwhile physical education activities can be included in the curriculum, efforts must be made to combine the concepts and competencies of those activities that have been included. For example, combining several rhythmical activities in an elementary curriculum may be accomplished by selecting unifying elements from several rhythmic skills and dances to produce an adequate experience and still provide time in the total program for content that may have previously been eliminated.

In the area of ball-handling skills, for example, numerous combinations can be considered while others can be omitted so that some other kind of physical education activity can be placed in the time frame assigned to the program. Therefore, all kinds of ball-handling skills for a particular grade level will be reviewed in an effort to combine common elements. Then when ball skills are employed in lead-up games, careful attention can be given to the select two or three skills. When this kind of planning is done for all parts of the program, including existing programs under revision, it may be possible to find time for a variety of activities. For example, touch football would no longer have to be played exclusively from September to November, or basketball exclusively from December to March, or softball exclusively from April to June.

Unfortunately, in many parts of the country, local schools put a physical education curriculum together piecemeal. It is common to find programs at a middle school or junior high school level that are merely thrown together, consisting of a little of this and a little of that. This problem is compounded for schools in which elementary and secondary school districts are organized and administered separately.

Broad and varied programs can be developed when physical education personnel and administrators see the need. Too often physical education programs lack breadth because the majority of the budget, staff time, and even class time are devoted to interscholastic sports. Physical education programs will continue to suffer as long as athletics are the primary concern of the school. In theory, this situation should not exist. A number of school systems exist where programs are very unbalanced.

STRUCTURING FOR QUALITY

Although the primary purpose of this book is to be concerned with activities and their organization in the physical education program, it is almost impossible to avoid teaching methodology. Ultimately, the wisdom in choosing an activity and the talent in teaching it go together. Keeping this in mind is essential when quality programs are being developed.

Being physically educated means the ability to use the body efficiently. However, too often the degree of recreation engaged in is directly proportional to the level of physical skill possessed for a given activity. This is vividly noticeable when a person considers that Americans are not exclusively sports spectators but first-degree participants when they have the abilities. Furthermore, knowledge and ability in a sport produce the best kind of spectators—bright, sophisticated observers who express judgment as a result of experiences. Participants and spectators, alike, seek excellence. Both are interested not only in scores, reputations, and action but also in quality of performance.

Because of inadequate planning, loose programming, and ineffective teaching, thousands of school children have missed learning the fundamental movement and basic game skills at an adequate level to experience a successful feeling. The level of exposure and concentration in these skills has been low. The actual learning period has been so shallow that only the idea of the skill has been brought up, with little opportunity provided to put muscles through their paces. The chance to practice physical skills and slowly perfect them has been treated too lightly. When physical education skills are properly learned the lasting value takes the form of a solid kinesthetic experience, the kind of learning that provides the student with a deep appreciation for the skills. It is this warm feeling for the skilled movement that furnishes the drive to engage in it again and again, perhaps throughout a lifetime.

SUMMARY

1. In this time of accountability, a thoroughly planned and designed physical education curriculum is a necessity.

2. Factors affecting curriculum development fall into one of three categories—personal, school, and non-school.
3. Because of the diversity among students, an understanding of their growth changes, characteristics, needs, and interests are essential when developing a physical education curriculum.
4. School factors affecting curriculum development include budget, facilities, time allotments, teaching faculty, class size, class composition, and administrative policy.
5. Non-school factors affecting curriculum development include state and federal policy/law, contemporary trends, and community.
6. Title IX has increased the sport and physical education opportunities for girls and women.
7. Public Law 94.142 mandated the physical education opportunities for all exceptional children.
8. Increased public awareness relative to legal liability has had an impact on curriculum planning.
9. The concepts approach to curriculum development helps provide students with a more complete understanding of what is to be learned.
10. To best meet the varied needs and interests of a diverse student body, a broad and varied program is recommended.

QUESTIONS AND LEARNING ACTIVITIES

1. In the last several years, curriculum changes have been more widespread and intensive than at any time in the history of U.S. schools. Are these changes in the curriculum really significant? Do children learn better in the new programs than they did in the old ones? Have curriculum modifications been made because it was popular to do so? Suggest ways of finding out how valuable changes occurred in a school.

2. Can a strong case be made for a national curriculum of physical education? What are the strengths and weaknesses of such a curriculum? Would you follow such a model if you had one?

3. React to the following statements:
   a. Planning the physical education curriculum with the instructors is far superior to planning for them.
   b. Planning is essentially an administrative function calling for energetic leadership.

4. *Education* is a means of improving society and the *curriculum* is the medium to bring about such improvement. Do you agree or disagree with this statement? Justify your decision.

5. Using Tyler's questioning approach to curriculum development, answer his four questions for a contemporary, large, multicultural, inner-city school and for a small, homogenous, rural school.

6. It has been said that the teacher of physical education is the *key* to curriculum development. Explain this view.

7. What specific community characteristics may have an impact on the curriculum development process?

8. Explain how you might go about amending a secondary school physical education curriculum that was heavily game-centered.

9. Consider the meaning of the word *innovation*. Read what some general educators have had to say about it, discuss it with your colleagues; and then try to respond to the following questions:

   a. Is movement education a form of innovation in physical education?
   b. Is substituting lacrosse for spring football practice an example of program innovation?
   c. Are there examples of innovation you can suggest that may be appropriate for junior high school?

REFERENCES

Annarino, A. A., Cowell, C. C., & Hazelton, H. W. (1986). *Curriculum theory and design in physical education*. Prospect Heights, IL: Waveland Press.

Bain, L. L. (1979). Perceived characteristics of selected movement activities. *Research Quarterly, 50,* 565–573.

Birch, D. A. (1992). Improving leadership skills in curriculum development. *Journal of School Health, 62*(1), 27–28.

Cowell, C. C., & France, W. L. (1963). *Philosophy and principles of physical education*. Englewood Cliffs, NJ: Prentice-Hall.

Durrant, S. M. (1992). Title IX: Its power and its limitations. *Journal of Physical Education, Recreation, and Dance, 63*(3), 60–64.

Engelman, S. (1969). *Conceptual learning*. Sioux Falls, SD: Adapt Press.

Hass, G. (1987). *Curriculum planning: A new approach*. Boston: Allyn & Bacon.

Jewett, A. E., & Bain, L. L. (1985). *The curriculum process in physical education*. Dubuque, IA: Brown & Benchmark.

Jewett, A. E., Bain, L. L., & Ennis, C. D. (1995). *The curriculum process in physical education*. Dubuque, IA: Brown & Benchmark.

Kirchner, G., & Fishburne, G. (1995). *Physical education for elementary school children*. Dubuque, IA: Brown & Benchmark.

Kliebard, H. (1968). The curriculum field in retrospect. In Paul W. F. Witt, (Ed.), *Technology and the curriculum*. New York: Teachers College Press.

Kruger, H., & Kruger, J. (1982). *Movement education in physical education*. Dubuque, IA: Wm. C. Brown Company Publishers.

McCarthy, C. (1990). Race and education in the United States: The multicultural solution. *Interchange, 21,* 45–55.

National Association for Sport and Physical Education. (1993). *Shape of the nation 1993: A survey of state physical education requirements*. Reston, VA: AAHPERD.

Siedentop, D. (1994). *Introduction to physical education, fitness, and sport*. Mountain View, CA: Mayfield.

Stevens, D. A. (1994). Movement concepts: Stimulating cognitive development in elementary students. *Journal of Physical Education, Recreation, and Dance, 65*(8), 16–23.

Straub, W. B. (1976). *The lifetime sports-oriented physical education program*. Englewood Cliffs, NJ: Prentice-Hall.

Thomas, J. R., Lee, A. M., & Thomas, K. T. (1988). *Physical education for children: Concepts into practice*. Champaign, IL: Human Kinetics.

Tyler, R. W. (1949). *Basic principles of curriculum and instruction*. Chicago: University of Chicago Press.

Tyler, R. W. (1981). Curriculum development since 1900. *Educational Leadership, 35,* 598–601.

Updyke, W. F. (1994). Fitness trends in a large population of 6–10 year old children. *Summary report of the Chrysler-AAU physical fitness testing program.* Bloomington, IN: Amateur Athletic Union.

Williams, Ted, & Underwood, J. (1969). *My Turn at Bat: The Story of my life.* New York: Simon & Schuster.

5
RESEARCH AND CURRICULUM CHANGE

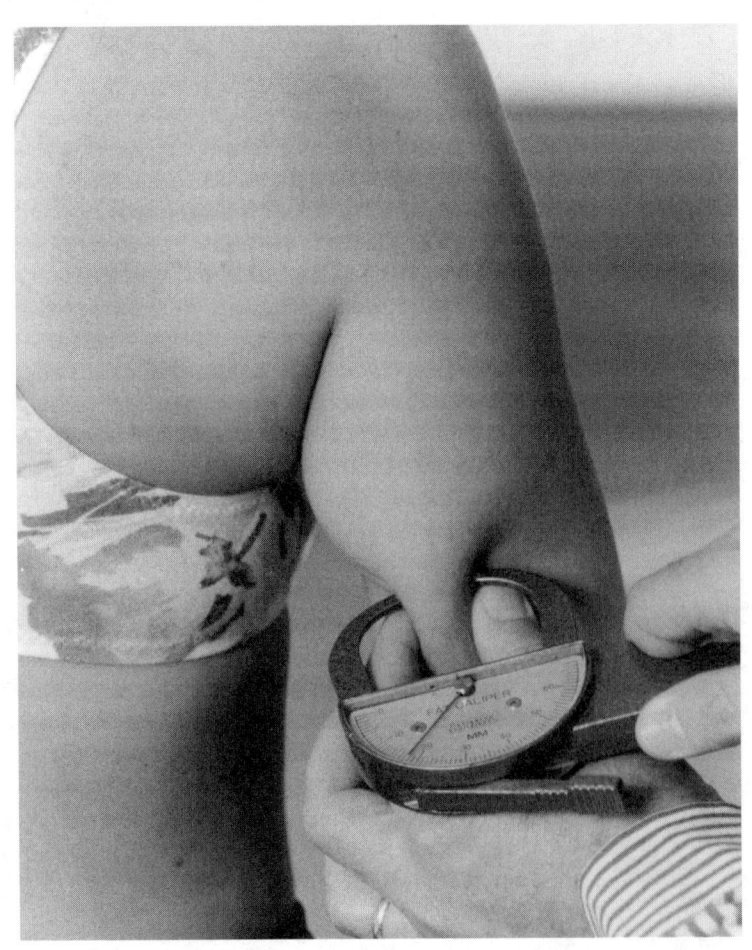

Outline

To Change or Not to Change
Curriculum Reform
Curriculum Research in Physical Education
Outside Influences
Local Assessment

Outcomes

After reading and studying this chapter, you should be able to:
- Define
  Curriculum reform
  Curriculum research
  Reform
  Research
- Discuss AAHPERD's purpose and identify its six member associations.
- Discuss how a physical educator's resistance to change can affect curriculum reform.
- Discuss how a physical educator's eagerness to change can affect curriculum reform.
- Explain why professionals are reluctant to become involved in curriculum research.
- Identify a variety of professional periodicals and journals.
- Identify a variety of professional organizations.
- Analyze selected research studies to determine how they may impact curriculum change.

Everything is a result of change. This statement embodies an essential consideration that is the basis for program development in physical education. In other words, change is inevitable and to face the educational implications arising from change is to also change.

Change is undoubtedly necessary; as society changes so do students and their needs and interests. In order for today's schools and the varied programs in these institutions to survive, especially in times of diminishing resources and overt criticism, these schools and the programs in them must also change. This precept embodies the essential consideration underlying program development, program evaluation, and/or program revision. This is especially true for physical education.

TO CHANGE OR NOT TO CHANGE

Two concerns need to be discussed when facing change. The first concern is the educator's *resistance* to change; and the second factor is the educator's *eagerness* to change.

Why don't we want to change? Shirley Jackson's short story, "The Lottery," portrays villagers who hold a lottery each year to decide whom they will stone to death. One character asks the villagers why they continue to carry out this inhumane ritual year after year. An elder quiets this inquisitive villager by answering "Because we have always had a lottery." For the same reason that Tevya continued to "fiddle on the roof," a tradition was being upheld.

This is also the case with a variety of physical education practices including inappropriate curriculum content, ineffective teaching methodology, and invalid evaluation procedures. Too many schools have not only practiced these traditions indefinitely but many have not seriously questioned these practices either. Under such circumstances little effort and thought has been given to change. This is partly true because the process of change, creative renewal, and curriculum reform implies a break from the traditional viewpoint of "as it has been" to the position of "as it ought to be."

To approach this renewal process takes human energy or a professional dedication because of the inherent resistance to change. Watson (1972) commented that all of the forces contributing to stability in an individuals personality and, in fact, in a social system can be perceived as a resistance to change. From a broader perspective, the tendencies of certain individuals and societies to resist change, to preserve present practices, or to "fiddle on the roof," is what ultimately threatens both individuals and the society in which they live.

The second concern regarding the eagerness to change gives meaning to the doctrine of overenthusiastic adaptability and supports the assertion of "changing for change sake." As previously mentioned, change is inevitable. Many educators view it as such, thereby equating change with progress. A result, is that educators often feel popular when associated with change whether the change is warranted or not.

To combat this popular identity problem educators must remember that curriculum reform should be based on some indication of need. To change just for the sake of changing is not always warranted. Therefore, basis for change is necessary. This basis may emerge from findings completed elsewhere or from local research. The tendency for individuals to move too fast, to abolish present practices, or to quickly accept *newness* may cause a change that is too radical. This type of change may also threaten individuals and society.

CURRICULUM REFORM

As population continues to grow, new school districts are aligned, new facilities are constructed, and new physical education curricula are developed. In addition, existing physical education curricula are selected, revised, and updated. To refer to these happenings as *revolutionary* would be an overstatement and this talk definitely exceeds the achievement.

Curriculum reform in the United States following World War II would have probably evolved much more slowly if it had not been for a prosperous middle class of ambitious parents who envisioned education as the means of achieving great expectations for their children. This *baby boomer* group not only developed new communities and new schools in these communities but also revitalized existing ones. Educators accepted this spirit of change and openly instituted school curriculum reform. Meanwhile, various influential factors including the population explosion, the knowledge explosion, and the media explosion—along with an increase in both the development of private foundations and the federal government's interest in local schools—made curriculum developers identify that the curricula being planned were both educationally sound and defensible.

CURRICULUM RESEARCH IN PHYSICAL EDUCATION

Anderson (1989) explains that curriculum research in physical education has been limited in recent years. On the other hand, research on teaching physical education has been prolific. This research is necessary because a teacher's effectiveness largely determines the degree of student learning. Anderson further states that the curriculum in which the teaching occurs also deserves attention. In fact, it is the physical education curriculum that provides not only the context for teaching but also the structure for student learning. Anderson indicates that some fundamental questions confronting physical education curriculum today need to be answered. The following items are among these questions:

- How are contemporary physical education curricula developed?
- How should physical education curricula be developed?
- What is occurring in today's physical education curricula?
- How effective are today's physical education curricula?
- What collaborative efforts between researchers and practitioners seem appropriate?

Siedentop (1994) has some additional questions to the ones Anderson provided:

- What is the ideal physical education curriculum?
- Why do students voluntarily take part in physical education?
- To what extent do physical educators achieve their curricular goals?
- What activities should be included in a contemporary elementary, middle school, and high school physical education curriculum?

These questions need answers and finding appropriate solutions is not an easy task. As a result, researchers are reluctant to get involved. Anderson

(1989) explains that just causes do exist for people who avoid curriculum research. First, a physical education curriculum—in addition to being extremely large—is an exceedingly complicated body for inquiry. For one physical educator teaching forty students, the number of events occurring in a one semester program is difficult to comprehend, much less record and then explain. This complexity shows inherent limitations not present in controllable, laboratory research. The second reason people avoid curriculum research, according to Anderson, pertains to the immense size of the physical education curriculum. Due to size, most research studies become intensive in nature because researchers are limited to a few programs in the overall curriculum or even a few cases in a single program. The third cause of research avoidance that Anderson provided regards the diversity of the physical education curriculum. The diverse nature of this type of curriculum presents a need for multiple data collection techniques including event recording, interview observation, and document analysis. Therefore, the results are multifaceted and lead to lengthy discussions and complex conclusions. However, curriculum research is necessary if providing the best curriculum to meet the needs of today's students is the desired outcome.

Regardless of how a person theoretically accepts the importance of curriculum research in physical education, it often becomes impractical due to the lack of time, funds, and/or expertise. In this situation, the very least a person can do is review existing research. This research is found in a variety of professional periodicals and journals (see Table 5.1). However, a consensus exists that practitioners (physical educators) tend to not use research in their work (Lawson, Bosel, & Belka, 1992; Locke, 1969; Ross, 1981; Rothstein, 1973). This is a distressing concept since the amount of research is prolific. Therefore Lawson (1992) asks:

- Why should research be supported and completed if it is not used for human betterment?
- Why locate professional education programs in colleges and universities if practitioners do not use the theory and research?
- If practitioners tend to not use theory and research in their work, on what basis do they make decisions about their work practices?
- How do practitioners know whether they are helping or harming people?
- Is it possible for practitioners who do not use research to become obsolete?

In a 1992 *Journal of Physical Education, Recreation, and Dance* (JOPERD) feature edited by Templin, the importance of research, specifically for and by practitioners, was discussed. The articles in this feature attempted to answer the following important questions:

- Why should practitioners be concerned about research?
- Are practitioners concerned about research?
- What is the knowledge base of HPERD practitioners relative to research?

TABLE 5.1 Professional Periodicals/Journals

Academic Papers
Adapted Physical Activity Quarterly
Aerobic Medicine
American Health
American Journal of Physical Medicine
American Journal of Public Health
American Journal of Sports Medicine
American Middle School Education
American Physical Education Review
American Physical Therapy Journal
ARETE: The Journal of Physical Education
Camping Magazine
Canadian Association of Health, Physical Education, and Recreation Journal
Canadian Journal of History of Sport and Physical Education
Child Development
Childhood Education
Children
Completed Research in HPERD
Corporate Fitness and Recreation
Early Childhood Research Quarterly
Ergonomics
Family Health/Today's Health
Grade Teacher
Health Education
Health Values
The Instructor
International Journal of Sport Biomechanics
International Journal of Sport Psychology
International Journal of Sport Sociology
Interscholastic Athletic Administration
Journal of American Medical Association
Journal of Educational Sociology
Journal of Health Education
Journal of Human Movement Studies
Journal of Leisure Research
Journal of Motor Behavior
Journal of Philosophy of Sport
Journal of Physical Education and Program
Journal of Physical Education, Recreation, and Dance
Journal of School Health
Journal of Sport and Exercise Psychology
Journal of Sport Behavior
Journal of Sport History
Journal of Sport Issues
Journal of Sport Management
Journal of Sport Psychology
Journal of Sports Medicine and Physical Fitness
Journal of Teaching in Physical Education
Journal of Youth and Adolescence
Leisure Today
Medical World News
Medicine and Science in Sports and Exercise
Middle School Journal
Motor Skills: Theory into Practice
Pediatric Exercise Science
Perceptual and Motor Skills
The Physical Educator
The Physical Fitness Newsletter
The Physical Fitness Research Digest
The Physician and Sports Medicine
Physiological Reviews
Play and Culture
Quest
Recreation
Research Quarterly for Exercise and Sport
Safety Education
Scholastic Coach
School Safety
Science
Sociology of Sport Journal
The Sport Psychologist
Strategies
Teaching Elementary Physical Education
Today's Education
Update
Young Children

- How can practitioners retrieve research information that may be useful to their practice?
- What are some useful strategies for practitioners to consider in data collection and data analysis?

In addition, Twine and Martinek (1992), Wessinger (1992) and Williamson (1992), discuss strategies and rationales for practitioners to do research while Culkin and Davis (1992), Gray (1992), and Keeney and Sunnarborg (1992) provide techniques for analyzing research. The reader is encouraged to study this *JOPERD* feature.

Although much of the published research may not relate directly to a specific curriculum, it may provide implications for curriculum change. Consider the following research studies and how each may influence curriculum reform.

- Brustad, R. J., & Zehrung, D. A. (1994). Effects of daily vs. every-other day physical education instruction upon indices of physical fitness, motor skill, and psychological characteristics of third grade children. *Research Quarterly for Exercise and Sport, 65,* A73.

Brustad and Zehrung (1994) examined the effects of daily physical education instruction on the physical fitness, motor skill development, and self-perception of third grade children. Two hundred thirteen children were assigned to either a daily or an every-other day physical education schedule for one year. Course content was identical except the daily classes received twice as many minutes of instruction for each content area. Pretests and posttests were conducted on a variety of physical fitness, motor skill, and psychological parameters. Results indicated that children receiving daily physical education instruction showed a greater improvement on the mile run and the fifty yard dash times. However, no significant changes were found on the other variables.

- Dulaney, N. M., & Corbin, C. B. (1993). Effects of flexibility training on school children. *Research Quarterly for Exercise and Sport, 64,* A40.

It has been generally accepted that regular stretching exercises improve adult flexibility. Dulaney and Corbin (1993) conducted a study to determine if five-day-a-week flexibility training would result in better sit and reach scores. The stretching occurred during the regular physical education class with one group of first, third, and fifth graders stretching two days a week. A second group had the same regimen but with additional stretching exercises for five minutes three days a week. The students were pre- and post-tested and then tested again following a six week latency period. The investigators found that significant improvements occurred for all grade levels but the gains disappeared after the latency period.

- Jay, D. (1991). Effect of a dance program on the creativity of preschool handicapped children. *Adapted Physical Activity Quarterly, 8,* 305–316.

Jay (1991) sought to determine the effects of a dance program on the creativity of three-to-five year-olds. The classes met thirty minutes a day, three days a week for twelve weeks. The focus was on sensory experiences utilizing Laban's effort action. The results indicated that imagination and element of creativity were significantly changed by the dance program.

- Lambdin, D. D., & Steinhardt, M. A. (1991). Elementary and secondary physical education teachers' perceptions of their goals, expertise, curriculum, and students' achievement. *Journal of Teaching in Physical Education, 11*, 103–111.

Lambdin and Steinhardt (1991) investigated the physical education curriculum from the physical educator's perspective. Teachers (K–12) completed a questionnaire to assess their level of agreement on statements associated with twelve commonly held goals of physical education. These goals included the development of basic motor skills, lifetime sports skills, and physical fitness. For each goal, the teachers assessed their commitment to the goal, their expertise in content related to the goal, whether they taught this goal, and their students' achievements of the goal.

Lambdin and Steinhardt found that teachers do not perceive their expertise as a limiting factor. Secondly, they showed a relationship with the teachers' commitment, his/her expertise, what was taught, and what was learned (student achievement). They concluded that teachers have a wide range of goals for teaching and, furthermore, the expertise they feel urges them to teach according to these goals. Most teachers rate *what is taught* lower than their commitment to the goals which indicates that barriers exist that prevent them from teaching what they would like and what they feel prepared to teach. The identification and examination of these barriers is recommended.

- Luke, M. D., & Sinclair, G. D. (1991). Gender differences in adolescents' attitudes toward school physical education. *Journal of Teaching in Physical Education, 11*, 31–46.

In the study that Luke and Sinclair (1991) conducted, the goals were to first identify and second examine the determinants of adolescents' attitudes toward school physical education. Luke and Sinlair were specifically seeking to find factors that contributed to the development of a positive/negative attitude. They found five major determinants that influenced both positive and negative attitudes. Curriculum content ranked first. The remaining determinants of a positive attitude toward physical education were (a) the class atmosphere—the tone of the class, (b) one's self perception, (c) the teacher's behavior, and (d) the facilities. The authors' conclusions indicated that if educators want to develop a positive attitude toward physical education with students, then the factors that have a direct influence on an individual's attitude—including the curriculum, the class atmosphere, and the teacher's behavior—need to be controlled in a systematic manner.

- MacDonald, D. (1990). The relationship between the sex composition of physical education classes and teacher/pupil verbal interaction. *Journal of Teaching in Physical Education, 9*, 152–163.

MacDonald (1990) was examining sex role stereotyping. He sought to determine the relationship between teacher expectations and teacher–student interactions in same-sex and mixed-sex classes. Coding and interview techniques were used. MacDonald found that sex role stereotyping by teachers was evident in mixed-sex classes. As a result, boys received a higher proportion of interactions with teachers. The teachers indicated that they received greater satisfaction teaching boys. Girls in single-sex classes were more satisfied with their efforts and perceived teachers as having higher expectations for them than girls in mixed-sex classes perceived.

- Mahon, D. A., Ignico, A. A., & Marsh, M. L. (1993). The effects of daily physical education on health-related physical fitness in first-grade children. *Research Quarterly for Exercise and Sport, 64,* A43.

Mahon, Ignico, and Marshe (1993) compared the health-related physical fitness levels of first-grade children who had daily physical education (DPE) with those having twice weekly physical education (TWPE). Children in the DPE program had aerobic conditioning activities three days per week and motor and sport skill development activities the remaining two days. The program for the TWPE group consisted of motor and sport skill development activities only. All classes met thirty minutes a day for the entire school year. Results showed that the DPE children performed better on the one-mile run, timed sit-ups, and the sit and reach tests. However, body fatness scores showed there were no improvements or differences between the two groups.

- Page, R. M. (1992). Lonely children: A special concern for exercise science professionals. *Research Quarterly for Exercise and Sport, 63,* A81.

Page (1992) assessed the loneliness of nearly six hundred elementary school children in grades 1–6. He then compared children who scored low, medium, and high to determine if loneliness affected performance on selected fitness components and on level of physical activity. He found that lonely children were (a) less fit on measures including the one-mile run/walk, shuttle run, and abdominal curls; and (b) less physically active than children who were not lonely. In addition the relationship between loneliness and physical fitness/activity was most profound at the third- and fourth-grade levels.

- Parker, J. (1995). Teacher and student beliefs about physical education. *Research Quarterly for Exercise and Sport, 66,* A67.

Parker (1995) investigated the beliefs held by both teachers and students about physical education and how these beliefs were translated into action in a class setting. One high school physical educator and three eleventh-grade students in the same physical education class served as subjects. Interviews were held and observational field notes were collected on each subject. Results of the qualitative analyses showed that one belief held by both the physical educator and the students focused on personal relationships. All agreed that learning to interact with others was more important than learning skills.

However, beliefs about the importance of physical education differed. The teacher believed that physical education was an essential component in the overall school curriculum while the students perceived physical education as nothing more than a recreational break. These students placed less importance on physical education and further indicated that including this in the curriculum would not contribute to future success. Parker identified that in addition to enabling the teacher and students to express individual beliefs, the study allowed them to react to each others' beliefs regarding physical education.

- Pizarro, D. C. (1990). Reliability of the health-related fitness test for mainstreamed educable and trainable mentally handicapped adolescents. *Adapted Physical Activity Quarterly, 7,* 240–248.

Pizarro (1990) investigated the suitability of the AAHPERD's 1980 Health Related Physical Fitness Test (HRPFT) for mainstreamed educable mentally handicapped (EMH) and trainable mentally handicapped (TMH) 15-year-olds. He indicated that it is understood that an appropriate level of physical fitness is important for everyone regardless of age, gender, or physical status. Widely accepted reliable field testing protocols for nonhandicapped individuals exist but little attention has been given to the development or modification of fitness tests for handicapped individuals.

At the time of Pizarro's research, the HRPFT was being used with handicapped individuals even though the HRPFT was developed and normed for nonhandicapped people. Therefore Pizarro wanted to determine (a) the HRPFT's reliability for EMH/TMH adolescents and (b) whether or not test modifications were necessary for obtaining the data. He found that three of the four items—skinfolds, sit-ups, and sit and reach tests—were both reliable and suitable for his subjects. The nine-minute run was inappropriate. Pizarro further added that proper orientation, an allowance for practice, and an appropriate test environment appear to be important aspects of test preparation for adolescents functioning at below normal intellectual level.

OUTSIDE INFLUENCES

A growing number of national and international organizations, institutions, and agencies have become instrumental in influencing educational research leading to curriculum reform (see Table 5.2). These organizations are concerned, in varying degrees, with the promotion and advancement of physical education and/or its allied fields including athletics, health, and physical fitness. Many of these agencies exist as professional units dedicated to improving physical education at all levels ranging from preschool to the university

TABLE 5.2 Professional Organizations

Amateur Athletic Union
American Academy of Physical Education
American Alliance for Health, Physical Education Recreation, and Dance
American Association of School Administrators
American Camping Association
American College of Sports Medicine
American Council on International Sports
American Heart Association
American Medical Association
American Public Health Association
American Red Cross
American School Health Association
American Sports Education Institute
Association for Supervision and Curriculum Development
Athletic and Recreation Federation of College Women
Athletic Institute
Boys Clubs of America
Boy Scouts of America
Bureau of Health Education, United States Public Health Service
Department of Classroom Teachers
Educational Sports Institute
Girl Scouts of America
International Association of Physical Education and Sports for Girls and Women
International Council for Health, Physical Education, and Recreation
International Society on Comparative Physical Education and Sport
National Association for the Education of Young Children
National Association for Physical Education in Higher Education
National Association of Governor's Councils on Physical Fitness and Sports
National Association of Secondary School Principals
National Council of Athletic Training
National Education Association
National Federation of State High School Athletic Associations
National Parent Teachers Association
National Recreation and Park Association
National Safety Council
President's Council on Physical Fitness and Sports
Society of State Directors of Health, Physical Education and Recreation
United States Office of Education
United States Public Health Service
Young Men's Christian Association
Young Men's Hebrew Association
Young Women's Christian Association

setting. One influential organization pushing for physical education improvements is the American Alliance for Health, Physical Education, Recreation, and Dance (AAHPERD).

Founded in 1885, the AAHPERD has been instrumental in promoting physical education through a variety of services including consultation, periodicals and special publications, and research. This educational organization is designed to support, encourage, and provide assistance to member groups

American Alliance for Health, Physical Education, Recreation and Dance

1900 Association Drive • Reston, VA 22091 • (703) 476-3400

Logo for the American Alliance for Health, Physical Education, Recreation and Dance

Reprinted by permission of American Alliance for Health, Physical Education, Recreation and Dance. 1900 Association Drive, Reston, VA 72467-0240.

and their personnel as they initiate, develop, and conduct programs in each of the allied fields. The Alliance specifically seeks to:

- Encourage, guide, and support professional growth and development in health, leisure, and movement-related programs based on individual needs, interests, and capabilities.
- Communicate the importance of health, leisure, and movement-related activities as they contribute to an individual's well-being.
- Encourage and facilitate research that will enrich health, leisure, and movement-related activities and to disseminate the findings of this research to both professionals and the general public.
- Develop and evaluate standards and guidelines for personnel and programs in health, leisure, and movement-related activities.
- Coordinate and administer a planned program of professional, public, and government relations that will improve education in the areas of health, leisure, and movement-related activities.
- Conduct other activities for public benefit.

AAHPERD's effectiveness, through its six member associations (see Table 5.3), is unsurpassed in its advancement of not only physical education but also its allied fields.

AAALF, founded in 1949 as the Association for Research, Administration, Professional Councils and Societies was renamed (ARAPCS) in 1994. This organization strives to (a) coordinate professional programs, projects, and activities through its eight councils that include the Adapted Physical Education Council, the College and Administrator's Council, and the Council on Aging and Adult Development; and (b) encourage and promote research activities of the AAHPERD. AAALF provides an avenue for members to share interests and concerns while shaping their futures.

The AALR was formed in 1974 in response to the growing public awareness of its importance to meet a fundamental need. The association develops

TABLE 5.3 AAHPERD's Member Association

American Association of Active Lifestyles and Fitness (AAALF)
American Association for Leisure and Recreation (AALR)
Association for the Advancement of Health Education (AAHE)
National Association of Girls and Women in Sports (NAGWS)
National Association of Sport and Physical Education (NASPE)
National Dance Association (NDA)

and promotes the organization of school, community, and national leisure activities and it is striving to improve individual's leisure lifestyle through increased recreational opportunities.

AAHE's primary objective is to improve the human condition (a) through program activities and federal legislation; and (b) by supporting dynamic health education programs in K–12 schools; colleges and universities; and business, industry, and community agencies. AAHE's strategy involves strengthening and fostering basic health knowledge, disseminating this knowledge not only among its membership but also to the general public, and putting this knowledge into action in both schools and communities across the United States.

NAGWS, founded in 1879, serves the interests of more than ten thousand professionals including teachers, coaches, and sports officials. NAGWS's primary goal is to provide support and foster the development of quality sports programs that will enrich the lives of all participants. A more contemporary concern is to serve as an advocate in promoting equity for females in all sports programs.

NASPE is AAHPERD's largest association with more than thirty thousand members. It is the only national association devoted exclusively to improving the total sport and physical education experience in the United States. It conducts research and education programs in areas such as sport psychology, sport sociology, philosophy, history, and curriculum development. NASPE further develops and distributes public information that explains the value of physical education programs.

NDA, which began in 1932, strives to promote arts education for all individuals ranging in age from preschoolers to older adults. This association promotes the development of sound philosophies and policies for dance as education through conferences, conventions, and publications. NDA serves the profession in academic, recreational, and professional preparation at local, state, and national levels.

Much of the scientific support for selected practices and activities in physical education school curricula today stems from the AAHPERD. This support includes curriculum items related to physical fitness, sports skills, and activities for the adapted physical education program. Moreover, its publications include *Health Education; Journal of Physical Education, Recreation, and Dance; Leisure Today; Research Quarterly for Exercise and Sport;* and *Strategies.*

In addition to the AAHPERD, a number of other energetic national groups exist that have a research influence. One such group is the President's Council on Physical Fitness and Sports (PCPFS). Established in 1956 under executive order by Dwight Eisenhower, this group serves as an independent presidential advisory council whose purposes are to:

- Enlist support of both individual citizens and private enterprise to promote physical fitness.
- Initiate programs that inform the public about the importance of exercise.
- Strengthen federal services and programs relating to fitness and sports.
- Encourage state and local governments to emphasize the importance of physical fitness.
- Develop cooperative programs among professional societies that encourage sound physical fitness practices.
- Assist educational agencies, national sports bodies, and business and industry in developing physical fitness programs.
- Encourage research in the sport and fitness area.

The American College of Sports Medicine (ACSM), with its more than twelve thousand members, promotes research and disseminates information dealing with the benefits and effects of exercise and the prevention and treatment of injuries incurred in sport and fitness activities. The ACSM's primary research publication is *Medicine and Science in Sports and Exercise.*

The National Association for the Education of Young Children (NAEYC), founded in 1926, has more than seventy-five thousand members. The primary focus of this organization is to provide educationally sound programs for preschool and primary school children. Members include individuals involved in or providing programs for young children such as teachers, directors, professors, and researchers. The NAEYC publishes the *Early Childhood Research Quarterly* and *Young Children,* journals covering developments in the practice, research, and theory of early childhood education.

The National Association of Secondary School Principals (NASSP) is largely involved in physical education curriculum support and development. It was founded in 1916 and has more than forty-three thousand members. The NASSP's primary publication is the *Bulletin: The Journal for Middle Level and High School Administrators* which contains news and research findings for public and private school principals as well as other individuals engaged in middle and secondary school administration and/or supervision.

The effects that such national groups have on school curricula are frequently underestimated. Physical education gets a boost several times each year, even though this area of study is not a foremost focus, from such organizations as the American Heart Association and the American Medical Association. These organizations disseminate both research funds and state and national health legislation information to its members and the general public.

In addition to the organizations, institutions, and agencies listed in this chapter, one additional state group exists whose influence is measurable. Individual state departments of education, under the leadership of state director or supervisor of physical education, are largely influential regarding physical education issues. Most states have one person in the director or supervisor position while others have several individuals assigned to assist individual school districts. This assistance typically takes the form of in-service programs, workshops, and clinics that are planned, promoted, and presented. It is these state department directors of physical education that, perhaps, are most effective in helping local physical educators improve their own programs.

LOCAL ASSESSMENT

A program is best improved when changes are promoted through careful examination of research findings. These changes can occur in program areas such as content selection and sequencing, teaching methodology, and leadership. Research findings become more meaningful if they are drawn from self assessment rather than from the examination of published findings done elsewhere. Therefore self assessment is encouraged. A number of assessment instruments are available including The LaPorte Health and Physical Education Score Card 1 and 2, AAHPERD's Assessment Guide for Secondary School Physical Education Programs, Bucher's Checklist of Selective Items for Evaluating a Physical Education Program, and Bucher's Checklist and Rating Scale for the Evaluation of the Physical Education Program. A complete description of these and other instruments is included in Chapter 12.

SUMMARY

1. As educators it is important to remember not to resist change or be too eager to accept change.
2. In recent years the research on teaching in physical education has been abundant, whereas curriculum research has not.
3. Curriculum research is important because it is the curriculum that provides the context for teaching and the structure for learning.
4. Even though published research may not relate directly to an individual's curriculum, it may provide implications for curriculum reform.
5. A variety of outside influences including national associations such as AAHPERD, NAEYC, and NASSP affect curriculum reform.
6. AAHPERD, with its six member associations, has been supportive in promoting research activities.

QUESTIONS AND LEARNING ACTIVITIES

1. Numerous people have said that teachers should read scholarly documents. It is a fact that too few physical educators read journals such as the *Journal of Teaching in Physical Education, The Physical Educator,* and *Research Quarterly for Exercise and Sport.* Interview several people who have been teaching physical education five

years or more. How do they feel about scholarly journals and the reading of research in general? Compare your findings with others.

2. A shortage seems to exist for research pertaining specifically to physical education program modification and the corresponding effect it has on students. Do you think this statement is correct? Give your reasons.

3. Define *reform*. How broad in scope is it? What does reform really mean when it is applied to educational practice?

4. Provide a situation in which curriculum revision can be brought about without research.

5. Define *innovation*. What is its derivation? Try applying the word to a certain grade level of physical education. List two or three ideas, procedures, or practices that would be innovative in a K–12 public school physical education curriculum.

6. Locate three current research articles and discuss how each may influence curriculum reform.

REFERENCES

Anderson, W. G. (1989). Curriculum and program research in physical education: Selected approaches. *Journal of Teaching in Physical Education, 8,* 112–114.

Brustad, R. J., & Zehrung, D. A. (1994). Effects of daily vs. every-other day physical education instruction upon indices of physical fitness, motor skill, and psychological characteristics of third grade children. *Research Quarterly for Exercise and Sport, 65,* A73.

Culkin, D., & Davis, H. (1992). Basic data analysis for non-researchers. *Journal of Physical Education, Recreation, and Dance, 63*(8), 29–31, 57.

Dulaney, N. M., & Corbin, C. B. (1993). Effects of flexibility training on school children. *Research Quarterly for Exercise and Sport, 64,* A40.

Gray, J. A. (1992). Creating and navigating a dance research database. *Journal of Physical Education, and Recreation, and Dance, 63*(8), 29–31, 57.

Jay, D. (1991). Effect of a dance program on the creativity of preschool handicapped children. *Adapted Physical Activity Quarterly, 8,* 305–316.

Keeney, G. L., & Sunnarborg, K. R. (1992). Strategies for identifying health information: One practitioner's experience. *Journal of Physical Education, Recreation, and Dance, 63*(10), 26–28.

Lambdin, D. D., & Steinhardt, M. A. (1991). Elementary and secondary physical education teachers' perceptions of their goals, expertise, curriculum, and students' achievement. *Journal of Teaching in Physical Education, 11,* 103–111.

Lawson, H. A. (1992). Why don't practitioners use research? Explanations and selected implications. *Journal of Physical Education, Recreation, and Dance, 63*(8), 36, 53–57.

Lawson, H. A., Bosel, V., & Belka, D. (1992). *Paradoxes in the work orientations and epistemologies of physical education teachers.* Paper presented at the American Educational Research Association Meeting, San Francisco.

Locke, L. F. (1969). *Research in physical education: A critical view.* New York: Teachers College Press.

Luke, M. D., & Sinclair, G. D. (1991). Gender differences in adolescents' attitudes toward school physical education. *Journal of Teaching in Physical Education, 11,* 31–46.

MacDonald, D. (1990). The relationship between the sex composition of physical education classes and teacher/pupil verbal interaction. *Journal of Teaching in Physical Education, 9,* 152–163.

Mahon, D. A., Ignico, A. A., & Marsh, M. L. (1993). The effects of daily physical education on health-related physical fitness in first-grade children. *Research Quarterly for Exercise and Sport, 64,* A43.

Page, R. M. (1992). Lonely children: A special concern for exercise science professionals. *Research Quarterly for Exercise and Sport, 63,* A81.

Parker, J. (1995). Teacher and student beliefs about physical education. *Research Quarterly for Exercise and Sport, 66,* A67.

Pizarro, D. C. (1990). Reliability of the health-related fitness test for mainstreamed educable and trainable mentally handicapped adolescents. *Adapted Physical Activity Quarterly, 7,* 240–248.

Ross, S. (1981). The epistemic geography of physical education: Addressing the problem of theory and practice. *Quest, 33,* 42–54.

Rothstein, A. (1973). Practitioners and the scholarly enterprise. *Quest, 20,* 56–60.

Siedentop, D. (1994). *Introduction to physical education, fitness, and sport.* Mountain View, CA: Mayfield.

Templin, T. J. (1992). Research for and by practitioners. *Journal of Physical Education, Recreation, and Dance, 63*(8), 11, 16.

Twine, J., & Martinek, T. (1992). Teachers as researchers: An application of a collaborative action research model. *Journal of Physical Education, Recreation, and Dance, 63*(8), 22–25.

Watson, G. (1972). Resistance to change. In G. Zaltman, P. Kotler, & I. Kaufman, (Ed.), *Creating social change.* New York: Holt, Rinehart & Winston.

Wessinger, N. P. (1992). Demystifying research for the practitioner: How do I find out what I want to know? *Journal of Physical Education, Recreation, and Dance, 63*(8), 12–16.

Williamson, K. M. (1992). Relevance or rigor: A case for teacher as researcher. *Journal of Physical Education, Recreation, and Dance, 63*(8), 17–21. 25.

6
PROGRAM ORGANIZATION

Outline

Interaction and Reform
Scope and Sequence
Scheduling the Curriculum
Teaching Stations
Staff Organization
Paraprofessionals
The Selective Program
Ability Grouping
Performance Contracts
Programmed Instruction
Computer-Based Instruction
Instructional Strategies Using Students

Outcomes

After reading and studying this chapter, you should be able to:
- Define
    Ability grouping
    Computer-based instruction
    Cycle plan
    Differentiated staffing
    Paraprofessionals
    Peer teaching
    Performance contracts
    Programmed instruction
    Scope and sequence
    Selective program
    Student assistant
    Team teaching
- Identify and define Bookwalter's criteria for organizing physical education activities.
- Distinguish between conventional and flexible scheduling.
- Describe the three approaches to team teaching.

- Identify advantages, disadvantages, and implications arising from the following innovations:
  Ability grouping
  Computer-based instruction
  Differentiated staffing
  Paraprofessionals
  Peer teaching
  Performance contracts
  Programmed instruction
  Student assistants
  Team teaching

Planning an effective instructional program requires the development and harmonious arrangement of curriculum content, teaching skills, and evaluation practices. As this is accomplished, a real opportunity exists for school systems to correct past errors, to be innovative, to regenerate the program, and to reform.

INTERACTION AND REFORM

The extent to which a program is reformed and improved depends largely on how much interaction occurs between individuals. Just as the first law of ecology is interaction, so is interaction the first rule of successful educational organization. Relationships between all individuals involved—administrators, teachers, parents, and students, as well as concerned community members—have no limits. As interaction increases, the belief in present and future programs becomes supportable. It may not *always* be clear, but in time it gets more focused. Moreover, throughout the interaction process the perspective of physical education becomes clearer. With a concise perspective, the organization of a program becomes easier particularly if the planning effort is related to all of the educational influences in the school and the community served.

Whitehead (1932) wrote about this concern for the whole learning experience involving the whole organism, and considered it so essential to effective teaching. This concern is repeatedly illustrated in physical education when a reasonably sound activity is skillfully taught but fails to carry over in any appreciable way. A game of volleyball, a round of golf, or a square dance may have a better chance of being experienced throughout a lifetime if the physical educator gives attention to the historical and intellectual influences, the immediate recreational opportunities afforded locally, and the instructional process.

SCOPE AND SEQUENCE

Scope relates to the *breadth* or *quantity* of movement experiences in the physical education curriculum. It refers to *what* should be taught at all grade levels. As previously mentioned, the scope of a program will vary depending on changes in society and the persistent and identifiable needs and desires of students of all ages. Sequence relates to the *quality* of movement experiences in the physical education curriculum. It refers to *when* activities should be taught, the order in which the content is to be delivered, and the grade placement of the physical education experiences. Sequence defines the curriculum vertically, whereas the scope defines it horizontally (see Figure 6.1).

In determining scope, it is a good practice to first view the entire physical education program, K–12, for both boys and girls. This view tends to put content in perspective and gives curriculum planners a chance to consider a broad and complete program of experiences for the lives of school children. Once the spectrum of activities is clearly visible, it is proper to break it down into categories of content appropriate for such organizational divisions as the elementary grades and senior high school grades. Content at these various levels will be discussed more thoroughly in Chapters 8 and 9.

In the past, judgments toward the scope of physical education were frequently subjective and often arbitrary. In some schools the director of physical education may have developed the program independently. Or perhaps each physical educator in the same school may have developed the program just for his/her classes. A newer development urges educators to derive content judgments from a wide discussion in larger and more representative groups. This concept is specifically discussed in Chapter 7.

Better school systems move beyond a static course of study to a wealth of new and different physical activities that, hopefully, will contribute to the needs of all students. In such cases, however, the scope of the program must be reviewed periodically. It is essential to see what has been omitted that should have been taught, or what should be omitted as a means of creating more time for something new. One way of determining scope is to lay out the content in broad categories (see Table 6.1) and then select the activities that are most appropriate for the school in question.

Bookwalter (1964) provides a valid set of selection criteria to use in dealing with the *scope* of a physical education program. Although they are more than thirty years old, the criteria state that the activity selected must:

- Contribute to the general objective(s) of physical education.
- Be selected according to their relative value(s).
- Be meaningful and purposeful to the learner.
- Be within the capacities (physical, physiological, intellectual, etc.) of the learner.
- Offer frequency of participation outside of the school environment.
- Have carry-over value and/or lead to further activity involvement.

Activities	Grade 7	Grade 8	Grade 9
Badminton			
Nature of game			
Court			
Rules			
Singles			
Strategy			
Rules			
Doubles			
Strategy			
Rules			
Alignment			
Court etiquette			
Grip			
Forehand			
Backhand			
Stance			
Skills			
Overhead clear			
Around the head clear			
Overhead drop			
Long serve			
Short serve			
Smash			
Block			
Footwork			
Front court			
Back court			
Golf			
Nature of activity			
Equipment selection			
Care of equipment			
Rules			
Etiquette			

FIGURE 6.1 Junior High School Scope and Sequence for Individual/Dual Activities

Continued

Activities	Grade 7	Grade 8	Grade 9
Golf (continued)			
Grip			
Stance			
Swing			
Skills			
Putting			
Chipping			
Short irons			
Long irons			
Woods			
Gymnastics			
Nature of activity			
Rules			
Safety			
Skills			
Tumbling			
Forward roll			
Backward roll			
Tripod balance			
Headstand			
Prone headstand			
Kip (neck spring)			
Cartwheel			
Round-off			
Back walkover			
Front walkover			
Headstand and forward roll			
Pommel horse			
Feint			
Front support and swing			
Single leg circle forward			
Simple travel			
Elementary combination			

FIGURE 6.1 *Continued*

Activities	Grade 7	Grade 8	Grade 9
Gymnastics (continued)			
Vaulting			
Squat vault			
Straddle vault			
Front vault			
Rear vault			
Handspring vault			
Elementary combination			
Rings			
Inverted hang			
Nest hang			
Forward single leg cut			
Backward double leg cut dismount			
Elementary combination			
High bar			
Backward hip circle			
Knee circle			
Kip			
Squat dismount from support			
Elementary combination			
Parallel bars			
Forward hand walk			
Hip roll			
Corkscrew mount			
Flank dismount			
Elementary combination			
Uneven parallel bars			
Back hip pullover			
Mill circle			
Pop-up			
Straddle sole circle			
Elementary combination			
Balance beam			
Squat mount			

FIGURE 6.1 *Continued*

Activities	Grade 7	Grade 8	Grade 9
Gymnastics (continued)			
Chasse			
Back shoulder roll			
Arabesque			
Leap			
Forward roll			
Cartwheel dismount			
Elementary combinations			
Swimming			
Water Orientation			
Holding Positions			
Entry			
Front			
Back			
Drafting			
Streamlining on front			
Streamlining on back			
Skills			
Bubble bobs			
Safety bobbing			
Front float			
Back float			
Front glide			
Back glide			
Front glide with kick			
Back glide with kick			
Front beginner stroke			
Back beginner stroke			
Jump from wall (shallow water)			
Tennis			
Nature of activity			
Court			
Rules			

FIGURE 6.1 *Continued*

Activities	Grade 7	Grade 8	Grade 9
Tennis (continued)			
Singles			
Strategy			
Rules			
Doubles			
Strategy			
Rules			
Alignment			
Court etiquette			
Grip			
Eastern			
Continental			
Stance			
Skills			
Forehand			
Backhand			
Serve			
Lob			
Volley			

FIGURE 6.1 *Continued*

TABLE 6.1 Senior High School Physical Education Content

Aquatics	Gymnastics	Individual Activities	Team Sports	Rhythms
Beginning swimming	Balance beam	Archery	Basketball	Creative dance
Intermediate swimming	Bars	Badminton	Field hockey	Folk dance
Advanced swimming	Floor exercise	Bicycling	Flag football	Modern dance
Synchronized swimming	Pommel horse	Bowling	Soccer	Social dance
Diving	Vault	Golf	Softball	Square dance
		Ice skating	Speedball	
		Karate	Volleyball	
		Roller skating		
		Tennis		
		Track and field		
		Weight training		
		Wrestling		

- Offer both leadership and followership opportunities.
- Be feasible for time, facilities, staff, etc.

The physical education curriculum content needs to be organized so that students will be able to progress toward an increasingly mature utilization of both their knowledge and skills. This kind of development calls for a careful presentation of activities in sequence. Bookwalter (1964) lists and defines the criteria for guiding the organization of activities. Still germane today, these criteria include:

- *Progression*—Not all physical education activities are equal in complexity regarding the type (individual, team, aquatic, etc.) or skills within an activity (tennis forehand, backhand, and serve). The form required, the skill level expected, the time, distance, and the repetitions needed to develop a skill or activity are all functions of its relative difficulty. The activity may be so easy that it is boring or so difficult that it is frustrating or unsafe.
- *Variety*—An adequately broad choice of activities is necessary to meet all of the objectives of a physical education curriculum. These activities can be classified into selected categories including individual, team, aquatics, gymnastics, and rhythms. Appropriating the proper amount of time for each category is necessary for a balanced program.
- *Seasonality*—To heighten student interest, it is necessary to give attention to fall, early winter, late winter, spring, and early summer activities. Flag football instruction in the early fall, basketball instruction in the late winter, and golf instruction in the spring better fit the customs and comforts of society, thereby creating a more conducive environment for learning.
- *Feasibility*—This is partly inherent and partly contrived. An inadequately prepared physical educator is not advised to teach gymnastics. A school without a swimming pool will be a difficult setting for an aquatics program. Possibilities are minimized when a two-day-a-week program exists instead of a five-day-a-week program. More can be taught with a one-to-one ratio of equipment-to-child than with a ratio of one to ten. Forty minute periods of physical education provide time for fewer movement experiences than a sixty minute period could avail. Classes of sixty students will undoubtedly allow less time-on-task for individuals than a class of twenty-five could provide.
- *Practice for Mastery*—Allowing ample time to learn (master) a movement is a function of sound organization. Other variables affecting mastery include class size, teacher effectiveness, availability of equipment and facilities, and the balance between a reasonable emphasis on all the basic skills and an intensive emphasis on a few skills in each activity. Students are adequately educated when they are no longer unskilled and when

they gain enjoyment from the learned skills. Using these skills both in school and outside of school shows that students are advancing to a desired level of competency.
- *Unity*—Placing selected activities and movement experiences together so that one supplements the other or that both complement each other. Unity leads to more effective teaching. Warm-up exercises that prepare students for participation, individual skill drills that prepare students for a game, and activities relating physical education and other school subject matter (such as art, music, and geography) are experiences that unify learning.

In addition, attention must be directed to a graduated (progressive) sequence of ideas and skills. There are too many instances of repetitious programs where the same activities and the same skills in these activities are taught *ad nauseam* from year to year. Little progression of content exists where selected activities can eventually be learned to a level that they can be considered adequate. If progress occurs, however, the time gained could be given to the mastery of new activities. This progression occurs in mathematics where the student studies algebra, completes it, and goes on to geometry. But in physical education, students are too often instructed in volleyball every year from grades four to twelve, with little, if any, change in content.

One advantage of a carefully planned skill sequence is that it relates to a sequence in the development of concepts. An important idea does not come immediately to a student. Rather, it comes as the result of a series of experiences in which aspects of the idea finally enable the individual to grasp the total idea conceptually. In health education, wanting to be healthy and understanding what it takes to be healthy gives rise to such an idea. In physical education, knowing how to keep physically fit and wanting to do so throughout a lifetime also gives rise to such an idea.

It is easy to put too much emphasis on one specific curriculum factor. Failure to provide for proper sequencing of learning experiences in physical education has probably been the biggest obstacle to quality programs. If curriculum developers and reformers would take time to develop a sequence of learning activities for all of the physical education activities, K–12, the ultimate consequences could be spectacular. Figure 6.2 presents an example of an ongoing activity that has been structured in the grades in which the activity will be taught.

Sequencing is just as important for content in the elementary school, such as that dealing with the fundamental movement skills, as it is for the more advanced, sport-specific skills associated with learning to play basketball or perform a contemporary dance in a middle school or high school program. Table 6.2 illustrates a sequence that ranges from easy to difficult tasks that can be organized for the fundamental locomotor skill of walking.

Skills	Grade 6	Grade 7	Grade 8
Underhand serve	I	R	–
Overhand serve	–	I	R
Underhand set	I	R	R
Overhead set	I	R	R
Block	–	–	I
Spike	–	I	R
Dink	–	–	I

I=Introduce   R=Review to competency

FIGURE 6.2 Progression for Volleyball Content

SCHEDULING THE CURRICULUM

It is necessary to schedule the program as an integral part of the total school curriculum since the scope of the program has been set and the content has been organized in a graduated sequence. Scheduling is an administrative procedure. No matter how perfect the physical education curriculum may appear on paper, its success will be determined by how well it is implemented. Its implementation involves scheduling to some degree. Many subjects other than physical education are a part of the modern school; therefore numerous questions arise.

- How much time should be set aside for a physical education program in a particular school?
- How should this time be scheduled at each level (elementary school, middle school, junior high school, and senior high school)?
- Should the time be the same length each period the classes meet?
- Should physical education be scheduled two days a week, three days a week, or five days a week?
- Should intramurals be scheduled as a part of the physical education class period or should they be held at another time?

TABLE 6.2 Handling the Body in Relation to Locomotor Skills

Walking

1. *Does the student:*

a. Know the difference between an erect and stiff walk?
b. Understand the effect of badly stacked blocks on balance?
c. Swing arms naturally with alternation of legs?

2. *Adapt walking, in relation to:*

a. Sound
   - Does the student recognize that walking is done to an even beat?
   - Can the student recognize the even beat in his/her foot pattern, and then adapt the rhythm to clapping and the use of percussive instruments?
   - Can the student walk correctly to the clapping rhythm?
b. Tempo
   - Can the student walk fast and slow?
   - Can the student walk with the beat using variations in tempo?
   - Does the student know that rapid walking makes use of considerable leg and arm action?
c. Movement
   - Can the student walk in different directions without bumping others?
   - Can the student walk while moving other body parts (arms, fingers, hips, etc.)?
   - Does the student know that strolling involves little upper body movement?
   - Does the student know that the entire body is in action in a racing walk?
d. Others
   - Can the student walk beside/behind a partner?
   - Can the student adapt steps to their partner?
   - Can the student walk in groups and adapt steps to those of others?
e. Music
   - Can the student walk in a group with various types of accompaniment?
   - Does the student recognize the phrasing of the music and walk only to certain phrases?
f. Space
   - Can the student walk freely among classmates?
   - Can the student walk as the play area decreases (modified by boundaries)?
g. Moods
   - Can the students express happiness by the way they walk?
   - Can the students express sadness by the way they walk?
h. Imaginative ideas
   - Can the students walk as if they were on ice?
   - Can the students walk as if they were in mud?
   - Can the students walk as if they were elephants?
   - Can the students walk as if they were soldiers?

3. *Games with emphasis on walking:*

a. Traffic Game
b. Magic Carpet
c. Posture Tag

4. *Singing games and dances with emphasis on walking:*

a. London Bridge
b. Oats, Peas, Beans & Barley
c. Loobey Lou

- Is the schedule flexible enough to vary according to both the nature of the activities and the facilities available?
- If scheduled, should such strategies as programmed instruction and performance contracts be done outside the regular class period or carried out during the assigned class time?
- Is the school exploring ways to make better use of its time?

Scheduling is time consuming. Frequently, an administrator may take most of the summer organizing a workable package of subjects. It is even more difficult to schedule when a particular department wants the freedom of moving students in and out of programs in order to better meet individual needs. Fortunately, computers make this task easier by digesting data input and formulating a conflict-free schedule. The fundamental decision of what goes into the computer is still the responsibility of the administrator.

Two organizational patterns used for scheduling essentially exist—the conventional (traditional) pattern and the flexible (modular) pattern. The conventional schedule divides the school day into an equal number of class periods that are all the same length. Annarino, Cowell, and Hazelton (1986) state that characteristics of the conventional scheduling pattern include:

- Class size remains relatively constant.
- Classes are heterogeneous.
- Classes are usually coeducational.
- The physical educator functions as the leader/director of class activities.
- The choice of content is limited and, generally, made by the physical educator.

An example of a schedule for a ninth grade student using the conventional pattern is illustrated in Figure 6.3.

The second scheduling approach is the flexible pattern. It emanated from a report by Trump and Baynham in the early 1960s, supported by the National Association of Secondary School Principals, and has been modified accordingly since that time. This schedule focuses on basic curriculum organization with attention being devoted to flexibility in scheduling for better learning. Of particular interest to physical educators today are the following items from the report:

- Some classes may be smaller. At times there may be fewer than fifteen students in a class. This will aid small-group discussion and give teachers an opportunity to explore a variety of teaching techniques. Students and instructors will have a better opportunity to get to know each other, and individual instruction can be provided in such activities as badminton, handball, and bowling.
- Independent study can be emphasized. It will be possible to focus on the special interests and abilities of individual students. In-depth study will be possible as the student develops a sense of inquiry. For physical education,

Conventional Schedule

Time	Monday - Friday Class
8:15 – 9:10	Algebra I
9:15 – 10:10	English I
10:15 – 11:10	Physical Education
11:15 – 12:10	Lunch/Study Hall
12:15 – 1:10	General Science
1:15 – 2:10	World History
2:15 – 3:10	Spanish I

FIGURE 6.3 Conventional Ninth-Grade Class Schedule

this means a chance to pursue a specific topic such as weight training by studying routines and conducting personal experimentation and library research. Moreover, individuals needing extra work in order to perfect selected sport specific skills can be encouraged to put in additional time.
- Some classes may be larger. Classes as large as one hundred fifty students may be brought together for general content. At the start of a physical education unit, it may be desirable and more effective for a large group to view an instructional video, observe an interactive video presentation, or witness a unique physical education demonstration.
- Three phases of instruction can be related. Large group, small group, and independent study phases can be carefully organized so that students can move from the gymnasium, to the library, to the classroom as needed.
- Paraprofessionals may be used. Team teachers can be employed for particular competencies and for specific tasks.
- Educational facilities may reflect change. The buildings of tomorrow, in order to permit flexibility, will need more small group rooms, more learning resource centers, and a teaching auditorium. In physical education, the requirement will be for more teaching stations and large multi-use activity areas.

- Schedules may be more flexible. Instead of six or seven class periods in the departmentalized school, there may be divisions of time into fifteen or twenty minute modules. At times, one module may be adequate for what is planned and at other times two or three modules may be necessary.
- Students' individual differences can be better addressed. How to accept and respect individual differences is often a problem. With a more flexible school day, the physical educator will be able to schedule students for adapted physical education more easily including boys and girls who are weak in basic skills and those who are poor in physical fitness.
- Curriculum may be reorganized. A strong movement away from compartmentalized programs may occur. Grade compartments, subject matter compartments, and fixed length periods have tended to stereotype education. More attention may be given to content and what the student knows. Nongraded schools will become more popular at the elementary level. Physical education skills will be taught to students who can learn them rather than to a particular age group. Experience here indicates, however, that physical education in the nongraded school is not without problems. Unfortunately, students varying in ages are sometimes put together for instruction without adequate teaching staff to handle wide differences in ability.
- Evaluation may be more complete. In physical education, not only the students, but also the total physical education curriculum, K–12, will be appraised periodically.

These suggestions do not call for alteration in the scope and sequence of a given physical education program. Rather it should cause the teacher to shift parts of the program for the purpose of becoming more flexible. In addition, the teacher should ask these questions:

- What activities, skills, and knowledge can students learn primarily by themselves?
- What activities, skills, and knowledge can students learn from the explanations of others?
- What activities, skills, and knowledge require personal interaction among students and teachers?

Flexible scheduling can take many forms, all of which are designed to expose the student to a more effective learning environment. Some attempts that have been made in an effort to move away from the more rigid structure are as follows:

- Formally extending the school so that all game skills can be practiced in game situations after regular class periods are over.
- Extending the school week to six days. For total school operation, this has not been proven popular. Where community recreation departments work closely with schools, cooperative efforts have been made to extend intramurals and other physical activities into Saturday time.

- Extending the school year. This has not been at all popular. Parental activities, vacations, and so forth tend to dictate the length of the school year.
- Assigning a large number of students to physical education in a time block. This works only when a number of teaching stations and staff members are available for the time block.
- Varying the length of the time block. For certain program elements the double period has numerous advantages. It is especially valuable if a school curriculum contains short periods (under forty-five minutes). If fifteen minutes are allocated for undressing, showering, and dressing, only thirty minutes are available for instruction. In this case, the double period allows more weekly exposure to physical education. However, it is not recommended to combine two periods of physical education per week into one double period. Five periods per week could be split into single periods on Monday, Tuesday, and Wednesday and a double period on Friday. Four periods could be split into single periods on Monday and Wednesday, and a double period on Friday.
- Assigning upper-level high school students to evening classes, particularly where elective activities may be practiced. Although this makes more time available for physical education, it tends to cut down on the time that students may be doing something else at home or in the community.
- Permitting study hall time to be used for needed instruction and practice in physical education activities when the individual student has a serious weakness. When carefully controlled, this practice can be worthwhile.

One advantage of flexible scheduling in physical education is the opportunity to vary the length of the activity period according to the needs of both the student and teacher through the use of time blocks called modules. The schedule is set up on the basis of blocks of time, usually ten to thirty minutes in length. This permits a variety of time arrangements for small group, large group, and individualized instruction. Once established, modules may be combined in many ways. An example of modular scheduling is shown in Figure 6.4. In this example, all students (N = 60–100) in groups A and B meet on Monday for a large group activity. During the first week of a unit, this initial meeting is to (a) provide an overview of the unit; and (b) assess entry-level behavior. On successive Mondays, class time is spent discussing, reviewing, and/or practicing previously learned content. On Tuesdays and Wednesdays for group B and on Tuesdays, Wednesdays, and Thursdays for group A, the students meet for large group introductory activity/review. The groups are then broken into smaller subgroups for skill instruction. The number of subgroups depends on both the number of teachers/paraprofessionals and, to a lesser degree, the availability of equipment and facilities. On Thursdays group B and on Fridays for group A, time is allotted for independent study. During this time stations are provided for students to work on specific skills. For group B, Fridays are designed for (a) lead-up/small-sided games for the first two or three Fridays of the unit and (b) tournament participation during the

Group	M	T	W	T	F
A	Large Group Activity (50 min.)	Large group introductory activity/review (10 min.)	Large group introductory activity/review (10 min.)	Large group introductory activity/review (10 min.)	Independent study (20 Min.)
		Two small group sessions (20 min. each)	Two small group sessions (20 min. each)	Two small group sessions (20 min. each)	Large group activity (40 min.)
	Closure (10 min.)	Closure (10 min.)	Closure (10 min.)	Closure (10 min.)	Closure (10 min.)
B	Large Group Activity (80 min.)	Large group introductory activity/review (10 min.)	Large group introductory activity/review (10 min.)	Independent study (20 min.)	Large group activity (80 min.)
		Three small group sessions (20 min. each)	Three small group sessions (20 min. each)	Two small group sessions (20 min. each)	
				Independent study (20 min.)	
	Closure (10 min.)	Closure (10 min.)	Closure (10 min.)	Closure (20 min.)	Closure (10 min.)

A=Freshman or beginning skilled students
B=Sophomores or intermediate skilled students

FIGURE 6.4 Modular Schedule

last one or two Fridays. The selection of content for Friday's lessons depends on the specific activity or unit being taught.

Modular scheduling not only works well in the attainment of cognitive and psychomotor objectives, but it also fosters affective development by facilitating socialization through various types of grouping. Annarino, Cowell, and Hazelton (1986) provide these characteristics that describe the flexible (modular) scheduling patterns:

- Class size may vary from one module to another, depending on the needs, interests, and/or ability levels of the students, the type of activity, the availability of equipment and facilities, and the availability and expertise of the staff.
- Students are grouped on the basis of needs and/or competencies.
- The teacher or course designer assumes a variety of roles including diagnostician, supervisor, and facilitator.
- Activities are based on an analysis of students' needs, interests, skill levels, and leadership abilities.

Outdoor scheduling is ideal for large-group activity.

For the majority of school districts the report by Trump and Baynham (1961) is still ahead of its time. In most places the traditional approach to scheduling is still practiced, and it is easy to understand why school administrators are reluctant to change to a more flexible scheduling of classes. It is much simpler to divide the school day into six or eight standard-length periods and assign the same set blocks of time for all subject matter areas. The assumption now, however, is that a better quality of physical education can be brought to students when more effective schemes of organizing school time are used.

The Cycle Plan

As previously mentioned, a tendency exists in physical education, and especially at the secondary level, to teach the same major activities each year. Sometimes repetition is good, particularly if it reacquaints students with topics or activities they may have missed the previous year. However, it may be more effective in terms of both student motivation and ultimate retention to teach certain seasonal activities every other year. This type of arrangement is called the cycle plan.

When the total physical education program has been carefully planned, real value in such a plan may surface. For example, instead of trying to teach short units of several fall, winter, and spring sports each year, effort could be concentrated on only half of these one year and on the other half the following year. This has practical application especially in climates where the outdoor season is short. This arrangement provides for more intensive study by allotting more time for each activity. Of course, the implication arising from this approach is that students must be enrolled in physical education for two successive years in order to truly benefit from all activities.

TEACHING STATIONS

Some physical educators think that the topic of class scheduling is closely related to facilities or *teaching stations*. Teaching stations are defined as any area used for the instruction of physical education. The more traditional teaching stations of both indoor and outdoor use are shown in Table 6.3. If the gymnasium and playing fields are small or nonexistent little room for flexibility occurs. If swimming pools, softball fields, and physical education classrooms are not available, the program often appears inflexible. As a result, the necessary activity modifications seldom take place. Exceptions exist, of course, but rarely. These schools are frequently fortunate for having dedicated physical educators who know how to make the most out of the least.

Evidence exists that supports the thesis that the finest examples of program flexibility, in both content and instruction, occur if large numbers of students are assigned to a class program where both indoor and outdoor multiple teaching stations are present. Therefore, the current increase in campus-type schools, consolidated schools, and centralized schools has much to offer physical education. In some instances more than twenty-five percent of the indoor space is assigned to physical education. With vastly improved outdoor playing fields and courts, it is possible to plan large-group, small-group, and individual activities in a program that is flexible.

The majority of elementary school buildings constructed in the last decade have bright, optimum-sized gymnasia and playing fields in addition to traditional playgrounds. Secondary schools have auxiliary gymnasia, separate weight training facilities, and dance studios. Increasingly, the most promising facility being constructed in the United States is the field house, with its wide-open spaces, multi-use fixtures, and portable floors. The field house sets the stage for a thoroughly organized, yet flexible program. With

TABLE 6.3 Physical Education Teaching Stations

Indoor	Outdoor
Gymnasium	Track
Swimming pool	Baseball/softball field
Classroom	Football field
	Playground

increased instructional staff assigned to large groups of students and the excellent variety of field house teaching stations, there is little reason for *not* conducting a superior program.

A quality program can be conducted even if the number of teaching stations is limited. Daughtrey and Lewis (1979) indicate that a physical educator in need of additional space should study the existing facility. Perhaps an old storage room, unused classroom, corridor, or oversized dressing room could be converted into a teaching station.

STAFF ORGANIZATION

To improve instruction with the hope of enhancing learner outcomes, staff organization is important. Two organizational patterns applicable to most schools—team teaching and differentiated staffing, will be discussed.

Team Teaching

The essential requirement for team teaching is that two or more teachers be scheduled in a way that enables them to work together to carry out the program more efficiently than if they were working by themselves. Rink (1993) explains that following the passage of Public Law 94.142 (see Chapter 10), many physical educators looked toward team teaching as a way of better meeting the needs of boys and girls, heterogeneously grouped, by having both a male and a female teacher share the responsibilities of planning, presenting, and evaluating. This is not a new concept but is a practice that has potential when appropriately used. Three approaches to team teaching can be employed (see Figure 6.5). The *unit team approach* is somewhat hierarchical. One teacher is designated the leader (master teacher) and the other(s) are assistant teacher(s). It is the master teacher's responsibility to organize and delegate duties to the assistant(s). These duties may include securing specific resources, teaching selected skills, and evaluating students. In the *skill event approach,* teachers select skills in specific units to teach. For example, in a seventh grade volleyball unit, one physical educator may teach the overhead set, another may teach the underhand set, and a third may teach the serve. In the *skill level approach,* students are grouped by ability and assigned to different teachers accordingly. For example, in a class of thirty eighth grade students, one physical educator may teach eighteen beginner tennis students, while a second may teach twelve advanced students.

Team teaching is an attempt to facilitate learning by reducing the student-to-teacher ratio. Also, the physical education department is able to use the best faculty for instruction by allowing them to teach in their area(s) of expertise. As well as providing more effective supervision and management, students are exposed to the talents of more than one teacher. In a unit team format, an assistant teacher can provide more individual help because that instructor does not have the responsibility of an entire class. In order for team

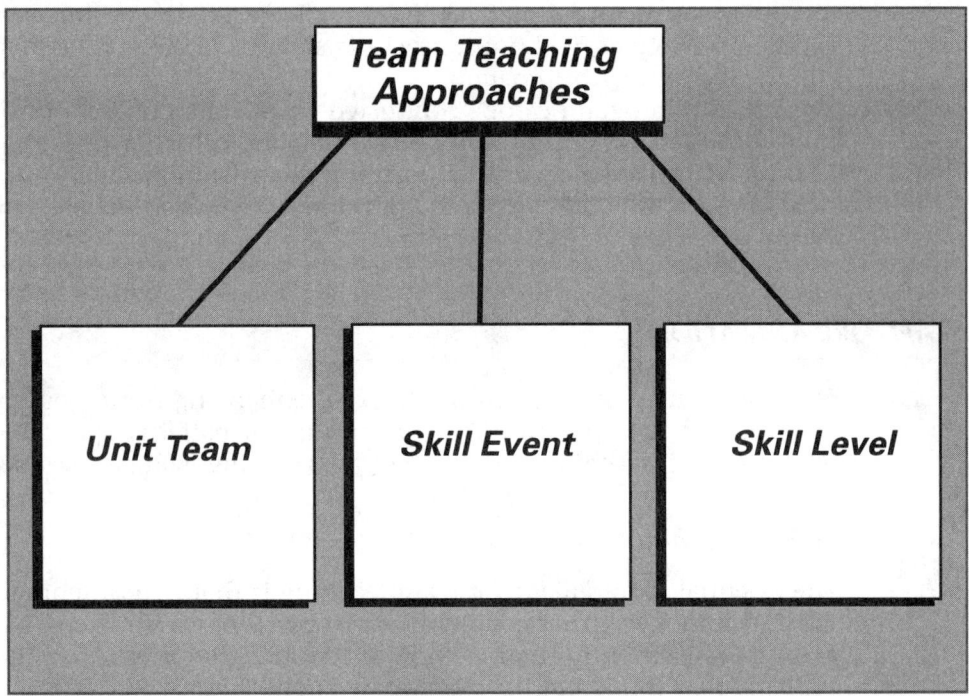

FIGURE 6.5 Approaches to Team Teaching

teaching to be an effective tool, it is essential that the physical educators establish interactive relationships that allow them to feel more comfortable teaching both with and before other colleagues (Rink, 1993). This approach offers teacher in-service, on-the-job training, an opportunity for professional growth, and the exchange of subject matter knowledge. This is especially advantageous for physical educators early in their careers. Teaching physical education in a team format is sound because it assures young teachers that they are not working alone.

Staffing

Differentiated staffing involves the selection and placement of the physical education staff at different levels of responsibility. This approach is an attempt to make the best use of the special competencies of each teacher. The first task in employing this pattern is to define these levels of responsibility.

Rand and English (1968) suggest a differentiated staffing plan that involves three levels with six different teachers each having different responsibilities. These staffing levels are shown in Table 6.4. Each of the six positions includes a job description. Individuals are selected and assigned according to education and experience. For example, a research associate position requires a doctorate degree, a staff teacher requires a bachelor's degree and one additional year of

TABLE 6.4 Differentiated Staffing Levels

Level 1	Level 2	Level 3
Teaching research associate Teaching curriculum associate Senior teacher	Staff (regular) teacher	Academic assistant Educational technician

education, and the educational technician position does not require a degree. This format is not applicable to all schools because it requires a faculty of at least six people. However, the levels, positions, and/or responsibilities can be modified. In order to achieve the full benefits of this type of program, the full complement of staff is necessary. Another concern when considering this organizational approach is cost, and Rand and English suggest that salary should increase as educators move up in levels.

PARAPROFESSIONALS

Paraprofessionals are personnel who have less formal educational background than a four-year baccalaureate degree (Mandell & Schram, 1983). These educators normally perform some professional-level functions under the supervision of a professional but because of insufficient training and/or experience they are not allowed total responsibility (Kelly & Vergason, 1978). A paraprofessional is defined as a person whose position is either instructional or delivers direct services to students and/or their parents, and who serves in a position for which a teacher or another professional have ultimate responsibility (Pickett, 1981).

Paraprofessionals include both paid individuals and volunteers who share a myriad of titles including teachers aides, teaching assistants, educational assistants, instructional assistants, and several others. Paraprofessionals are used either because the demand or need for qualified physical educators is greater than the supply or because the means of delivering educational services for less money will be possible by using this type of personnel.

A dramatic increase in the use of paraprofessionals has occurred in the last twenty years (Vogler, French, & Bishop, 1989). Using these individuals can maximize effectiveness by decreasing the student-to-teacher ratio. If utilized, three items worthy of consideration exist:

- The selection of the paraprofessional.
- The role of the paraprofessional.
- The training of the paraprofessional.

A paraprofessional's responsibilities need to be clearly defined and understood by both the physical educator and the aide. Frith (1982) provides a list of *do's* and *don'ts* for outlining recommended job expectations (see Table 6.5).

TABLE 6.5 Paraprofessional Do's and Don'ts

Don't

- Assume the role of a substitute teacher
- Conduct unsupervised activity
- Make curricular decisions
- Make instructional decisions
- Decide on discipline methods
- Administer corporal punishment
- Assign final grades
- Initiate parental contact

Do

- Assist with planning (lesson/units)
- Secure necessary equipment
- Modify activities with teacher
- Administer selected tests (fitness, skill, etc.)
- Demonstrate selected skills
- Assist in behavior management
- Assist in clerical duties (grade exams, record scores, etc.)
- Provide one-on-one instruction

From Frith, G.H. *The Role of the Special Education Paraprofessional: An Introductory Text.* (1982). Courtesy of Charles C. Thomas, Publisher, Springfield, IL.

The don'ts are those responsibilities of the certified teacher, whereas the do's are suggested tasks for the paraprofessional.

Once the role has been clearly defined, the selection criteria need to be developed. In physical education the following minimum qualifications are suggested:

- High school diploma
- Twenty-one years of age (or older)
- Emotionally mature
- Completed a standard first aid course
- In good health
- Interested in physical activity

To derive the most from a paraprofessional Vogler, French, and Bishop (1989) indicate that professional development is a necessity. Pickett (1981) stated that paraprofessionals are the fastest growing and least prepared professionals in education. Perhaps the best approach to assuring that paraprofessionals have the knowledge necessary for supporting a physical education program is pre-service education. Therefore, the paraprofessional arrives on the first day of work having completed a program of study involving, at a minimum, the knowledge of (a) the learner, (b) the content, and (c) instructional strategies. Too often, however, paraprofessionals with few or any of these qualifications are employed. If an underqualified individual is hired the responsibility then turns to the physical education department and/or the school for providing in-service education to better prepare the paraprofessional.

THE SELECTIVE PROGRAM

From a traditional viewpoint, it has been considered sound practice to require a designated program from K–12. This requirement has insured a breadth of experiences for all students. This "we know what's best for you" approach has frequently reduced students' motivation to participate. During the formative years from kindergarten through middle school, a required physical education program that will facilitate the student's optimum development and understanding of a variety of games, skills, and movement experiences is recommended. The physical education program is the only part of the school's total curriculum that focuses on the study of human movement. Furthermore, the required program is more apt to lead to larger percentages of physically fit, healthy students.

Vergerio (Woodward, 1963), an influential educational humanist during the Italian Renaissance, expressed his concern for a liberal education, more than five thousand years ago, a concern discussed today. A trend exists that encourages individual choice in one's curriculum. Generally accepted today, individual choice generates student interest which leads to continued involvement in physical activity. To achieve this end, the selective curriculum is recommended. This program allows students to choose or select specific activities in which they have an interest from a listing. Students can then concentrate on these selected activities. This approach has the greatest application at the senior high school level but also can be used successfully with a middle school program. When secondary schools have abandoned a rigid, structured required physical education program and have allowed students to choose activities, a better understanding and a greater appreciation for the program emerges.

ABILITY GROUPING

Ability grouping involves the placement of students in groups according to levels of performance. As early as 1967 the American Medical Association's Committee on Exercise and Physical Fitness promoted the importance of proper grouping in physical education (Chambers, 1988). It was the committee's opinion that in order to encourage participation and thereby achieve physical education values, some degree of homogeneity needs to exist.

The primary purpose of grouping students with similar abilities is to establish an instructional setting to facilitate learning. Grouping has been accomplished on the basis of everything from chronological age, to grade level, to interest, to anthropometric assessment, and so on. With the increasing range of ability found in coeducational classes a growing need to provide equal opportunity for all students has emerged in recent years. Too often, however, when a wide range of ability exists, frustration on the part of the physical educator occurs. This frustration leads to a practice of engaging almost wholly in recreational games instead of involving more demanding physical education skills and fitness improvement activities.

Ability grouping in a physical education program has proven to be advantageous because it provides the teacher with a better opportunity for meeting the needs of all students. In addition, it allows students to more easily (a) develop leadership skills, (b) attain success in a movement environment, and (c) learn skill through more effective teaching. By grouping students homogeneously, it is possible to focus instruction at the appropriate level of individual ability. Why should a good tumbler repeat forward rolls just because it is the lesson of the day for everyone in class? If more than one teaching station is present, a second teacher or student assistant could help the skilled student in learning more advanced skills. In addition students grouped heterogeneously are often more difficult to manage and motivate. Evidence shows that when students are ability grouped, high-ability individuals improve more than when they are taught in a mixed-ability class (Lockhart & Mott, 1981).

While working with younger children, Schurr (1980) noted that poorly skilled individuals are frequently discouraged as they watch those who are constantly successful. In this scenario, ability grouping would be recommended. However, young children often learn by imitation and segregating them from their better-skilled peers could deprive them of a significant source of models. Separation may also lead to stereotyping and/or labeling.

Beneficial game experiences and motivational techniques may also be found in a heterogeneous set-up, and it could be difficult to allow students these experiences in a limited, homogeneous situation. Evidence shows (Lockhart & Mott, 1981) that low-ability students do not significantly benefit from ability grouping. Hellison and Templin (1991) state that ability grouping may be useful only if the physical educator (a) can effectively interact with different groups, (b) is able to validly assess students for placement, and (c) is flexible following the initial placement of reassigning students as the need arises.

Concerns on how to group and how much time to devote to this ability grouping of students are legitimate. The use of student self ratings, teacher rating scales, and game performance are all appropriate techniques for judging ability. To achieve accurate ability grouping, Kneer (1982) supports the use of criterion-referenced skill tests which are interpreted in terms of specific performance standards. Ultimately, the decision regarding ability has to be resolved locally, keeping in mind the resources that are available. Certain teachers can advance curriculum concepts and skills in a mixed group successfully because of observation and encouragement, while other teachers can work more effectively with students who are similar in ability.

PERFORMANCE CONTRACTS

Using performance contracts, the physical educator and the individual student *agree* on a specific behavior in order to fulfill a certain requirement. It is an instructional strategy whereby a reward, usually a grade, is awarded to the student at the completion of the contract.

Contracting is a form of individualized study whereby the student embarks on a self-directed learning experience (Bucher & Koenig, 1983). Contracting allows students to be responsible for their own learning while progressing at their own pace. Contracts are appropriate for both psychomotor and cognitive behaviors.

Bucher and Thaxton (1979) state that contracts may be drawn up for a total unit of activity or for a single skill within a unit of activity. Figure 6.6 (Fast, 1971) is an example of a contract at the middle or senior high school level requiring both in-class and outside-of-class participation. In addition, contracting can be used at the elementary school, middle school, and high school levels. Examples of contracts at these various levels are illustrated in Figures 6.7, 6.8, (Bucher & Thaxton, 1979) and 6.9 (Annarino, Cowell, & Hazelton, 1986). Students may be allowed to do both in-class and/or outside-of-class work on their contracts. Contracting is a useful strategy but it is essential that both the teacher and the student understand the terms of the contract. In addition, it requires that the teacher hold each student accountable for fulfilling the contract.

PROGRAMMED INSTRUCTION

The opportunity for self-paced learning, self assessment, and decision making is the essence of programmed instruction. It allows for individual differences and gives the student responsibility for his/her own behavior. The subject matter is organized sequentially so the student can learn independent of the teacher. Both psychomotor skills and cognitive information can be programmed effectively through a step-by-step format. Figure 6.10 is an example of programmed instruction involving volleyball rules. An example of a programmed approach for learning the volleyball overhead pass is shown in Figure 6.11 (Gustafson, 1973). An example of a programmed approach for learning the basketball jump shot is shown in Figure 6.12 (Mueller, 1976).

Programmed instruction has been used sparingly in physical education. Its best application is probably in a supplement approach to complement other teaching strategies. The major obstacle to overcome is the lack of published programmed materials. Another concern is the lack of training for developing programmed knowledge and skills on the part of the physical educator.

Programmed instruction in a physical education program is worthy of use. It allows for more teacher efficiency, flexibility, and student individuality especially for those students who are independent, self-motivated, and whose goals are congruent with the learning program (Heitmann & Kneer, 1976).

Bowling Contract

Required

1. Bowl six games at any local bowling alley. Bring your score sheet back as part of your report. On a separate sheet of paper list and define the symbols used in scoring. Also list the two basic rules for scoring.
2. Write a paper detailing the development of bowling as a sport. Use at least four library references and include them in a bibliography. The paper should be equivalent to two double-spaced, typed pages.
3. At brief practical examination with the instructor, be able to demonstrate appropriate grip, correct hold of the ball, footwork for the approach, and proper form at release. Also, be ready to demonstrate how these features differ when the bowler wants to throw a hook ball, a straight ball, or a back-up ball.

Elective (complete any combination that totals 75 points)

1. Observe one complete session of any local bowling league for adults. Write a two-page, double-spaced typed paper on your impressions. (20 points)
2. At a brief practical examination with the instructor, be able to demonstrate the appropriate technique and strategy for picking up various splits and spares. (15 points)
3. Bowl three games with a friend or classmate. Describe in detail the technique used by the bowler including an analysis of the errors committed. Based on the analysis, suggest specific practice strategies to help this person improve. Prepare in writing both the analysis and the suggestions for improvement. (20 points)
4. At a brief practical examination with the instructor, be able to explain how to select a ball. Be sure to include information about weight of the ball in relation to the bowler, fitting the hand to the ball, and what options exist for a person purchasing a ball. (15 points)
5. Read any published instructional book on bowling. Write a brief summary of the book including a summary of the contents and a critique of how the information was presented. (20 points)
6. Practice bowling by completing six additional games, not including those in the required contract. Keep a journal of what spares and splits you had to pick up and how successful you were. Based on these games, analyze your strengths and weaknesses as a bowler. Turn in the journal and the analysis. (20 points)
7. Watch a professional bowling match on television. In a two-page, double-spaced typed paper, describe in detail how your local league differs from what you observed. (15 points)
8. Interview at least three bowlers from an adult league. Ask each bowler why they bowl, what pleasure they derive from the sport, what they think is important about being a good bowler, and their recommendations on how to have fun at it. Write a two-page, double-spaced typed paper on your interviews. (20 points)

FIGURE 6.6 In-Class and Outside-of-Class Contract

Fast, B. (1971). Contingency contracting. *Journal of Health, Physical Education, Recreation, and Dance.* 42(8), 31–32. Reprinted by permission.

Name: _____ Grade: _____
Room: _____ Date Completed: _____

Contracts 1, 2, 3, 5, and 6 are required.

Contract 1 (10 points). Research and write a paper (two pages) on the history of basketball. The paper may be either typed or legibly handwritten. A minimum of two references must be used, and a bibliography must be included.

Contract 2 (5 points). Explain any three of the following rules and/or fouls:
 a. Throw in from out-of-bounds
 b. Player positions for free throws
 c. Three-second violations
 d. Dribbling infractions
 e. Charging and blocking
 f. Personal and technical fouls

Contract 3 (20 points). Pass a written test with a score of eighty percent or higher. The test will cover basic rules, terminology, and the history of basketball.

Contract 4 (10 points). Devise a lead-up game to basketball and include rules, number of players, and the equipment and facilities needed.

Contract 5 (10 points). Demonstrate and explain the following skills to the teacher:
 a. One-hand push pass
 b. Two-hand push pass
 c. Two-hand bounce
 d. Set or push shot
 e. Lay-up shot
 f. High and low dribble
 g. Defensive stance and movement

Contract 6 (35 points). You will be expected to pass a skills test covering the skills listed in Contract 5. (The specific test is in the packet on the basketball contract.) In order to receive the total point value, you must make a score of ninety percent or higher.

Contract 7 (5 points). Play a game of one-on-one basketball with a classmate. By counting each basket as one point, play a twenty-one-point game.

Contract 8 (10 points). Officiate a basketball game during the intramural basketball tournament.

Contract 9 (5 points). Construct a single elimination tournament for eight teams. Explain the tournament, emphasizing why it would be used instead of other types of tournaments.

Contract 10 (5 points). Watch a high school basketball game and a professional basketball game during the next two weeks and write a few paragraphs explaining three rules that are different and three rules that are the same for both games. Also make a general statement regarding the basic difference in the games as you view them.

Contract 11 (10 points). Teach a student a basketball skill that he or she cannot perform until that student is able to pass a performance test on that skill.

Contract 12 (5 points). Explain any two of the following concepts:
 a. "Giving with the ball" as it is caught.
 b. Taking a step in the direction of the pass and shifting the weight when passing.
 c. Following through after the pass or shot.
 d. Putting backspin on the ball when shooting.

FIGURE 6.7 Basketball Contracts for Grades 7–12

From C. A. Bucher & N. A. Thaxton, *Physical Education for Children: Movement Foundations and Experiences*. New York, NY: Macmillan. Copyright by C. A. Bucher & N. A. Thaxton. Reprinted by permission.

Name: _____ Grade: _____
Room: _____ Date Completed: _____
Check when you have performed the skill successfully five out of five times.

( ) 1. Spin hoop on one arm.
( ) 2. Spin hoop on the other arm.
( ) 3. Pass hoop from one arm to the other while spinning it.
( ) 4. Hold hoop high over head and drop it so hoop hits the ground without touching the body.
( ) 5. Throw hoop into the air and catch it.
( ) 6. Throw hoop into the air, let it bounce, and then catch it.
( ) 7. Throw hoop into the air and catch it on your foot.
( ) 8. Roll hoop on the floor so it will come back to you.
( ) 9. When hoop comes back after a roll, run through it.
( ) 10. When hoop comes back after a roll, jump over it.
( ) 11. Throw hoop into the air and lasso yourself with it.

FIGURE 6.8 Hoop Contract for Grades 2–3

From C. A. Bucher & N. A. Thaxton, *Physical Education for Children: Movement Foundations and Experiences*. New York, NY: Macmillan. Copyright by C. A. Bucher & N. A. Thaxton. Reprinted by permission.

COMPUTER-BASED INSTRUCTION

A constant search for the most effective pedagogical method to deliver content exists in education. Johnson and Morris (1981) state that the desire to move from the passive lecture approach to the interactive student participation approach exists. Perhaps the greatest influence has stemmed from the rapid development and increased utilization of computer-based instruction (CBI). From its initial development on the large main-frame computers in the early 1960s to the contemporary microcomputer usage, CBI has proven to encompass a variety of instructional components. The two components providing the greatest impact are computer-assisted instruction (CAI) and interactive video instruction (IAV).

CAI utilizes the computer by providing instruction through a computer screen presentation of the content to be learned. This information is typically presented in the form of text and/or graphics. Technological developments have led to the ability of merging full motion video, quality audio, and enhanced graphics to produce the more advanced IAV, commonly called the multimedia approach.

Kelly (1987) indicated that computer-based instruction, including CAI and IAV, can fall into one of the following three categories:

- Drill and practice
- Tutorial
- Simulation

To the student: The following contracts are for you to work on and complete at your own pace. Choose the contracts you want to work on. Each contract is worth a certain number of points. There are one hundred points total. Below is the point scale to be used:

86–100	A
66–85	B
50–65	C
Below 50	Unsatisfactory

Your contract will be due on _____.

Contract 1 (Level 2 = 10 points). On a piece of paper draw a diagram of a track field. Draw a start and finish line for the fifty-yard dash. Using the same start line, draw a finish line for the two hundred twenty-yard run. You may use colors.

Contract 2 (Level 3 = 15 points). On a piece of paper list all of the field events you can think of. Next to each event write a few sentences about what you do in that event.

Contract 3 (Level 3 = 15 points). Make four batons for your relay team. Choose the materials you would like for the batons.

Contract 4 (Level 2 = 10 points). Write a short paper on how the sport of track and field began. The librarian will show you how to find the books needed.

Contract 5 (Level 3 = 15 points). The inside of the track oval is where field events take place. On a piece of paper draw in where you would put all of the field events you can think of. Be sure to label each event.

Contract 6 (Level 2 = 10 points). Go to a high school track meet and write a short paper on what you saw while you were there.

Contract 7 (Level 2 = 10 points). Go to a middle school track meet and act as a helper in two events of your choice.

Contract 8 (Level 1 = 5 points). Go to a middle school track meet and act as a helper in one event of your choice.

Contract 9 (Level 2 = 10 points). Pick one event in either track or field and show a fourth-grade student how to perform that activity. Work together to help this person as much as possible. Write down which event you picked and what you did to help that person learn more about the event.

I received _____ points on my written contract.

My grade for the written contract is _____.

FIGURE 6.9 Track and Field Contracts for Grades 4–8

Reprinted by permission of Waveland Press, Inc. from Annarino, A. A., Cowell, C. C., and Hazelton, H. W. *Curriculum Theory and Design in Physical Education.* (Prospect Heights, IL; Waveland Press, Inc. 1980 [reissued 1986]. All rights reserved.

Paragraph 12
The game of volleyball is played between two teams hitting the ball back and forth across a net. The object of the game is to hit the ball in such a way that the opposition cannot return it. Play is started when the ball is served across the net and the volleying continues back and forth until one team fails to return the ball in accordance with the rules.
   Read and answer question #1.

Question #1 The activity in volleyball continues until:
1. A certain time limit expires. (If you choose this answer, go to paragraph 16.)
2. One team becomes tired. (If you choose this answer, go to paragraph 11.)
3. One team fails to legally return the ball over the net. (If you choose this answer, go to paragraph 14.)

Paragraph 11
Indirectly your answer may be right. If a team becomes tired this may cause them to make a mistake and fail to return the ball. However, being tired in itself is not the reason the activity stops. Go back to paragraph 12 and select another answer.

Paragraph 16
Your answer implies that the activity stops in volleyball at the end of a certain time. You must be confused with some other game (possibly basketball) because nothing stated indicates this. Go back to paragraph 12, read the paragraph and question #1 again, and select another answer.

Paragraph 14
Your answer is correct and this indicates your understanding of how the game is played. The team starting the play is known as the serving team. When the serving team fails to serve the ball over the net into the receiving court, side out is called and the receiving team becomes the serving team. Only the team serving may score points. If the receiving team fails to return the ball over the net legally, one point is given to the serving team.
   Read and answer question #2.

Question #2 Which team scores a point when side out is called?
1. Receiving team. (If you choose this answer, go to paragraph 17.)
2. Serving team. (If you choose this answer, go to paragraph 13.)
3. No point is scored when side out is called. (If you choose this answer, go to paragraph 20.)

FIGURE 6.10 Programmed Volleyball Rules

In drill and practice programs, the content is initially presented and then followed by one or more questions. Following the student's response, the computer will evaluate it and provide immediate feedback. Tutorial programs are similar but call for greater student interactions. Beyond just reading text and answering questions, students can periodically review prior content and/or take an exam. Simulation programs provide real life situations involving student interaction. Simulation programs are most effective in an IAV format because of the ability to show full-motion video.

Station: Gymnasium wall

Skill: Volleyball overhand pass

Behavioral objective: To be able to execute the two-handed, overhead volleyball pass by making a minimum of eight consecutive passes against a wall.

Instructions: Await the ball with hands at face height, fingers spread, knees slightly bent. (The body slightly crouched and positioned directly under the ball.) The ball should be contacted with the fingertips and thumbs about a foot above the head and in front of face. The pass should be hit approximately fifteen feet in the air and directly on top of the head of the teammate for whom the pass is intended. Uncoil into the ball, rather than jump at it.

Practice: Throw the ball over your head and practice hitting the ball to yourself, keeping it high and directly over your head.

Skill assignment: Make consecutive passes against the wall; each pass must hit the wall above the white ten-foot line.

Number of consecutive passes (circle one)

Level 1	Level 2	Level 3
8	12	16

Date completed: _____

Initials: _____

FIGURE 6.11 Programmed Overhead Pass in Volleyball

Computer-based instruction is an effective tool.

Select one of the following sources for gaining information on the jump shot:
1. Live demonstration and explanation.
2. A textbook on basketball skills.
3. Silent loop film—analyze the movement.

You may memorize the movements or write them down. Regardless, after ten shots and fifteen shots, return to the sources and review your insights.

Description of the task: After you attain the information, select a basketball and a basket and choose one of the distance arcs marked on the floor. On this paper mark your selected arc before you start. You will take twenty shots from your selected distance.

Hints to the learner:
1. Stay with your selected distance—don't change it. Take all twenty shots.
2. If you have problems, think about the techniques and go back to the source if necessary.
3. Remember that you are responsible for your own self-evaluation.
4. Return to the source after the tenth shot.

Indicate the distance from the basket by crossing one out.

3'	5'	7'	9'	11'	15'	17'	18'	19'	20'

Indicate the number of baskets made by crossing one out.

1	2	3	4	5	6	7	8	9	10
11	12	13	14	15	16	17	18	19	20

Comments
1. Were you pleased with your results? _____
2. What was the most consistent part of your jump shot? _____
3. What part of the jump shot did you change after returning to the source following shot #10? _____
4. Were you more successful as a result of your change? _____
5. Are you ready to move on to a new skill? _____

FIGURE 6.12 Programmed Jump Shot in Basketball

From Mueller, R. (1976). *Personalized learning in physical education.* Washington, D.C.: AAHPERD. Reprinted by permission.

Although K–12 physical education seldom employs the passive lecture methodology, cognitive components exist that enhance this more traditional approach. These components include the history, rules, terminology, and strategy of various games and sports. Passive lecture methodology has been presented through both CAI and IAV (Adams, et al., 1991; Justen, Adams, &

Waldrop, 1988; Kerns, 1989; Steffen & Hansen, 1987). The use of CBI has also been used in the psychomotor domain.

INSTRUCTIONAL STRATEGIES USING STUDENTS

Using students for instructional purposes is a common occurrence in physical education. The transfer of instructional responsibility from the teacher to the student has obvious benefits. Using students allows the physical educator more time for content organization, class supervision, and the utilization of different teaching techniques. These experiences provide an opportunity for students to nurture desirable personality traits including self-confidence and responsibility and allow students to develop leadership qualities. Rink (1993) adds that student involvement has the potential to aid students in developing skills of observation and analysis and a better understanding of the motor skills being taught.

Two approaches for using students as *teachers* exist—student assistants and peer teaching. The student assistant approach uses older students as a means of complementing younger students; for example, having eighth and ninth grade students assist in the primary grades. This approach can be successful in motivating both the younger students being taught and the older students doing the teaching. The implementation of student assistants can enrich the overall physical education program. The responsibilities for student assistants include the following:

Students can:

- Teach content selected by the physical educator.
- Supervise group activity as assigned by the physical educator.
- Provide individual attention.
- Assist in pre-class organization (preparing an area for activity).
- Assist in post-class clean up.

One student is used to explain and/or demonstrate a skill to another student in the same class with peer teaching exercises. Rink (1993) explains that it is best to match skilled or experienced students with novice, less experienced performers. It often works well, because peers have a communication advantage over the teacher. Peer teachers can be utilized to convey content to the entire class, to a portion of the class, or to one student. When the class is organized in pairs, peer teaching becomes reciprocal (Mosston & Ashworth, 1994). This requires one student to be the performer while the other student is the observer. While one student performs the skill, the second student provides feedback based on criteria provided by the teacher. This feedback can occur during or immediately following the performance.

Peer teaching can be used for an entire lesson (see Figure 6.13) or for part of a lesson (see Figure 6.14). Rink stresses that the key to using this strategy is the development of a productive peer relationship. This will happen only if the responsibilities of the students are understood and they are held accountable for these responsibilities.

Gymnastics (high school)

1. The physical educator divided the students into ability groups of four people. Using previously learned floor exercise skills, each student in the group is expected to teach his/her routine to the other members of the group.
2. The physical educator explains that the student who is teaching the routine (the peer teacher) is responsible for the quality of performance of the learners and that groups will not be evaluated on the level of difficulty but rather on the following criteria:
   - Clarity of body shape throughout the routine
   - Smoothness of transition from one move to another
   - Control of movement
   - Dynamic quality of execution
3. The peer teacher is encouraged to first demonstrate and explain how each part of the routine is done and then give students practice on each part. When students can do each part with quality, the peer teacher puts the parts together. Groups move at their own pace but are encouraged to practice one routine until it is done successfully before moving onto another routine.

FIGURE 6.13 Entire Lesson Peer Teaching

Adapted from *Teaching Physical Education for Learning* (p.173) by Judith E. Rink, St. Louis, MO: Mosby. Reprinted by permission of Mosby.

Volleyball

1. The physical educator works with the entire class on the volleyball underhand serve. The teacher then divides the class into groups of four people. One student serves the ball from one side of the net, and one student serves the ball from the other side of the net. One student on each side (peer teachers) coaches the server. The coach's job is to check for the following teaching cues that have been given for underhand serve:
   - Using up and back stance with body lean
   - Hitting the ball out of the hand with no toss
   - Finishing with weight on the front foot
2. Each group has a skill card with the cues listed. Coaches are told to look for only one cue each time the ball is served and then tell the server whether that cue has been observed.

FIGURE 6.14 Part of a Lesson Peer Teaching

Adapted from *Teaching Physical Education for Learning* (p.174) by Judith E. Rink, St. Louis, MO: Mosby. Reprinted by permission of Mosby.

SUMMARY

1. Curriculum reform is best accomplished when all individuals, including administrators, teachers, parents, and students become involved in the process.

2. Scope refers to *what* is to be taught and sequence refers to *when* it is to be taught.
3. To guide the development of a scope and sequence, Bookwalter provides six criteria—progression, variety, seasonality, feasibility, practice for mastery, and unity.
4. When scheduling the physical education program, two organizational patterns are typically used—traditional and flexible.
5. The cycle plan allows for more intensive study of a specific activity.
6. Both indoor and outdoor facilities are used for the instruction of physical education.
7. Team teaching is an approach to staffing that can be beneficial to students by reducing the student-to-teacher ratio, providing more effective supervision and management, and exposing students to the talents of more than one teacher.
8. Differentiated staffing is an approach to staffing that can prove beneficial to students by making the best use of the competencies of all the teachers.
9. The use of paraprofessionals has grown in these times of shrinking resources. Of specific concern is the selection, training, and role delineation of individuals.
10. Allowing secondary school students to select what activities they want to be taught may lead to a better understanding of and appreciation for physical education.
11. Homogeneity in physical education can be accomplished through ability grouping.
12. Three approaches to individualized study in a physical education curriculum are contracting, programmed instruction, and computer-based instruction.
13. Students can be useful for instruction either as assistants or peer teachers.

QUESTIONS AND LEARNING ACTIVITIES

1. Interview the physical education director of a large school. Ask how the total curriculum is put together and how the physical education faculty carries it out. Examine the program for seasonal content, time allotment, variety of activities, and electives available for both boys and girls.

2. Examine literature pertaining to ability grouping, performance contracts, programmed instruction, and computer-based instruction. List two or three advantages and disadvantages for each. Be prepared to discuss what implications need to be considered when using one of these innovations.

3. Provide a description of a scope and sequence. Visit selected schools to secure a copy of existing scopes and sequences.

4. Suppose you are employed by a large urban school system as the director of physical education. You have been asked to become involved in curriculum reform for the entire school. Indicate in several steps how you may participate in such a project and how your participation may benefit physical education.

5. Using Bookwalter's six criteria for the organization of physical education activities, determine which criteria is exemplified in the following statements. Place the letter(s) of your response in the space provided.

    A. Progression   D. Feasibility
    B. Variety   E. Practice for Mastery
    C. Seasonability   F. Unity

_____ 1. Adapting the choice of the activity to suit weather and the prevailing interest in sports.
_____ 2. Allowing more than three volleys in volleyball for beginners.
_____ 3. Assigning a series of forward rolls after the single roll is learned.
_____ 4. Avoiding the boring repetition of activities.
_____ 5. Combining a variety of related stunts into a routine.
_____ 6. Equipment is available for the activity.
_____ 7. Extensive rather than intensive treatment.
_____ 8. Gradual increase in performance, difficulty, or complexity in accordance with individual or class readiness.
_____ 9. Integrating the dance and history topics.
_____ 10. Intensive rather than extensive treatment.
_____ 11. Lowering the basketball goals for the intermediate grades.
_____ 12. Planning a specific activity for early spring.
_____ 13. Playing soccer in the fall.
_____ 14. Repeating the same stunt or exercise reasonably often.
_____ 15. Selecting activities that are practical under the conditions.
_____ 16. Selecting activities that contribute to all of the objectives.
_____ 17. Staying with an activity until ease of function is acquired.
_____ 18. Sufficient drills to assure learning.
_____ 19. The inclusion of all activities essential for the needs, interests, and capacities of all pupils.
_____ 20. Within the ability of the teacher.

REFERENCES

Adams, T. M., Kandt, G. K., Throgmartin, D., & Waldrop, P. B. (1991). Computer-assisted instruction vs. lecture methods in teaching the rules of golf. *The Physical Educator, 48*(3), 146–150.

Annarino, A. A., Cowell, C. C., & Hazelton, H. W. (1986). *Curriculum theory and design in physical education.* Prospect Heights, IL: Waveland Press.

Bookwalter, K. W. (1964). *Physical education in secondary schools.* New York: The Center for Applied Resources in Education.

Bucher, C. A., & Koenig, C. R. (1983). *Methods and materials for secondary school physical education.* St. Louis, MO: Mosby.

Bucher, C. A., & Thaxton, N. A. (1979). *Physical education for children: Movement foundations and experiences.* New York: Macmillan Publishing Company.

Chambers, R. L. (1988). Legal and practical issues for grouping students in physical education classes. *The Physical Educator, 45*(4), 180–185.

Daughtrey, G., & Lewis, C. (1979). *Effective teaching strategies in secondary physical education.* Philadelphia: Saunders.

Fast, B. (1971). Contingency contracting. *Journal of Health, Physical Education, Recreation, and Dance, 42*(8), 31–32.

Frith, G. H. (1982). *The role of the special education paraprofessional: An introductory text.* Springfield, IL: Charles C. Thomas, Publisher.

Gustafson, J. (1973). Making programmed instruction practical. *The Physical Educator, 30*(2), 91–92.

Heitmann, H. M., & Kneer, M. E. (1976). *Physical education instructional techniques: An individualized humanistic approach.* Englewood Cliffs, NJ: Prentice-Hall.

Hellison, D. R., & Templin, T. J. (1991). *A reflective approach to teaching physical education.* Champaign, IL: Human Kinetics.

Johnson, W. S., & Morris, D. C. (1981). Students as active participants: The case for student oriented research. *Educational Research Quarterly, 6,* 38–45.

Justen, J. E., Adams, T. M., & Waldrop, P. B. (1988). Effects of small group versus individual user computer-assisted instruction on student achievement. *Educational Technology, 28*(2), 50–52.

Kelly, L. J. (1987). Computer assisted instruction: Applications for physical education. *Journal of Physical Education, Recreation, and Dance, 58*(4), 74–79.

Kelly, L. J., & Vergason, G. A. (1978). *Dictionary of special education and rehabilitation.* Denver, CO: Love Publishing Company.

Kerns, M. M. (1989). The effectiveness of computer-assisted instruction in teaching tennis rules and strategies. *Journal of Teaching in Physical Education, 8,* 170–176.

Kneer, M. E. (1982). Ability grouping in physical education. *Journal of Physical Education, Recreation and Dance, 53*(9), 10–13.

Lockhart, A., & Mott, J. (1981). An experiment in homogeneous grouping and the effect on achievement in sports fundamentals. *Research Quarterly, 22,* 58–62.

Mandell, B. R., & Schram, B. (1983). *Human services: An introduction.* New York: John Wiley & Sons.

Mosston, M., & Ashworth, S. (1994). *Teaching physical education.* New York: Macmillan Publishing Company.

Mueller, R. (1976). *Personalized learning in physical education.* Washington, DC: AAHPERD.

Pickett, A. L. (1981). *Paragraphs in special education: The state of the art.* New York: New Careers Training Laboratory.

Rand, J., & English, F. (1968). Towards a differentiated teaching staff. *Phi Delta Kappan, 49,* 264–268.

Rink, J. E. (1993). *Teaching physical education for learning.* St. Louis, MO: Mosby.

Schurr, E. L. (1980). *Movement experiences for children.* Englewood Cliffs, NJ: Prentice-Hall.

Steffen, J., & Hansen, G. (1987). Effect of computer-assisted instruction on development of cognitive and psychomotor learning in bowling. *Journal of Teaching in Physical Education, 6,* 183–191.

Trump, J. L., & Baynham, D. (1961). *Guide to better schools: Focus on change.* Chicago: Rand McNally.

Vogler, E. W., French, R., & Bishop, P. (1989). Paraprofessional: Implications for adapted physical education. *The Physical Educator, 46*(2), 69–76.

Whitehead, A. N. (1932). *The aims of education: And other essays.* London: Williams & Northgate.

Woodward, W. H. (1963). *Vittorino da Feltre and other humanist educators.* New York: Teachers College Press, Columbia University.

7
THE CURRICULUM GUIDE

Outline

Defining the Guide

Preliminary Considerations

The Administrator's Role

The Curriculum Coordinating Committee

Curriculum Subcommittees

Faculty Involvement

Constructing the Guide

Outcomes

After reading and studying this chapter, you should be able to:
- Define
  Curriculum guide
  Curriculum coordinating committee
- Discuss the importance of developing a curriculum guide.
- Describe the procedure for developing a curriculum guide.
- Explain the administrator's role in development.
- Explain the responsibilities of the planning and the curriculum coordinating committees in developing a curriculum guide.
- Provide examples of faculty involvement for enhancing the development of a curriculum guide.
- Provide a content format of a curriculum guide.

Leland Stanford was correct when he stated, "The world stands aside for the man who knows where he is going." If an individual knows where he/she is headed, that person will certainly know if and when he/she gets there. In education, however, it is not enough to merely know where you are going. In the age of accountability, this information must be available for all people concerned including administrators, parents, and students. Unfortunately, too many physical educators exist who have known where they have wanted to go but have failed to effectively communicate this information. Furthermore, educators have failed to document this intent or direction as a matter of record.

Writing a course of study or curriculum guide is time consuming and often tedious. When completed, however, the project becomes an administratively sound document that gives direction to the program. The curriculum guide contains *what* a physical education program purports to do and *how* it purports to do it.

Regardless of the school system's size, a need exists to structure the physical education program on paper for everyone to see, review, and periodically revise. This planning may initially appear to be a major task, but if it is approached logically and sequentially, it will not be a big ordeal. Acknowledge the necessity of written materials, seek administrative support (including resources), and begin. As the initial planning begins, it is recommended that the guide be designed for the entire K–12 physical education program.

DEFINING THE GUIDE

Cooking with a "pinch of this" and a "dash of that" in the manner reminiscent of grandma baking molasses cookies is hardly appropriate for the homemaker today. A detailed recipe is required so that guesswork is eliminated. For the same reason that an actor needs a script or an orchestra conductor needs a score, a physical educator needs a curriculum guide.

A curriculum guide is a plan for an educational program. Annarino, Cowell, and Hazelton (1986) define the guide as a document for both teachers and students of physical education that indicates how educational philosophy and theory are translated into action. Rink (1993) states that the curriculum guide should specify what a student should learn and behaviorally be able to do after the educational program is completed. Existing for teachers individually and collectively, the curriculum guide is a framework that often contains an individual's philosophy, aims, objectives, as well as the scope of offerings and the sequence in which these offerings will be presented.

Melograno (1996) states that a curriculum guide should provide answers to the following three questions:

- *Where are we going?* This question is best answered by establishing a sound philosophy and a list of general objectives for the physical education program.
- *How will we get there?* This question is best answered by (a) planning and establishing student outcomes and explicit content, and (b) devising meaningful learning experiences.
- *How will we know we have arrived?* This question is best answered by selecting and/or developing valid evaluation procedures for determining the effectiveness of the program.

PRELIMINARY CONSIDERATIONS

A useful curriculum guide requires forethought and planning, but even then it will have limitations. The guide is not a solution to a weak program. The most important element for a quality program is instruction, and it is the teacher's responsibility to successfully promote this instruction. A well developed curriculum guide could provide a strong beginning. The curriculum guide will hopefully increase the effectiveness of the program by five percent. A five percent increase may not sound like a significant improvement, but many businesses today either succeed or fail on less than a five percent margin.

An organizational flow chart for curriculum development in physical education is illustrated in Figure 7.1. Before constructing a guide, a number of preliminary issues should be considered. The appointment of a planning committee may accommodate many of these considerations. It may be advantageous to appoint a planning committee/group, particularly in larger school systems, during the development stages of a new curriculum guide or during the revision cycle of the existing guide.

This committee (see Figure 7.2) is an initiating group, generally led by the superintendent of schools or the director of physical education, whose goal is to probe into practical ways of developing a comprehensive physical education program. The committee should be comprised of one school administrator (in most instances a building principal) and a physical education representative from each level (primary, intermediate, middle or junior high, and senior high). This is an appropriate number of members to meet with the physical education director, who will probably serve as the chair of the

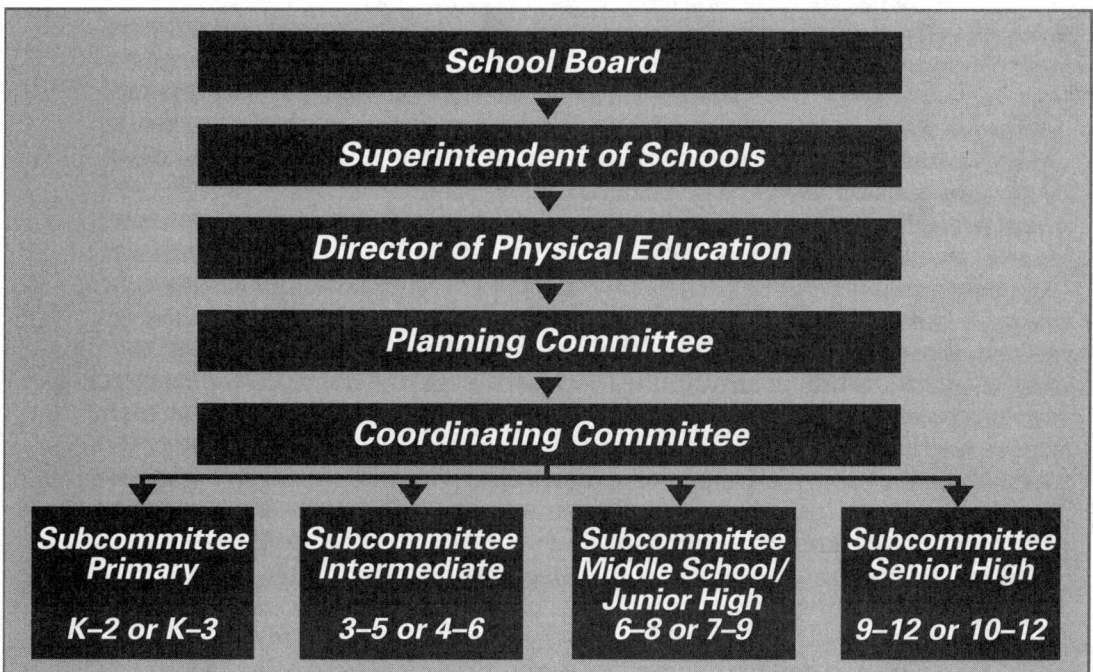

FIGURE 7.1 Flow Chart for Curriculum Development in Physical Education

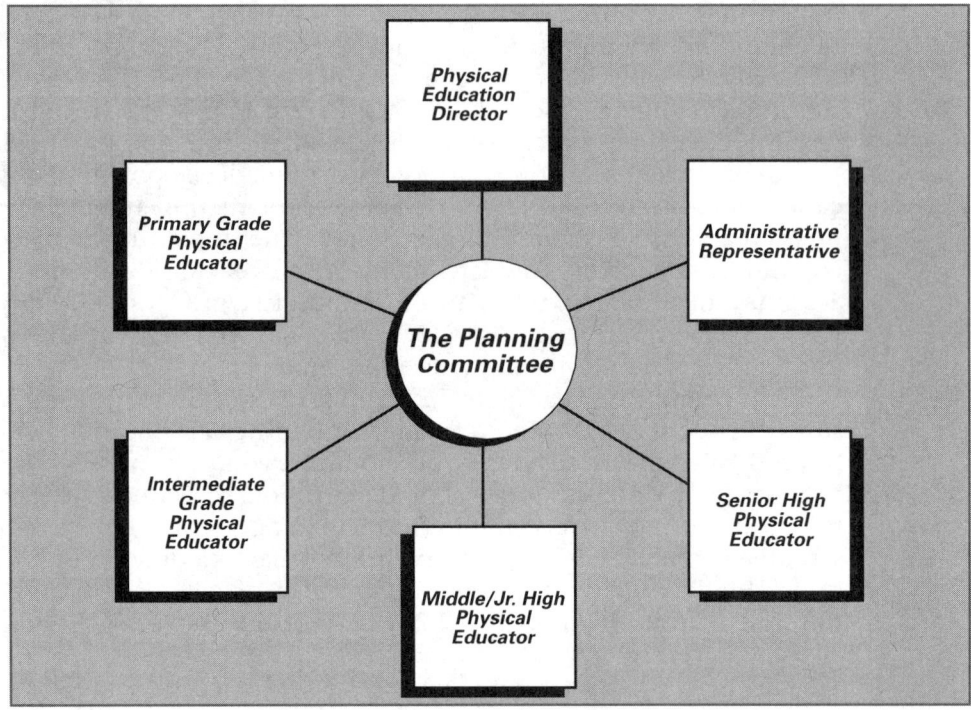

FIGURE 7.2 Planning Committee Personnel

committee and will give thought to the scope and depth of the development or revision about to be undertaken.

The two steps the planning committee intends to use to initiate this curriculum project include:

- Exploring the degree of dissatisfaction with the present curriculum. A simple curriculum survey can be prepared so that all members of the physical education faculty and fellow teachers may respond. Each physical educator should be able to respond regarding the activities offered at his/her level and what is considered the strengths and weaknesses of these offerings.
- Meeting with separate school principals and eventually with the school board in order to establish necessary administrative procedures. These procedures may include:
- Obtaining release time for selected physical educators to (a) attend in-service programs, professional clinics, conferences, and/or conventions, and/or (b) visit other school systems similar in size as a means of bringing these new program ideas and practices back to the faculty.
- Making budget provisions for the employment of a curriculum consultant for assisting the faculty in whatever capacity deemed appropriate.

THE ADMINISTRATOR'S ROLE

The support of the school system's administration is crucial if the development of the curriculum guide is to be successful. This support can best be shown by the principal serving on the planning committee. This administrator's specific responsibilities are to:

- Arrange meeting places for the curriculum coordinating committee and the subcommittees.
- Provide a list of the school system's total educational goals for the curriculum coordinating committee.
- Arrange release time, if necessary, for curriculum coordinating committee and subcommittee members to meet.
- Make necessary resources available, including instructional materials, printed references, and consultant services.
- Arrange for necessary equipment, supplies, and secretarial services.
- Cooperate with committee personnel in both raising questions and seeking answers relating to the impact of the new curriculum guide on the rest of the school curriculum.
- Inform the local public of the progress being made in developing the curriculum guide and why both the guide and physical education, in general, are important for the community and its future citizens.
- Encourage scientific inquiry in general.
- Assist in the appraisal of the results of the curriculum project.

THE CURRICULUM COORDINATING COMMITTEE

Once the planning committee has arranged the development of the physical education curriculum guide, the organization of the curriculum coordinating committee should be established. This group will eventually write the guide and should consist of five or six individuals acting as coordinators of the efforts of various subcommittees. The make-up of the curriculum coordinating committee is similar to that of the planning committee (see Figure 7.2); it should contain one administrator and one representative from each of the four levels of the physical education program. The only representative missing is the physical education director.

The immediate tasks of the curriculum coordinating committee are to:

- Appoint faculty to each subcommittee.
- Establish appropriate procedures underlying the guide construction effort.
- Standardize the progression of learning experiences for various grade levels.
- Formulate work schedules for all of the subcommittees.
- Encourage the subcommittees to perform their functions in a professional manner.

- Encourage both physical education and nonphysical education faculty to be supportive in the guide development.
- Coordinate the work of the subcommittees and when completed, fit it into the complete curriculum.
- Provide the subcommittees with the results of (a) a community survey including its historical background, social and economic structure, and the availability of its recreational facilities; and (b) a school survey including the availability of indoor and outdoor facilities, equipment, class size, and faculty qualifications.
- Provide the subcommittees with regulations and/or requirements from the state department of education.
- Formulate the foundations on which the guide should be written, including a definition of physical education, a statement of the school's philosophy of physical education, a listing of the program's general objective, and information on the characteristics, needs, and interests of the community's youth (Annarino, Cowell, & Hazelton, 1986).
- Collect, review, and collate all materials from the subcommittees.
- Write the curriculum guide.

CURRICULUM SUBCOMMITTEES

The subcommittees (see Figure 7.3) should be comprised of one physical educator, one principal, one nonphysical education teacher from the specific level, one parent, and one student. The regular classroom teacher can be an asset during the content selection and arrangement process because he/she views this content differently than the physical educator. Parents are generally helpful because they are keenly aware of the needs and interests of the children in the specific community. A concerned parent who is willing to work diligently is the ideal. However, the selection of this individual may cause problems if chosen arbitrarily. It is recommended that the responsibility of selecting which parents should serve on each of the four subcommittees be given to the school system's parent group. Most communities have this type of parent group, which is generally called either the Parent Teacher Association (PTA) or Parent Teacher Organization (PTO). At both the junior high and senior high school levels a student should be added to the subcommittee.

Each subcommittee should:

- Determine the most effective curriculum model for that grade level.
- Select and organize the physical education activities for that grade level.
- Provide a scope and sequence for these activities.
- Establish student behavioral objectives or outcomes.
- Determine effective instructional strategies.
- Select appropriate methods for the evaluation of students.

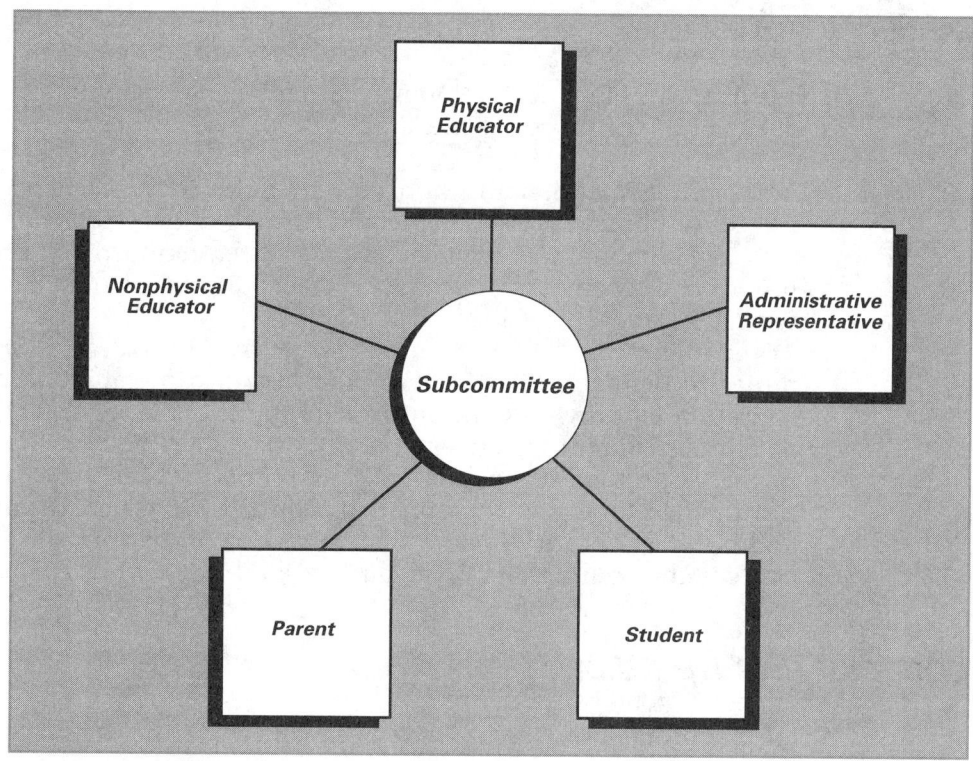

FIGURE 7.3 Subcommittee Personnel

The work of specific subcommittees is time consuming. The exchange of educational philosophies, the debate over personal beliefs and convictions, and the arrival at behavioral outcomes for youth at various age levels cannot be accomplished in a matter of days or even weeks. Proceeding slowly and carefully in the initial meetings is important in order to lay the foundation that all physical education teachers will accept and build on when the guide becomes a reality.

The secret of group action is that if several people of different backgrounds are involved in a cooperative effort, some common agreement and enthusiasm for the content of the guide is likely to occur. The task of teachers and parents working cooperatively for the purpose of planning a physical education program should result not only in a meaningful curriculum for the students but also in professional growth for the teachers. In addition, an awareness of the place and importance of physical education for the parents may result. In fact the cooperative effort of developing a curriculum guide is capable of providing a rich professional experience for everyone involved, including administrators, teachers, parents, and students.

FACULTY INVOLVEMENT

At various stages of guide development it may be necessary for other faculty involvement in the process. For example:

- At the primary level, both a noncommittee classroom teacher and a physical educator may be asked to prepare a sequence of integrated movement activities combining academic concepts (letter, number, and color recognition) and locomotion that will be placed in the instructional program at a later date.
- At the intermediate level, a music teacher may be added to the subcommittee to define music education and how it can compliment physical education by providing meaningful rhythmic activities and eliminating repetitious content for students.
- At the senior high school level, an interscholastic coach may be asked to assist in developing an appropriate basketball unit. Where the unit begins and how in depth it develops will be related, in part, to the amount of content and instruction at previous levels.

CONSTRUCTING THE GUIDE

When the curriculum materials have been collected from the subcommittees, but before the writing begins, an examination of other curriculum guides should take place. Libraries at most teacher education colleges and universities contain examples of curriculum guides from local school systems. Also useful are guides prepared at the state level. Identified in a survey by Stillwell and Reneau (1992), twenty-eight of the state agencies have developed a recommended curriculum guide or course of study. Many of these guides can be obtained free of charge by writing to the respective state agency. Table 7.1 is a listing of state agency curriculum materials and where they may be obtained. In addition, a variety of curriculum materials including guides are available from the ERIC Clearinghouse on Teacher Education. Table 7.2 provides twelve such guides. A third source for curriculum guides is the Kraus Curriculum Development Library (KCDL). It was created in 1983 and is a comprehensive curriculum development resource. KCDL contains a collection of current curriculum guides from North America. Those guides in the publication are selected on one criterion—the usefulness to teachers and teachers-in-training. A listing of selected physical education KDCL curriculum guides is shown in Table 7.3.

Curriculum guides often contain consistent content but varied formats. Content is generally categorized by grade level. The most common format separates content into the following grade levels: elementary school, middle or junior high school, and senior high school. Some guides further subdivide the elementary school content into primary (K–2 or K–3) and intermediate

TABLE 7.1 State Agency Curriculum Materials

Guide Title	Source
A Guide for Instruction in Physical Education	South Dakota State Department of Education Kneip Building 700 North Illinois Street Pierre, SD 57501
A Tool for Assessing and Designing a K–12 Physical Education Program (1985)	Iowa State Department of Public Instruction Grimes State Office Building East 14th and Grand Street Des Moines, IA 50319
Alabama Course of Study: Physical Education (1989)	Alabama State Department of Education 483 State Office Building 501 Dexter Avenue Montgomery, AL 36130
Elementary & Secondary Physical Education Model Curriculum Guides (1986)	Alaska State Department of Education P. O. Box F Juneau, AK 99811
Handbook for Physical Education (1986)	California State Department of Education 721 Capitol Mall P. O. Box 944272 Sacramento, CA 94244
Kansas Physical Education Curriculum Guidelines	Kansas State Department of Education Kansas State Education Building 120 East 10th Street Topeka, KS 66612
Mississippi Curriculum Structure for Health and Physical Education (1991)	Mississippi State Department of Education Sillers Building P.O. Box 771 Jackson, MS 39205
Montana in Action: Physical Education Curriculum Guide, Grades K–12 (1988)	Montana Office of Public Instruction Room 106, State Capitol Helena, MT 59620
Physical Education and Recreation Curriculum Guide: Grades K–10 (1981)	Louisiana State Department of Education P. O. Box 94064 Baton Rouge, LA 70804

Continued

TABLE 7.1 *Continued*

Guide Title	Source
Physical Education Guide, Grades K–12 (1988)	New York State Department of Education 111 Education Building Washington Avenue Albany, NY 12234
Physical Education Curriculum Guide: K–12 (1985)	North Dakota Department of Public Instruction 600 Boulevard Avenue E Bismarck, ND 58505
Physical Education Curriculum Guidelines: K–12 (1985)	Washington State Department of Education Old Capitol Building Mail Stop FG–11 Olympia, WA 98504
Physical Education Program Guide, K–12 (1979)	Hawaii State Department of Education Queen Liliuokalani Building P. O. Box 2360 Honolulu, HI 96804
South Carolina Physical Education Curriculum Guidelines, Volume I K–6 & Volume II 7–12 (1989)	South Carolina State Department of Education Rutledge Building 1429 Senate Street Columbia, SC 29201

(3–5 or 4–6), as illustrated in Figure 7.1. Regardless of the number of levels, the content must be coordinated to avoid undue repetition and to insure that the activities are sequenced progressively. Of course, this is the task of the curriculum coordinating committee.

If the guide is intended for the total physical education program, this format may be employed for its construction:

    I. Title
   II. Introduction
  III. Definitions Specific to Physical Education
  IV. Philosophy of Physical Education
      A. Physical Education Defined
      B. Justification for Physical Education
   V. Need for Physical Education
      A. Aim(s)
      B. General Objectives
         1. Behavioral objectives/outcomes by grade level
         2. Concepts by grade level

TABLE 7.2 ERIC Clearinghouse Curriculum Materials

A Guide to Curriculum Planning for Visually Impaired Students. (1991). Madison, WI: Wisconsin State Department of Public Instruction. 197pp. (ERIC No. ED 337 942).

A Guide to Curriculum Planning in Physical Education. (1989). Madison, WI: Wisconsin State Department of Public Instruction. 142 pp. (ERIC No. ED 267 024).

Arizona Essential Skills for Performing Arts, K–12 Dance. (1990). Phoenix, AZ: Arizona State Department of Education. 144 pp. (ERIC No. ED 324 302).

Michigan K–12 Program Standards of Quality. (1984). Lansing, MI: Michigan State Board of Education. 79 pp. (ERIC No. ED 253 941).

Middle School Physical Education. (1989). Fort Worth, TX: Fort Worth Independent School District. 172 pp. (ERIC No. ED 317 515).

Model Learner Outcomes for Physical Education. (1989). St. Paul, MN: Minnesota State Department of Education. 94 pp. (ERIC No. ED 329 552).

Montana Rural Education Curriculum Guide. (1982). Helena, MT: Montana Office of Public Instruction. 30 pp. (ERIC No.ED 224 635).

PACE IV: The Developmental Physical Education Curriculum from Theory to Practice. (1990). Bloomington, IN: Indiana University. 120 pp. (ERIC No. ED 355 188).

Physical Education Grade 1. Physical Education Grade 2. (1989). Fort Worth, TX: Fort Worth Independent School District. 122 pp. (ERIC No. ED 317 516).

Physical Education Grades 3–5. (1989). Fort Worth, TX: Fort Worth Independent School District. 179 pp. (ERIC No. ED 317 513).

Physical Education Syllabus, Grades K–12. (1986). Albany, NY: New York State Education Department. 88 pp. (ERIC No. ED 272 461).

Responsible Healthy Lifestyles. Teacher Resource Guide: Movement-Fitness (K–6). (1989). Farmington, UT: Davis County School District. 114 pp. (ERIC No. ED 323 182).

    VI. Program Content
        A. Time Allotment
        B. Class Size and Composition
        C. Scope and Sequence
           1. Primary grade level
           2. Intermediate grade level
           3. Middle school level
           4. Senior high school level
   VII. Instructional Strategies by Level
  VIII. Resources and Instructional Materials
    IX. Evaluation in Physical Education
        A. Student
        B. Teacher
        C. Program
     X. Selected References
        A. For Students by Level
        B. For Teachers by Level

TABLE 7.3 KCDL Curriculum Materials

Elementary Physical Education Curriculum Guide. (1986). Florence, KY: Boone County Schools. 154 pp. (PE K*–061).

Elementary Physical Education Guide. (1987). Wichita, KS: Wichita Public Schools. 254 pp. (PE K*–062).

Fundamentals of Fitness: An Exercise Concepts Curriculum. (1987). Needham, MA: Stay Fit. 186 pp. (PE K*–027).

Physical Education: Basic Course of Study. (1985). Sacramento, CA: Sacramento City Unified School District. 42 pp. (PE K*–063).

Physical Education: A Comprehensive Curriculum Guide for Kindergarten–Grade 12. Auburn, NY: Cayuga–Onondaga BOCES. 126 pp. (PE K*–066).

Physical Education Course of Study. (1985). Chagrin Falls, OH: Chagrin Falls Exempted Village Schools. 25 pp. (PE K*–053).

Physical Education Curriculum Guide K–10. (1986). Bloomington, MN: Bloomington Public Schools. 226 pp. (PE K*–056).

Physical Education Curriculum Guide (K–12). (1984). Wheaton, IL: Wheaton Warrenville District 200. 549 pp. (PE K*–048).

Physical Education Curriculum Guide (Resources K–5). (1985). Fountain Valley, CA: Fountain Valley School District. 128 pp. (PE K*–052).

Physical Education Curriculum Guide (Resources 6–8). (1985). Fountain Valley, CA: Fountain Valley School District. 154 pp. (PE K*–006).

Physical Education: A Guide for 7th and 8th Grades. (1983). Eugene, OR: Eugene Public Schools. 210 pp. (PE K*–024).

Physical Education: Middle School. (1982). Columbus, OH: Columbus Public Schools. 311 pp. (PE K*–004).

In addition to these basic components, the following information may be included in a specific curriculum guide:

- The developmental characteristics of students
- Organizational formats, both unit and lesson
- A map of the school, highlighting the teaching stations
- Grading policy
- Accident policy

Jewett, Bain, and Ennis (1995) state that the contents and the degree of specificity of the curriculum guide reflect the philosophy about the students within the program and the teachers who will implement the program. The curriculum guides that are more flexible and/or less detailed will allow all teachers the autonomy to make decisions regarding content, methodology, grading, and so on. Whereas the curriculum guides that are precise in content and well detailed will provide all teachers, especially the new ones, a firm foundation from which to teach.

SUMMARY

1. A curriculum guide presents the physical education program in written form and provides a framework from which to review and/or revise.
2. The development of a curriculum guide is the responsibility of all individuals involved including administration, teachers, parents, and students.
3. Before the curriculum guide is written it is recommended that example guides be obtained from public schools and/or state departments of education.

QUESTIONS AND LEARNING ACTIVITIES

1. Examine curriculum guides from schools of different sizes. List the strengths and weaknesses of each guide. List similarities and the differences as they relate to both the content and organization of the guides.
2. Once a school has developed a curriculum guide, is there a danger that the program may become too rigid? If so, how can this be combated?
3. What are some of the circumstances that prevent a physical educator from teaching content as it appears in the curriculum guide?
4. To what extent should classroom teachers become involved in developing a curriculum guide?
5. As the director of physical education for twelve elementary schools, three junior high schools, and two high schools, your task is to develop a comprehensive curriculum guide. Explain the process you would follow for completing this task.

REFERENCES

Annarino, A. A., Cowell, C. C., & Hazelton, H. W. (1986). *Curriculum theory and design in physical education*. Prospect Heights, IL: Waveland Press.

Jewett, A. E., Bain, L. L., & Ennis, C. D. (1995). *The curriculum process in physical education*. Dubuque, IA: Brown & Benchmark.

Melograno, V. J. (1996). *Designing the physical education curriculum*. Champaign, IL: Human Kinetics.

Rink, J. E. (1993). *Teaching physical education for learning*. St. Louis, MO: Mosby.

Stillwell, J. L., & Reneau, P. (1992). A survey of state agency physical education curriculum material. *The Physical Educator, 49*(4), 170–173.

8

THE ELEMENTARY PHYSICAL EDUCATION PROGRAM, K–6

Outline

Children Moving

The Elementary School Child

Curriculum Content for the Elementary Grades

Time Allotment

The Middle School

Outcomes

After reading and studying this chapter, you should be able to:
- Define

  Basic rhythms

  Body awareness

  Cooperative games

  Creative rhythms

  Folk dance

  Lead-up games

  Locomotor skills

  Low organized games

  Manipulative skills

  Movement education

  Movement qualities

  Nonlocomotor skills

  Relationships

  Relays

  Self-testing

  Singing rhythms

  Social dance

  Spatial awareness

  Sports

  Square dance

  The middle school concept

  Traditional and contemporary dance
- Identify the five content categories for an elementary physical education program.

- Describe the physical characteristics of elementary school students.
- Describe the intellectual characteristics of elementary school students.
- Describe the social/emotional characteristics of elementary school students.
- Provide specific examples in each of the five elementary physical education content categories.
- Discuss the place and importance of games in an elementary physical education curriculum.
- Discuss the time allotment for each of the elementary physical education content areas for grades K–6.
- Select physical education activities for a K–6 program based on the students' physical, intellectual, and social/emotional characteristics.

The concept that children's play is as old as culture itself is supported by the disciplines of the classics, archeological findings, and the antiquities of civilization. From Rousseau to Piaget it has been called priceless—the children's way of life. Play is what children do when they are not eating, sleeping, or complying with the wishes of adults (Gallahue, 1996). It is through play that children learn about themselves and their movement capabilities. More importantly is the concept that children learn about the people and the world around them by means of playing. Children have not waited for others to teach them how to play. Rather, children have learned themselves in a manner that is serious and meaningful. This "self teaching" is a profound dimension because the naturalness, innocence, and lack of sophistication that exists in children facilitates a valid observation showing how children feel not only about an activity but also about each other while at play.

CHILDREN MOVING

One goal of children's play, much of which is in a movement setting, is the efficiency of movement. The movement learning process is partly an intellectual one because the gaining of both perceptual-motor skills and rich sensory experiences is paramount to young people's understanding of themselves and their adjustment to the world of people, things, and ideas. It is through the early acts of moving, both individually and collectively, that children learn to associate competence with social acceptance. Cratty (1986) states that this association is an important dimension of the value system surrounding youngsters. Research supporting this concept shows that for over the last quarter century studies have repeatedly demonstrated the positive relationship between motor skill ability and social status, self-concept, and popularity.

Movement and how a person moves is the essence of existence itself to a child. The self-discovery, freedom, kinesthetic feeling, and sheer enjoyment of movement signify a lot to a child. These reasons should urge the development of a balanced physical education curriculum at the elementary school

TABLE 8.1 Fundamental Skills

Locomotor	Nonlocomotor	Manipulative
Gallop	Bend	Catch
Hop	Fall	Dribble
Jump	Pull	Kick
Leap	Push	Strike
Run	Rise	Throw
Skip	Stretch	
Slide	Sway	
Walk	Swing	
	Turn	
	Twist	

level. This curriculum should provide numerous ways—individually, with a partner, or in groups—for children to learn the fundamental locomotor, nonlocomotor, and manipulative skills. These skills are shown in Table 8.1.

THE ELEMENTARY SCHOOL CHILD

Both program planning and effective teaching require a familiarity with the signs of growth and development in the psychomotor, cognitive, and affective domains. From this perspective it is better to group children rather than attempt to pinpoint behavior at one particular year. In addition, a time never exists when all boys and girls in a particular class are at the same growth age.

Developmental characteristics (Gallahue, 1996; Kirchner & Fishburne, 1995; Wall & Murray, 1994) are presented to provide a more complete view of the elementary school child (see Tables 8.2, 8.3, and 8.4). Both a thorough understanding of and the implications arising from these characteristics will make it easier and more educationally sound when selecting the elementary physical education content. It is important to remember prior to teaching *who* will be taught.

CURRICULUM CONTENT FOR THE ELEMENTARY GRADES

If the objectives of the curriculum (see Chapter 2) are to be met, a broad scope of physical education offerings must be available. Figure 8.1 shows the scope of the physical education curriculum for a K–6 elementary school. Each of the movement experiences shown in this figure can assist children in the attainment of their total development. In addition Figure 8.1 presents an overview of content that could easily be adapted to fit most schools employing the K–6 organizational structure.

TABLE 8.2 Characteristics of Students Ages 5–7 Years

Physical/Physiological

- Growth is relatively slow but steady in both height and weight as students grow from two to three inches and gain from five to seven pounds per year, respectively.
- The resting heart rate may exceed ninety beats per minute while the respiration rate is eighteen breaths per minute.
- Endurance is poor causing students to fatigue easily.
- The development of both strength and muscular endurance is steady.
- Reaction time is slow showing gradual improvement with an increase in age.
- Perceptual-motor abilities are incomplete but developing. Because the eyes are slow to focus and students are farsighted at this age, hand-eye coordination is poor.
- Gross motor control is developing rapidly and at a more advanced rate than fine motor control.
- The development of fundamental movement skills, both locomotor and manipulative, is occurring rapidly.
- Rhythmic skills show a gradual increase in quality.
- Bones, still developing, are relatively soft and pliable.
- Pelvic tilt is evident in the early stages of this developmental group.
- Static (stationary) and dynamic (moving) balance show steady improvement.
- Students are active and energetic.
- Gender differences are insignificant.

Intellectual/Social/Emotional

- Attention span is short.
- Play is more individual/partner rather than group-oriented.
- Students are creative, imaginative, and imitative.
- Students are curious and adventurous yet exhibit a fear of new situations.
- Students are shy and self-conscious.
- Students are egocentric while most behaviors are self-satisfying.
- Adult approval becomes important as they are developing a desire to please.
- Students do not accept criticism well.
- Self-concept is rapidly developing.
- The ability to reason, exercise judgment, and solve problems is developing, but intuition is used more than logic in the thinking process.

Implications

- Provide daily, vigorous activity while limiting extended periods of inactivity.
- Provide a variety of large muscle movement experiences.
- Provide activities of short duration while refraining from enduring activities.
- Make certain that initial instruction includes shorter distances and lower speeds.
- Provide frequent rest intervals, if necessary.
- Provide activities involving a change in speed, force, and level of movement.
- Provide activities requiring balance and agility, employing both large and small apparatus.
- Incorporate a variety of rhythmic activities including creative dance experiences.
- Provide a variety of manipulative activities. Use large (seven inch) balls for ease in tracking.

TABLE 8.2 *Continued*

Implications (Continued)

- Provide wholesome coeducational activities.
- Provide abdominal strengthening exercises and activities.
- Provide activities employing imagery, drama, and problem solving to foster creativity.
- Incorporate bilateral skills (e.g., skipping and galloping) once unilateral skills have been somewhat well developed.
- Stress the development of fundamental locomotor and manipulative skills that progress from simple to complex.
- Emphasize process as the quality of the movement, rather than product as the end result of the movement. Correct execution should be the primary goal.
- Provide for individual differences by letting students progress at their own rates.
- Take time to explain selected components of the class.
- Include ample, genuine positive reinforcement.
- Limit negative comments.
- Continually stress safety.

TABLE 8.3 Characteristics of Students Ages 8–9 Years

Physical/Physiological

- Height and weight gains continue to be steady.
- The heart and lungs continue to develop slowly with a steady decrease in both resting rates.
- Strength improvement is steady as muscle mass will nearly double from ages five to ten.
- Reaction time is slow but becomes established by the end of this stage.
- Hand-eye coordination, balance, and other perceptual-motor abilities are improving.
- Fundamental movements are well developed and nearing refinement.
- Poor posture is common, more often in girls.
- Rhythmic skills are nearing refinement.
- Hand preference is firmly established.
- Flexibility has decreased slightly, especially in boys.
- Students are still active and easily fatigued.

Intellectual/Social/Emotional

- Attention span continues to increase. At the end of this stage, children often become focused.
- Students seek independence.
- A shift from individual/partner to group activities occurs.
- Students remain curious, adventurous, and eager to know *why*.
- Students have become both self-conscious and self-critical.
- A strong desire to please adults exists. As a result, children are responsive to authority.
- Students exhibit an eagerness to learn.

Continued

TABLE 8.3 *Continued*

Intellectual/Social/Emotional (Continued)

- Students are eager to try new activities but become frustrated if the required movements are beyond their capabilities.
- Group identity, loyalty, and acceptance become important.
- Students exhibit fear of failure especially in selected movement skills.
- Students are not capable of abstract thinking.
- Students become aggressive, boastful, and sometimes argumentative.

Implications

- Continue to provide daily, vigorous activity.
- Provide exercises and/or activities for improving flexibility.
- Provide more complex balance and agility activities.
- Provide more complex locomotor and basic game skill activities.
- Introduce a variety of sport-specific skills through drills and lead-up games.
- Provide activities that incorporate music to enhance the understanding of rhythmic components and to refine coordination.
- Provide more complex rhythmic skills including structured folk, square, and contemporary dance.
- Continue to provide activities that stress the antigravity muscles.
- Encourage students to maintain proper posture. Also instruct them on proper body mechanics.
- Provide group activities to enhance both interaction and appropriate social behavior.
- Provide abundant opportunities for encouragement and positive reinforcement. Assure children they are important and valued.
- Provide a variety of self-testing activities so students can independently determine their skill level.
- Focus on skill acquisition while allowing ample time for practice.
- Integrate academic concepts with movement.
- Encourage children to think before they become involved in an activity.
- Provide concrete examples and situations for enhancing cognition.

TABLE 8.4 Characteristics of Students Ages 10–12 Years

Physical/Physiological

- At the onset of puberty and into adolescence, children experience a rapid growth spurt affecting both height and weight. Girls will reach puberty between ages ten to eleven while boys will reach puberty around ages twelve to thirteen.
- Heart and lungs have increased in size which is proportionate to an increase in overall growth. As a result cardiovascular endurance has increased.
- Reaction time is improved.
- Overall coordination, although continually developing, may slowly regress due to a rapid growth spurt.
- Hand-eye coordination is fully developed.
- Most of the fundamental movements are refined and, as a result, have become overlearned.
- Gender differences appear with girls as they become taller and more physiologically advanced.
- Girls may be more developed in selected sport-specific skills.

TABLE 8.4 *Continued*

Intellectual/Social/Emotional

- Students continue to seek independence.
- Interest in specific movement activities broadens.
- A concern for fitness and refinement of sport-specific skills is keen.
- Students are self-conscious of motor inadequacies.
- Group loyalty is strong as indicated by the formation of *cliques*.
- Students seek social acceptance from their peers rather than their teachers.
- Competition becomes important.
- A difficulty in controlling emotions occurs, often causing students to over-react.
- Sexual modesty and an interest in the opposite sex is developing, as is sex antagonism (e.g., hitting, teasing, and chasing).
- An interest in appearance is apparent.
- Students enjoy being challenged, both physically and mentally.
- The activity interest of boys and girls that was similar in earlier stages begins to diverge now.
- Fads in food, clothes, and movement experiences often influence interests.
- Students exhibit a capacity for self evaluation.
- Individual differences are many and varied.
- Students have developed an ability to deal with abstract concepts.

Implications

- Continue to provide daily, vigorous activity.
- Provide strenuous activities to work the muscles, heart, and lungs.
- Continue to provide a variety of perceptual-motor activities.
- Provide ample opportunities for students to refine all of the locomotor and basic game skills. In addition, increase opportunities for students to combine selected fundamental skills so their movements become efficient.
- Promote self-reliance by exposing students to experiences requiring responsibility.
- Allow students leadership opportunities.
- Provide activities that foster fair play and sportsmanship.
- Continue to provide group activities to enhance both interaction and appropriate social behavior.
- Provide challenging experiences.
- Continue to integrate academic concepts with movement.
- Provide experiences that are developmentally appropriate and foster skill acquisition.
- Stress accuracy and form during skill instruction.
- Incorporate timely activities that have contemporary interest.
- Provide activities that are geared to both the needs and interests of the students.
- Provide assistance so students can more easily make the transition from the fundamental movement phase to the sport-specific movement phase.
- Encourage students to participate in youth sport activities that are developmentally appropriate.

Thomas, Lee, and Thomas (1988) place the elementary physical education content into three categories: games, rhythmic activity, and gymnastics. These categories of learning experiences are further defined in Table 8.5.

Annarino, Cowell, and Hazelton (1986) provide a seven category listing of elementary physical education content for grades 1–6 (see Table 8.6) and a five category listing for kindergarten (see Table 8.7). A discussion of each

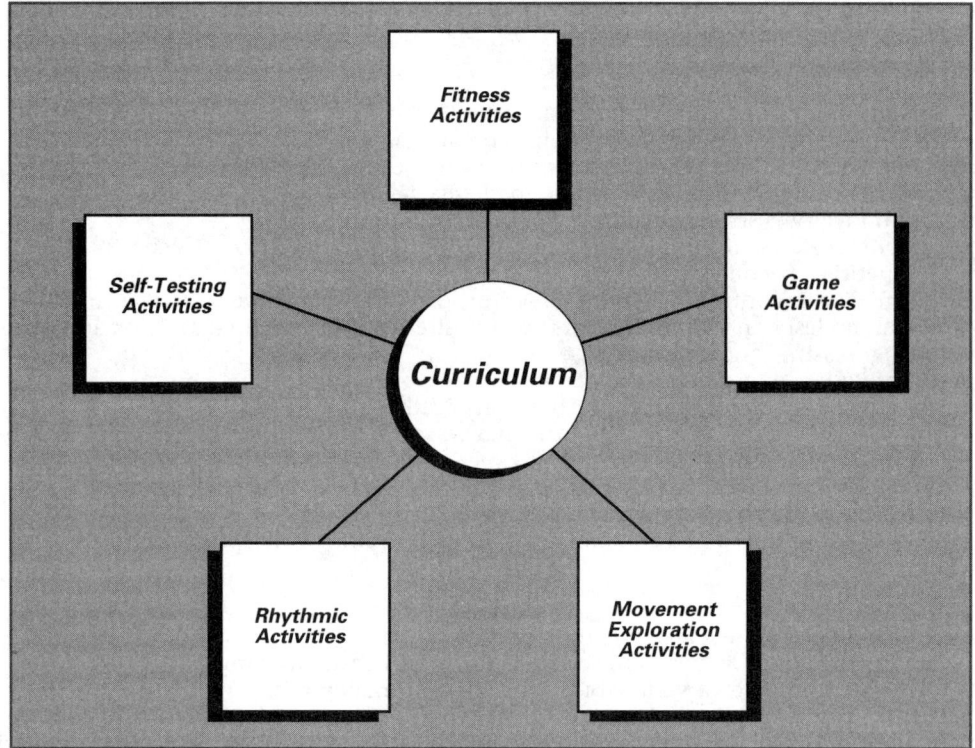

FIGURE 8.1 Elementary Physical Education Content

category shown in Figure 8.1 is provided to show a better understanding of the elementary physical education scope.

Fitness Activities

Even though many of the activities in the physical education curriculum contribute in some way to the development and maintenance of physical fitness, it is still necessary to include fitness as a separate content area. Moreover, since the formation of the President's Council on Physical Fitness, under the Eisenhower administration in 1956, a vigorous, cooperative effort has existed in this country to raise the physical capacity of our youth. As long as both men and women need the physical capacity to perform a day's work and have a reserve to recreate and/or meet any emergency that may arise, our schools need to be seriously concerned with the topic of physical fitness.

A person's level of physical fitness can be enhanced through a variety of content including games, rhythmic activities, and gymnastics. However, fitness activities are designed to develop and maintain a student's aerobic capacity, strength, muscular endurance, flexibility, and a favorable body composition. This category includes such specific activities as jogging, weight

TABLE 8.5 Categories of Learning Experiences in Games, Rhythmic Activity, and Gymnastics

Games	Rhythmic Activity	Gymnastics

Low organized games
  Cooperative games
  Creative games
Relays
Lead-up games
Team sports
  Basketball
  Football
  Hockey
  Soccer
  Softball
  Volleyball
Individual sports
  Badminton
  Golf
  Tennis
  Track and field
Recreational games
	Creative dance
	  Imitating living things
	    (animals, clowns)
	  Imitating things in nature
	    (wind, rain)
	  Imitating objects
	    (train, blender)
	  Moving to words
	    (melt, sizzle)
	  Moving to feelings
	    (happy, sad)
	Story play
	Folk dance
	Novelty dance
	Square dance
	Aerobic dance
	Routines to music (jump rope,
	  balls, wands, exercise)
	Country dance
		Individual and creative
		  stunts
		Group stunts
		Mat tumbling
		Balance stunts
		Small apparatus skills
		  Balance boards
		  Hoops
		  Ropes
		  Stilts
		  Wands
		Large apparatus skills
		  Bars
		  Beam
		  Bench
		  Cargo nets
		  Climbing ropes
		  Horizontal bar
		  Latters
		  Parallel bars
		  Vaulting box

From Thomas, J. R., Lee, A. M., & Thomas, K. T. (1988). *Physical education for children: Concepts into practice.* (p. 91). Champaign, IL: Human Kinetics. Copyright 1988 by Jerry R. Thomas, Katherine T. Thomas, and Amelia M. Lee. Reprinted by permission of Human Kinetics.

TABLE 8.6 Grades 1–6 Activity Classification

Aquatics
Developmental activities
Games and sports
Outdoor education activities
Recreational activities
Rhythmical activities
Self-testing activities

TABLE 8.7 Kindergarten Activity Classification

Developmental activities
Games (low organized)
Movement exploration
Rhythmical activities
Self-testing activities

training, rope jumping, and free exercise. For a more detailed description of free exercises, see the book *More Fitness Exercises for Children* by Stillwell and Stockard (1988).

Game Activities

Games have significance to the elementary physical education program not only because of their popularity with children of all ages but also because of their potential developmental value. When used properly, games become an important educational tool. Because of the possible contribution to the physical, social, and recreational objectives, close scrutiny of games is recommended. This is especially true when the games are either improperly taught or built into the curriculum at an inappropriate grade level. A carefully selected program of games can aid in the development of (a) fundamental movement skills such as running, jumping, and skipping; (b) basic games skills including throwing, catching, and kicking; (c) selected components of fitness; and (d) acceptable social behavior.

Games may be classified in a variety of ways. Perhaps the most common classification includes low organized games, relays, cooperative games, creative games, lead-up games, and sports.

Low Organized Games

Low organization games have few rules; require little, if any, equipment; may be played with a brief explanation; and may be easily modified. Five low organized games are presented in Figures 8.2, 8.3, 8.4, 8.5, and 8.6.

Name: Crows and Cranes

Skills: Selected locomotor

Equipment: None

Formation: Double-line partner

Students are divided into two equal groups facing each other as shown. One group represents the crows and the other group represents the cranes. On the command *crows*, the crows turn and run toward their free line. The cranes chase the crows trying to tag them before they cross the free line. If tagged, the student joins the other group. This becomes a dramatic game as students listen carefully for the teacher's cue of *Crrrr . . . ows* or *Crrrr . . . anes*.

FIGURE 8.2 Crows and Cranes

Name: *Partner Tag*

Skills: *Selected locomotor*

Equipment: *None*

Formation: *Random/scattered*

From a random formation as shown, students are paired. In each pair, one student is *it*. On the command, the students who are *it* must count to five while their partner is free to run. If tagged, the partner becomes *it* and must count to five as the other person flees.

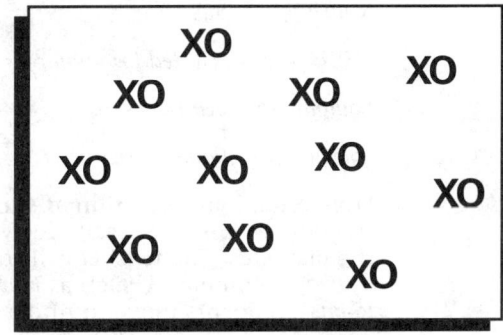

FIGURE 8.3 Partner Tag

Name: *Everybody It*

Skills: *Selected locomotor*

Equipment: *None*

Formation: *Random/scattered*

From a random formation as shown, everyone is *it*. On the command, each student (a) attempts to tag as many other students as possible, and (b) moves to prevent from being tagged by other students.

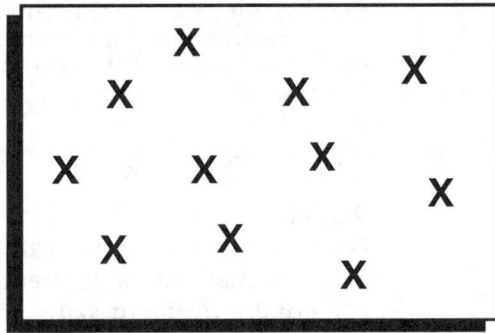

FIGURE 8.4 Everybody It

Name: *Loose Caboose*

Skills: *Walking and sliding*

Equipment: *None*

Formation: *Random/scattered*

Students are grouped in threes forming a train while holding the waist of the person in front of them. The first student is the engine, the second is the baggage car, and the third is the caboose. Two or three students are called *loose cabooses* or chasers. From a random formation as shown, each train moves to prevent its caboose from being tagged. However, if tagged, the engine must break away to become a new loose caboose.

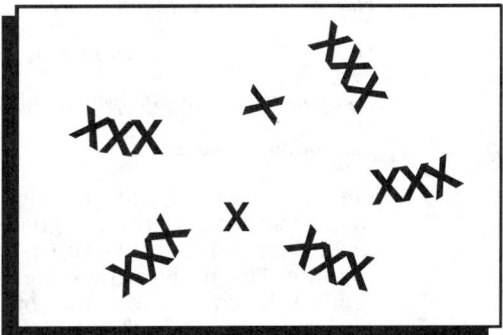

FIGURE 8.5 Loose Caboose

Name: Busy Bee

Skills: Selected locomotor

Equipment: Bean bags

Formation: Random/scattered

From a random formation as shown, students *buzz* as they walk freely in the play area. The teacher calls out a specific command, such as *back-to-back*. Students move to find a partner and stand back-to-back. The teacher then calls out *Busy Bee*. On the command, the students move from their partner and buzz as they again walk about the play area. The game continues as the teacher alternates partner commands, such as *hip-to-hip, foot-to-foot,* and *elbow-to-elbow,* with the *Busy Bee* commands.

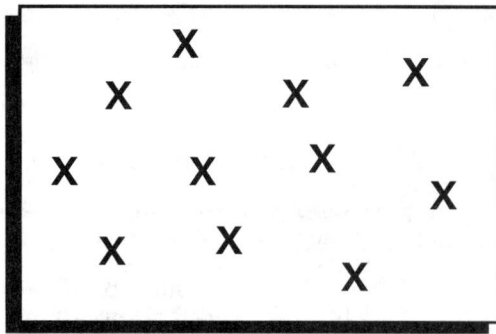

FIGURE 8.6 Busy Bee

Relays

Relays are small-group, team-oriented activities. They provide an organizational format that is different from games in that relays aim to develop fundamental movement skills. Five relays are presented in Figures 8.7, 8.8, 8.9, 8.10, and 8.11.

Name: Locomotor Relay

Skills: Selected locomotor

Equipment: One cone per squad

Formation: Relay

On the command, the first student in each squad uses the designated locomotor skill to move to the turning line. The student then goes around the cone, and comes back to the starting line. The student touches the next person in line who repeats this process. This procedure continues until each member of the squad has had a turn.

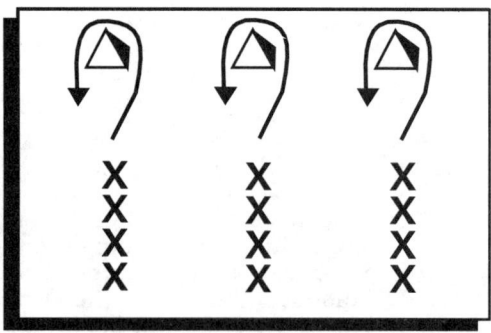

FIGURE 8.7 Locomotor Relay

Name: *Figure Eight Dribble Relay*

Skills: *Hand/foot dribble*

Equipment: *One ball and three to five cones per squad*

Formation: *Relay*

On the command, the first student in each squad weaves around the cones in a figure eight pattern while dribbling a ball with the hand or foot. On returning to the starting line, he/she gives the ball to the next person in line who repeats this process. This procedure continues until each member of the squad has had a turn.

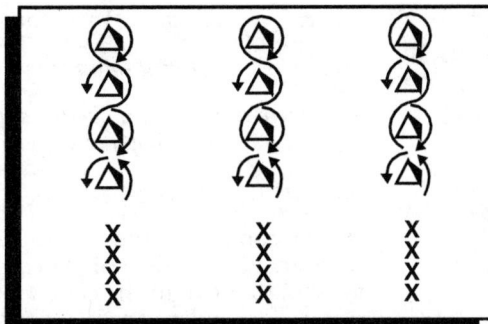

FIGURE 8.8 Figure Eight Dribble Relay

Name: *Rescue Relay*

Skills: *Selected locomotor*

Equipment: *None*

Formation: *Relay*

On the command, the first student at the starting line uses the designated locomotor skill to move to the turning line. The student then grasps the first squad member's hand (rescuing him/her) and returns to the starting line. The rescued student returns to the turning line and rescues the next person in line. This procedure continues until the last student is rescued.

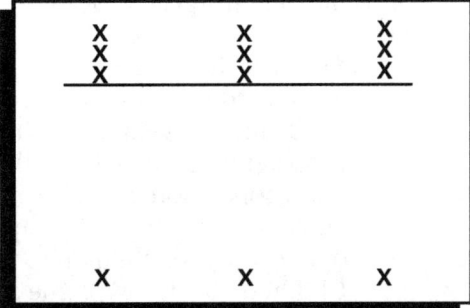

FIGURE 8.9 Rescue Relay

Name: *Shuttle Pass Relay*

Skills: *Passing and catching*

Equipment: *One ball per squad*

Formation: *Shuttle*

On the command, the first student in line A passes (bounce, chest, or overhead) the ball to the first person in line B. After releasing the ball, the student moves to the end of the approaching line. After catching the ball, the first student in line B passes the ball to the next person in line A. This procedure continues for a designated amount of time or for a designated number of passes.

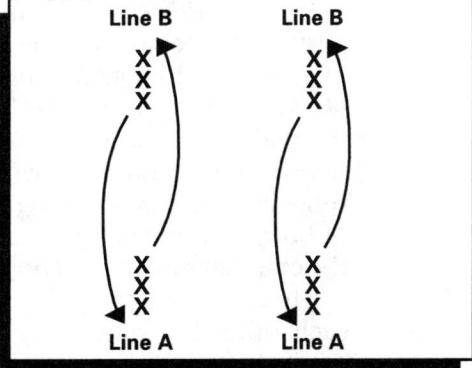

FIGURE 8.10 Shuttle Pass Relay

Name: Clean Up Your Plate Relay

Skills: Selected locomotor

Equipment: One bean bag per student and one hoop per squad

Formation: Relay

On the command, the first student in each squad uses the designated locomotor skill to move to the center circle (the plate). The student then picks up one bean bag, returns to the starting position, places the bean bag in his/her hoop, and tags the next student in line who repeats this process. This procedure continues until each student has had a turn and the plate is clean.

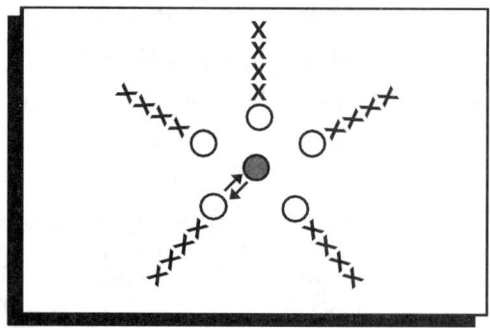

FIGURE 8.11 Clean Up Your Plate Relay

Cooperative Games

Cooperative games have become popular from work by Orlick (1977, 1978, and 1982) and Fluegelman (1976, 1981). Popularity has grown in recent years because cooperative games are nonthreatening and noncompetitive and not only emphasize cooperation but also require it for successful participation. Orlick (1982) describes this cooperative approach to game usage by stating that it provides an opportunity for children to play *with* each other, rather than *against* one another. Children play to overcome a challenge, not an opponent. These games allow the participants, merely by their structure, to enjoy the play experience itself. More specifically, cooperative games provide freedom from competition and exclusion and freedom to choose and create. Cooperative games are classified as being (a) games without losers, (b) collective score games, or (c) reversal games.

Games without losers require students to work cooperatively toward accomplishing a specific task. These games provide an alternative approach to the various elimination games used in elementary physical education. The game *Musical Hoops* (see Figure 8.12) is an example. *Musical Hoops* is a modification of the traditional *Musical Chairs* in that children need to step inside any occupied hoop, thereby sharing it with one or more classmates, rather than eliminating those children not standing inside a hoop when the music stops. As the number of hoops diminishes, the game presents a challenge to the entire class because the children must work cooperatively to assure that everyone gets inside a hoop.

In *collective scoring games* the individuals/teams do not compete to outscore each other but rather work cooperatively to attain a designated score. For example, rather than compete individually in *Bean Bag Horseshoes* (see Figure 8.13) to outscore an opponent, the points for each student are totaled to either beat a previous score or reach a predetermined score. In a team game such as *Newcomb Serve* (see Figure 8.14), rather than compete to outscore an opponent, a game point is awarded each time the ball is successfully caught.

In *reversal games,* children are rotated from squad to squad during a game so that emphasis is placed on each child's performance rather than the team's

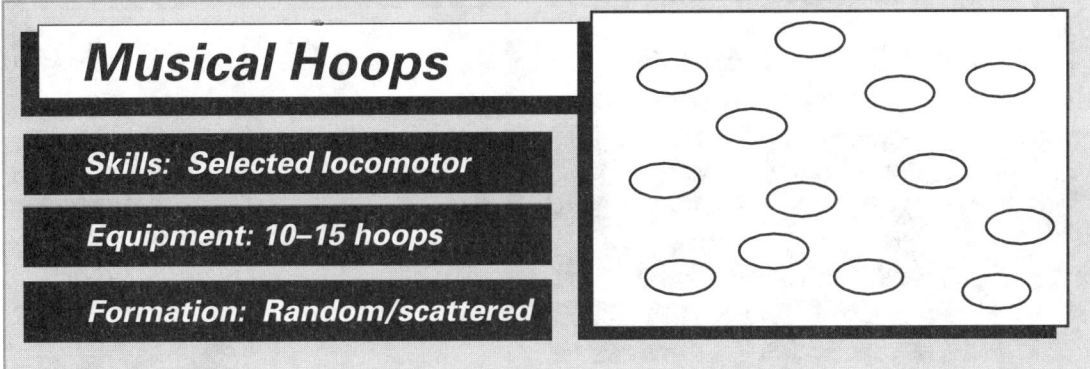

FIGURE 8.12

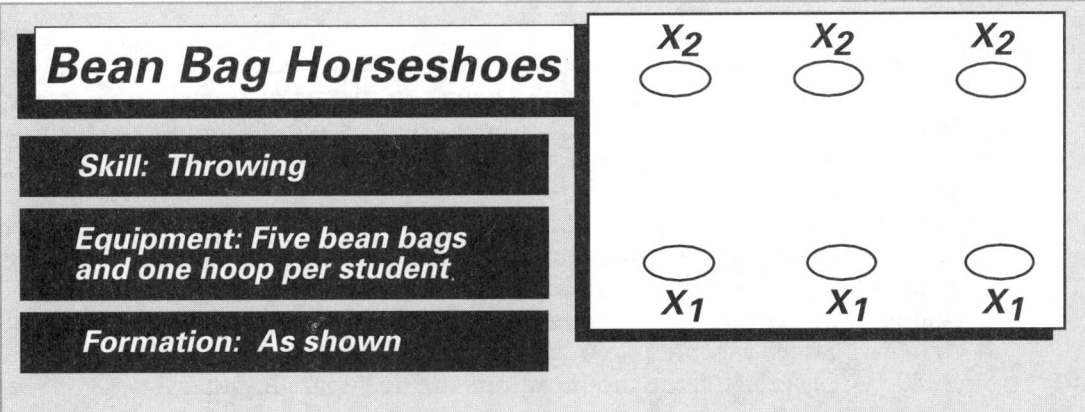

FIGURE 8.13

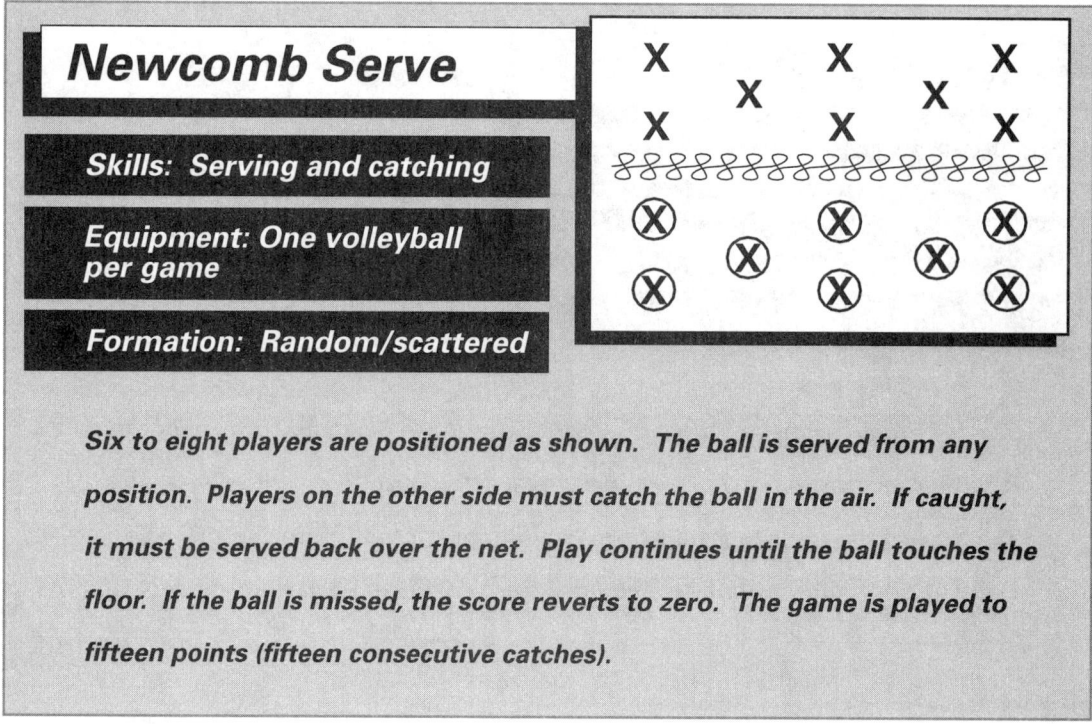

FIGURE 8.14

outcome. For example, the game of *Four Goal Soccer* (see Figure 8.15) is modified by having the scoring player change teams every time he/she scores. Therefore, if player A scores, he/she immediately becomes a member of team B.

Creative Games

Creative games have derived from one of two sources—the modifications of existing games or the development of an original game. A published or existing game often may need to be modified because of class size, the availability of equipment, or to better meet the objective(s) of the lesson. The concept of changing games was presented by Morris (1976, 1980) and Morris and Stiehl (1989). Appropriate game modifications include changing the:

- Movement pattern
- Number of players
- Equipment used
- Formation
- Space
- Time allotment
- Scoring procedures

Gabbard, LeBlanc, and Lowy (1994) describe original games as those created by the teacher, the teacher and the students, or by the students

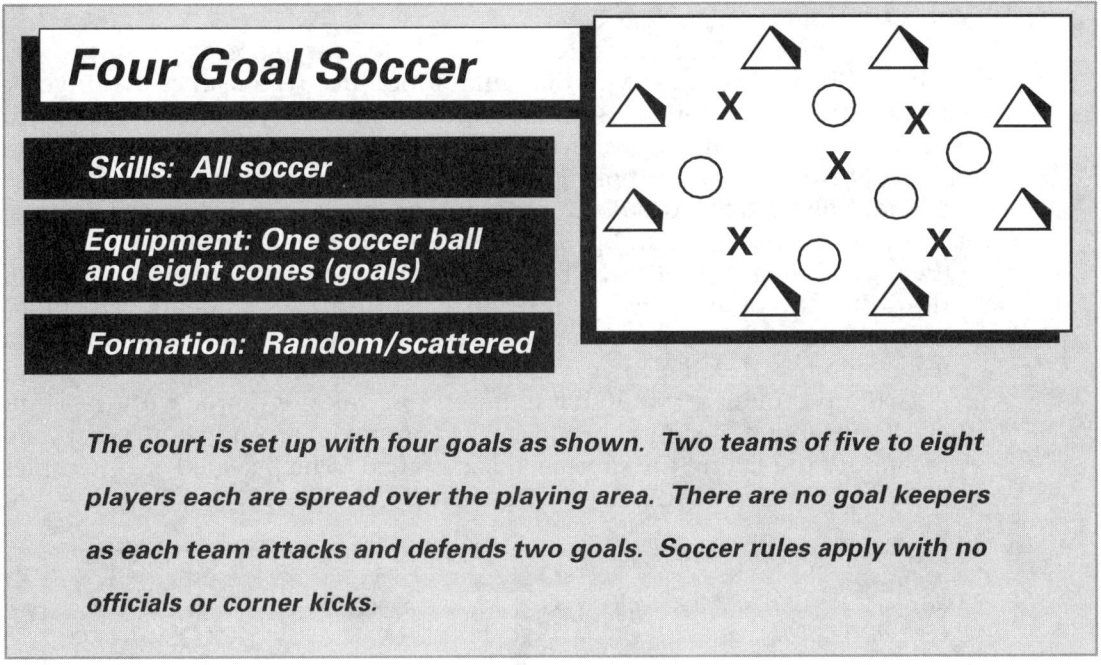

FIGURE 8.15

alone. In order for the teacher-student and the student-alone approaches to be effective, everyone involved needs an understanding of what should be learned from the game. When working cooperatively on a creative game, the teacher should act as a facilitator by presenting general guidelines for the game. The teacher and students then work together to determine the game specifics, including the rules, equipment, boundaries, and so on. For student-designed games, the teacher's primary role is to supervise and maintain a safe environment. However, the teacher should not interfere. Graham (1977) provides the following guidelines when using creative games:

- Progress gradually. More structure is needed early but as students become more adept, the teacher should lessen the imposed structure.
- Limit interference. Allow students to make meaningful decisions in order to promote responsibility.
- Allow students to enforce their own game rules. If allowed the opportunity to make the rules, students should then be involved with enforcing them.
- Be patient. The creative process does not unfold quickly. Remember that the process is just as important as the product. Once students have mastered the general idea of the game components and how to manipulate them, the quality of responses will increase.
- Be flexible while encouraging students to be creative. The primary rule is that the game can always be changed.

Lead-Up Games

Lead-up games deserve special attention. A definite place exists in the elementary physical education curriculum for modified team games that involve one or more of the sport skills, rules, or procedures used in official sports such as basketball, softball, and volleyball. Lead-up games present an alternative to the repetitive and often boring skill drills. Lead-up allow students to go beyond drills of isolated skills in order to play a modification of the game at a level in which success and personal enjoyment go hand-in-hand. Gallahue (1996) recommends that once the sport skill has been reasonably mastered, skill drills may be modified to take on game form. As students gain proficiency, make the lead-up games increasingly complex by incorporating a greater number of skill elements and/or more involved strategies.

Lead-up games are a way that children can link the simple with the complex. These activities should be viewed as a means to an end because they are preparatory to playing the sport as it is designed to be played. Four examples of lead-up games are presented in Figures 8.16, 8.17, 8.18, and 8.19.

Name: Sideline Basketball

Skills: All basic basketball skills

Equipment: One ball and two goals

Formation: Random/scattered and line

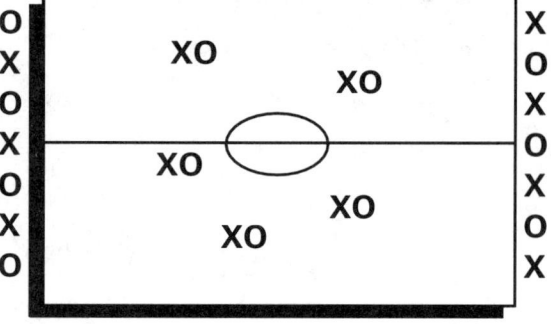

FIGURE 8.16 Sideline Basketball

Each team consists of eight to twelve players. Half of the players are on the playing court while the remaining players are along each sideline. The object of the game is to move the ball down the court by passing and/or dribbling in order to score a goal. Following a throw-in by either team, standard basketball rules apply. The ball may be passed to a teammate on the sideline who must pass it to a teammate on the court. Following a goal, a defensive rebound, or a stolen ball, the ball must be passed to a sideline player.

Name: Zone Soccer

Skills: Basic soccer skills

Equipment: One soccer ball per game

Formation: As shown

Each team consists of eight to twelve players. The playing area is separated into thirds with each team divided into three groups and positioned as shown. The object of the game is to kick the ball over the opposing team's goal line. Following a kickoff, players must remain in their respective zones. As a result,

x_1 o_3	x_1 o_3	x_1 o_3
x_2 o_2	x_2 o_2	x_2 o_2
x_3 o_1	x_3 o_1	x_3 o_1

FIGURE 8.17 Zone Soccer

the only way to move the ball down the field and attempt to score is by passing it ahead to a teammate in another zone. X_1 and O_1 players are goal keepers who are responsible for defending their goal line. X_2 and O_2 players are midfielders who receive passes from the goal keepers and relay them to the forwards (X_3 and O_3) who attempt to score.

Name: Straight Base Ball

Skill(s): Throwing, catching, and striking

Equipment: Three bases, one plastic bat, and two plastic balls

Formation: Random/scattered

Each team consists of eight to twelve players. The object of the game is to outscore the opponent. The first player on the batting team has only two opportunities to hit a pitched ball. The pitcher is a member of the batting team. After hitting the ball, the batter tries to run to first or second base and return home. The runner cannot stop on a base, and if the player makes it to home safely after touching first base, one run is scored. In addition, if the player touches second base, two runs are scored. The runner is out if (a) a fly ball is caught, or (b) the batter is forced out at home. After each member of the batting team has batted, they take the field.

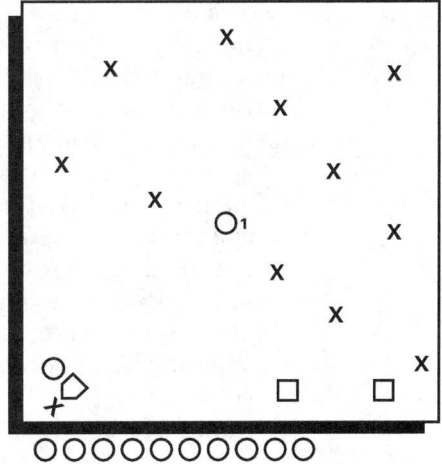

FIGURE 8.18 Straight Base Ball

Name: Volley Volleyball

Skills: Serve and/or volley

Equipment: Volleyball/beach ball, and net

Formation: Random/scattered squad

Each team consists of six to nine players. The game is played with either a volleyball or a beach ball. The object of the game is to outscore the opponent. The game begins with a serve from anyone on the court. Teams must then volley the ball back and forth across the net. The ball may be volleyed as many times as needed to get it back over the net. In addition, any player may hit the ball as many times as necessary. The serving team scores one point each time the receiving team (a) fails to return the ball, (b) volleys the ball out of bounds, or (c) touches the net. The game is played to eleven or fifteen points.

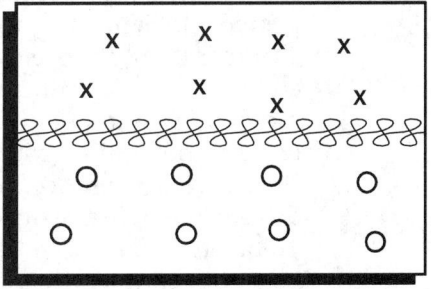

FIGURE 8.19 Volley Volleyball

Sports

Sports are classified as (a) individual, such as bowling, golf, and gymnastics; (b) dual, such as badminton, racquetball, and tennis; and (c) team, such as basketball, softball, and volleyball. According to Gallahue (1996), official sports are those activities governed by a specific set of rules and regulations and are recognized and interpreted by an official governing body as the standard for performance and play. Many educators agree that official sports are inappropriate for an elementary physical education program. Elementary students do not have the physical/physiological or cognitive development to play official sports as they are designed to be played.

Thoughtful selection and use of games is essential since games have such a potential benefit for the elementary physical education program and because hundreds of games exist from which to choose. For these reasons, Gallahue (1996) provides the following guidelines for today's teacher:

- Choose games that are appropriate for time allottment, class size, space availability, and lesson objective(s).
- Plan in advance so the play area and equipment is ready for use.
- Make necessary explanations clear, concise, and brief with children in game formation.
- Demonstrate or combine the demonstration with the explanation, whenever possible.
- Avoid stopping the game too frequently to make corrections.

Movement Exploration Activities

Read (1945) said that education could be defined as the cultivation of modes of expression—teaching children and adults how to make sounds, images, and movements. Furthermore, the aim of education is the creation of artists—people efficient in these various modes of expression. These significant statements by Read elevate an education for movement to new heights. In addition, they encourage both young and old people to ask why humans move, how humans move, and how movement can help them to discover, understand, and adjust to the environment.

Educators agree on what movement exploration can do even though some disagreement exists on both its name and interpretation. Laban (1948) and Tillotson (1970) both called it movement education, stressing the development of a kinesthetic awareness of movements that have both expressive and educational value. Fait (1976) prefers to call it movement exploration partly because problems are posed that focus on the discovery of movement potentials. These potentials include movement in a stationary position, movement while in locomotion, movement as a means of communication, and movement as a way to explore one's environment. Others call it basic movement. Bucher and Thaxton (1979) indicate that the spectrum of interpretations of movement education ranges from those who view it as curriculum content to those who interpret it to mean the total scope of human movement.

Schurr (1980) sets the stage for movement education by writing:

> *In the primary grades the focus of the physical education program is the exploration and refinement of basic patterns and the understanding of environmental factors that affect movement. Emphasis is placed on the* why *of movement,*

on understanding one's own capacity in movement, and on acquiring proficiency in a wide range of movement skills. Indirect styles of teaching are utilized to help children develop the processes of exploration, experimentation, simple problem solving, and evaluation. Consistent with the stage of development, children are given a great deal of freedom and responsibility for learning to adapt to movements of skills to elements of intensity; different shapes of small and large objects and obstacles; and in relationship to others as they experience the joy and fulfillment that can accompany movement.

Movement education, therefore, may simply be defined as a means of achieving body management through an understanding of movement factors and the ways they effect the body in motion. While movement exploration is the general term given to the methodology employed for meeting these two objectives, supporters of movement education have made it clear that:

- Individual development of each student is the chief concern.
- Successful movement experiences contribute to an individual's self-confidence and enhance a person's self-image.
- Movements are introduced as age-appropriate challenges.
- Students use personal movements, making them more meaningful.
- Creativity is encouraged, especially in solving selected movement problems.

The movement education concepts are shown in Figure 8.20. *Body awareness* is a knowledge of the various body parts and how these body parts can move. It leads to an understanding of how to move and control the body as a whole or as different body parts in a variety of situations. *Spatial awareness* is a knowledge of space and an orientation of the body in space, specifically personal, general, and restricted space. It leads to an understanding of the different directional pathways and varying levels in which the body can move. *Movement qualities* include time, force, and flow. A knowledge of these concepts leads to an understanding of how the body can move from one position to another. *Relationships* to others and to both small and large apparatus occur often in an elementary physical education program. Learning how to move in relation to each of these concepts is a goal of movement education. These concepts are often presented to students in an exploratory manner by the teacher who provides verbal cues in the form of commands, questions, and challenges. Examples of each follow.

Commands:

- Walk in a circle without touching anyone.
- Run quietly on your toes.
- Skip with a partner while holding hands.
- Jump two times with your hands on your knees.
- Catch the bean bag on the back of your hand.
- Put your elbows together.
- Raise your body from a lower level to a higher level.

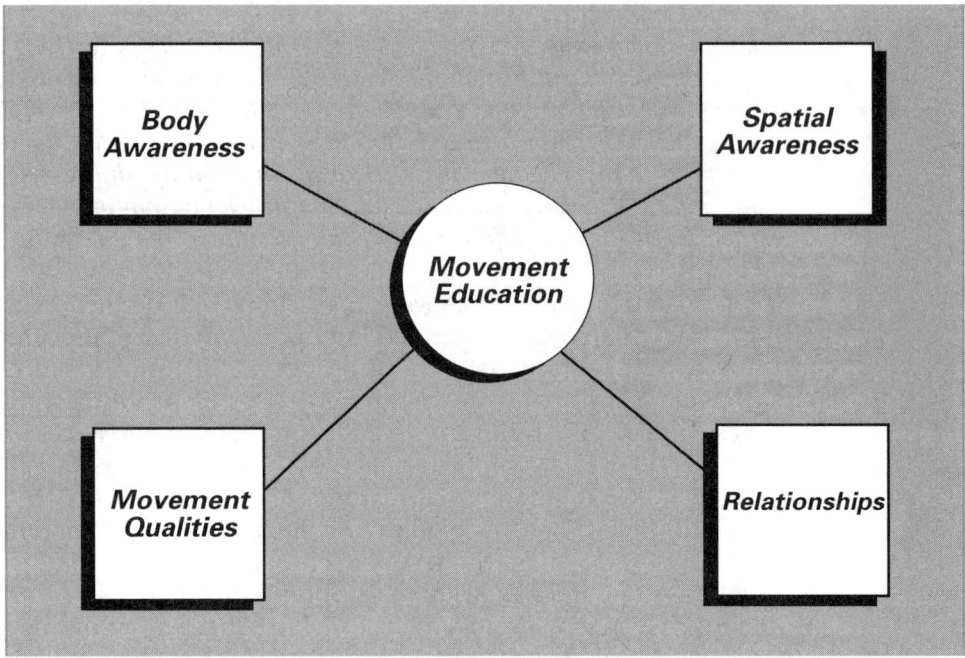

FIGURE 8.20 Movement Education Concepts

- Dribble the ball without using your hands.
- Make your body shake.
- Walk with heavy feet.

Questions:

- Can you walk without swinging your arms?
- Can you move quickly around the play area and stop when you hear the whistle?
- Can you run like an elephant?
- Can you show me how a butterfly moves?
- Can you make believe you are riding in a roller coaster?
- Can you make yourself look like a flower?
- Can you catch the bean bag with one hand?
- Is it possible to kick the ball with your other foot?
- Can you skip with a bean bag on your head?
- How can you catch the bean bag without using your hands?

Challenges:

- Show that you can balance on five body parts.
- Try to move across the play area without walking.
- Try to clap your hands five times before you catch the tossed ball.
- Show how you would walk if it was raining.

- Show that you can catch the ball standing on one foot.
- Show three different ways to move your hand.
- Show that you can dribble the ball with your elbow.
- Show a different way to kick the ball.
- Try to walk across the balance beam backwards.
- Show that you can toss and catch the bean bag from a seated position.

It is important to note that in the process of exploring the fundamental movement skills, whether they be locomotor, nonlocomotor, or manipulative, the student should eventually arrive at a satisfied state of knowing how to execute these skills correctly. For example, a student may have experimented with walking fast, walking slow, or walking with the arms in different positions, but the individual should emerge from these activities with an erect, relaxed, rhythmical walk. In addition, a student may explore how to dribble with the palm of the hand, from a stiff-legged position, or while keeping the ball at eye level, but the individual should eventually dribble using the finger pads, with knees flexed, and with the ball at waist level. From the movement education perspective it is appropriate to contrast very quick and very slow movements, movements with specific spatial restrictions, and movements from different levels. By using these types of skills, students can (a) learn how to move efficiently, and (b) understand the impact of time, force, flow, and space on the body. Furthermore, it allows students to discover the appropriate or skillful way of performing the fundamental movements by experiencing inappropriate ways of doing these skills.

Rhythmic Activities

A rich, social inheritance embodied in rhythms and dance exists. In virtually all cultures, dance has been a part of the lives of the people. Dances have been executed formally as an art form and as a means of self-expression for such events as birth, death, marriage, war, and worship. They have served as a form of recreation, have been used to communicate individual's feelings and ideas, and have been performed spontaneously for pure joy.

Rhythm is a distinctive and essential quality inherent in all coordinated movements including walking, skipping, and even dribbling a ball. Rhythmic activities are perceived as an ideal means of self-expression for young children, are an excellent medium for developing appropriate social behavior. They furnish an opportunity for children to express almost any emotion that can be isolated. Furthermore, rhythms and dance tend to steer both boys and girls away from self-consciousness and timidity and toward confidence and poise.

The rhythmical activities in the elementary physical education curriculum may be classified into the following four areas:

- Basic rhythms
- Creative rhythms
- Singing rhythms
- Traditional and contemporary dance

Enhancing self expression through rhythmic activities

Basic Rhythms

Basic rhythms are not altogether different from selected activities associated with movement education. The primary distinction is that these activities are performed rhythmically. Locomotor movements such as walking, running, and skipping, and nonlocomotor movements such as swinging, swaying, and twisting, can be done to an accompaniment of rhythm sticks, a tambourine, a drum, or an appropriate record or cassette. Furthermore, Gallahue (1996) assures that a close rhythmic parallel between music and movement exists. With few exceptions, children enjoy both of these activities.

Examples of Basic Rhythm Activities Are:

With students sitting in a random/scattered formation, play a record or cassette with a 4/4 meter and a relatively slow tempo. As the students listen, have them:

- Clap on the first beat.
- Clap on the first and third beats.
- Clap on all four beats.
- Slap their thighs on the first beat.
- Slap their thighs on the first and third beats.
- Slap their thighs on all four beats.
- Slap the floor on the first beat.
- Slap the floor on the first and third beats.
- Slap the floor on all four beats.
- Tap their knees on the first beat.
- Tap their knees on the first and third beats.
- Tap their knees on all four beats.
- Do selected combinations of the previous activities such as:

  Clapping their hands four times, followed by slapping their thighs four times.

  Clapping their hands on the first and second beats, and slapping their thighs on the third and fourth beats.

  Clapping their hands on the first and third beats and slapping their thighs on the second and fourth beats.

  Clapping their hands on the first beat, slapping their thighs on the second beat, slapping the floor on the third beat, and tapping their knees on the fourth beat.

- Modify the previous activities by having the children perform them as partners facing each other; in groups of three, four, or five facing each other; and while using equipment such as bean bags, paddles, or rhythm sticks.

Creative Rhythms

According to Hankin (1992), in a world where discursive language is the primary mode of communication, creative rhythms provide the student an alternative expressive medium. Creative rhythms allow the student (a) the freedom of choice in rhythmical movements, thereby promoting creativity; (b) to use a familiar movement vocabulary (fundamental movement skills) rather than having to learn new movements; (c) to expand their understanding of the basic rhythms; and (d) to express their feelings, ideas, and emotions.

Creative exploration through rhythms may be accomplished in a number of ways such as performing an exercise routine in time to music, creating

TABLE 8.8 Singing Rhythms

Did You Ever See a Lassie	Loobie Loo
Farmer in the Dell	Mulberry Bush
I'm a Little Teapot	Ring around the Rosie
London Bridge	Ten Little Indians

locomotor and/or nonlocomotor movements to the reading of a poem, and making up a dance routine to music selected by the student. It is important to remember that if the development of creativity is an objective of the elementary physical education program, it should not be left to chance. Instead, the physical educator should encourage curiosity, be respectful of unusual ideas, recognize original creative behavior, ask questions that require thinking, build on skills that students already have, and give opportunities for learning in creative ways.

Singing Rhythms
Singing rhythms are activities that enable students to perform prescribed movements to a poem or song while saying or singing the words. Gallahue (1996) indicates that singing rhythms are especially appealing to students because they (a) tell a story, (b) develop an idea, (c) have a pleasing rhythmic pattern, (d) stimulate imagination, and (e) have dramatic possibilities. Furthermore, these simple repetitive rhythms allow the student to learn the words easily and respond through movement while doing so. Examples of singing rhythms are shown in Table 8.8.

Traditional and Contemporary Dance
Traditional and contemporary dance is the final category of rhythmical activities. By definition, this category includes structured dances that require students to perform specific patterns including folk, square, and social dances. Bucher and Thaxton (1979) explain that elementary children should be exposed to traditional and contemporary dances because they aid in the development of (a) an understanding and appreciation of the people and cultures of other countries, (b) the ability to transform directions into movements, and (c) desirable social skills and attitudes.

Folk dances are structured dances that are specific to a country. Square dances are specific to North America, reflecting the culture of these countries forefathers. Social dances reflect the mores of American culture during the times in which they were popular. These dances are done with a partner; therefore, it is recommended that they be introduced in the upper elementary grades. In addition, the interest in contemporary social dances is often short lived, such as disco. The interest in other kinds of dances is cyclic, such as the jitterbug. A listing of traditional and contemporary dances is shown in Table 8.9.

TABLE 8.9 Traditional and Contemporary Dances

Folk	Square	Social
Greensleeves—England	Oh Johnny	Bus Stop
Seven Jumps—Denmark	Birdie in the Cage	Cotton Eye Joe
Virginia Reel—United States	Ladies Chain	Electric Slide
Hora—Israel	Heads and Sides	Fox-trot
La Rospa—Mexico	Red River Valley	Jitterbug
Bleking—Sweden	Dive the Rug	Texas Two Step
Schottishe—Scotland	Duck for the Oyster	Twist
Tinikling—Philippines		Waltz
Patty Cake Polka—Poland		

Self-Testing Activities

Homer (Fagles, 1990) stated that "greater glory hath no man than that which he wins with his own feet and hands." It is not uncommon to hear the modern elementary school criticized because students spend so much time working on teacher-directed activities. This approach is not necessarily harmful especially if the students become physically involved in the process. What students do, in physical education or any other discipline, should be related to them in a personal way.

People cannot underestimate the significance of a student's immediate self-appraisal in an activity. Self-testing activities specifically allow the student to perform individually; therefore, the individual is given an opportunity to compare (a) personal activity from performance to performance, and (b) peers to himself/herself.

Self-testing activities are important for primary-aged students because they often find it difficult to work cooperatively in group activities. However, these activities also benefit intermediate-aged students by allowing them to learn new skills without having to rely on another student or team as a prerequisite for participation.

Numerous self-test motor activities have great appeal as students strive for recognition. The improvement in an individual's ability to perform selected self-testing activities brings on feelings of adequacy, security, and acceptance. Therefore, setting aside a definite amount of time in the elementary physical education curriculum for self-testing activities is an important practice.

Self-testing activities may be classified in a variety of ways, but they typically include stunts and tumbling activities such as a log roll, a forward roll, and a frog stand; large apparatus activities such as those done on a balance beam, parallel bars, and a horizontal ladder; small apparatus activities using bean bags, hoops, and balls; and additional activities that develop the fundamental movement skills shown in Table 8.1.

Examples of large apparatus activities on a balance beam include having the student walk across the beam:

- On the balls of the feet.
- On the tiptoes.
- With hands on the head, hips, or knees.
- With the body rigid or relaxed.
- With the right or left foot leading.
- While balancing a bean bag on the head, hand, or shoulder.
- While balancing two bean bags on different body parts.
- While tossing a bean bag from hand to hand.
- While dribbling a basketball on the floor.
- While stepping through a hoop.

Examples of small apparatus activities using bean bags include having the student toss the bean bag into the air and:

- Catch it with both hands.
- Catch it with the right or left hand only.
- Catch it on the back of the hand.
- Catch it on the elbow.
- Catch it on the back.
- Clap the hands two, three, or more times before catching it.
- Count to five, ten, or more before catching it.
- Do two, three, or more jumping jacks or jills before catching it.
- Say as much of the alphabet as possible before catching it.
- Spell designated words before catching it.

The self-testing activities selected will depend primarily on class size, the availability of equipment, and the space utilized. However, the age level, ability level, and characteristics of students should be the most important factors when selecting these activities.

TIME ALLOTMENT

After the educator has decided *what* to teach, the next logical question is *how much* of it to teach? More specifically, what percentage of time should be allotted to fitness activities, game activities, movement exploration activities, rhythmic activities, and self-testing activities? When progressing from kindergarten to grade six, should more or less time be allotted for a specific content area?

Table 8.10 provides suggested time allotment percentages for the five content areas by grade level. The numbers listed are *recommended* percentages. Where the emphasis should be placed is not only dependent on the school and nonschool factors discussed in Chapter 4 but more importantly on where

TABLE 8.10 Time Allotment for Elementary Physical Education Content (in percentages)

Content Area	Grade Level						
	K	1	2	3	4	5	6
Fitness activities	10	10	15	15	20	20	20
Game activities	10	10	10	15	30	30	30
Movement exploration activities	25	25	25	20	10	10	10
Rhythmic activities	25	25	20	20	15	15	15
Self-testing activities	30	30	30	30	25	25	25

students range in both skills and knowledge at any grade level. In addition, the movement experiences in which students have already been exposed should be considered. The suggested percentages in Table 8.10 are based on the general characteristics and generally accepted needs of elementary school students.

A closer look at the amount of time allocated to the major elements of the elementary physical education curriculum reveals that:

- Games and the subsequent development of sport-specific skills grow considerably in importance from the primary to the intermediate level.
- Movement education activities receive less attention in the intermediate grades.
- A small but gradual decrease in emphasis is placed on rhythmic activities from kindergarten to grade six.
- Self-testing activities remain fairly constant in importance across all grades and appeal to all children.

THE MIDDLE SCHOOL

In recent years the number of school districts embracing the middle school concept has been increasing. Middle schools emerged in response to a perceived need of better bridging the gap between elementary and high school—a need the junior high school was not meeting (Kelly & Kelly, 1990). The majority of middle schools in the United States are organized with either a fifth to eighth grade or sixth to eighth grade structure, having no junior high school. As a result, the responsibility of helping young students make a satisfactory transition from the child-centered philosophy of elementary school to the more subject-centered philosophy of high school is assumed by the middle school.

Traditionally the middle school program has been student-centered. Advocates believe that the middle school organizational structure can better meet the needs and interests of students by allowing for developmental, rather than chronological, grouping. Kelly and Kelly (1990) indicate that the main goals of middle schools are to better meet the needs of the quickly developing adolescent through a unique organization, program, and instructional system. The middle school was described by Alexander (1971) to include (a) a home base and teacher for every student to provide the continuing guidance and assistance for helping students make the decisions they face, almost daily, regarding special needs and learning opportunities; and (b) a program of learning opportunities offering balanced attention to three major goals of the middle school—personal development of the between-ager, skills of continued learning, and effective use of appropriate knowledge.

In most instances the physical education program has not been modified to any significance. The grade 5–6 program is simply extended to grades 7 and 8 with more attention given to (a) the development of sport-specific skills (for example, the volleyball serve or the basketball pass), and (b) the depth of instruction.

SUMMARY

1. Movement is a medium through which students learn about themselves and the world in which they live.
2. A knowledge of the characteristics of elementary school students and the implications arising from these characteristics are essential for developing a physical education curriculum.
3. To meet both the needs and interests of elementary school students, as well as the general objectives of the curriculum, a variety of movement experiences is essential.
4. Fitness activities are included in the elementary physical education curriculum to help develop and maintain strength, muscular endurance, flexibility, aerobic endurance, and a favorable body composition.
5. Games are a means of enhancing a student's overall development and well-being. Specifically, games can help students develop the fundamental movement skills and the basic game skills essential for successful participation in sport activities not only during the secondary school years but throughout adulthood.
6. Movement exploration activities provide a medium for the student to achieve body management through an awareness and understanding of movement concepts and how they affect the body while moving. These concepts include body awareness, spatial awareness, the qualities of movement (time, force, and flow), and relationships.
7. Rhythmic activities provide a means of self-expression and are germane to an elementary physical education curriculum because rhythm is an inherent quality in all movement.
8. Self-testing activities, include stunts and tumbling, large apparatus activities, and small apparatus activities.
9. A slowly decreasing percentage of time should be devoted to both movement exploration and rhythm activities from kindergarten to grade six, while an increase should occur for both fitness activities and games. Time for self-testing activities should remain fairly constant from K–6.

QUESTIONS AND LEARNING ACTIVITIES

1. Arnold Gessell, writing in *The Child from Five to Ten,* spoke about the need for free, unregimented play activities for children. His feeling was that this kind of activity "taps the deeper springs of personality." How do you feel about this concept? Is there a difference between *aimless play* and *organized play*? Also, do values exist in both kinds of play for K–6 boys and girls?

2. Explain the concept that dance is indeed a *basic educational technique.*

3. Review a number of sources dealing with movement education. From your reading, formulate your own definition.

4. Find out about play in other cultures. Are games of low organization about the same everywhere?

5. It has been said that the development of motor performance in primary grade students can be advanced more effectively through a program of specific instruction than it can through free play and movement exploration. How would you ascertain the truth of this statement? What kind of experiment would you set up?

6. The primary objective for an elementary physical education program is the development of health-related fitness. Do you agree or disagree with this statement? Provide published support for your view.

7. After reading from the work of Orlick, justify a place for cooperative games in an elementary physical education curriculum.

8. Survey a number of elementary schools to determine the extent that games are used in the physical education curriculum. Prepare a list of the different low organized and lead-up games used.

REFERENCES

Alexander, W. (1971). How fares the middle school? *National Elementary Principal, 51,* 8–11.

Annarino, A. A., Cowell, C. C., & Hazelton, H. W. (1986). *Curriculum theory and design in physical education.* Prospect Heights, IL: Waveland Press.

Bucher, C. A., & Thaxton, N. A. (1979). *Physical education for children: Movement foundations and experiences.* New York: Macmillan Publishing Company.

Cratty, B. J. (1986). *Perceptual and motor development in infants and children.* Englewood Cliffs, NJ: Prentice-Hall.

Fagles, R. (1990). *Homer's the iliad.* New York: Viking.

Fait, H. (1976). *Experiences in movement: Physical education for the elementary school child.* Philadelphia: Saunders.

Fluegelman, A. (1976). *The new games book.* Garden City, NY: Dolphin Books.

Fluegelman, A. (1981). *More new games.* Garden City, NY: Dolphin Books.

Gabbard, C., LeBlanc, E., & Lowy, S. (1994). *Physical education for children: Building the foundation.* Englewood Cliffs, NJ: Prentice-Hall.

Gallahue, D. L. (1996). *Developmental physical education for today's children.* Dubuque, IA: Brown & Benchmark.

Graham, G. (1977). Helping students design their own games. *Journal of Physical Education, Recreation, and Dance, 48*(7), 35.

Graham, G., Holt/Hale, S., McEwen, T., & Parker, M. (1987). *Children moving: A reflective approach to teaching physical education.* Palo Alto, CA: Mayfield.

Hankin, T. (1992). Presenting creative dance activities to children: Guidelines for the nondancer. *Journal of Physical Education, Recreation, and Dance, 63*(2), 22–24.

Kelly, B., & Kelly, N. (1990). *Physical education for the middle school.* Springfield, IL: Charles C. Thomas, Publisher.

Kirchner, G., & Fishburne, G. (1995). *Physical education for elementary school children.* Dubuque, IA: Brown & Benchmark.

Laban, R. (1948). *Modern educational dance.* London: McDonald & Evans.

Morris, G. S. D. (1976). *How to change the games children play.* Minneapolis, MN: Burgess.

Morris, G. S. D. (1980). *How to change the games children play.* Minneapolis, MN: Burgess.

Morris, G. S. D., & Stiehl, J. (1989). *Changing kids games.* Champaign, IL: Human Kinetics.

Orlick, T. (1977). *Winning through cooperation: Competitive insanity.* Washington, DC: Hawkins & Associates.

Orlick, T. (1978). *The cooperative sports and games book: Challenge with competition.* New York: Pantheon Books.

Orlick, T. (1982). *The second cooperative sports and games book.* New York: Pantheon Books.

Read, H. (1945). *Education through art.* New York: Pantheon Books.

Schurr, E. L. (1980). *Movement experiences for children.* Englewood Cliffs, NJ: Prentice-Hall.

Stillwell, J. L., & Stockard, J. R. (1988). *More fitness exercises for children.* Durham, NC: Great Activities Publishing Company.

Thomas, J. R., Lee, A. M., & Thomas, K. T. (1988). *Physical education for children: Concepts into practice.* Champaign, IL: Human Kinetics.

Tillotson, J. (1970). A brief theory of movement education. In R. T. Sweeney (Ed.), *Selected readings in movement education.* Reading, MA: Addison-Wesley.

Wall, J., & Murray, N. (1994). *Children and movement: Physical education in the elementary school.* Dubuque, IA: Brown & Benchmark.

9

THE SECONDARY PHYSICAL EDUCATION PROGRAM, 7–12

Outline

Secondary School Organization

The Secondary School Student

Practical Considerations

Planning and Organizing the Content

A Closer Look at Content

Outcomes

After reading and studying this chapter, you should be able to:
- Define

  Aquatics

  Ballroom/social dance

  Circuit training

  Conditioning activities

  Contra dance

  Folk dance

  Free exercises

  Gymnastics

  Individual/dual activities

  Junior high school

  Modern dance

  Outdoor education

  Senior high school

  Square dance

- Identify the six content areas for a secondary physical education program.
- Describe the physical, intellectual, and social/emotional characteristics of secondary school students.
- Select physical education activities for a program for grades 7–12, based on the students' physical, intellectual, and social/emotional characteristics.
- Discuss the time allotment for each of the physical education content areas for grades 7–12.
- Organize and plan a yearly physical education program for grades 7–12.

In 1941 Rogers wrote:

> *Physical education is a kind of teaching, a special method of modifying body and mind, a particular way of transforming character, which achieves the aims of education predominately by means of pupils' large-muscle activities. The purposeful employment of sports to change permanently the behavior of pupils is physical education. The use of team games to improve strength and courtesy is physical education. But the use of any of these types of large-muscle activity to* amuse or recreate *is not educational, as we have defined education. It is merely entertaining or recreational.*

More than half a century has passed since Rogers cautioned physical educators to distinguish between the physical activities that were educational and those that were not. The reason for most teaching failures, according to Rogers, is the indefiniteness of aim.

It is barely necessary to indicate that secondary school physical education has to be a carefully planned program of human development if its aim is to achieve predetermined goals. Without direction at the curriculum level, colleagues may not only cross purposes but adversely affect other's efforts. Therefore, physical educators should examine what is taught under the title of *physical education.* Siedentop (1994) indicates that this is especially important today because the responsibility for education is delegated to the states. Laws governing how much of any subject matter is required within our schools are primarily determined by state legislation. Siedentop explains that because states differ dramatically on both their views on education and to what degree they are willing to support this education, it should be no surprise that laws governing the amount of K–12 physical education differ markedly. In fact, more than half of the states have either no requirement for physical education at the secondary school level or require only one semester or one year for graduation. With today's financial status and an increased sense of accountability, it is essential that quality physical education programs are offered.

Physical educators are often aware of certain program shortcomings. So, too, are observant general educators aware of inadequate curriculum content. These educators frequently refer to physical education as *aimless play.* This criticism is not without foundation since programs exist that represent everything from disorderly free play to the highly organized, inflexible routine. Programs exist in which sport skills and fitness development activities are kept in the background—programs where games are played period after period as an end, rather than as a means to an end; and programs where little, if anything, is done to spark the imagination of students or to challenge them. The worst thing about such conditions is that both parents and students can identify a poorly developed curriculum. Today's parents are educated and their secondary students are mature so the recognition of a weak program and a weak teacher is evident. During these years, students are either preparing for college or deciding on the termination of their education after grade 12. It is impossible to determine which students will choose to continue their formal education and so physical educators must prepare all students as if this secondary school experience will be their last exposure to physical education. Moreover, since college and university physical education programs differ so much in both course offerings and the depth of instruction within these offerings, it is nearly impossible to know how far to go and when to limit instruction in order to complement a particular higher education curriculum. Regardless, these variables should provide the necessary stimuli for educators to closely examine what they are doing in order to better prepare for what should be occurring.

SECONDARY SCHOOL ORGANIZATION

Regarding pure logic and, to some degree, tradition, it is understandable why the K–6 elementary school years and the 7–12 secondary school years are separated. In addition this logic is used to further separate the junior high school years from the senior high school years. This separation will be visible only if the programs are treated distinctly. A problem arises with the concept—by studying the two programs in an isolated manner, the significant ingredient of continuity is apt to be ignored or slighted.

If the physical education curriculum for grades 7–12 is viewed as a continuum, it is possible to (a) appreciate the need for progression in both the selection and presentation of activities, and (b) more effectively observe and assess student progress. Moreover, a number of activities exist in the junior high school physical education program that are repeated in greater depth in the later secondary school years. These activities, and the effects and outcomes caused by them, need to be examined over the years of the secondary school physical education curriculum.

The common format for today's junior high schools is either (a) two years, grades 7 and 8, or (b) three years during grades 7, 8, and 9. These formats are designed to prepare students for four-year (grades 9–12) or three-year (grades 10–12) senior high schools. In addition, the traditional K–8 grammar school still exists which directly prepares students for high school years. Even though these are the traditional organizational patterns, an increasing number of middle schools exist (see Chapter 8). Educators favoring the middle school structure subscribe to the concept that seventh and eighth graders have more in common with upper elementary students than they have with ninth graders.

THE SECONDARY SCHOOL STUDENT

A time in the lives of young people occurs when students are curious and possess an eagerness to discover and try something new. It is a time when *teachable moments* are clearly apparent. The junior high school (grades 7, 8, and 9) stage is such a time; when both boys and girls are capable of extensive physical activity. Students are willing to struggle, perspire, and concentrate on skill acquisition.

To better plan a properly functioning program, both a thorough understanding of the learner's characteristics (Gabbard, 1996; Pangrazi & Darst, 1991; Rink, 1993) and the implications arising from these characteristics are essential (see Tables 9.1 and 9.2).

TABLE 9.1 Characteristics of Students Ages 13–15 Years

Physical/Physiological

- Growth is rapid especially in the long bones of the arms and legs.
- Muscular development is rapid often resulting in poor coordination or awkwardness.
- Posture is poor.
- Acne period begins.
- An apparent unlimited source of energy exists.
- Boys broaden at the shoulders, as girls broaden at the hips.
- Voice changes and the appearance of pubic hair occurs in boys, as secondary sexual characteristics changes become apparent.
- Bone ossification is still incomplete.
- In most cases sexual maturity is reached in the later junior high school years.
- Girls are a year and a half to two years ahead of boys in maturation.
- Menstrual cycle is irregular in girls.
- Girls are more concerned with personal appearance and posture.

Intellectual/Social/Emotional

- Strong desire for independence.
- Somewhat rebellious toward those in positions of authority including parents and teachers.
- Great interest in group membership and loyalty to group leaders.
- Intense interest in self improvement of sport skills, occurring in boys more than girls.
- Interest in impressing the opposite sex.
- A move from fantasy to reality, giving way to intellectual analysis.
- Keen interest in clothes.
- Boys are more self-conscious of physical inadequacies.
- Keen interest in competition.
- Exuberant, boisterous, outgoing.
- Intense need for friends.

Implications

- Provide both individual and group activities.
- Provide a variety of self-testing activities.
- Provide activities to develop strength and flexibility.
- Discuss correct technique in skill drills.
- Provide coeducational activities.
- Maintain a safe and well supervised physical education environment.
- Provide opportunities for the development of responsibility and leadership.
- Employ skill drills to enhance learning and/or improvement.
- Provide ample encouragement in all activities.
- Match teams accordingly in competitive events.

TABLE 9.2 Characteristics of Students Ages 16–18 Years

Physical/Physiological

- Improvement in motor coordination occurs.
- Muscular growth in boys continues as it tapers off in girls.
- Bone growth is nearly complete.
- Maturity in both height and weight is nearly complete.
- Students are relatively free from infectious diseases.
- Improvement in muscular strength occurs.
- Secondary sex characteristics are complete.
- Increase in endurance occurs.
- Poise, grace, and grooming are more important to girls.

Intellectual/Social/Emotional

- Intensely emotional and complex.
- Sensitive to limitations in the psychomotor domain.
- Well adjusted to the secondary school environment.
- Enjoy exciting, adventurous activities.
- Attempts are made to gain status through social activities.
- Conformity to peer group standards is a dominating influence.
- Highly critical of peers as well as adults.
- Keen interest in the opposite sex.
- Boys have a growing interest in competition through contemporary sports. Girls have a narrowing interest in sports.
- Strong interest in personal appearance.

Implications

- Continue vigorous physical activity.
- Stress proper form in sport activities.
- Cognizant of helping students learn appropriate social behavior.
- Provide both coeducational and separate activities.
- Provide a cognitive component as to *why* an active lifestyle is important.
- Survey students, so as to provide high interest activities.
- Place a greater emphasis on the quality rather than the quantity of skills learned.

The secondary school years should be viewed as a continually evolving period of growth and maturation. This time of adolescence will gradually come to fruition in the later high school years in the form of a young adult who is ready to take a place in the college or university environment or in the workforce. Therefore, some of the characteristics of the junior high school student already discussed will apply at the senior high school level. The selected characteristic is still apparent but may have changed in degree. For example, students in grade 10 will be more interested in their physical ability and recreational skills than they were previously, yet they will still seek peer approval. Throughout the secondary school years, opportunities should be presented to guide and encourage individual and group participation in the types of activities fostering personal security. Ultimately, on graduation, students should leave school satisfied that their physical education experience has helped in self-understanding and has given them both the desire and the skills to recreate.

PRACTICAL CONSIDERATIONS

Perhaps the foremost concern is knowing exactly what behavioral changes educators want to observe in students following participation in a program. In other words, what are the physical educator's objectives? In previous chapters both program planning and organization were discussed in detail. Earlier chapters emphasized that for the best physical education results, curriculum content needs to be directly related to specific grade level objectives. Specific objectives need to be highlighted in order to ensure that the curriculum content will lead to student attainment, since both the physical and social/emotional characteristics already listed and the developing needs of today's secondary school students are an issue. These objectives are shown in Table 9.3.

Another secondary school level consideration that is missing at the elementary school level is maintaining a balance between the instructional program and the extra-class program. The instructional program is the portion of the curriculum that provides educational experiences for all students during a regularly scheduled time. The extra-class program is the portion of the curriculum that is conducted beyond the regularly scheduled school day. Examples of extra-class activities are intramurals and interscholastic athletics, and these are discussed more thoroughly in Chapter 11.

TABLE 9.3 Objectives for Junior High School and Senior High School

Junior High School	Senior High School
• Development of the physical/physiological system through vigorous physical activities adapted to the individual	• Continued
• Development of motor skills specific to a variety of sports and sport-related activities	• Refinement of these same motor skills as a means of yielding greater satisfaction
• Development of self-confidence, self-direction, initiative, and feelings of personal worth and belonging	• Continued to a greater degree by programming students into extra class activities including intramurals and/or interscholastic athletics
• Development of appropriate social behavior, including proper boy-girl relationships	• Continued to a greater degree through the promotion of co-educational participation
• Development of an understanding of cooperative, democratic living through leadership and followership experiences	• Continued
• Development of an understanding of sports and sport-related activities	• Continued by a greater degree to enhancing an individual's appreciation of sport activities in order to affect post-school physical education choices

According to Jewett and Bain (1985) the development and implementation of a quality secondary school physical education program requires special attention toward maintaining this balance. To foster this requirement, the following guiding statements should be adhered to while carrying out the instructional program:

- Both boys and girls should be exposed to an instructional program.
- There should be no substitute for the instructional program.
- The instructional program should be scheduled to allow:
    —for maximum participation
    —ample time for each student to have an opportunity to be challenged
    —and gain satisfaction that comes from achievement
- A daily quality physical education experience is recommended, but becomes mandatory if an educator is going to grasp the depth of teaching the requirements of secondary school students.
- A variety and significant number of activities should be included in the secondary school physical education program in order to meet all of the objectives.
- A majority of the activities should be introduced at the middle school/junior high school level to allow for acquainting students with the activities. Students will hopefully participate in them in extra-class programs and/or in selected community programs.
- The physical educator should allow time for preparation and planning.
- Interscholastic athletics should first and foremost be viewed as an educational experience and secondly as a challenging, enrichment program for the physically gifted.

PLANNING AND ORGANIZING THE CONTENT

Three major considerations should be addressed when discussing the mechanics of organizing curriculum content at the secondary school level. The first consideration involves designating the content areas and placing the various activities into appropriate categories. The more commonly accepted content areas for secondary school physical education are shown in Figure 9.1. Additional categories include outdoor pursuits such as backpacking, hiking, and orienteering; and combative activities, such as martial arts and wrestling. A list of commonly taught content activities is shown in Table 9.4.

The second consideration pertains to the percentage of time assigned to each of the major content areas. Recommended percentages are shown in Table 9.5.

The final consideration relates to both the selection of and the percentage of time allotted to the specific activities in each of the six content areas. The instructional framework should be established at this point. In developing a structure for the secondary school physical education program, it is generally advantageous to initially organize the major content areas into blocks of time (units) according to the degree of emphasis considered appropriate for each

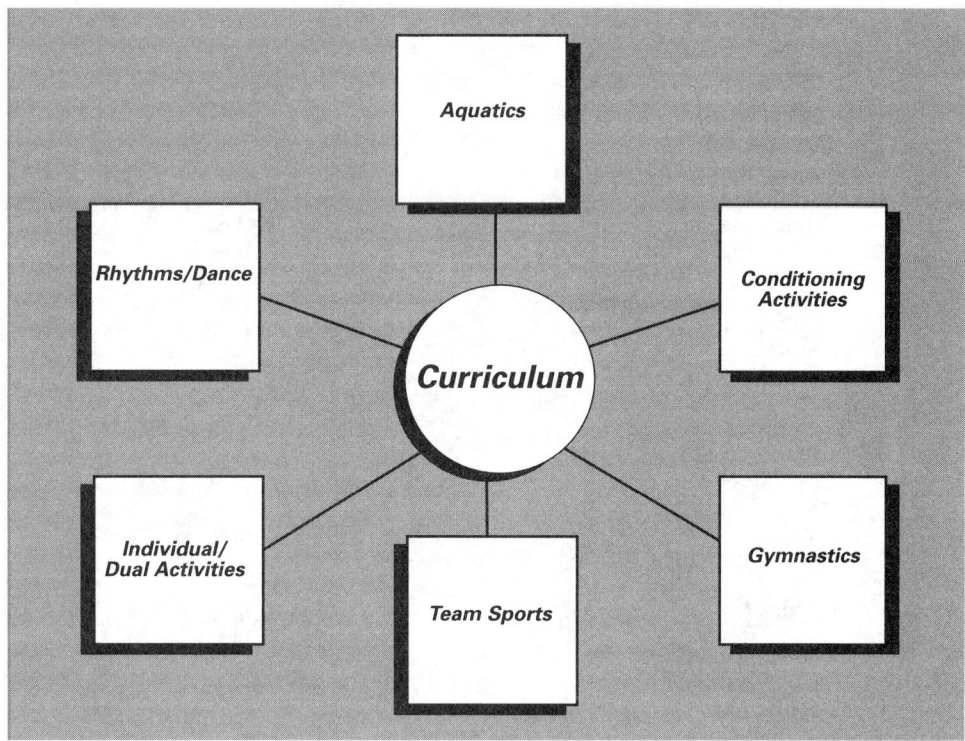

FIGURE 9.1 Secondary School Physical Education Content Areas

grade level. After this development has been accomplished, a further breakdown of time may be determined for the selected activities in each content area. This breakdown will depend on many variables including the number and length of classes per week, the availability of facilities and equipment, and staffing.

In many schools the selection of activities in each major content area tends to merely follow what other schools have done. The result may be either a major mistake or a genuine blessing depending on what the other school(s) used for guidelines and how soundly its curriculum was developed. Some validity exists, however, in (a) making a list of those schools with exemplary programs at the state level, if not at the national level, and (b) collecting curriculum materials from these schools. It may be advantageous to carefully examine these materials in order to ascertain what these curricula have in common. With a listing of major program elements, the physical education faculty should be able to better determine how well these elements coordinate with the local philosophy and how they may best meet local needs.

The validity of a physical education program is often determined by referring to *experts*—the individuals in positions to judge a program's worth. In addition, referring to the state department of education for assistance should not be undervalued. Many times state supervisors of physical education have been working in both the design and revision of curriculum for years.

TABLE 9.4   Secondary School Physical Education Activities

Aquatics

Diving (basic)
Diving (scuba)
Lifesaving
Snorkeling
Swimming (beginning)
Swimming (intermediate)
Swimming (advanced)
Synchronized swimming
Water polo

Conditioning Activities

Aerobic exercise
Circuit training
Free exercise
Interval training
Jogging
Weight training

Gymnastics

Balance beam
Horizontal bar
Parallel bars
Pommel horse
Rings
Stunts
Trampoline
Uneven parallel bars
Vaulting horse

Individual/Dual Activities

Archery
Badminton
Bowling
Cycling

Individual/Dual Activities (Continued)

Deck tennis
Fencing
Golf
Handball
Horseshoes
Racquetball
Shuffleboard
Skating (ice)
Skating (roller)
Table tennis
Tennis
Track and field
Wrestling

Rhythms/Dance

Ballroom/social dance
Contra dance
Folk dance
Modern dance
Square dance

Team Sports

Basketball
Field hockey
Flag football
Flickerball
Hockey (floor)
Hockey (ice)
Lacrosse
Soccer
Softball
Speedball
Team handball
Volleyball

TABLE 9.5   Time Allotment for Secondary School Physical Education Content

Content Area	Grade Level					
	7	8	9	10	11	12
Aquatics	10	10	10	10	10	10
Conditioning activities	10	10	10	15	15	15
Gymnastics	15	15	15	10	10	10
Individual/dual activities	20	20	20	30	30	30
Rhythms/dance	15	15	15	10	10	10
Team sports	30	30	30	25	25	25

Curriculum recommendations exist in the states of Alabama, California, Kansas, Montana, North Dakota, South Carolina, and South Dakota. The titles of these guides and addresses for obtaining them are listed in Table .9.6. Reviewing these guides is recommended for physical educators before any local revision is undertaken. Alabama provides a course of study that includes a well designed conceptual framework for the K–12 physical education program. California's comprehensive *Handbook for Physical Education* moves from developing a philosophy of physical education to assessing the physical education program. The handbook section dealing with developing and implementing a balanced secondary school physical education program is especially well done. The Kansas State Department of Education provides an excellent discussion of developing a scope and sequence in its guide. In *Montana in Action: Physical Education Curriculum Guide Grades K–12,* a well outlined program of content for

TABLE 9.6 State Agency Curriculum Materials

A Guide for Instruction in Physical Education
   South Dakota State Department of Education
   Kneip Building
   700 North Illinois Street
   Pierre, SD 57501

Alabama Course of Study: Physical Education (1989)
   Alabama State Department of Education
   483 Street Office Building
   501 Dexter Avenue
   Montgomery, AL 36130

Handbook for Physical Education
   California State Department of Education
   721 Capitol Mall
   P. O. Box 944272
   Sacramento, CA 94244

Kansas Physical Education Curriculum Guidelines
   Kansas State Department of Education
   Kansas State Education Building
   120 East 10th Street
   Topeka, KS 66612

Montana in Action: Physical Education Curriculum Guide, Grades K–12 (1988)
   Montana Office of Public Instruction
   Room 106 State Capitol
   Helena, MT 59620

Physical Education Curriculum Guide K–12 (1991)
   North Dakota Department of Public Instruction
   600 Boulevard Avenue E
   Bismarck, ND 58505

South Carolina Physical Education Guidelines (1989)
   South Carolina State Department of Education
   Rutledge Building
   1429 Senate Street
   Columbia, SC 29201

grades 7–12 is presented. The North Dakota Department of Public Instruction provides a detailed discussion of both content and content sequencing. The South Carolina State Department of Education guide and South Dakota's *A Guide for Instruction in Physical Education* includes further information on content and content sequencing.

A CLOSER LOOK AT CONTENT

One reason that curriculum planning is so difficult is because each of the major content areas has to be carefully organized yet balanced with other areas. In addition, the curriculum must be set up as a means of providing innovation and modification, as well as flexibility. Under such demanding circumstances it would be relatively easy for the administrator to merely select a number of activities from each major content area and then leave the rest to the physical educator. This occurs too often and results in programs that are nearly impossible to defend. A more solid practice would be structuring a somewhat firm and detailed course of study that contains thorough and balanced coverage. This framework may allow some departure by those physical educators who desire to implement innovative activities. However, an individual first needs a thorough understanding of the content areas discussed next.

Aquatics

The need for swimming, survival skills, and water-related activities is essential to a physical education curriculum. Public education concerning swimming instruction and water survival techniques should be taught. Nearly 15,000 water-related accidents occur each year, making this the second most frequent cause of death up to age forty-four. Aquatic education has been effective in lessening this frequency (Smith, 1982). Additional justification for including aquatics in the secondary school program is provided by Siedentop, Herkowitz, and Rink (1984), which include the following:

- Swimming is, perhaps, the perfect activity for developing overall physical fitness. All swimming strokes require use of the limbs and most body joints, resulting in improved strength, muscular endurance, and flexibility. In addition, the energy expenditure associated with swimming helps achieve and maintain an appropriate level of percent body fat.
- Because such a broad spectrum of swimming activities exists, ranging from basic to more advanced strokes, aquatics can easily provide challenging experiences for all students.
- Aquatics provide an excellent medium for socialization. In a well organized aquatics program, students have the opportunity to observe peers, compare their performance with others, help others, and develop both leadership and followership skills.

One variable limiting aquatic instruction in today's schools is the lack of a swimming pool, yet a pool on site is not necessary for an aquatics program.

Arrangements can often be made to use pools located in public and/or private recreational areas.

Conditioning Activities

A unique goal of physical education is the development and maintenance of health-related fitness—an optimum level of physical condition. This *capacity for activity* has concerned physical educators for centuries. In fact, long before games and recreational activities were accepted as educational activities, medical doctors and educators in Europe were proclaiming the virtues of personal exercise as a key contributor to good physical condition and well-being. Since then, a variety of activities specifically designed to promote health-related fitness have been proposed.

What conditioning activities should be included in a secondary school program? The answer must relate to both *if* and *how well* the conditioning activities develop the components of health-related fitness. Fortunately, many activities employed for building health-related fitness also develop selected components of motor fitness including agility, power, and speed. Therefore, it is possible to develop motor fitness skills along with a variety of sport, dance, and game skills while simultaneously developing a gradual but satisfactory level of physical conditioning. The individual development of physical condition should not be left entirely to game and sport participation. Other, more specific, health-related fitness activities should be used in the program such as aerobic exercise, circuit training, free exercise, and weight training.

Aerobic exercise, which leads to an aerobic lifestyle, is a significant curriculum dimension in today's schools. However, the carry-over into adulthood is the essential part of aerobic exercise. Aerobic endurance is synonymous with maximal oxygen consumption. This dimension can be measurably improved through repetitive physical activity including jogging, bicycling, and swimming. This component of health-related fitness is especially valuable during childhood and the adolescent years because people who exercise regularly during the formative years reach adulthood in a state of aerobic fitness, both physiologically and psychologically. In addition, individuals striving to achieve their physical potential must have some training before full growth and development have been reached (Falls, 1980).

Circuit training is a conditioning activity that enables a large number of students to be active at the same time in a small area, with limited equipment. In addition, circuit training may be easily structured to accommodate students with disabilities since it applies the principle of progressive overload. A circuit of consecutively numbered task stations (eight to twelve, depending on space) is laid out. Students must progress through the circuit completing the prescribed amount of work at each station. A list of tasks for a junior high school circuit program is shown in Figure 9.2. Although the basic tasks in the circuit are the same for each student, the intensity at each station will differ depending on the individual student's level of fitness. Therefore, all students can work through the circuit at their own degree of intensity.

Station	Level 1	Level 2	Level 3
Pull ups	1–3 Reps.	4–6 Reps.	Maximum
Run in place	30 Strides	40 Strides	60 Strides
Sit ups	5 Reps.	11–20 Reps.	21–30 Reps.
Bench steps	10–15 Reps.	16–20 Reps.	21–25 Reps.
Push ups	5 Reps. (bent knee)	6–10 Reps.	6–10 Reps. (with hand clap)
Jump rope	15 Reps.	25 Reps.	35 Reps.
Curls	4 Reps./25 pounds	5 Reps./30 pounds	6 Reps./35 pounds
Pogo springs	30 Reps.	40 Reps.	50 Reps.

* All stations must be completed in 30 seconds.

FIGURE 9.2 Circuit Program for Junior High School Students

Free exercises, also called warm-ups and calisthenics, provide a traditional set of movements for enhancing general body conditioning. Called *developmental exercises* by Stillwell and Stockard (1988), these activities are designed to provide proper stimulation to both the musculoskeletal and the cardiorespiratory systems. Since exercises are designed to be performed in work bouts of either ten to twenty-five repetitions or thirty- to sixty-second intervals, these activities are not generally accepted as *appropriate* for the development of cardiorespiratory endurance. Most of these exercises are categorized as isotonic. In recent years, however, isometric exercises have been introduced in the secondary school curriculum. A listing of commonly used developmental exercises is shown in Table 9.7.

Weight training has gained popularity with both boys and girls to such an extent that a majority of junior and senior high schools have nicely equipped weight rooms. Due to increased interest, it is important to remember that the emphasis be placed on overall conditioning and not on weight lifting for competition.

Achieving a comfortable, aerobic lifestyle involves complications especially in a society that does nearly everything for us. The likelihood of students developing an aerobic lifestyle is minimal since they live in a society where *soft living,* fast foods, and physical comforts are readily at hand.

TABLE 9.7 Developmental Exercises

Flexibility	Strength/Muscular Endurance
• Elbow knee benders	• Back kicks
• Elbow pullers	• Bent knee sit ups
• Forward lungers	• Crab walkers
• Head/trunk rotators	• Jump turns
• Hurdle stretchers	• Jump twisters
• Inch worms	• Leg circles
• Needle threaders	• Let downs
• Overhead benders	• Pogo springs
• Side straddle hops	• Push ups
• Side stretchers	• Reverse push ups
• Toe touches	• Reverse sit ups
• Windmills	

Rink (1993) explains that both *incorporating* aerobic fitness and *teaching* aerobic fitness in a school curriculum are difficult for a variety of reasons. Some of these difficulties include:

- Many schools lack sufficient time for developing fitness, much less maintaining it.
- Many older students dislike the work that is necessary for developing/maintaining fitness.
- Fitness gains are short-lived unless the student maintains a level of activity.

To combat these difficulties, Rink lists the following five curriculum alternatives that may assist physical educators in achieving the fitness objective:

1. Choose specific grades throughout the curriculum that will focus primarily on fitness. Rather than devoting a small percentage of time to fitness each year, target particular grades (K–12) and strive to meet the fitness objectives in all three behavioral domains.
2. Employ school time outside of the instructional program by implementing fitness activities before school, at lunch time, after school, and/or in the classroom when appropriate.
3. Approach the development of fitness as a health maintenance behavior by stressing the benefits of leading an aerobic lifestyle. The emphasis is thereby placed on the *why* rather than the *how*.
4. Include activities that have a high fitness value in the curriculum. Therefore, activities with a minimal aerobic component such as archery, bowling, and golf would be excluded.
5. Include some vigorous activity in each lesson. Either incorporate some unrelated fitness activity in the lesson or modify the lesson content to be more aerobic in nature.

Greene (1989) provides examples of such modifications in his book *Sport Specific Aerobic Routines* by combining aerobic exercise with sport-specific skills. The modification attempts to improve an individual's level of skill while increasing the heart's ability to pump blood more efficiently. Greene includes routines for basketball, soccer, softball, tennis, track and field, touch football, and volleyball.

The goal of Rink's five alternatives is for students to not only become fit but to also value fitness. Developing an attitude that will precondition students to be aerobically active is essential.

Gymnastics

Pangrazi and Darst (1991) define gymnastics as specific movements, a performance, or a routine done on either a large mat or large apparatus. Activities done on a mat are called stunts or tumbling when done individually, but they are called floor exercise when grouped together to form a routine. A listing of apparatus and selected stunts is shown in Table 9.8. Gymnastic activities for boys include floor exercises, horizontal bar, parallel bars, pommel horse, rings, trampoline and vaulting horse, while activities for girls include balance beam, floor exercises, trampoline, uneven parallel bars, and vaulting horse.

Gabbard, LeBlanc, and Lowy (1994) support the inclusion of gymnastics in the curriculum by stating that gymnastics:

- Are inherently challenging
- Are self-testing
- Provide opportunities for creative movement
- Enhance the development of selected health-related fitness components
- Offer a medium for understanding the laws of motion
- Foster cooperation among students

Individual and Dual Activities

A large percentage of time is allotted to games in the upper elementary and early middle school years. These games are generally like lead-up games to

TABLE 9.8   Secondary School Gymnastic Activities

Apparatus	Stunts
Balance beam	Back walkover
Horizontal bar	Backward roll
Parallel bars	Cartwheel
Pommel horse	Forward roll
Rings	Front walkover
Trampoline	Headstand
Uneven parallel bars	Kip
Vaulting horse	Prone headstand
	Round-off
	Tripod balance

both team sports and individual/dual activities. The existence of individual/dual activities in the secondary school physical education program is well established. By definition, these activities can be done independently such as archery, bowling, and golf, or they require either two or four individuals in competition with each other such as badminton, racquetball, and tennis. Individual/dual activities allow a student to compare his/her performance with other students or with a standard that has been set by a teacher or by the student. At the secondary school level, a generous allotment of time to these activities seems advisable (see Table 9.5). The progressive development and perfection of the skills and knowledge involved in these life-time activities provide a wholesome, enjoyable, physically satisfying form of recreational activity. This has become important in a culture characterized by a shortened work week, technology, and the tension syndrome.

Rhythms/Dance

The value of rhythms and dance in elementary education is very important in the physical education curriculum. Much of the previous discussion in this book regarding rhythms and dance tie together the elementary physical education experiences with those at the secondary school level. Activities for grades 7–12 should be an extension of what was experienced in lower grades, in both depth and scope.

Planning a secondary school rhythms and dance program requires physical educators to know what has been offered to students in previous years. It is frequently assumed that students entering junior high school have experienced instruction involving fundamental rhythms that include basic and singing rhythms. In many instances this is not the case. As a result, the physical educator must begin by having students walk, jump, skip, and so on to a variety of audible accompaniments before the various structured dances can be taught.

Montague (1972) explains that one of dance's strongest potentials is that it allows students to release human feelings in ways that are significant to the doer, enabling the individual to make a personal statement of what life feels like. It is through the dance medium that students can sort out impressions and sensations by initially internalizing them and then by externalizing them in movement. One of the primary objectives of the National Dance Association (1988) is to make dance a part of every individual's experience from early childhood through the retirement years, since it is through this medium that every person has the opportunity to experience self-expression and aesthetic development. In addition the association's guiding statement explains that every person has the right to move in ways that are expressive, imaginative, primal, and transformational.

The importance of dance in the secondary school curriculum as a means of expression, as an art form, and as a way of physical conditioning is apparent, yet it has been a content area reflecting little emphasis in many schools. One reason for this lack of emphasis has been the belief that dance is only for girls. This judgmental factor should not exist toward dance since the joy this activity has to offer can and should be shared by both. In addition, dance is the ideal coeducational activity for a secondary school physical education curriculum. Fallon (1977) supports this belief by stating:

> *But what does a society think of a boy's performance in dance? Does a boy dance gracefully or does he dance effeminately? In a society where his performance in physical activity is measured quantifiable, man has received little encouragement to express himself aesthetically in movement. There are few Bannisters in the athletic world who run with an awareness of self and universe that produces harmony with nature and satisfaction from a race well run regardless of victory or defeat. While it may be unproductive and therefore unlikely for the athlete, male or female, to strive for aesthetic expression, such expression is the essence of dance. And in dance, where performance is motivated by intrinsic satisfaction, a young man without orientation to creative, spontaneous expression stands barren and ignorant of his own body. With no apparent alternative, he shamefully rejects his bodily impulses to become the ultimate athlete.*

The types of dances that may be included in the secondary school curriculum are varied. Different dance types are included in Table 9.4 and discussed next. Specific dances within selected categories are shown in Table 9.9.

The selected dances will be dependent to some degree on the teacher's knowledge of and expertise in the dance; however, this should not be the limiting factor. Individuals are often present within the school and/or the community with the expertise and interest to teach a dance unit.

Ballroom/Social Dance

Ballroom/social dances are structured dances of a recreational nature usually done by couples in a social setting. Harris, Pittman, and Waller (1988) explain that ballroom/social dance has passed through six phases, each motivated by a specific style of music. These phases include: Foxtrot, Charleston, Swing, Latin, Rock and roll, and Country-western. These dances are somewhat cyclic—the interest comes and goes from time to time—and because the availability of social settings that offer a variety of music (big band, rock and roll, country-western, rhythm and blues, etc.) are limited, the need to include them in the secondary school physical education curriculum is apparent.

Contra Dance

More than two thousand American contra dances appear in publication today. A contra dance is one that is performed by many couples facing each other in a double-line formation. This type of dance only requires students to be able to count to eight and to move in time with the music. Therefore, contra dances are excellent precursors to the more refined, complex dances.

Folk Dance

As defined in Chapter 8, folk dances are structured dances that are specific to a country—they are one expression of a country's heritage. Folk dances pro-

TABLE 9.9 Secondary School Dances

Ballroom/Social Dance	Folk Dance
Cha Cha	Alexandrovska—Russia
Charleston	Corrido—Mexico
Country-western	Flowers of Edinburgh—Scotland
Disco	Hambo—Sweden
Foxtrot	Hava Nagila—Israel
Mambo	Man in the Hay—German
Merengue	Miserlou—Greece
Rumba	Sicilian Tarantella—Italy
Samba	Three Meet—England
Swing (Jitterbug)	Totuv—Denmark
Tango	
Waltz	*Modern Dance*
Contra Dance	*Square Dance*
All the Way to Galway	A Long Way Over
Broken Sixpence	Arkansas Traveler
Brown-Eyed Maid	Five Hands
Chorus Jig	Four in the Middle
Lady of the Lake	Gents Star Right
One for the Money	Go the Route
Portland Fancy	Just a Breeze
Ragged Mountain Reel	Promenade the Ring
Virginia Reel	Sail Away
Willow Tree	There's Your Corner

vide students with both an appreciation for and an understanding of the role that dance has played in the cultural development of various countries. When taught, the teacher is encouraged to include cognitive content including the history, geography, and climate of the specific country. According to Harris, Pittman, and Waller (1988) these details will allow students to (a) better understand the customs and traditions of other cultures, (b) appreciate the idea that the language of folk dancing may be a common bond between people of all cultures, and (c) learn that cultural differences can become adventures in discovering cultural similarities.

Modern Dance

Modern dance, as defined, incorporates the components of technique, improvisation, and composition. According to Lockhart (1977), *technique* provides the skills of dance movement. It is through technique that students learn how to control the body, which make it an instrument of movement. *Improvisation* is the spontaneous response by the student following the teacher's suggestion(s) which can be verbal, visual, tactile, and so on. A dance *composition* is merely a series of spontaneous (improvised) movements. Modern dance allows students complete freedom, relative to each of these components, to move.

Square Dance

Square dance has been proclaimed America's folk dance. Its popularity in the United States is so apparent that a commercial market exists that (a) supports full-time professionals tending to the square dancer's calling and instructional needs, (b) offers square dance vacationing packages, and (c) creates a complete line of fashion wear. Square dance requires students to learn a select number of movements that are fundamental to most dances. Some of these moves include honor (bow), do-si-do, promenade, allemande left, and grand right and left. Once the students learn these moves only one or two additional moves need to be taught in order to learn a new square dance.

The five dance categories just discussed are not all inclusive. Depending on the availability of time and the teacher's expertise, other dances could be taught in the secondary school physical education curriculum including ballet, clogging, jazz, round dance, and tap dance.

Team Sports

Sports have become an important element in American culture. As a result, the need for sports education at the secondary school level is also important. Team sports are learned and subsequently played in junior and senior high

Team sports in the secondary physical education curriculum

school for more than just recreation. Team sports are played as a means of developing a quality of *social efficiency* in students—the ability to get along with others and to exhibit desirable standards of conduct. Abundant evidence exists that validates the positive relationship between motor performance in sport-specific areas and the character traits of leadership and cooperation. During the adolescent years, a student's level of physical conditioning, paired with the development of sports skills, combine to provide a capacity of understanding others. This capacity leads to greater social acceptance.

Too often team sports are taken lightly, at least from an instructional perspective. They are viewed as free-play content, whereas they are played with minimal instruction. This type of activity results in poorly learned skills because students rush onto courts and fields merely to play. Skills and knowledge must be properly taught if the sport experience is aimed at successful development.

A high concentration of teams sports is needed in the secondary school with a modest tapering off beginning with grade 10 (see Table 9.5). Slowly tapering off allows time for instruction in activities that tend to have a greater degree of carry-over value into the adult years. Refer to Table 9.4 for the most frequently taught team sports. The sports selected from Table 9.4 will be determined partly by the availability of facilities and equipment, geographic location, and, to some degree, student interest.

Outdoor Education

A content area not listed in Table 9.4 that has gained popularity in recent years is outdoor education, also called adventure activities and outdoor pursuits. Smith et al. (1972), define outdoor education as learning *in* and *for* the outdoors. They do not view outdoor education as a separate discipline but rather a means of extending the existing curriculum and thereby enriching the lives of students through outdoor experiences. Specifically, outdoor education is a medium to (a) identify and resolve real life problems, (b) acquire the skills needed to enjoy a lifetime of creative living, and (c) develop a concern about one's natural environment.

A more recent definition by Siedentop, Herkowitz, and Rink (1984) indicates that outdoor education includes all pursuits that provide experiences related to the various components of our natural environment including hills, rocks, streams, rivers, trees, and so on. These outdoor pursuits involve adventure, exploration, and a personal contact with nature. Miles and Priest (1990) explain that outdoor education includes structured activities that use natural or artificial environments to identify both individual and group intrapersonal and interpersonal strengths and weaknesses in order to better promote positive personal growth. Specific activities in this content area include backpacking, camping, and orienteering. Additional adventure activities are shown in Table 9.10.

Darst and Armstrong (1991) indicate that the addition of outdoor education activities in physical education is one of the most significant curricular

TABLE 9.10 Adventure Activities

Angling	Orienteering
Backpacking	Rappelling
Bicycling	Rock climbing
Boating	Ropes courses
Camping	Sailing
Canoeing	Sculling
Fishing	Skiing
Fly casting	Sledding
Kayaking	

innovations in this century. They add that physical educators have a reluctance to offer outdoor activities because they (a) are unfamiliar with the content, its purposes, and its benefits, and/or (b) perceive outdoor education as having a different set of educational objectives that requires a different set of teaching skills. Support for including outdoor education activities in the secondary school physical education program is given by Annarino, Cowell, and Hazelton (1986) who warn that in the midst of this technological explosion, individuals must be careful not to forget the deep-rooted, long-established relationship between humans and nature. To strengthen this relationship, outdoor pursuits are needed since they provide a medium for developing communication skills, self-concept, self-confidence, cooperation, leadership, followership, and trust (Hammersley, 1992). Further justification is provided by Siedentop, Herkowitz, and Rink (1984) who indicate that adventure activities provide:

- Active participation regardless of skill level.
- Success in challenging activities.
- Experience in a different competitive setting, since the student is competing with nature.
- A need for responsible behavior, since concern for safety, cooperation, and equipment exists.

If outdoor education is intended for inclusion in the secondary physical education curriculum, the percentage of time devoted to these activities must come from another content area (see Table 9.5). The choice of which content area to modify, whether it be aquatics, gymnastics, or team sports, should not be made arbitrarily.

SUMMARY

1. A knowledge of the characteristics of secondary school students and the implications arising from these characteristics is essential for an individuals developing a physical education curriculum.

2. At the secondary school level it is essential to maintain a balance between the instructional program and the extra-class program.
3. In order to meet both the needs and interests of secondary school students, as well as the general objectives of the curriculum, it is necessary to offer a variety of activities .
4. If facilities are available, then sound justification for including aquatics in the secondary school program exists.
5. Conditioning activities are included in the secondary physical education curriculum to help develop and maintain strength, muscular endurance, flexibility, aerobic endurance, and a favorable body composition.
6. Gymnastics include floor and apparatus activities that challenge students to learn to move in a way different from most sport activities.
7. Individual and dual activities provide a wholesome, enjoyable, physically satisfying means of recreating.
8. Rhythms/dance activities at the secondary school level should be an extension of those experiences included in the K–6 program. The student should have exposure to a variety of dances including ballroom/social, contra, folk, modern, and square.
9. Team sports are an important content area in a secondary physical education curriculum since students can learn (a) a variety of skills for use in their post-school years and (b) appropriate sport behavior (sportsmanship).

QUESTIONS AND LEARNING ACTIVITIES

1. Determine how well Title IX practices are going in your area? Where are the strengths? Where are the problems?
2. Visit a school where adventure activities are included. Interview students and physical educators who relate to the value of these activities as a part of the total physical education curriculum.
3. Review two or three references who are experienced with the problems of young adolescents. List five or six of these problems and show how physical education may contribute to solutions.
4. Examine literature relating to *extra class programs,* and *alternative schools.* What advantages and disadvantages do you find with these programs in secondary school education? What can you discover relative to physical education? Are local schools involved in these programs?
5. Survey the recreational facilities in a particular community, both commercial and public. To what extent do the junior and senior high school curricula in physical education provide the appropriate skills, and how do they stimulate interest in the use of these facilities?
6. Is any purpose served by carefully developing an aquatics program on paper if no swimming facilities exist in the community?

7. In your opinion, where does ballroom/social dance fit best in the secondary school physical education program? Support your answer with the viewpoint of at least one reference.

8. Justify the place and importance of a rhythms/dance program at the secondary school level.

REFERENCES

Annarino, A. A., Cowell, C. C., & Hazelton, H. W. (1986). *Curriculum theory and design in physical education.* Prospect Heights, IL: Waveland Press.

Darst, P. W., & Armstrong, G. P. (1991). *Outdoor adventure activities for school and recreation programs.* Prospect Heights, IL: Waveland Press.

Fallon, D. (1977). A man unchained. *Journal of Physical Education and Recreation, 48*(5), 43–45.

Falls, H. B. (1980). *Essentials of fitness.* Philadelphia: Saunders.

Gabbard, C. (1996). *Lifelong motor development.* Dubuque, IA: Brown & Benchmark.

Gabbard, C., LeBlanc, E., & Lowy, S. (1987). *Physical education for children: Building the foundation.* Englewood Cliffs, NJ: Prentice-Hall.

Greene, L. (1989). *Sport specific aerobic routines.* Dubuque, IA: Eddie Bowers Publishing Company.

Hall, G. S. (1965). *Health, growth, and heredity.* New York: Teachers College Press.

Hammersley, C. H. (1992). If we win, I win: Adventure education in physical education and recreation. *Journal of Physical Education, Recreation, and Dance, 63*(9), 63–67, 72.

Harris, J. A., Pittman, A. M., & Waller, M. S. (1988). *Dance a while: Handbook of folk, square, contra, and social dance.* New York: Macmillan Publishing Company.

Jewett, A. E., & Bain, L. L. (1985). *The curriculum process in physical education.* Dubuque, IA: Wm. C. Brown Publishers.

Lockhart, A. S. (1977). *Modern dance: Building and teaching lessons.* Dubuque, IA: Wm. C. Brown Publishers.

Miles, J., & Priest, S. (1990). *Adventure education.* State College, PA: Venture Publishing.

Montague, M. E. (1972). Dance is affective and therefore effective education. *Journal of Health, Physical Education, and Recreation, 43*(3), 87–88.

National Dance Association. (1988). *Dance curricula guidelines K–12.* Reston, VA: AAHPERD.

Pangrazi, R. P., & Darst, P. W. (1991). *Dynamic physical education for secondary school students: Curriculum and instruction.* New York: Macmillan Publishing Company.

Rink, J. E. (1993). *Teaching physical education for learning.* St. Louis, MO: Mosby.

Rogers, F. R. (1941). *Dance: A basic educational technique.* New York: Macmillan Publishing Company.

Siedentop, D. (1994). *Introduction to physical education, fitness, and sport.* Mountain View, CA: Mayfield.

Siedentop, D., Herkowitz, J., & Rink, J. E. (1984). *Elementary physical education methods.* Englewood Cliffs, NJ: Prentice-Hall.

Smith, D. S. (1982). Drownproofing and the water safety spectrum. *Journal of Physical Education, Recreation, and Dance, 53*(5), 56–58.

Smith, J. W., Carlson, R. E., Donaldson, G. W., & Masters, H. B. (1972). *Outdoor education.* Englewood Cliffs, NJ: Prentice-Hall.

Stillwell, J. L., & Stockard, J. R. (1988). *More fitness exercises for children.* Durham, NC: Great Activities Publishing Company.

10

THE ADAPTED PHYSICAL EDUCATION PROGRAM

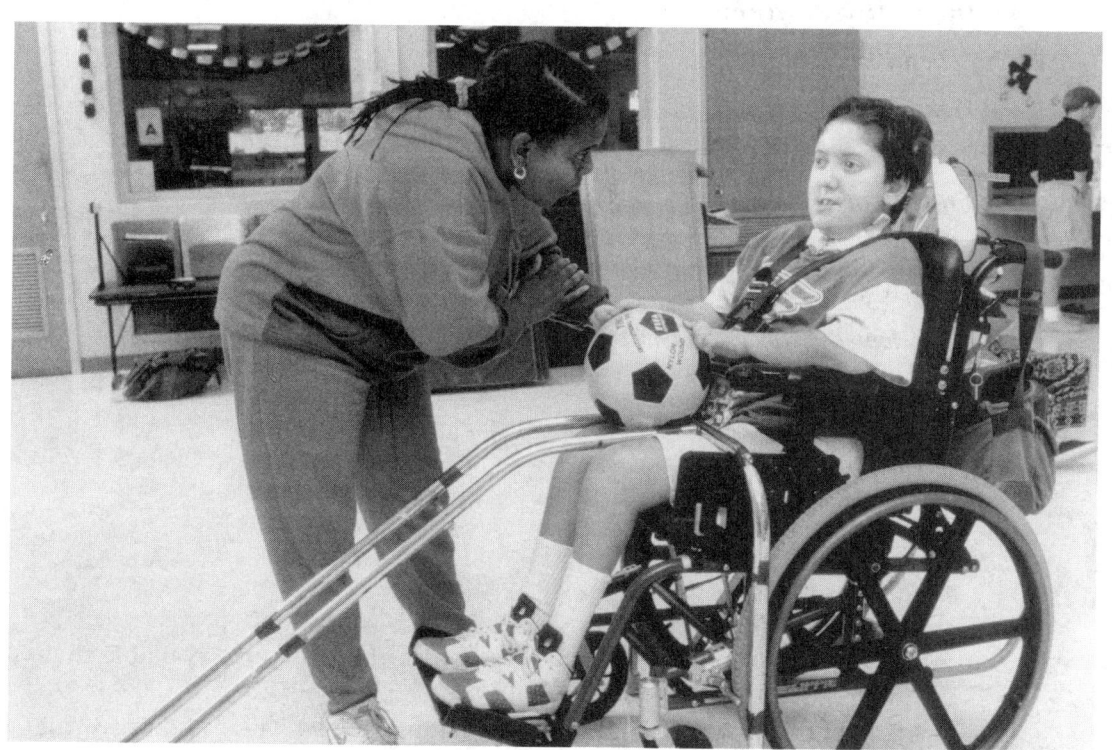

Outline

Definitions

Benefits of an Adapted Physical Education Program

The Mandate for Adapted Physical Education

Public Law 94.142

The Individualized Education Program

Cooperative Planning and the Coordination of Professionals

Classification and Organization

Inclusion

Additional Programming

Innovative Programs

Scheduling

Helpful Resources

Outcomes

After reading and studying this chapter, you should be able to:
- Define

  Adapted physical education

  Disabled

  Exceptional

  Handicapped

  Impaired

  Inclusion

  Mainstreaming

  Special education
- Distinguish among the various organizational structures available that provide for students with disabilities.
- Identify the various components of Public Law 94.142 and discuss their implications for the physical education curriculum.
- Develop and design an IEP.
- Modify and adapt physical education activities to meet the student's individual needs.
- Discuss the individual benefits that can be derived from an adapted physical education program.

Physically, mentally, socially, and emotionally impaired youth have been unfairly subjected to inactivity in the past and often been considered exempt from physical education. The result is the unrealized potential and a social injustice to these youth.

This chapter emphasizes not only the development of a program that concentrates on flexibility and innovation, but one that is specifically designed to account for individual differences. This kind of program addresses ways of providing active participation for those students who cannot participate safely and successfully in the unrestricted activities of a regular physical education program. This group of students includes more than youngsters with minor orthopedic difficulties, postural problems, or low levels of physical fitness. The comprehensive adapted physical education program will provide opportunities for all students who need individualized and specialized instruction regardless of the disabling condition (see Table 10.1). In addition, the program is a diversified one of developmental movement activities, games, sports, and rhythms suited to the needs and interests, as well as the limitations, of all students.

DEFINITIONS

In order to better understand the need and importance of the adapted physical education program, the following terms are defined:

- *Adapted physical education*—A diverse program of developmental activities, exercises, games, rhythms, and sports designed to meet the unique physical education needs of handicapped individuals (Winnick, 1996).
- *Adapted physical educator*—A professional with specialized training in designing, implementing, and evaluating specialized physical education programs (Auxter & Pyfer, 1989).

TABLE 10.1 Disabling Conditions

Chronically impaired	Emotionally disturbed
Anemia	Hearing impaired
Arthritis	Learning disabled
Asthma	Mentally retarded
Cardiac disorders	Multi-handicapped
Cerebral palsy	Neurologically impaired
Diabetes	Obese
Epilepsy	Orthopedically impaired
Hemophilia	Overweight
Multiple sclerosis	Socially maladjusted
Muscular dystrophy	Speech impaired
Poliomyelitis	Terminally ill
Spina bifida	Visually impaired
Convalescing injury	

- *Disabled*—Individuals who have lost physical, social, or psychological functioning that significantly interferes with normal growth and development (Hardman, Drew, & Egan, 1987).
- *Exceptional*—Individuals so different in mental, physical, emotional, or behavioral characteristics that in the interest of equality of educational opportunity, special provisions must be made for their proper education (Daniels & Davies, 1982).
- *Handicapped*—A limitation that is imposed on the individual by environmental demands and that is related to the individual's ability to adapt to these environmental demands (Hardman, Drew, & Egan, 1987).
- *Impaired*—Individuals with an identifiable organic or functional condition that adversely affects their educational performance (Seaman & DePauw, 1989).
- *Inclusion*—Placement of students with disabilities in regular education classrooms, with appropriate support personnel, to receive an education and related services alongside peers (Miller, 1994).
- *Mainstreaming*—Placement of handicapped students into the regular physical education class with an Individualized Education Program (Auxter & Pyfer, 1989).
- *Special education*—Specially designed instruction, at no cost to the parents or guardians, to meet the unique needs of a handicapped student including classroom instruction, instruction in physical education, home instruction, and instruction in hospitals and institutions (Public Law 94.142, 1975).

BENEFITS OF AN ADAPTED PHYSICAL EDUCATION PROGRAM

Before developing an adapted physical education program, it is important to answer the following questions:

- What behavioral changes do educators want to see in students with disabilities?
- What accomplishments may be expected from each student as a result of being involved in the program?
- What individual benefits may be derived from such a program?

The following list includes benefits that may be derived from participation in an adapted physical education program:

- Development of a variety of recreational skills.
- Development of physical capacity and joint function.
- Alleviation of corrective, atypical physical conditions.
- Improvement of overall physical fitness.

- Development of an understanding of one's movement capabilities and limitations.
- Development of both satisfaction and a sense of pride in one's ability to overcome limitations.
- Development of a positive self-image.
- Development of effective interpersonal relationships.
- Development of an understanding, appreciation, and enjoyment of movement.

THE MANDATE FOR ADAPTED PHYSICAL EDUCATION

Theoretically, physical education offers something to every student. Merely excusing disabled students—individuals unable to perform in the regular physical education curriculum—is to sidestep responsibility. What must be provided is a physical education curriculum that specifically allows for individual differences.

The need for adapted physical education has never been greater than it is today. Students with a variety of disabilities are attending this nation's schools (see Table 10.2). As reported in 1990 in the Tenth Annual Report to Congress on the Implementation of the Education of All Handicapped Children Act:

- More than four million handicapped children received special education during the 1988–1989 school year.
- Among these children, ninety-four percent had one of the following four handicapping conditions: learning disability, speech impairment, mental retardation, or emotional disturbance.
- Handicapped children comprised nearly eleven percent of all school-aged children during the 1988–1989 school year.

TABLE 10.2 Special Education School Children in 1992–1993

Disability or Impairment	Total Cases
Learning disabled	2,364,000
Speech/language impaired	998,000
Mentally retarded	532,000
Emotionally disturbed	402,000
Multi-disabled	103,000
Hearing impaired	61,000
Orthopedically impaired	53,000
Other health impaired	50,349
Visually impaired	24,000
Deaf-blind	1,000

Beginning in 1961 with Public Law 87.276 Special Education Act, continuous governmental support for the education of handicapped persons has occurred (see Table 10.3).

The passage of these legislative acts has direct implications not only for the physical education curriculum, but also for the physical education instructor. In order to both help disabled students and to operate within the federal mandate, today's physical educator needs special knowledge and skills. Among these are:

- Knowledge of disabling conditions.
- Knowledge of the laws which directly affect teachers.
- Knowledge of special equipment and its use.
- Knowledge of available resources.
- Skills in managing student behavior.
- Skills in selecting and administering motor, perceptual-motor, and fitness tests for diagnostic assessment.
- Skills to develop an individualized education program.
- Skills to formulate learning progressions, especially in motor skills (Jansma, 1977).

PUBLIC LAW 94.142

In 1973 Congress enacted the Rehabilitation Act in which Section 504 guaranteed the civil and personal rights of handicapped individuals in all programs for which the sponsoring group(s) received federal funds. The responsibility is on the local education agency through the individual school to see that appropriate and necessary accommodations are made and the individual is not withheld from, discriminated against, or excluded from activities because of a handicapped condition. Section 504 prohibits "handicapism" in the same manner that Title VI of the Civil Rights Act prohibits racism.

The rules pertaining to the implementation of the Rehabilitation Act were enforced in December, 1976 as a part of Public Law 94.142 Education for All Handicapped Children Act, which was signed into law by President Gerald Ford on November 29, 1975. At that time the act was designed to ensure that all handicapped students had the availability of a free, appropriate public education including special education and related services for meeting their unique needs. In addition, the law (a) insured that the rights of the handicapped student and the parents would be protected; (b) gave assistance to states and localities that provided for the education of all handicapped students, and (c) required assessment to ensure the effectiveness of efforts for educating these students.

The school curriculum was intended to be fully operational by 1980. Student needs were supposed to be met by:

- Conducting a needs assessment program that would establish realistic goals for each learner. Individual testing would determine the extent to

TABLE 10.3 Federal Legislation Impacting Individuals with Disabilities

Name	Focus
1961 Public Law 87.276 Special Education Act	Designed to train professionals to prepare teachers of deaf children
1965 Public Law 89.10 Elementary and Secondary Education Act	Enabled states and local school districts to develop programs for economically disadvantaged children through federal funds for economically disadvantaged
1966 Public Law 89.750 Amendments to the Elementary and Secondary Education Act	Created the Bureau of Education for the Handicapped
1973 Public Law 93.112, Section 504 Rehabilitation Act	Declared that handicapped people cannot be excluded from any program or activity receiving federal funds on the sole basis of being handicapped
1975 Public Law 94.103 Developmental Disabilities Assistance and Bill of Rights Act	Affirmed the rights of the mentally retarded and other developmentally disabled individuals
1975 Public Law 94.142 Education for All Handicapped Children Act	Required that an individual education program be developed for each handicapped child and that handicapped students receive their programs in the least restrictive environment
1983 Public Law 98.199 Amendments to the Education for All Handicapped Children Act	States were required to collect data to determine the anticipated service needs for handicapped children
1986 Public Law 99.372 Handicapped Children's Protection Act	Attorney's fees were reimbursed to parents who were forced to go to court to secure an appropriate education for their handicapped child
1986 Public Law 99.457 Education for All Handicapped Children Amendment	States were instructed to develop comprehensive interdisciplinary services for handicapped children from birth to age two and to expand services for handicapped children ranging in ages from three to five
1990 Public Law. 101.336 Americans with Disabilities Act	Extended Section 504 of the Rehabilitation Act to the private sector, thereby providing a clear and comprehensive mandate to eliminate discrimination against individuals with disabilities
1990 Public Law 101.476 Individuals with Disabilities Education Act	Replaced and extended provisions of Education of the Handicapped Act to further guarantee the educational rights of students with disabilities

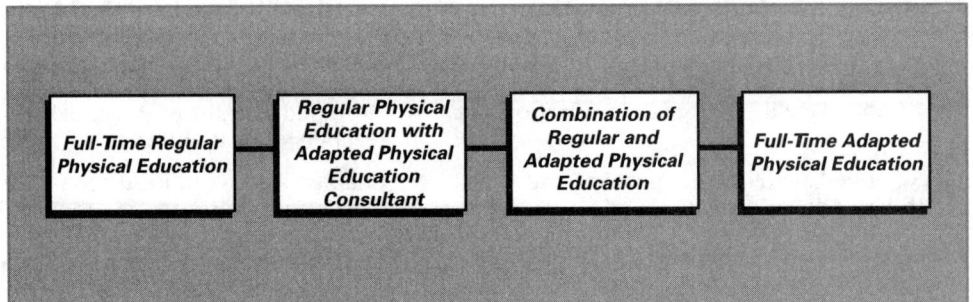

FIGURE 10.1 Adapted Physical Education Placements

which the individual had attained the goals. The gaps between the established goals and the level of the learner would be identified and put in statement form.
- Planning and initiating the Individualized Education Program (IEP).
- Evaluating learner progress at least once annually.
- Placing each learner in the least restrictive environment, the setting in which the student is likely to have the most productive learning experiences (see Figure 10.1).
- Keeping the parents or guardians advised at periodic intervals as to the progress of the student.

For the purposes of this act, physical education includes special physical education, adapted physical education, movement education, and motor development. It entails the development of physical and motor fitness, fundamental motor skills and patterns, body mechanics, individual and group games and sport skills such as intramural lifetime sports, aquatics, and dance. In addition, each disabled student must be given the opportunity to participate in the regular physical education program that is available to nondisabled students unless the student is enrolled full-time in a special facility. If specially designed physical education is prescribed, then the public agency responsible for this education must provide services directly or make arrangements for them through other public or private programs.

THE INDIVIDUALIZED EDUCATION PROGRAM

In Section 602 of the Education for All Handicapped Children Act considerable attention is directed to the special education process of designing instruction and activities that meet the unique needs of students through an Individualized Education Program (IEP). Carefully defined in the regulations, the IEP must include a written statement for each handicapped student including annual goals, short-term objectives, and services to be provided (see

Figure 10.2). The Office of Special Education (1980) indicates that the IEP will serve as:

- A focal point for parent-school communication and can be used as a tool in resolving differences between the two parties.
- A basis for evaluation in determining the extent of the student's educational progress.
- A monitoring device for governmental agencies attempting to determine if a student is truly receiving a free, appropriate education.
- A source for listing all services that must be provided to the student and, as such, is used to determine the appropriate placement of, as well as the appropriate curriculum for, the student.

Individualized Education Program (IEP)

Name: _____

Date: _____

School: _____

Grade: _____
_____

Age: _____

  a. Performance level assessment

  b. Annual student goals

  c. Short-term instructional objectives

  d. Educator in charge

     Role of special education (including physical education)

     Role of general education and related services

     Program starting date

     Program ending date

     Date of review procedure

  e. Program particulars: placement, curriculum, time assigned to regular physical education class (least restrictive environment), time assigned to adapted physical education

  f. Committee recommendations: learning styles, teaching materials, etc.

  g. Evaluation criteria

  h. Members of the IEP Committee

  i. Committee meeting dates

FIGURE 10.2 Worksheet for Developing an IEP

Prior to the start of the student's program, six IEP procedures progress as follows:

1. A formal parental consent and preplanning of objectives.
2. An assessment of the student and a specific description of the disabling condition(s).
3. A mandatory conference between the parents and the teachers responsible for the student's education to discuss the IEP pertaining to the student's level of educational performance including instructional goals and objectives, special education, related services, and projected time schedules.
4. A discussion of services available for meeting the needs resulting from the assessment.
5. Program implementation, carefully written and disseminated to all personnel participating in the student's IEP.
6. Evaluation of the student's progress and the suitability of the existing program and instructional objectives.

COOPERATIVE PLANNING AND THE COORDINATION OF PROFESSIONALS

Any worthwhile program that meets the legislative requirements for disabled learners must involve a close working arrangement between all individuals responsible for instruction. Within the school, the need for a cooperative effort involving the school health personnel, classroom teachers, special education teachers, physical educators, family physicians, and parents is essential. Davis and Davis (1994) indicate that to ensure that all students with disabilities receive the appropriate physical education, a communication network across all disciplines must be established. Cooperative curriculum planning can make it possible to provide appropriate and challenging movement experiences involving individual, partner, small group, and large group activities. Such planning may be time consuming but is not an unusual occurrence for the professionals teaching students who require special attention and services. The challenge for the professionals who deliver services to students with disabilities is considerable and requires cooperation if the outcome is aimed at being done correctly.

Cooperation is also essential between individuals providing services outside the school. In addition to the direct medical services provided for the disabled student by physicians and nurses, psychological services are frequently provided by a counselor or a clinical social worker. Providing a specific rehabilitation program with the goal of returning the disabled student to an effective level of overall well-being, requires a number of available additional personnel, including those engaged in art therapy, dance therapy, music therapy, and vocational counseling. Individuals specifically concerned with movement include physical therapists, occupational therapists, recreational therapists, corrective therapists, and developmental specialists. Problems arising in the delivery of the related services and redundant efforts existing among the many professionals involved may be due to a lack of adequate coordination in planning these services (Auxter & Pyfer, 1989).

After studying the variety of functions and services most frequently provided to students with disabilities, Cratty (1989) suggests that the adapted physical educator (1) assumes the major responsibility of handling the more complex motor skills; (2) works with groups of students rather than individuals; and (3) provides motivational activities for a cross-section of disabled students, including those with emotional problems, learning disabilities, and varying degrees of mental retardation.

Although a wider variety of students requiring the attention of the physical educator exists today, the traditional tasks still remain. Such tasks include working with children who have low levels of fitness and postural problems, guiding the slow learner of general motor skills, and planning programs for the obese. For the most part, these students are not considered special education students, as defined in the Education for All Handicapped Children Act. Most of these individuals will be students who have no restrictions relating to their ability to move, yet attention to their needs is just as important as to the needs of students who are in need of special education under the act.

CLASSIFICATION AND ORGANIZATION

As previously stated, children with disabilities should be placed in a physical education class that will provide the most productive learning experiences. When a special education teacher and a physical education teacher work together, students should be classified and placed for participation accordingly. The assessment techniques used for this placement must be valid to ensure that the most productive and appropriate procedures are being done. The family physician should be consulted since this health professional may provide the medical information that an adapted physical education program can be based. Dunn and Fait (1989) indicate that this meeting allows the physical educator an opportunity to share with the physician both the goals of the adapted program and the commitment to providing quality physical education for the disabled student. To meet this objective, it is recommended that the family physician complete a medical referral form. Figures 10.3 and 10.4 are examples of departmental letters dealing with activity expectations and should be completed by the attending physician.

A variety of organizational structures are available that provide for students with disabilities ranging from the informal to the more formal arrangement of students, and from the small homogeneous grouping to the larger heterogeneous grouping. This is partly due to the fact that no single structure can provide for the various disabling conditions. One structure for grouping disabled students for instruction is to use the least restrictive environment approach previously discussed in this chapter. Following an

---

Referral Form

Physician's Recommendation for Physical Education

Dear Physician:
All students enrolled in public schools participate in physical education activities that are designed to meet their growth and developmental needs. In addition many students participate in other types of physical activities, including intramurals, athletics, and band. To identify the specific needs of students, all school personnel, parents, and the physician must work cooperatively. Please provide the information below so that the most appropriate activities may be provided.

I have examined _____ and find the following disability(es): _____
_____

I recommend the following (please check all that apply):
_____ 1. No activity restrictions.
_____ 2. Participation in all activities except athletics.
_____ 3. No restrictions in physical education.
_____ 4. Adaptations in physical education:
    _____ a. Limited running and jumping
    _____ b. No running and jumping
    _____ c. No activities involving body contact
    _____ d. Strenuous conditioning exercises
    _____ e. Exercises designed for rehabilitation only
_____ 5. Other adaptations (please specify):
_____
_____

I recommend these adaptations for:
    ____ 2 weeks   ____ 2 months
    ____ 1 month   ____ Other (please specify)

Date: _____

Physician: _____ Address: _____

Please return this form to:
_____
                                                                                                 (School name and address)

FIGURE 10.3 Student with Disability Activity Form

assessment process, each student will receive the necessary instruction in one of the four categories shown in Figure 10.1.

As a result of the mandated implementation of PL 94.142, Ersing (1974) suggested the following categorical structure:

- Unrestricted prcgram (totally mainstreamed)
- Modified program (partially mainstreamed)

ABC High School
Department of Physical Education

Name: _____
Date: _____

The physical education department at ABC High School believes that every student who is able to attend should also be able to benefit from the program. After allowing time for undressing, dressing, and showering, the daily activity time ranges from twenty-five to thirty minutes.

Please either (X) one general activity category or (X) specific activities you would recommend for this student.

Mild	**Moderate**	**Strenuous**
( ) Aerobic exercise	( ) Aerobic exercise	( ) Aerobic exercise
( ) Archery	( ) Apparatus (bars)	( ) Basketball
( ) Corrective exercise	( ) Apparatus (horse)	( ) Cageball
( ) Golf skills	( ) Badminton	( ) Field hockey
( ) Horseshoes	( ) Badminton skills	( ) Soccer
( ) Mild dance	( ) Bowling	( ) Speedball
( ) Shuffleboard	( ) Corrective exercise	
( ) Table tennis	( ) Dance	
( ) Tennis skills	( ) Golf	
( ) Tumbling	( ) Softball	
	( ) Tennis	
	( ) Volleyball	
	( ) Volleyball skills	
	( ) Weight training	

Note: If strenuous activity is recommended, it is accepted that mild and moderate are permissible unless exceptions are indicated. Likewise, if moderate activity is recommended, it is accepted that mild is permissible. If you think the student should be doing only mild activities, but find that one or more moderate activities such as bowling and golf should be included, then check them. If non-activity is desirable at this time for this student, please make this notation and provide the number of days this status should continue.

Up to the date of _____, please excuse this student from all activity.
Signed _____
Attending Physician
Comments: _____
_____
_____

FIGURE 10.4 Adapted Physical Education Referral Form

—Vigorous activity
—Moderate activity
—Mild activity

- Remedial program (partially mainstreamed)
- Developmental program

A similar classification system that the American Medical Association supports is based on the type of activity presented in the curriculum. It includes the following four categories:

- *Unrestricted activity*—Full participation in all physical education activities.
- *Moderately restricted activity*—Participation in designated physical education activities.
- *Severely restricted activity*—Participation in a limited number of physical education activities.
- *Reconstructive or rehabilitative activity*—Participation in a concentrated program of corrective and adapted physical education activities.

These categories not only apply to the identifiably disabled student but also to (a) students convalescing from an illness or injury who need a gradual return to unrestricted activity; (b) students with certain muscle groups in need of strengthening; and (c) students with postural deviations that have been determined as subject to improvement through prescribed activity.

Thomas, Lee, and Thomas (1988) suggest grouping students by the disabling condition. This format includes the following three categories related to physical education:

- Those conditions not influencing motor skill.
- Those conditions impairing performance and motor-skill learning but amenable to change (functional).
- Those conditions impairing performance that require permanent adaptation (structural).

INCLUSION

By law, students with disabilities cannot be excluded from physical education. In the past, programming for these students has typically taken one of the two following forms:

- A segregated special education class.
- An integrated class.

Segregated programming was commonplace prior to the enactment of PL 94.142, but since its enactment in 1975 the move from separate special education programming to inclusion has resulted. Kirchner and Fishburne (1995) indicate that two additional factors have led to this change. The first factor involves an increased awareness by today's parents of their children's educational rights. Secondly, dwindling resources have forced administrators at the state level to reduce monetary support for special programs. As a result, public schools must assume more of the responsibility for providing both the programs and the individuals to address the educational needs of the special student.

Making adaptations in activity enhances learning.

Whenever possible, it is recommended that students with disabilities be integrated—placed in their regular physical education class. Originally called *mainstreaming* in the 1970s, it provided the foundation for what is now called *inclusion*. Mainstreaming focused on placing the student in the least restrictive environment, whereas inclusion focuses on the learned outcomes achieved by the student. Block and Vogler (1994) call this process *full inclusion* and define it as educating all children with disabilities, whether mild or severe, in regular classroom settings even if it requires special resources and/or curricula. Inclusion suggests that students with disabilities receive their IEP in physical education in the context of general physical education with the necessary adaptations and support to ensure appropriateness, safety, and success (Block, 1994). Miller (1994) indicates that inclusion allows all students, regardless of disabling condition, to be included in every aspect of school life in order for them to feel like a true part of their school community.

As mentioned, inclusion was developed to allow for specially designed instruction for students with disabilities. Inclusion has become widespread because of its benefits, which include the following:

- The availability of age-appropriate role models.
- Students learning appropriate social skills.
- Students having ample opportunity to participate in a variety of school activities (Stainback & Stainback, 1990).

Further support for inclusion is provided by the Child Advocacy Center (1991) which states that inclusion is important because:

- It provides benefits to disabled students in terms of peer role models as well as the opportunity to interact socially.
- It provides benefits to the general school population in terms of tolerance, acceptance, and the valuing of differences in people.
- Separation often causes stigmatization.
- Separation leads to the lowering of expectations (self-fulfilling prophecy).

To better meet the needs of students in an inclusive physical education environment, it often becomes necessary to make changes in various aspects of the curriculum. Block and Vogler (1994) discuss the following three changes that have proven useful:

1. Changing what is taught.
2. Changing how it is taught.
3. Changing who does the teaching.

Changing the content or *what is taught* may be accomplished in either a multi-level or an overlapping format. In the multi-level format, all students are involved in the same unit (basketball) and the same skill (dribbling, passing, or shooting) within that unit. However, the learning experiences used are selected in relation to each student's abilities. For example, in a basketball unit, students without disabilities may be working at the application level by using both complex game skills and strategies in a 3-on-3, game-like drill. In the same class, disabled students may be working at the comprehension level by learning basic skills and a lower-level strategy in a 2-on-1, game-like drill. In the overlapping format, students work toward meeting the same goal. In other words, a shooting objective for all students in a basketball unit may be to make three out of five lay-ups. To ensure that disabled students can attain this goal, the basket may need to be lowered and/or the size of the basketball may need to be changed.

The second factor involves changing *how the content is taught*. This format is based on the game/activity modification work of Morris and Stiehl (1989). Existing sports such as basketball, soccer, and volleyball are modified; and lead-up games such as sideline basketball, zone soccer, and volley volleyball are further modified to allow all students to participate successfully.

The third format focuses on changing *who will teach the content*. Rather than having the educational services delivered only by the physical educator, additional individuals are employed to better meet the needs of disabled students. Adapted physical education specialists, paraprofessionals, parents, and peers are among the people providing these services. Craft (1994) reminds that it is important to remember that inclusion changes the assumption that the physical educator is employed to deliver normal curriculum content to students. Instead, the educator is employed to teach content that is appropriate for each student and that content may vary greatly among students.

Helion and Fry (1995) indicate that when modifying an activity, the teacher may take two approaches. The physical educator may manipulate either the task or activity itself or the environment in which the task is being done. The task or activity may be manipulated by modifying the (a) required movements; (b) number of attempts; (c) time limits; (d) scoring procedures; and (e) team size and/or composition. The environment may be manipulated by modifying the (a) play area; (b) number and/or size of goals; and (c) type and/or amount of equipment.

ADDITIONAL PROGRAMMING

Whether students are integrated through mainstreaming or inclusion, there are times when the disabling condition either restricts or prohibits complete participation in the regular physical education class. As a result, a special program may need to be provided. To meet the needs of the disabled students needing special attention, Gallahue (1996) offers three such programs: the adapted program, the remedial program, or the developmental program.

The Adapted Program

This program consists of modified activities based on the physical, mental, and emotional limitations of the disabled student. Modifications may be made specific to the activity being used (see Table 10.4) or specific to the participant(s) involved in the activity (see Table 10.5). A variety of ways to modify an activity exist, but the modifications should be planned and not made carelessly. To lessen this task, Berryman et al. (1974), provide an activity analysis model shown in Table 10.6. This model allows the physical educator to analyze the activity to be used and make only those modifications necessary to meet the student's needs.

The Remedial Program

This program consists of specific exercises and movement activities for correcting defective body mechanics and perceptual-motor functioning. Objectives include the improvement of such basic skills as sitting, standing, and moving through space.

The Developmental Program

This program contains the elements of both the adapted and the remedial programs. It is comprised of movement activities designed to improve the basic skills, physical fitness, and socialization.

TABLE 10.4 Activity Modifications

1. Reduce playing area
2. Use larger equipment
3. Use lighter equipment
4. Shorten distances
5. Shorten playing time
6. Reduce point requirements for winning
7. Eliminate competition by not keeping score
8. Allow balls to bounce or be caught in games like volleyball
9. Use special devices to accommodate (handrails, guide ropes, and textured floors)
10. Lower baskets and nets
11. Substitute skill practice for game participation
12. Decrease number of repetitions in exercises
13. Reduce tempo in rhythmic activities
14. Soften landing area with mats
15. Increase size of striking implements and targets
16. Substitute accuracy for distance in throwing/kicking activities
17. Use stationary ball handling activities
18. Simplify cues
19. Stress process (technique) rather than product (performance)
20. Change the formation

TABLE 10.5 Participant Modifications

1. Use extra players
2. Use free substitutions
3. Rotate players frequently
4. Allow frequent rest periods
5. Allow two hands instead of one when accuracy/power is involved
6. Allow substitute runners
7. Substitute walking for running
8. Eliminate movements of specific body parts
9. Take fewer turns
10. Restrict playing area to half court or less
11. Play a team position requiring less activity
12. Allow peer assistance

INNOVATIVE PROGRAMS

Innovative physical education programs for students with disabilities can be found throughout the United States. In many of these programs the orientation and teaching have taken place in the school setting, and the specific activity has been put into practice in a community recreation or similar program. Selected innovative programs are discussed next.

I CAN

This comprehensive, instructional program was developed at Michigan State University under the direction of Janet Wessel (1979). I CAN is an acronym

TABLE 10.6 Activity Analysis Model

Physical Demands

1. Primary body position required
2. Movement skills required
3. Amount of fitness required
4. Amount of coordination required
5. Amount of energy required

Social Demands

1. Number of participants required
2. Type of interaction
3. Type of communication
4. Type of participant leadership required
5. Cooperative or competitive activity
6. Amount of physical contact required
7. Noise level

Cognitive Demands

1. Rule complexity
2. Strategy level
3. Concentration level
4. Academic skills required
5. Verbal skills required
6. Directional concepts required
7. Scoring system complexity
8. Memory required

Administrative Demands

1. Time required
2. Equipment required
3. Facilities required
4. Leadership required
5. Safety considerations

---

for "**I**ndividualized instruction, **C**reate social leisure competence, **A**ssociate all learning, **N**arrow the gap between theory and practice." It is based on individual needs, establishes objectives, and utilizes activities that have been field tested. The I CAN program was developed for mentally impaired individuals, but may be adapted for any disabled individual. It is developmental in nature, offering a balance between the acquisition of psychomotor skills and appropriate affective behavior. The program is organized into the following four areas:

- *Health and fitness*—Includes activities to develop muscular strength and endurance, flexibility, aerobic endurance, and posture.
- *Fundamental skills*—Includes locomotor skills such as walking, running, and jumping; and game skills such as throwing, catching, and kicking.
- *Body management*—Includes body awareness and control.
- *Aquatics*—Includes basic skills such as adjustment to water, breathing, and buoyancy; and swimming skills such as treading water, crawl stroke, and backstroke.

IMP Program

The IMP (**I**ndividual **M**otor **P**rogram), developed by Loovis and Ersing (1979), provides a direct link between mandatory testing and the curriculum. Following diagnostic assessment, a performance-based curriculum that is comprised of a sequence of progressive, instructional activities for each motor skill is developed.

Perceptual-Motor Programs

Children with specific learning disabilities exhibit a disorder in one or more of the basic psychological processes involved in understanding or in using spoken or written language. These difficulties may be manifested in disorders like listening, thinking, talking, reading, writing, spelling, or doing mathematical functions. The motor development view suggests that the dynamics of learning are involved in movement and body management.

Research indicates that perception is multi-sensory and that all modes of perception are dynamically tied to the neuromuscular system and the movements of the body. In addition, the role of motor activity in the perceptual process is significant in (a) both directing and correcting perception; (b) relating kinesthetic information to essential changes in visual orientation; (c) influencing cognitive development through a sophisticated link with language and communication skills; and (d) advancing self-concept. Haubenstricker (1982) has shown that students with learning disabilities can be immensely helped in the adapted physical education program.

Perceptual-motor activities can make a valuable contribution to the adapted physical education program primarily because of their numerous associations with disabling conditions. For example, the improvement on laterality and directionality tends to advance both reading and mathematics skills and enhances both auditory and visual perception especially in young children.

In recent years a fair amount of attention has been given to perceptual-motor development and activity programs to enhance this development. Four such programs will be discussed next.

1. In the Alameda Unified School District in California, the perceptual-motor program meets the needs of students in grades K–3 and in special education classes by concentrating on the acquisition of efficient movement, sensory function, and the development of a positive self-image. This is accomplished through the utilization of activities for developing balance skills, body awareness, hand-eye coordination, locomotor skills, and spatial awareness.
2. In the Crown Point Community School Corporation in Indiana, a perceptual-motor program was developed for educationally handicapped students ranging in age from six to twelve. Activities were designed to develop balance, ball handling skills, locomotor skills, and visual perception.
3. In the Dayton Public Schools in Ohio, the program operates for students in the primary grades under the direction of the body-management instructor in the physical education department. Research indicates that students participating in the program made gains well above those not in the program. Gains were noted in the areas of academic achievement, self-image, self-concept, sense of worth, and peer acceptance.
4. In the Riverside County Schools in California, a successful program for perceptually handicapped students was developed. The students are exposed to carefully selected movement experiences designed to improve their competencies in balance, body rhythm, and attention-concentration span.

PREP Play Program

This program, developed in Edmonton, Alberta, Canada has the primary goal of developing the play skills of moderately, mentally retarded, young students. It is based on the idea that improving one's play skills will enable the student to participate more successfully in a non-structured play setting. The instructional phase is comprised of the teacher's prompts, the student's behavior, and the teacher's feedback.

Project ACTIVE

This nationally recognized, individualized physical activity program (**A**ll **C**hildren **T**otally **InV**olved **E**xercising) was developed in Oakhurst, New Jersey under the direction of Thomas Vodola (1973). The primary goal of this program is to ensure that all students, regardless of disability, would have the opportunity to participate in a quality physical education program. Teachers receive in-service training in a forty hour course to teach all students with disabilities including the mentally retarded, learning disabled, visually impaired, hearing impaired, and orthopedically impaired, as well as students with low motor ability, postural abnormalities, nutritional deficiencies, breathing difficulties, and low physical fitness. The training prepares teachers to write individualized prescriptions, prepare information on individual strengths and weaknesses, and carry out appropriate activities commensurate with the student's needs.

Project Adventure

This physical activity program was developed in the Hamilton-Wenham Regional School District (1977) in Massachusetts. This program's purpose is to help disabled students develop a sense of adventure and the satisfaction of solving problems together. Specific objectives are to increase:

- Agility and coordination
- Confidence
- Mutual support within a group
- The sense of joy in oneself and in being with others
- Familiarity and identification with nature

Project PEOPEL

This peer teaching program was developed in Phoenix, Arizona and is designed to provide "**P**hysical **E**ducation **OP**portunity for **E**xceptional **L**earners." Trained student aides are paired with disabled students in small, mainstreamed classes. To qualify for an aide position, students must complete a one semester training course provided by the school.

SCHEDULING

The scheduling of special classes for students with disabilities depends not only on the nature of the disabling condition but also on the availability of both a teaching station (gymnasium, classroom, playground, and so on) and an instructor. When the intent is to clearly help a student in need of individual attention, a way will be found. A few students can be easily accommodated during or after school hours, but if numbers are large, problems arise. If faculty are available and at least two teachers are assigned to a class, one should be able to work primarily with the disabled students who need special attention. If only one physical educator handling the class is available, the use of student leaders may require the teacher to direct some attention toward students who can profit from individual attention.

Although noon hour, after school, and study periods are times that have been used for special scheduling, the most efficient programs are preplanned and taught during the regular school day. Scheduling a separate adapted physical education class at the same time as a regular class is an acceptable method. For disabled students who need additional services but are placed in an inclusion curriculum, additional classes may be scheduled (a) on alternate days from the regular class; (b) during alternate periods; or (c) during elective periods. In order to not disrupt the established school schedule, it is advantageous to assess the disabled students in May before school is dismissed for the summer. At this time, a determination can be made as to which students will profit most from an adapted physical education program that would begin the following September. This allows ample time to develop a workable schedule and answer questions relating to faculty, class size, and teaching stations.

HELPFUL RESOURCES

In addition to the chapter references, the following list provides a number of informational sources dealing with disabled individuals.

Selected Organizations

Adapted Sports Association, Inc., Communications Center, 6832 Marlette Road, Marlette, MI 48453

American Academy for Cerebral Palsy, 1255 New Hampshire Avenue NW, Washington, DC 20036

American Academy for Cerebral Palsy and Developmental Medicine, P. O. Box 11083, 2405 Westwood Avenue, Richmond, VA 23230

American Alliance for Health, Physical Education, Recreation, and Dance, 1900 Association Drive, Reston, VA 22091

American Association for the Blind, 1511 K Street NW, Washington, DC 20005

American Athletic Association for the Deaf, 3916 Lantern Drive, Silver Spring, MD 20902
American Coalition of Citizens with Disabilities, 1200 15th Street NW, Washington, DC 20036
American College of Sports Medicine, 1440 Monroe Street, Madison, WI 53706
American Congress of Rehabilitation Medicine, 30 North Michigan Avenue, Chicago, IL 60602
American Dance Therapy Association, Suite 216E, 1000 Century Plaza, Columbia, MD 21044
American Diabetes Association, 2 Park Avenue, New York, NY 10016
American Epilepsy Society, Box 341, University of Minnesota, Minneapolis, MN 55455
American Foundation for the Blind, Inc., 15 West 16th Street, New York, NY 10011
American Heart Association, Inc., 7320 Greenville Avenue, Dallas, TX 75231
American Medical Association, 535 North Dearborn Street, Chicago, IL 60610
American Occupational Therapy Association, Inc., 600 Executive Boulevard, Rockville, MD 20852
American Physical Therapy Association, 1156 15th Street NW, Washington, DC 20005
American Psychiatric Association, 1700 18th Street NW, Washington, DC 20006
American Psychological Association, 1200 17th Street NW, Washington, DC 20036
An Association for Children and Adults with Learning Disabilities, Resource Library, 4156 Library Road, Pittsburgh, PA 15234
Association for Education of the Visually Handicapped, 1604 Spruce Street, Philadelphia, PA 19103
Association for Retarded Citizens, 2501 Avenue J, Arlington, TX 76011
Clearinghouse on the Handicapped, Office of Special Education and Rehabilitative Services, Room 3106, Switzer Building, Washington, DC 20202
Council for Exceptional Children, 1920 Association Drive, Reston, VA 22091
Epilepsy Foundation of America, 1828 L Street NW, Suite 406, Washington, DC 20036
Foundation for Child Development, 345 East 46th Street, New York, NY 10017
Joseph P. Kennedy, Jr. Foundation, 1350 New York Avenue NW, Washington, DC 20005
March of Dimes Birth Defects Foundation, Division of Health Information and School Relations, 1275 Mararoneck Avenue, White Plains, NY 10605
Muscular Dystrophy Association, 27th Floor, 810 7th Avenue, New York, NY 10019
National Association for Music Therapy, Inc., Box 610, Lawrence, KS 66044

National Association for the Visually Handicapped, 305 East 24th Street, New York, NY 10010

National Association of Sports for Cerebral Palsy, 66 East 34th Street, New York, NY 10016

National Association of the Deaf, 814 Thayer Avenue, Silver Spring, MD 20919

National Association of the Physically Handicapped, 76 Elm Street, London, OH 43140

National Center for a Barrier Free Environment, 1140 Connecticut Avenue NW, Washington, DC 20036

National Consortium on Physical Education and Recreation for the Handicapped, Seton Hall, University of Kentucky, Lexington, KY 40506

National Handicapped Sports and Recreation Association, 4105 East Florida Avenue, Denver, CO 80222

National Hemophilia Foundation, 25 West 39th Street, New York, NY 10018

National Mental Health Association, 1800 North Kent Street, Rosslyn, NY 22209

National Multiple Sclerosis Society, 205 East 42nd Street, New York, NY 10017

National Therapeutic Recreation Society, 3101 Park Center Drive, Alexandria, VA 22302

National Wheelchair Athletic Association, 2107 Templeton Gap Road, Suite C, Colorado Springs, CO 80907

Office of Special Education, 400 Maryland Avenue SW, Donahoe Building, Washington, DC 20202

People-to-People Committee for the Handicapped, 1522 K Street NW, #1130, Washington, DC 20005

President's Committee on Employment of the Handicapped, 1111 20th Street NW, Washington, DC 20201

Special Olympics, Inc. 1350 New York Avenue NW, Suite 500, Washington, DC 20006

Spina Bifida Association of America, 343 South Dearborn, Chicago, IL 60604

United Cerebral Palsy Association, Inc., 66 East 34th Street, New York, NY 10016

United States Amputee Athletic Association, Route 2, County Line, Fairview, TN 37062

United States Association for Blind Athletes, 55 West California Avenue, Beach Haven Park, NJ 08008

Wheelchair Sports Foundation, 40–24 62nd Street, Woodside, NY 11377

SUMMARY

1. To better meet the needs of students with disabilities, physical education activities often need to be adapted.

2. Teaching in an inclusive physical education setting requires that teachers promote acceptance of all students, modify the curriculum to better meet students' needs, and work collaboratively with all involved.
3. Public Law 94.142 ensures that all disabled students be provided a free, appropriate education and the related services to meet their needs. To meet these needs, an Individualized Education Program (IEP) is required to be developed for each student.
4. More than one individual, both school and nonschool, is often involved in organizing, implementing, and evaluating the IEP for the disabled student. For the best results, these individuals including the physical educator, classroom teacher, and physical therapist must collaborate and work cooperatively.
5. A variety of organizational structures are available to aid in physically educating disabled students. The structure selected should be one that can provide for the most effective learning.
6. Inclusion has become the accepted method of programming adapted physical education.
7. A variety of innovative programs exist throughout the United States to aid in the total development of the disabled student.

QUESTIONS AND LEARNING ACTIVITIES

1. Prepare a statement that will support the premise that a proper program of physical education will provide an opportunity for the development of physical expression to counteract the lack of verbal expression in mentally retarded students.

2. Why is the word *adapted* a better term to use than *remedial* or *corrective?*

3. What do you think of relaxation exercises? Should they be designed strictly for the chronically fatigued and hypertense or for everyone?

4. What are the obstacles to overcome in establishing an adapted physical education curriculum in a school system that has never had this kind of program?

5. Survey small and large schools to determine the quality of their physical education programs for students with disabilities. Find out their objectives, content, and evaluative techniques.

6. Interview several teachers of special education. Determine their views relating to the value of physical education as compared to a free-play period for students with disabilities.

7. Through your study, prepare a description of an innovative program for disabled students not found in your text.

8. List what you think are the three major advantages and disadvantages of inclusion programming. Provide published support for your belief.

REFERENCES

Auxter, D., & Pyfer, J. (1989). *Principles and methods of adapted physical education and recreation.* St. Louis, MO: Mosby.

Berryman, D., Lefebve, C., Kinney, W., & Dickason, J. (1974). *Systems utilization for comprehensive modular planning of therapeutic recreation services for disabled children and youth.* New York: New York University.

Block, M. E. (1994). Why all students with disabilities should be included in regular physical education. *Palaestra, 10*(3), 17–24.

Block, M. E., & Vogler, E. W. (1994). Inclusion in regular physical education: The research base. *Journal of Physical Education, Recreation, and Dance, 45*(1), 40–44.

Block, M. E., & Vogler, E. W. (1994). Innovative and adaptive curriculum models for full inclusion. *Teaching Elementary Physical Education, 5*(5), 6–7.

Child Advocacy Center. (1991). *Mainstreaming . . . integration . . . inclusion: What does it mean and how can we make it happen?* Cincinnati, OH: Child Advocacy Center.

Craft, D. (1994). Strategies for teaching inclusively. *Teaching Elementary Physical Education, 5*(5), 8–9.

Cratty, B. J. (1989). *Adapted physical education in the mainstream.* Denver, CO: Love Publishing Company.

Daniels, A. S., & Davies, E. (1982). *Adapted physical education.* New York: Harper & Row Publishers.

Davis, R., & Davis, T. (1994). Inclusion and least restrictive environments. *Teaching Elementary Physical Education, 5*(5), 1, 4–5.

Dunn, J. M., & Fait, H. F. (1989). *Special physical education: Adapted, individualized, and developmental.* Dubuque, IA: Brown & Benchmark.

Ersing, W. F. (1974). The nature of physical education programming for the mentally retarded and physically handicapped. *Journal of Health, Physical Education, and Recreation, 45*(2), 89–91.

Gallahue, D. L. (1996). *Developmental physical education for today's children.* Dubuque, IA: Brown & Benchmark.

Hass, G. (1987). *Curriculum planning: A new approach.* Boston: Allyn & Bacon.

Hardman, M. L., Drew, C. J., & Egan, M. W. (1987). *Human exceptionality, society, school and family.* Boston: Allyn & Bacon.

Haubenstricker, J. L. (1982). Motor development in children with learning disabilities. *Journal of Physical Education, Recreation, and Dance, 53*(5), 41–43.

Helion, J. G., & Fry, F. F. (1995). Modifying activities for developmental appropriateness. *Journal of Physical Education, Recreation, and Dance, 66*(7), 57–59.

Jansma, P. (1977). Get ready for mainstreaming. *Journal of Physical Education and Recreation, 48*(7), 15–16.

Karper, W. B., & Martinek, T. J. (1983). Motor performance and self-concepts of handicapped children and nonhandicapped children in integrated physical education classes. *American Corrective Therapy Journal, 37*(3), 91–95.

Kirchner, G., & Fishburne, G. (1995). *Physical education for elementary school children.* Dubuque, IA: Brown & Benchmark.

Loovis, E. M., & Ersing, W. F. (1979). *Assessing and programming gross motor development for children.* Cleveland Heights, OH: Ohio Motor Assessment Associates.

Miller, S. E. (1994). Inclusion of children with disabilities: Can we meet the challenge? *The Physical Educator, 51*(1), 47–52.

Morris, G. S. D., & Stiehl, J. (1989). *Changing kids' games.* Champaign, IL: Human Kinetics.

National Center for Education Statistics. (1995). *The condition of education, 1994.* Washington, DC: U.S. Department of Education.

PEOPEL Project Materials. 3839 West Camelback Road, Phoenix, AZ, 85091.

Rizzo, T. L., & Vispoel, W. P. (1992). Changing attitudes about teaching students with handicaps. *Adapted Physical Education Quarterly, 9*(1), 54–63.

Rohnke, K. (1977). *Cowstails and cobras.* Hamilton, MA: Project Adventure.

Seaman, J. A., & DePauw, K. P. (1989). *The new adapted physical education: A developmental approach.* Mountain View, CA: Mayfield.

Stainback, W., & Stainback, S. (1990). *Support networks for inclusive schooling: Interdependent integrated education.* Baltimore: Paul H. Brookes.

Thomas, J. B., Lee, A. M,, & Thomas, K. T. (1988). *Physical education for children: Concepts into practice.* Champaign, IL: Human Kinetics.

U. S. 94th Congress. (1975). *Public Law 94.142.*

Vodola, T. M. (1973). *Individualized physical education program for the handicapped child.* Englewood Cliffs, NJ: Prentice-Hall.

Wessel, J. (1979). I CAN: *Locomotor and rhythmic skills.* Northbrook, IL: Hubbard Scientific.

Winnick, J. P. (1996). *Adapted physical education and sport.* Champaign, IL: Human Kinetics.

11

THE EXTRA-CLASS PROGRAM: INTRAMURALS AND INTERSCHOLASTIC ATHLETICS

Outline

Moral and Ethical Behavior
Balance in Programming
The Need for Planning
The Intramural Program
The Interscholastic Athletic Program

Outcomes

After reading and studying this chapter, you should be able to:
- Define
  Coaching certification
  Exclusionary varsity model
  Interscholastic athletics
  Intramurals
  Pay-to-play
  Role conflict
  Sport
  Sport specialization
- Distinguish between an intramural and an interscholastic athletic program.
- Discuss the importance of sports in our society.
- Explain how sports may affect the moral and ethical behavior of students.
- Discuss current interscholastic athletic issues including coaching certification, the pay-to-play policy, and specialization.
- Justify the need for both an intramural program and an interscholastic athletic program.
- Discuss both the strengths and weaknesses of an interscholastic athletic program.
- Discuss the effect that role conflict can have on both the physical education curriculum and the interscholastic athletic program.
- Discuss the effect the exclusionary varsity model can have on students.

Sport is as old as civilization itself. Its prominence, especially in western cultures, is signified by the ever-increasing number of both participants and spectators, the increasing number of sports publications, and the number of radio and television programs geared solely towards sports. Siedentop (1994) explains that sport has an almost religious significance. During the seventh game of the World Series, throughout the NCAA Final Four, or on Super Bowl Sunday, the nation seems to stop momentarily. Attention seems completely focused on these sporting events.

Higgins (1979) wrote nearly twenty years ago that American society places far more emphasis on its sports than, perhaps, any civilization since ancient Rome. In fact, sports have attained such a prominent position of influence in American society that propagation now involves nearly the total socialization of its many participants. Sports have become an element of American life so pervasive that virtually no individual either directly or indirectly is untouched by them.

It is apparent that sports are far more than a simple part of the American way of life. They are a social institution consisting of numerous complex and varied activities, values, and relationships. As a social institution, sports function in the development and reinforcement of appropriate values, the regulation of acceptable behavior, and the attainment of desired goals with the chief focus on the quality of performance by the participants.

Sports have an impressive quantitative and qualitative aspect that enables them to become a major force in the promotion of acceptable practices and attitudes if presented appropriately. Evidence suggests that as school sports are conducted in a more serious and businesslike fashion, closely resembling the professional scene, the cherished values may exceed the grasp of too many participants. As a result, a significant number of students will miss what Pindar, the Greek poet, wrote about in 409 B.C.:

He who wins of a sudden, some noble prize in the rich years of youth is raised high with hope; his manhood takes wings, he has in his heart what is better than wealth.

Interestingly, in the days of the early Greeks, both Spartan and Athenian philosophers focused on the dangers inherent in overemphasis and specialization in athletics. The intellectuals tolerated sports chiefly because sports (a) prepared male citizens to defend the land from external aggression and/or internal revolution; (b) contributed to the advancement of an individual's physical condition; and (c) fostered unity as teams came together to compete in national athletic festivities. Although such major sporting and game activities were accepted by the Romans, the concern persisted that sports could get out of control and defeat the sportsmanship objective. As a critic of society, Cicero saw some real value in sport but warned that it also symbolized, in a general way, the moral degradation of the society of Rome. In discussing Cicero's views, Fielding (1977) related sports to the twentieth century by stating that:

He was talking to a society that needed desperately to learn how to use its leisure. A leisure similar to our own, in that for the few it was partly earned, while for the many it was imposed. A leisure that had markedly political overtones and which could be used as an opiate to lull the masses into passivity. At the center of the leisure, Cicero saw competitive sport, oriented to the spectator and impoverished of ethical overtones. He saw all too clearly what might happen to a society which becomes seduced by its pursuit for pleasure, particularly when this pursuit of pleasure becomes divorced from the desire for good and results in the view that pleasure is the sole object of existence.

Some concern exists today that too many youth programs are imperfect copies of professional sports in which the organizers and coaches are familiar and the business is to win. Under these circumstances, the ennobling contribution of sport to education that Vergerio (Woodward, 1963) wrote about during the Renaissance would be considerably weakened.

Fortunately, in numerous school situations the athletic goals are set high so that students engaged in sports not only become very aware of their limits and concepts of self but also experience a real appreciation of a quality performance, in terms of both lasting skills and the essence of fair play. Therefore, encouraging participation in appropriate extra-class sporting activities is sound educational practice. This part of the curriculum is a well-tested experience consistent with the broad purposes of education.

The benefits and satisfaction derived from sports participation during the upper elementary grades (4–6) and the junior and senior high school years do carry over into adult life. Skilled, unskilled, and exceptional students all need the opportunity to participate in extra-class programs, whether they are through intramural and/or interscholastic programs. In addition, the school should provide financial support.

MORAL AND ETHICAL BEHAVIOR

Sports are popular both in and out of school. Sport sociologists continue their research because of the positive and negative implications arising from sports. Moreover, the popularity of sports and an individual's association with sports will continue to grow in upcoming years as the interest in sport science and health-related fitness continue to increase. However, the effect that sports participation has on a student's affective development is a concern.

For a number of years researchers have been seeking more productive ways of affecting the moral and ethical behavior of youth through sports participation. Criticisms are increasing regarding the unethical abuses in sports. Observed in both intramurals and interscholastic athletics, these criticisms are due to an overriding emphasis on winning at any cost. Striving to win a sports contest while exhibiting morally responsible behavior has always been an educational concern. However, the real issue is teaching values in connection with the personal needs of young people.

Arnold (1980) states that the true importance of a sport

lies not in its outward characteristics and procedures so much as in the needs, cravings, and satisfactions of its participants. The fact that participants try to win when playing competitive games in no way suggests that to win is their sole purpose, and least of all their chief purpose. For many, the attempt to win is but a procedural feature of competing.

When not unduly influenced by overenthusiastic parents and coaches, most young people indicate that they would rather play on a losing team than sit on the bench of a winning team. As of old, the game's the thing. Thus, if critics identify intramural and/or interscholastic athletic programs as having too much emphasis on competition and winning then the curriculum planners must clarify that the sports are scheduled for educational reasons. Therefore, these programs are designed to meet the same objectives as the instructional program. Furthermore, sports in both programs are a means to achieving these objectives. These sports can be designed to make use of both competitive and cooperative processes.

Competition between opponents occurs when rules and tactics are enforced, and cooperation among teammates occurs when their overall responsibilities and the tasks performed are implemented. As a result, moral and ethical behavior associated with sports should receive increased emphasis in physical education programs in schools. In addition, the school's concern should be extended to parents and others in the community. Highly structured leagues and overenthusiastic parents have not always been helpful in promoting ethical behavior. Wholesome parental influence as a socializing agent in sports can be considerable especially when motivation for participation in sports and recreation is emphasized.

BALANCE IN PROGRAMMING

In order for all students, boys and girls alike, to have equal opportunity to participate in a variety of sport-related activities, a careful balance must be maintained between offerings in intramurals and interscholastic athletics. Conflict between these two programs should not occur if the resources (budgets, time, facilities, equipment, and personnel) are apportioned impartially—that is, according to how well each meets the overall objectives of the total program. Bucher and Koenig (1983) state that if each program is conducted properly then it can contribute to and complement the other. Through an overall, well-balanced program, all students can enjoy and respect sports and the potential they have for improving an individual's physical, mental, social, and emotional development.

If a proper balance between programs at both the junior and senior high school levels is not maintained then program emphasis should center primarily on interscholastic athletics. This is a natural occurrence in localities where school and community spirit run high and people take pride in their teams. The result is for teachers and coaches to diligently prepare their teams for the spectators who come to see intense competition in a contest where their school will reign supreme. Unfortunately, this reaction causes one part of the overall program to overshadow the rest. This is especially upsetting when a hundred percent of the students are exposed to the instructional program, while as few as fifteen to twenty percent actually take part in interscholastic activities. In addition, the remaining eighty to eighty-five percent need encouragement and a chance to participate in extra-class activities suited to their abilities and interests. The traditional model illustrating the relationships among the three programs is shown in Figure 11.1.

As shown, the instructional program provides the base of the pyramid and reaches every student in the school. The second level of the pyramid is the intramural program and provides opportunities for students to further their skill development. The top of the pyramid is the interscholastic athletic program and it reaches the fewest number of students, although these individuals will be more highly skilled.

Intramural experiences are capable of promoting lasting values. They are completely voluntary and the participants work at achieving a common objective. Therefore, the inclusion of these experiences in the educational program is really important. In addition, when students are properly motivated to win a contest fairly, they use all of their mental and physical powers, their cooperative abilities, and their individual perseverance to complete the job.

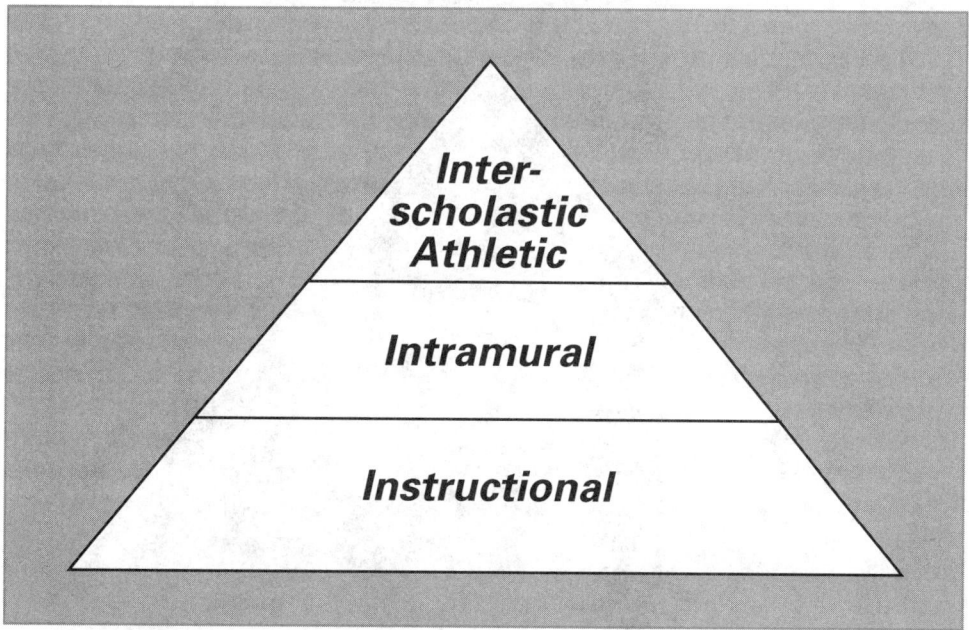

FIGURE 11.1 Model for Programming Physical Education

THE NEED FOR PLANNING

An extra-class program must be carefully planned in order to yield good results. This is especially true in large school systems where the cocurricular activities are extensive in both number and quality. Too often, intramurals and interscholastic athletics compete with each other for the student's free time, requiring such a concentration of effort that to participate fully in more than one or two experiences is nearly impossible. For example, a member of the school's band can hardly engage in varsity football, nor can a cross-country aspirant give much attention to an after-school photography club.

Another factor affecting the programming of extra-class activities is the growing number of students committed to working after school hours. An impaired economy and the desire among many students to enter the adult world as soon as possible have led to a high percentage of secondary school students preferring to work rather than take part in after-school activities.

Despite the fact that many other attractive after-school activities exist in the upper elementary, junior, and senior high schools, it is possible to build extra-class physical education experiences that will reach students. The planning committee's task is to structure both components of the extra-class program so that they are an extension of and supplemental to the developmental instruction program.

Intramurals at the elementary school level

THE INTRAMURAL PROGRAM

It has been said that children are permanently tuned to activity; they are born with an urge to play. Children like to move and, in fact, they have an inherent need to move. In previous years, children had chores to do; they climbed trees, ran through the fields, skated on ponds, and organized their own sandlot ball games. Today's children, however, are subjected to an "easy society" where the once natural opportunities for large muscle movement have been programmed out of their lives. A quality physical education program involving intramural experiences is one way to compensate for these lost movement opportunities of the past.

The intramural program should be an integral part of the total curriculum thereby receiving the same support in terms of planning, implementation, and evaluation that the instructional program receives. It should be a logical extension of a quality instructional program—one of the objectives of the instructional program is to provide instruction for all students, whereas the intramural program exists to provide the students with an opportunity to use and/or further refine the skills learned in the instructional program. Intramurals can be seen as a laboratory period for sports and other activities whose fundamentals have been taught in the regularly scheduled physical education program (Bucher & Koenig, 1983). This program, which is voluntary in nature, should provide activity opportunities for all students, male and female, skilled and unskilled, big and small. Emphasis should be placed on skill application (play) with an instructional component relative to rules and the application of strategy, if necessary. A quality intramural program should enrich the expression of this natural, inherent urge to play. The unique purposes of the intramural program, as outlined by Bookwalter (1964), are to:

- Provide an opportunity for each student to compete in sports of choice at specific levels of competency.
- Provide additional time and experience that will advance the student's development in activities begun in the basic instructional program.
- Promote school and group loyalties and cooperation through participation in and observation of the scheduled activities.
- Assure greater leisure education and carry-over from class instruction.
- Promote sportsmanship and ability in self-management and self-control in future recreation.

This list states the ideal situation. As Siedentop (1994) indicates, the ideal is seldom achieved. In fact, too often the intramural program is nonexistent which results, primarily, from the insufficient resources of time, facilities, personnel, and budget.

Providing a time for intramural activities is a frequent problem. Intramural activities may be scheduled before school, during the school day, after school, on weekends, during vacation periods, and are occasionally associated with selected community recreation programs. Early morning programs are becoming increasingly popular as students opt to begin their day with activity. Intramural activities are often scheduled during the school day either over an extended lunch hour or during a regularly scheduled intramural period. Although used sparingly, weekend and vacation time scheduling is an option. This demands a strong commitment on the part of not only those directing and supervising the program, but on the students as well. Perhaps the best time for scheduling intramurals is immediately after school; however, this is also the most convenient time for scheduling *all* other extra-curricular activities including interscholastic athletics and club activities. This compounds the problem of scheduling not only in terms of competing for students but also in the competition for facilities.

In order for the intramural program to be successful and to thrive, it needs strong leadership. This leader, commonly a physical educator in the school system, should be paid and given specified responsibilities. A listing of such responsibilities is shown in Table 11.1. One duty that warrants further explanation is the topic of dealing with promotion. Regardless of how well the activities are planned, if students do not participate then the intramural program will eventually fail. Daughtrey and Lewis (1979) provide the following promotional techniques to ensure public awareness:

- Develop a public relations program through the use of television, radio, local and school newspapers, parental newsletters, school announcements, and bulletin boards.
- Provide coverage of scheduled events, contest results, and outstanding individual/team performances.
- Include faculty by scheduling contests between students and teachers.
- Encourage parents to attend scheduled events.
- Incorporate an awards system that gives recognition to all participants.

Additional guidelines to foster a successful program are listed in Table 11.2.

Intramural sports can be presented in two different formats—organized and self-directed. The organized format is the most common. Typically students sign up to participate in a particular sport and are subsequently assigned to teams. The teams are placed in leagues and then they play in some tournament format (see Figure 11.2) with awards at the end. This format is most appropriate for team sports including basketball, soccer, and volleyball.

TABLE 11.1 Intramural Director's Duties

- Prepare and administer the budget
- Chair the committees specifically responsible for the selection, organization, and implementation of activities
- Arrange schedules
- Evaluate the program on a regular basis
- Promote the program

TABLE 11.2 Intramural Guidelines

- The program should supplement and not replace either the instructional or the interscholastic athletic program.
- The program should be broad enough in scope to interest and attract most students.
- The activities selected should afford individual and group experiences for both boys and girls.
- The program should include corecreational as well as both individual and team activities for disabled students.
- The program should include both organized and self-directed activities.
- The program should include both strenuous and non-strenuous activities.
- No student should be exempt from or denied the opportunity to participate in the program due to low academics or poor skill ability.
- Competition should be arranged between students of equal skill whenever possible.
- The program should provide opportunities for skill practice.
- Individual and group instruction should be provided on students' requests.
- The program should be conducted according to a regular schedule.
- The program should make use of more than one available time period whenever possible (before, during, and after school) to better accommodate students.
- Officials should be well trained and qualified in order to maintain safety and promote fair play.
- Complaints and protests should be handled in an equitable and democratic manner.
- Tournaments that offer continuous participation (round robin and ladder) rather than limited participation (single elimination and double elimination) should be utilized.
- Intramural records should be kept not only for public relations purposes but also for making program evaluations.
- The program should have an awards system that recognizes all participants but should not be the primary motive for participation.
- The program should not be perceived as a proving ground for interscholastic athletic candidates.

Round 1	Round 2	Round 3	Round 4	Round 5
Teams	Teams	Teams	Teams	Teams
1 vs 2	1 vs 6	1 vs 5	1 vs 4	1 vs 3
6 vs 3	5 vs 2	4 vs 6	3 vs 5	2 vs 4
5 vs 4	4 vs 3	3 vs 2	2 vs 6	6 vs 5

FIGURE 11.2 Six Team Round Robin Tournament

The organized format is also appropriate for selected individual/dual activities such as badminton, golf, and tennis.

The self-directed format is a more informal approach. Students are still required to sign up for a specific activity. Following the sign-up stage, students are then provided with (a) a list of participants; (b) a required number of participants to compete against; and (c) a time-frame within which to complete the number of games. It then becomes the student's responsibility to contact opponents and play. This format is best used with individual/dual activities.

The selection of activities for inclusion in the intramural program should be carefully planned. Recall that the intramural program, although extra-class, still needs to provide wholesome educational experiences. As a result, Annarino, Cowell, and Hazelton (1986) explain that intramural activities should be carefully examined according to the following ten criteria:

1. To what extent do the intramural activities satisfy students' interests and needs for:
    a. Adventure, new experiences, and excitement
    b. Recognition, acceptance, and approval by peers
    c. Group status with a feeling of belonging
    d. Mastery and achievement
    e. Affection and close friendships
    f. Autonomy, self-realization, self-direction, and individual integrity
2. To what extent do the intramural activities help bridge the gap between school and community by the arrangement of games and having parents participate actively in school affairs?
3. Are boys and girls learning to play together, managing their friendships, and preparing for family living through coeducational intramural activities?
4. Does the intramural program enrich the opportunities for students to participate in the policy-making and administrative aspects of the program?
5. Is the intramural program open to all students regardless of race, socioeconomic status, or absence of proficiency in activities?
6. Are guidance possibilities based on the observance and appraisal of students in intramural activities used to a high degree?
7. Do the intramural activities contribute to the student's physical, cognitive, psychomotor, and affective development?
8. Is some effort made to evaluate the extent to which desirable educational outcomes have resulted from the intramural program?
9. Is participation in intramural activities engaged in by a large number of students with different backgrounds?
10. To what extent is the supervision of the intramural program by trained leadership?

As previously stated, the intramural program should be an extension of the instructional program. However, this is not always possible. In addition, some people argue that offering novel activities is a means of increasing participation. A successful approach for Pine Mountain Middle School in Cobb

TABLE 11.3 Suggested Seasonal Intramural Activities for Students in Grades 4–12

Fall	Winter	Spring
Archery	Badminton	Golf
Backpacking	Basketball	Horseshoes
Bicycling	Bowling	Miniature golf
Field hockey	Floor hockey	Shuffleboard
Flag football	Gymnastics	Softball
Flickerball	One-on-one basketball	Tennis
Jogging	Roller skating	Track and field
Soccer	Swimming	
Speedball	Table tennis	
	Volleyball	
	Wrestling	

County, Georgia provides a month of "supermural" activities including clogging, karate, and drill team to the existing intramural program (Tenoschok, 1995). Supermurals utilize a combination of intramural and community education resources to expose the Pine Mountain students to a variety of unique experiences. Qualified volunteer professionals from the community provide the instruction for students who are willing to participate after school. This well accepted addition to the intramural program has (a) allowed students to enjoy nontraditional activities that could not have been presented otherwise; and (b) strengthened school-community relations thereby fostering future combined efforts.

Table 11.3 is a listing of some of the more traditional activities that are appropriate for students in grades 4–12. Table 11.4 is a listing of intramural activities from the S-T-R-E-T-C-H (Students and Teachers Relaxing, Exercising, Talking, Computing, and Helping) program at Blue Valley Middle School (BVMS) in Overland Park, Kansas. The final decision regarding what intramural activities are offered will be affected by the school's resources including budget, time, and the availability of equipment and facilities. At the upper elementary school level (grades 4–6) the activities selected should pertain to

TABLE 11.4 BVMS Intramural Activities Used in the S-T-R-E-T-C-H Program for Blue Valley Middle School

Basketball	Six bases
Basketball one-on-one	Soccer
Basketball two-on-two	Softball
Board games	Tetherball
Coneball	Ultimate
Four square	Volleyball
Horseshoes	Walking and talking
Mumball	Win-loose-draw

the noncontact variety. Although exceptions arise, most researchers indicate that because of the possibility of damage to maturing bodies, collision and contact sports should be excluded.

THE INTERSCHOLASTIC ATHLETIC PROGRAM

In many communities, the crowning point of the overall physical education curriculum is the opportunity provided to physically gifted students for competition in the interscholastic athletic program. This program undoubtedly provides both boys and girls a valuable educational experience. School personnel—teachers and administrators alike—who have constructed and soundly implemented a K–12 physical education curriculum should perceive the interscholastic athletic program as surpassing the limits of an intramural program to a more competitive, more demanding, and more concentrated experience.

Siedentop (1994) indicates that the large, diversified interscholastic athletic program is unique to the American junior high school and senior high school model. Most secondary schools have teams at the freshman, junior varsity, and varsity levels in a variety of sports. The importance that interscholastic athletics play in our culture and the ultimate effect they have on our youth regardless of whether or not they compete is unmistaken.

Sage (1990) estimates that more than five million adolescent boys and girls in the United States are involved in approximately thirty different high school sports each year (see Table 11.5). Although this number is relatively large, it is a small proportion to the total number of students. In a 1990 published study funded by the Athletic Footwear Association and conducted by the Youth Sports Institute at Michigan State University, it was indicated that

TABLE 11.5   Interscholastic Sports

Archery	Judo
Badminton	Lacrosse
Baseball	Riflery
Basketball	Skiing (alpine)
Bowling	Skiing (cross country)
Canoeing	Soccer
Crew	Softball
Cross country	Swimming
Diving	Team tennis
Equestrian	Tennis
Fencing	Track and field
Field hockey	Volleyball
Football	Water polo
Golf	Weight lifting
Gymnastics	Wrestling
Ice hockey	

at age ten, forty-five percent of young people say they participate or intend to participate in some form of organized sports program (Ewing & Seefeldt, 1990). Among eighteen-year-olds, this percentage drops to twenty-six percent. The data for this study were collected from nearly ten thousand young people in eleven different states. Additional data revealed that:

- Fun was the primary reason for sports participation and, subsequently, lack of fun was the leading reason for dropping out (see Table 11.6).
- Winning was not the leading motivator for participation, nor was it seen as a major benefit of participation.
- Social activities increased in importance as young people matured and often replaced sports participation.

In a 1993–1994 survey, the National Federation of State High School Athletic Associations reported that participation in high school athletics increased for the fifth consecutive year. The federation indicates that this increase is partly due to a record number of more than 2.1 million female participants. With 3,478,530 male participants, the combined total is more than five and a half million participants. The number of male and female participants for the ten most popular sports is shown in Tables 11.7 and 11.8, respectively.

The interscholastic program provides an opportunity for physically gifted students to compete at the highest level of ability against boys and girls from other schools. This competition is often under the auspices of the school and an interscholastic athletic conference, if not the state. Well organized and properly controlled competition between schools can make a valuable contribution to the overall goals of education but more specifically to the goals of physical education. According to Bookwalter (1964) the more commonly accepted purposes of an interscholastic athletic program are to:

- Contribute to the maximum development of physical fitness.
- Contribute to self-discipline and self-control even under the most trying circumstances.

TABLE 11.6 Ten Most Important Reasons for Sports Participation

1. To have fun
2. To improve skills
3. To stay in shape
4. To do something I am good at
5. For the excitement of competition
6. To get exercise
7. To play as part of a team
8. For the challenge of competition
9. To learn new skills
10. To win

TABLE 11.7 Most Popular Male Sports

Sport	Participants
1. Football	928,134
2. Basketball	530,068
3. Baseball	438,846
4. Track and field	419,758
5. Soccer	255,538
6. Wrestling	233,433
7. Cross country	162,188
8. Tennis	135,702
9. Golf	131,207
10. Swimming and diving	81,328

- Afford the maximal attainment of an individual's social traits of leadership and followership.
- Provide an opportunity to compete with others who have similar abilities in sports.
- Provide wholesome outlets for recreational activity for students and adults as participants and as spectators, respectively.
- Contribute to school loyalty and morale.

Unlike the instructional and intramural programs, interscholastic athletics are characterized by a higher degree of organization, an increased number of spectators, considerable publicity, and too often, commercialism. As a result, interscholastic athletics have become a part of the total physical education curriculum that requires close scrutiny. Two specific concerns arise regarding interscholastic athletics. First, the interscholastic athletic program should be included in the curriculum only after both the instructional and intramural programs are firmly established. Secondly, due to the emotional atmosphere surrounding a competitive event and the desire to win by players and coaches alike, athletics are more subject to manipulation than either the instructional or intramural programs. This overemphasis to win often leads to

TABLE 11.8 Most Popular Female Sports

Sport	Participants
1. Basketball	412,576
2. Track and field	345,700
3. Volleyball	327,616
4. Softball (fast pitch)	257,118
5. Soccer	166,173
6. Tennis	136,239
7. Cross country	124,700
8. Swimming and diving	102,652
9. Field hockey	53,747
10. Softball (slow pitch)	41,118

coaching pressures, player exploitation, and other abuses that can threaten the entire physical education curriculum. The interscholastic athletic program should not be viewed as either community entertainment or a school business. It is nothing more than an opportunity for students to pit their sports skills and knowledge against students with equal or greater ability.

The values and benefits derived from the interscholastic athletic program do not come automatically from participation. These experiences must be (a) well planned under the leadership of knowledgeable and dedicated school personnel; and (b) well established on sound policies whether or not they are developed by the school, the athletic conference, and/or based on the Cardinal Athletic Principles of the National Federation of State High School Athletic Associations (see Table 11.9) first published in 1947. Even in the best of situations, problems

TABLE 11.9   Cardinal Athletic Principles*

1. Be closely coordinated with the general instructional program and properly articulated with other departments of the school.
2. Be sure that the number of students accommodated and the educational aims achieved justify the use of tax funds for its support. Also justify use of other sources of income, provided the time and attention which is given to the collection of such funds, is not such as to interfere with the efficiency of the athletic program or of any other department in the school.
3. Be firm on the spirit of nonprofessionalism so that participation is regarded as a privilege to be won by training and proficiency and to be valued highly enough to eliminate any need for excessive use of adulatory demonstrations or of expensive prizes or awards.
4. Confine the school athletic activity to events that are sponsored and supervised by the proper school authorities so that exploitation or improper use of prestige built up by school teams or members of such teams may be avoided.
5. Be planned so as to result in opportunity for many individuals to explore a wide variety of sports and in reasonable season limits for each sport.
6. Be controlled in order to avoid the elements of professionalism and commercialism which tend to grow up in connection with widely publicized "bowl" contests, barnstorming trips and interstate or interjectional contests that require excessive travel expenses or loss of school time or that are bracketed with educational travel claims in an attempt to justify privileges for a few at the expense of decreased opportunity for many.
7. Be kept free from the type of contest that involves a gathering of "all-stars" from different schools to participate in contests that may be used as a gathering place for representatives of certain colleges or professional organizations who are interested in soliciting athletic talent.
8. Include training in conduct and game ethics to reach all nonparticipating students and community followers of the school teams in order to ensure a proper understanding and appreciation of the sports skills and of the need for adherence to principles of fair play and right prejudices.
9. Encourage a balanced program of intramural activity in grades below ninth grade to make it unnecessary to sponsor contests of a championship nature in these grades.
10. Engender respect for the local, state, and national rules and policies under which the school program is conducted.

*The National Federation of State High School Associations authorized the listing of these principles in 1947 and included them in their handbook up through 1975.

arise. Jewett, Bain, and Ennis (1995) report that from a historical perspective, physical education and athletics have been closely related. From a practical viewpoint, both programs have shared facilities, if not equipment. In addition, it is not uncommon to find that both programs are conducted by the same individual, serving as both the physical educator and the coach. One or both of these situations has led to the following problems:

- The athletic program abandonment of educational goals for an emphasis on winning
- The physical education program being used to identify and/or develop potential athletes
- Athletic participation serving as a substitute for the physical education requirement
- Diminished administrative support for physical education as athletic visibility increases
- Role conflict as the physical educator attempts to be both teacher and coach
- The development of the exclusionary varsity model (Siedentop, 1994)

Two of the problems in the previous list—role conflict and the exclusionary varsity model—will be discussed in detail next.

Many individuals choosing to coach in today's schools are hired as teachers. Therefore, they are filling two similar but distinctly different roles and the result is *role conflict,* a condition that arises when incompatible expectations for different roles exist (Locke & Massengale, 1978; Sage, 1987). Figone (1994) states that role conflict is the result of a teacher-coach attempting to fulfill the expressed expectations of both roles. Too often the individual either (a) falls short of the expectations of both roles; or in most instances (b) devotes time and energy to one role thereby neglecting the other. Role conflict flourishes because the rewards and the expectations for coaching are so much greater than for teaching. Coaches are in the public eye. Even though both the teacher and the coach come under close scrutiny by administrators and parents, too often the teacher's accomplishments go unnoticed while the coach is admired, praised, and much more socially accepted. Therefore, it is easy to understand why the teacher-coach devotes more time to the coaching role.

Sports participation for elementary school children is generally community based through YMCA, YWCA, and PARA programs. As Siedentop (1994) indicates, these programs are, for the most part, widely available. Sports participation for secondary school students is programmed primarily by the schools. In addition, this participation is geared toward varsity participation which is exclusionary in nature—it acts to identify and cater to the highly skilled athlete. The secondary school students excluded have few opportunities to continue their sports participation, at least until they are old enough to take part in a community-based adult program. Unless an adolescent is highly skilled, the result is little opportunity to further develop those skills the individual had an interest in developing.

Further discussion of both the strengths and weaknesses of an interscholastic athletic program is provided by Annarino, Cowell, and Hazelton (1986) as shown in Table 11.10.

The selection of activities (sports) for the interscholastic athletic program may come from the list of sports presently sponsored in secondary schools throughout the country (see Table 11.5). This list is rather extensive because regional and even local needs, interests, and facilities may vary somewhat according to climate, geography, and traditions. The total number of interscholastic sports offered in any one school depends primarily on budget, student interest, and the availability of competition. For example, if the budget allows for and student interest warrants the inclusion of soccer in the interscholastic athletic program but no opponents within a one hundred mile radius exist, it would not be advised to include soccer in the program.

The appropriateness of athletics for junior high school students has been discussed for years. The effects of both collision sports (football, ice hockey, and lacrosse) and contact sports (basketball, soccer, and wrestling) and the undesirable pressures from intense athletic competition have also been debated. The stand taken by many sport leaders is that highly organized interscholastic athletic programs are questionable for junior high school students.

Bucher and Koenig (1983) contend that the main concentration at the junior high school level should be on a broad intramural program. These young people are in a transitional stage between elementary school and high school. It is at this time that students are gaining an increased interest in sports, but their physical and social immaturity make it unwise for them to participate in an interscholastic athletic program. This fact does not significantly lessen the number of junior high school programs that exist. In addition, the junior high school programs that do exist must face a set of problems not found in a good intramural program including unqualified coaches, specialization at ages that are too young, and developmentally inappropriate sports. If interscholastic sports are intended to be a part of the junior high school program, it is essential that they follow sound principles. Bucher and Koenig (1983) propose the following four recommendations:

- The primary objective should be healthful participation.
- A certified teacher with knowledge of both the participant and the sport should provide leadership.
- Students should be encouraged to participate in many sports rather than specialize in just one.
- Selected sports should be modified pertaining to the developmental age of the participants.

These principles apply to athletics at any educational level but especially at the junior high school level.

In the past two decades a variety of trends have impacted high school athletics. Four such trends, as shown in Figure 11.3, will be discussed next.

TABLE 11.10 Strengths and Weaknesses of Interscholastic Athletics

Strengths

- Athletics have long been recognized as a means to group unity. The athletic team is a unifying agent that can bring all participants into a common loyalty and community of interests.
- Athletics offer appropriate opportunities for self-testing which are important in the development of adolescents.
- Athletics offer experiences for students to recognize that groups can sometimes achieve what individuals cannot; the achievement of a goal depends on using the contribution of each member; and each individual needs to be in a position where he/she can make a unique contribution.
- Athletics can develop a sense of belonging—being a member of a group. Young people can share difficult undertakings and establish personal bonds.
- Athletics provide common experiences so that students interact with students from other schools.
- Young people are sensitive to the judgment of peers. They desire not to be different. The lack of an athletic program makes students, both as spectators and as participants, feel strange in a sports-conscious community.
- Skillful students need competition on a high level. Interschool competition provides this need.
- Athletic participation encourages healthful living practices and self-sacrifice in training and practicing.
- Basic ethics can be taught through rules of conduct and fair play. The opportunity for the development of sportsmanship, self-control, and self-responsibility is also afforded.
- Athletics can motivate intramural participation through example by raising the level of aspiration of younger students and less skilled students.

Weaknesses

- Athletics emphasize the physical development of a few skilled performers thereby neglecting the ordinary student.
- Participation may sometimes disrupt the regular school routine with contests in the middle of the week.
- Interschool rivalry is not always wholesome. It can encourage gang-like behavior between students from different schools.
- Competition with a win-at-all-cost attitude can place undue pressure on both coaches and athletes.
- Booster clubs that view winning as the most important objective often gain too much influence and persuade players to become professional in attitude.
- Post-season tournaments and all-star competitions unduly prolong a season.
- Athletics are given an importance that preempts the proper use of budgets often to the detriment of the instructional and/or the intramural program.
- The need for financing the program often leads to commercialism.
- The undue attention given to athletics in terms of awards, banquets, and so on, gives maturing youths a distorted sense of values and may prompt questions regarding self-importance.
- Demands of an athletic season may adversely affect the academic growth of students.

Reprinted by permission of Waveland Press. From Annarino, A. A., Cowell, C. C., & Hazelton, H. W. (1986). *Curriculum theory and design in physical education.* Prospect Heights, IL: Waveland Press. 1980 (reissued 1986). All rights reserved.

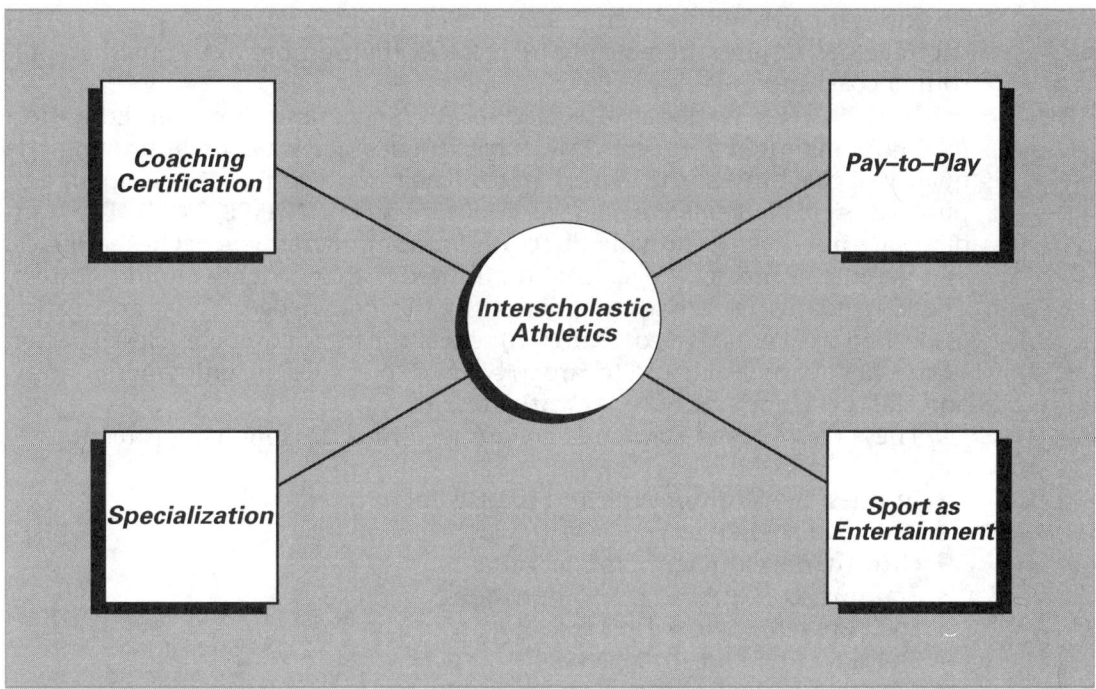

FIGURE 11.3 Current Trends in Interscholastic Sports

Coaching Certification

The United States is the world's only major sporting nation without a certification program for its coaches. A need to have a means of insuring that student-athletes are under the leadership of qualified individuals exists at the state level if not also at the national level. As previously stated, more than five million students in the United States participate in interscholastic sports yearly, requiring nearly 200,000 teams. The number of coaches required to staff this many teams is substantial (Stewart & Sweet, 1992). The majority of these students are coached by individuals who are certified just to teach. However, this has changed dramatically since the number of certified teachers who want to coach is fairly low. The result is what the American Sport Education Program (1996) has termed the *accidental occupation,* meaning that coaching in U.S. schools is an occupation that many have drifted into by accident. In fact, it is estimated that more than two-thirds of interscholastic coaches have received little formal coaching education, if any at all.

There are no national certification requirements for someone wanting to coach at the secondary school level. Although requirements for coaches do exist in some states, they vary from state to state and are often related to teacher certification, not to coaching preparation. In fact, only a few states have coaching certification requirements (Sisley & Wiese, 1987). Paired with the expansion of sports at all levels and the continued growth of interscholastic programs for girls and women, a shortage of qualified coaches is present. This shortage has resulted in a steady increase in the number of unqualified personnel coaching today's youth.

In 1992 the National Association for Sport and Physical Education (NASPE) appointed a special task force to consider ways of improving the quality of coaching in the United States. The result was the development and publication of *National Standards for Athletic Coaches* (NASPE, 1995). The standards are intended to provide direction for administrators, coaches, athletes, and parents regarding the skills and knowledge that coaches should possess. These standards (a) are a compilation of the knowledge, skills, and values associated with effective coaching; (b) reflect the basic competencies expected of coaches at any level; and (c) are to be used to ensure the enjoyment, safety, and skill development of today's athletes.

These thirty-seven standards are grouped into the following categories:

- Injuries: Prevention, care, and management
- Risk management
- Growth, development, and learning
- Training, conditioning, and nutrition
- Social/psychological aspects
- Skills, tactics, and strategies
- Teaching and administration
- Professional preparation and development

The need for qualified coaches is evidenced by the support for this project from the National Alliance for Youth Sports, the National Association for Girls and Women in Sports, the National Association for Sport and Physical Education, the National Federation of State High School Associations, the United States Sports Academy, the Women's Sport Foundation, and the Youth Sports Institute.

A second attempt to rectify this questionable situation has been the development and marketing of coaching education programs. Four such programs are shown in Table 11.11.

The American Coaching Effectiveness Program (ACEP), begun in 1976, is the most widely used coaching education program in the United States (Partlow, 1992). This program has three phases:

- *Clinic phase*—Designed (a) to raise the participants' awareness that education is important; and (b) to motivate the participants to want to learn.
- *Self-study phase*—Involves learning in a textbook format.
- *Self-test phase*—Requires participants to recall and apply learned material.

The Coalition of Americans to Protect Sports (CAPS) primary purpose is to provide information regarding effective risk management practices and safety measures to administrators, coaches, and others involved in sports programs (Lincoln, 1992). The goal is to reduce the number of sports injuries to youth.

TABLE 11.11   National Coaching Education Programs

American Coaching Effectiveness Program (ACEP)
Box 5076
Champaign, IL 61825

Coalition of Americans to Protect Sports (CAPS)
200 Castlewood Drive
North Palm Beach, FL 33408

National Youth Sports Coaches Association (NYSCA)
2611 Old Okeechobee Road
West Palm Beach, FL 33409

Program for Athletic Coaches Education (PACE)
Institute for the Study of Youth Sports
Michigan State University
East Lansing, MI 48824

More specifically, the program is designed to educate coaches on how to (a) identify potential hazards; (b) upgrade safety for athletes; and (c) reduce liability. These objectives are met through an educational format.

The National Youth Sports Coaches Association (NYSCA) is a nonprofit association designed to educate coaches about their importance in the physical, psychological, and emotional development of youths (Engh, 1992). To become certified, prospective coaches must complete a three-year, three-phase program of study:

- *Year 1*—The study of sport psychology, sports medicine, and exercise physiology.
- *Year 2*—The study of the physical and psychological characteristics of youths.
- *Year 3*—The study of the mechanics of sport-specific skills.

This program includes studies on a variety of content including sports injuries and first aid, sport psychology, and sport skill instruction.

The Program for Athletic Coaches Education (PACE) emanated from the establishment of the Michigan Institute for the Study of Youth Sports by the state legislature in 1978 (Seefeldt & Milligan, 1992). From the legislature three mandates were proposed:

- To conduct research dealing with the effects of sports on youth.
- To provide educational materials to those involved with youth sports.
- To promote continuing education for those involved with youth sports through clinics, conferences, and workshops.

Few people would argue that a need exists for our sport-minded youth to learn in a wholesome educational environment. Furthermore, the most significant component of this environment, perhaps, is the coach. The development and implementation of these four educational programs is an attempt to provide better, qualified coaches for today's youth.

Pay-to-Play

Even in the best times, school districts across the United States find it difficult to provide a quality education with funds available. School districts search to find creative ways of generating revenue to prevent programs from being reduced or eliminated altogether. One approach is to require a user's fee for extracurricular activities. Students who elect to participate in these activities, in which athletics is one, must pay for this experience, with fees ranging from twenty-five to one hundred dollars per sport. This pay-to-play policy is illegal in some states because it is seen as discriminatory to those students who lack the resources to participate (Swift, 1991).

A solid argument against user's fees is made by the National Federation of State High School Athletic Associations. The organization states that interscholastic athletics are included in the school's overall program because of their educational value. Therefore, if they are seen as such, athletics should be funded and made available to all students. Yet, because of the rising costs of administering a comprehensive athletic program, compounded with recurring budget cuts, user's fees may provide a viable and valuable source of new revenue to help fund interscholastic athletic programs.

Specialization

Sage (1990) explains that the days of an athlete participating in three or four sports are all but over. With coaches demanding more from their athletes and athletes striving for a competitive edge, a need to devote more time to just one sport arises. This specialization at the high school level has occurred as a result of the following two developments (Siedentop, 1994):

- The national acceptance of off-season training
- The increased availability of athletic scholarships at the college/university level

Sport as Entertainment

At the professional level, sports are entertainment (see Chapter 1). This view has also reached the collegiate level as millions of dollars are spent annually on the marketing and televising of college athletics. On a lesser scale, this view has now reached the high school level and as a result, interscholastic athletics are becoming a business. This has caused administrators to look at sports as a means of producing revenue rather than as a means of educating students. This adversely affects the program and the objectives the program was designed to achieve.

SUMMARY

1. Sports in America have developed an unparalleled contemporary prominence.
2. Interscholastic sports involvement is unmatched by any other country with more than 5.5 million participants.
3. The intramural program, often viewed as an extension of the instructional program, must be accepted as integral to the physical education curriculum.
4. Intramurals can be presented in an organized and/or self-directed format.
5. Sports, whether scheduled through an intramural or an interscholastic athletic program, are educational—that is, they are designed to achieve predetermined objectives.
6. A balance needs to be maintained between intramural and interscholastic athletic programs.
7. For educational benefits to be derived from participation in interscholastic athletics, a need for both leadership and planning exists.
8. Various trends have impacted interscholastic athletics including coaching certification, the pay-for-play policy, specialization, and sport as entertainment.

QUESTIONS AND LEARNING ACTIVITIES

1. From your experience, what are the benefits in providing athletic competition for children with disabilities?
2. Why do athletes seem to belong to more clubs, have wider interests, and be more extroverted and better adjusted socially then nonathletes? Does participation in athletics develop these qualities or do students with these qualities tend to participate in athletics?
3. Should a school sponsor a wide variety of intramural and interscholastic athletic activities if the community through its YMCA, YWCA, and PARA programs has a fairly extensive program? Explain your answer.
4. It has been said that it is no longer a desirable practice to divide sports into established seasons. What may be the reasons for this viewpoint?
5. Interview two or three directors of physical education relating to broadening the girls' intramural and athletic programs. What problems have arisen as a result of compliance with Title IX regulations? Interview two or three women coaches, relating to the same problem. How do their answers compare with those of the directors of physical education?
7. Indicate why it is important that coaches, players, students, and the community understand the school's philosophy of interscholastic athletics.
8. Interview three or more high school athletic directors regarding what they view as the key issues/concerns in today's interscholastic athletics.

9. What effect can interscholastic athletics have on the development of ethical behavior? In answering this question, list both the positive and the negative implications arising from sports in today's society.

10. Provide support for the placement of the three components of the physical education curriculum as illustrated in Figure 11.1.

REFERENCES

American Sport Education Program. (1996). *Raising the standard: The 1996 national interscholastic coaching requirements report.* Champaign, IL: Human Kinetics.

Annarino, A. A., Cowell, C. C., & Hazelton, H. W. (1986). *Curriculum theory and design in physical education.* Prospect Heights, IL: Waveland Press.

Arnold, P. J. (1980). Values of being in sport. The Academy Papers. Reston, VA: AAHPERD, (14), 31–33.

Bookwalter, K. W. (1964). *Physical education in secondary schools.* New York: The Center for Applied Research in Education.

Bucher, C. A., & Koenig, C. R. (1983). *Methods and materials for secondary school physical education.* St. Louis, MO: Mosby.

Daughtrey, G., & Lewis, C. (1979). *Effective teaching strategies in secondary physical education.* Philadelphia: Saunders.

Engh, F. (1992). National youth sports coaches association (NYSCA): More than just a certification program. *Journal of Physical Education, Recreation, and Dance, 63*(7), 43–45.

Ewing, M. E., & Seefeldt, V. (1990). *American youth and sports participation.* North Palm Beach, FL: Athletic Footwear Association.

Fielding, L. W. (1977). Marcus Tullius Cicero: A social critic of sport. *Canadian Journal of History of Sports and Physical Education, 8,* 16–27.

Figone, A. J. (1994). Teacher-coach role conflict: Its impact on students and student-athletes. *The Physical Educator, 51*(1), 29–34.

Girls' participation reaches all-time high. (1994). *National Federation News,* November/December, *12*(3), 12–13.

Higgins, R. J. (1979). American athletic mentality: Identities and conflict. In A. Yiannakis (Ed.), *Sport sociology: Contemporary themes.* Dubuque, IA: Kendall/Hunt Publishing Company.

Jewett, A. E., Bain, L. L., & Ennis, C. D. (1995). *The curriculum process in physical education.* Dubuque, IA: Brown & Benchmark.

Lincoln, S. M. (1992). Sports injury risk management and the keys to safety: Coalition of Americans to protect sports (CAPS). *Journal of Physical Education, Recreation, and Dance, 63*(7), 40–42, 63.

Locke, L., & Massengale, J. (1978). Role conflict in teacher/coaches. *Research Quarterly, 49,* 162–174.

National Association for Sport and Physical Education. (1995). *National standards for athletic coaches.* Washington, DC: AAHPERD.

Partlow, K. (1992). American coaching effectiveness program (ACEP): Educating America's coaches. *Journal of Physical Education, Recreation, and Dance, 63*(7), 36–39.

Sage, G. H. (1987). The social world of high school athletic coaches: Multiple role demands and their consequences. *Sociology of Sports Journal, 4,* 213–228.

Sage, G. H. (1990). High school and college sports in the United States. *Journal of Physical Education, Recreation, and Dance, 61*(2), 59–63.

Seefeldt, V. D., & Milligan, M. J. (1992). Program for athletic coaches education (PACE): Educating America's public and private school coaches. *Journal of Physical Education, Recreation, and Dance, 63*(7), 46–49.

Siedentop, D. (1994). *Introduction to physical education, fitness, and sport.* Mountain View, CA: Mayfield.

Sisley, B., & Wiese, D. (1987). Current status: Requirements for interscholastic coaches. *Journal of Physical Education, Recreation, and Dance, 58*(7), 73–85.

Stewart, C., & Sweet, L. (1992). Professional preparation of high school coaches: The problem continues. *Journal of Physical Education, Recreation, and Dance, 63*(6), 75–79.

Swift, E. M. (1991). Why Johnny can't play. *Sports Illustrated,* 75(13), 60–64, 66–68, 70–72.

Tenoschok, M. (1995). Adventures in supermurals. *Teaching Middle School Physical Education, 1*(4), 13.

Woodward, W. H. (1964). *Vittorino da Feltre and other humanist educators.* New York: Teachers College Press, Columbia University.

12
CURRICULUM EVALUATION

Outline

Definitions

The Intent of Measurement and Evaluation

Evaluation Guidelines

An Overview of Evaluation

Student Evaluation

Evaluation of Students with Disabilities

Portfolio Assessment

Teacher Evaluation

Program Evaluation

Outcomes

After reading and studying this chapter, you should be able to:
- Define
  Affective domain
  Cognitive domain
  Evaluation
  Formal knowledge assessment
  Informal knowledge assessment
  Measurement
  Physical domain
  Process assessment
  Product assessment
  Program evaluation
  Psychomotor domain
  Student evaluation
  Teacher evaluation
  Test
- Discuss the principles for guiding your approach to evaluation.
- Describe evaluation procedures that can be used to assess program effectiveness.
- Describe evaluation procedures that can be used to assess teaching effectiveness.

- Describe evaluation procedures that can be used to assess students in each of the four domains.
- Identify the four purposes for assessment of students in the adapted physical education program.
- Discuss why on-going teacher evaluation is important.

A teacher's primary function is to bring about desirable behavioral changes in students. These behavioral changes should be based on stated educational objectives. The search for indications that these educational objectives have been achieved is the essential concept of evaluation and the process whereby teachers demonstrate accountability to parents and school board members.

Combs (1979) stated that as the United States struggles to update the educational system—which is a never ending process—educators are becoming accountable for their expenditures of both human and financial resources. No one can oppose accountability; however, it is possible that the means individuals choose to determine this accountability may impede or even destroy the goals of education. If people agree with Combs' premise, then the need to think carefully about the *means* chosen for assessment in today's ever-changing world should be examined. As assessment becomes more efficient, evidence of student shortcomings should decrease, such as graduating from high school with the inability to complete an application for employment. Fewer students should leave physical education programs with (a) the inability to perform lifetime sport skills; (b) an inadequate level of fitness; and (c) a lack of appreciation for the role that physical activity plays in the maintenance of a healthful lifestyle.

Today's teachers are not always fully aware of shortcomings in their work. They do not struggle with cost-benefit programs, nor do they measure their successes by health care costs over a person's lifetime. The teaching profession does not have a *tremble factor* with which to deal, a concept that was employed in ancient Rome. When the scaffolding of a building was removed from a completed arch, the Roman engineer responsible for its construction stood beneath it. If the arch came crashing down, then the engineer was the first to know. As a result, the concern for the quality of the arch was intensely personal which may explain why so many Roman arches have survived for more than two thousand years. If today's teachers had to stand under the educational *arch* set forth for the students, how many would survive the tremble factor?

DEFINITIONS

Whenever evaluation is discussed, it is difficult not to mention both tests and measurement. These three terms—evaluation, tests, and measurement—are often used interchangeably. They do not mean the same thing but are closely related. The following definitions are given to form a basis for the content that follows.

- *Measurement*—The process of collecting data (Kirkendall, Gruber, & Johnson, 1987).
- *Evaluation*—A decision-making process involving the collection of data and the determination of the worth of this data (Dunham, 1994).
- *Test*—Form of assessment to measure the acquisition and retention of knowledge or ability in some mental or physical endeavor (Johnson & Nelson, 1986).

The relationship between these three terms can be best explained as the use of an instrument (test) for the collection of data (measurement) that allows one to make a more appropriate decision (evaluation).

THE INTENT OF MEASUREMENT AND EVALUATION

Measurement in education is related to preconceived aims and objectives. It is a process of making comparisons and relating them to one's needs in an effort to find where an individual is headed.

To evaluate, states the Merriam-Webster dictionary, is to appraise carefully and to appraise is to establish a value. This value is determined by relative worth, excellence, or importance. The process of evaluating, therefore, should be considered along with measurement. Measurement answers the questions of how much, how many, and how often and is concerned with quantities and qualities in evidence. Evaluation goes beyond the mechanics of testing and measuring to judgment in light of preconceived aims and objectives.

Evaluation answers the question of whether or not a particular experience has value. It is a continuous process and should be fully integrated with the teaching-learning process. In its broadest sense, it concerns the advancement of the total program and involves data about not only the excellence of the school plant and the students but also the way in which the school serves the community.

The current emphasis is not placed too heavily on tests themselves but rather on the application of these tests for solving problems in physical education. In the end, therefore, measurement devices and evaluation techniques become an administrative means to aid teachers in helping their students. As a result, the most common purpose of measurement for evaluation in physical education is to determine the status, progress, and/or achievement of the student. Measurement for evaluation provides other valuable services. Measurement can be used to:

- Classify students.
- Determine student status for grading.

- Aid in the diagnosis of student weaknesses in fitness, skill development, and so on.
- Predict student success.
- Motivate students.
- Determine program effectiveness.
- Determine teacher effectiveness.
- Contribute to research.
- Improve public relations with students, colleagues, administrators, parents, and the community.

EVALUATION GUIDELINES

Dunham (1994) explains that one's general approach to the instructional process and to evaluation within that instructional process is dependent on one's philosophical perspective. This philosophy, which envelops the values held concerning selected aspects of life, governs a person's actions. In physical education, a person's philosophy dictates not only the curriculum content selected but also the instructional procedures employed and the evaluation system utilized.

To ensure for a more effective physical education curriculum, Dunham (1994) provides a comprehensive list of principles for guiding the physical educator's approach to evaluation. Three important principles from this list state that the evaluation should be:

- Accepted as an integral part of the teaching process
- Employed to assist students in achieving terminal competencies (psychomotor, cognitive, and affective)
- Based on the status of the individual student

AN OVERVIEW OF EVALUATION

The financial burden of supporting today's schools rests primarily on the taxpayer. During inflationary times, schools are called on to justify the worth of their educational programs. If schools intend to provide an education worth justifying, then both educators and administrators must continually evaluate all aspects of the program in order to highlight areas that are worthy and strengthen areas that are not.

Important trends in evaluation and a widespread concern for adopting higher standards in both public and private institutions exist today. Nationwide, school children are repeating grades and classes as school districts have stiffened promotion and graduating standards. The notion today is to appraise progress carefully in all subject matter areas and work harder with those students needing special attention.

Current educational trends in physical education have brought about (a) an increased use of physical fitness tests and (b) further study of the factors contributing to lifetime, health-related fitness. Motor development is being appraised through appropriate measures of general motor ability for all students. Sport-specific skills are being measured. Written tests for the assessment of knowledge in physical education are now common. The quality of the extra class programs such as intramurals and interscholastic athletics is being measured in terms of personal student goals.

Total health behavior, academic achievement, self-concept, and personal happiness are being related more to physical performance and such specific factors as body mechanics, strength, muscular endurance, and aerobic endurance. Also significant is the fact that a majority of state departments of education have now suggested a course of study or curriculum guide with achievement standards or outcomes for sport skills, general motor ability, social behavior, and fitness. The users of such guides and courses of study are expected to compare their students with these standards in order to obtain some indication of immediate student needs.

Physical education competencies for grades 3, 6, 9, and 12 are contained in the curriculum booklet from the Pennsylvania Department of Education. These competencies are minimal—that is, what students should be expected to do according to age and physical development. They are written within the three domains of learning.

The Office of Instructional Services in the Hawaiian Department of Education provides a list of achievement standards for children in grades K–6. They are contained within the categories of skill, understanding, and social learning. The outcome standards are stated in terms of known child growth and development and what schools may expect from a well executed, individualized physical education program. Examples of expected outcomes in each category for children in grades K–2 are in the following list.

Skills—Students should be able to:
- Walk five hundred yards without stopping.
- Run a thirty-yard dash in six seconds or less.
- Jump a standing broad jump a distance of approximately their own height plus three inches.
- Bounce a ball to 2/4 or 4/4 music count.
- Roll an eight-inch diameter ball over an eighteen-inch square from a distance of ten to twelve feet in two out of five tries.
- Bounce a ball continually for two minutes or twenty-five times using both the right and left hands.
- Throw a ball a distance of twenty to thirty feet using a single, over-arm throw.
- Throw and catch a ball fifteen times in succession with a partner fifteen feet away without a miss.

- Jump a short rope, turned by self, ten times using a variety of foot patterns.
- Do ten sit ups without stopping.

Understanding—Students should know:
- The body needs daily, vigorous, large muscle activity.
- Vigorous running activities help strengthen muscles and increase endurance.
- Games require cooperation as well as competition.
- Rules for a game are made for a purpose.
- A wide stance makes for better balance.

Social Learning—Students should be able to:
- Follow directions and respond quickly to signals for attention.
- Play and cooperate with other children without fighting, quarreling, or battling.
- Use supplies and equipment properly and safely.
- Create and organize their own activities.
- Willingly help others and not laugh at their mistakes.

In 1990 the Arizona Department of Education developed a Comprehensive Health Essential Skills document. It contains essential health and physical education skills for children in grades K–12. The physical education skills are listed by grade levels K–3, 4–6, 7–8, and 9–12. The document contains key indicators and suggested evaluation procedures for each skill. Table 12.1 presents the seven essential skills for grades 4–6.

The Rhode Island Department of Elementary and Secondary Education has developed a comprehensive set of behaviorally stated, instructional outcomes (objectives) for grades K–12 physical education.* The outcomes are contained in the following instructional areas:

- Fitness
- Movement exploration
- Rhythmic activity and dance
- Game skills and team sports
- Stunts, tumbling, and gymnastics
- Individual and dual sports
- Aquatics

The outcomes are written for each grade level with some grades combined. In the *game skills and team sport* instructional topic for grade eight, outcomes are written for basketball, flag football, soccer, softball, and volleyball. The instructional outcomes for basketball are in the list on page 298.

*Reprinted by permission of the Rhode Island State Department of Education.

TABLE 12.1 Essential Skills for Arizona Children in Grades 4–6

Skill	Key Indicators	Suggested Evaluation
1. Students will understand the benefits and principles of exercise and the components of an effective exercise program	1(a). State the benefits of exercise 1(b). Describe exercise principles 1(c). List the components of an effective exercise program	Oral and/or written response
2. Students will develop and maintain an adequate level of physical fitness	2(a). Participate in activities to improve: • cardiovascular endurance • flexibility • muscular strength/endurance • body composition	Pre-test and post-test students in: • mile walk/run • sit and reach • pull ups-flexed arm-hang • skinfolds
3. Students will be proficient in fundamental movement activities	3(a). Participate in activities to improve: • locomotor movements • non-locomotor movements • hand-eye coordination • foot-eye coordination • fundamental balance • partner and group stunts • tumbling skills	Teacher observation of student performance in a variety of activities and settings; teacher observation of student performance in a variety of individual, dual, and team sport activities
4. Students will be competent in a variety of sport skills	4(a). Participate in drills and lead-up games in a variety of sports 4(b). Participate in the sport	Teacher observation of student performance; teacher-made skill tests; written tests
5. Students will develop body management skills	5(a). Demonstrate competency in a variety of individual stunts 5(b). Accomplish a variety of partner and group stunts 5(c). Safely perform a basic progression of tumbling skills 5(d). Perform a variety of fundamental performances	Teacher observation of student performance
6. Students will be proficient in a variety of rhythmic activities	6(a). Participate in a variety of folk dances 6(b). Participate in a variety of line dances	Teacher observation of student performance
7. Students will be proficient in a variety of leisure activities	7(a). Participate in such sports as aquatics, badminton, cycling, deck tennis, racquetball, orienteering, tetherball, archery, golf, and tennis	Teacher observation of student performance; student report on leisure activities in which they participate, in and out of school

From Arizona Department of Education. (1990). *Comprehensive health essential skills*. Phoenix, AZ: Arizona Department of Education. Reprinted with permission.

The student in grade 8 will demonstrate the ability to participate in basketball by:

- Scoring twelve points from the foul line. Two points are awarded for a successful attempt; one point is awarded for hitting the rim if the ball hits the rim before it touches the backboard. A total of fifteen shots will be taken. (Maintain or improve the grade seven score.)
- Scoring eleven points by taking ten shots on each side of the court fifteen feet from the basket. Two points are awarded for a successful attempt; one point is awarded for hitting the rim. A total of twenty shots will be taken. (Maintain or improve the grade seven score.)
- Scoring seven field goals by shooting any way desired continuously for thirty seconds. Each basket made scores one point. Two trial shots will be given. (Maintain or improve the grade seven score.)
- Passing the ball continuously ten times against a wall in thirteen seconds or less. Each student will stand behind a line nine feet from the wall. Time starts when the first pass hits the wall. Two trial passes will be given. The ball must be caught and passed, not batted.
- Dribbling in and out of six cones, alternating hands to keep the ball on the outside, in twelve seconds or less. Cones will be placed eight feet apart with the first cone placed five feet from a line. Two trial dribbles will be given.
- Integrating basketball skills in an active game situation (one-on-one, two-on-two, three-on-three, or half court).
- Demonstrating, through written tests and participation, a knowledge of history, rules, scoring, terminology, safety, care of equipment, and etiquette.

Forethought is essential to the evaluation process. Planning and organization of time and resources is necessary to prevent a haphazard approach to the measurement of program effectiveness. It is a good practice to measure student physical fitness twice a year—once at the beginning of the year for diagnostic assessment and again at the end of the year to determine student progress and both teacher and program effectiveness. Students in adapted physical education may need to have their progress checked more often. Tests of skills and knowledge generally should be given at the end of each unit of instruction or at the end of each six- or nine-week grading session. It is recommended that students, especially in the middle school, junior high, and high school grades, be measured at least once in the affective domain—the domain dealing with the development of a sound understanding of the nature and value of the physical education experience. Ideally, the testing procedures should be as carefully planned and carried out as the curriculum itself. It is recommended that the testing procedures be shared with both students and their parents.

Another point related to the educational competencies of students exposed to a particular curriculum relates to the need for school-based research. If an individual is to ideally evaluate anything, including a physical education program, attention should be given to an experimental design that will be instrumental in showing the general effectiveness of the program. Such a design should consist of (a) a representative sample of program participants; (b) a pretest of abilities; (c) a control or exposed group for comparison; (d) a random assignment of the sample to the experimental and control groups; and (e) a post-test to measure the effect(s) of the experimental element. This experimental approach to program improvement can be accomplished in most schools. Moreover, in many schools specialized personnel is available to assist teachers in setting up such a design.

A complete evaluation of the curriculum involves an assessment of the student, the teacher, and the program. A discussion of each assessment follows.

STUDENT EVALUATION

The evaluation of student performance and progress is becoming an increasingly important and integral part of all physical education programs and has therefore become an essential responsibility of all teachers. In addition to measuring students to determine a grade, data is necessary for determining overall teacher and program effectiveness. In order to best accomplish this task, the student needs to be evaluated in the four areas illustrated in Figure 12.1.

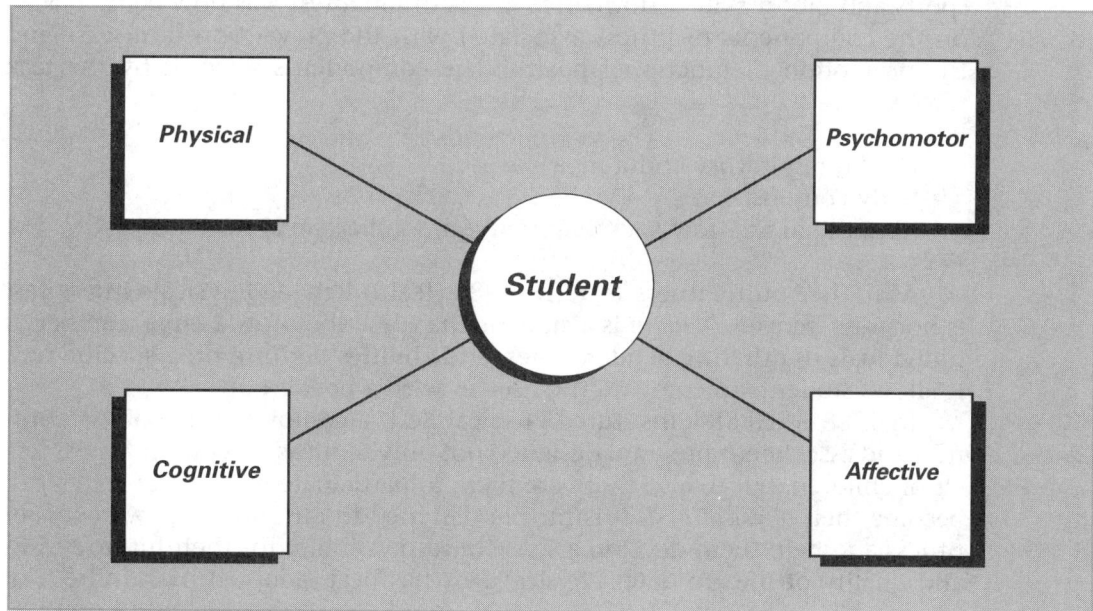

FIGURE 12.1 Domains for Evaluation

The Physical Domain

Assessment in this domain deals with growth and development, and with the specific measures of height, weight, posture, and fitness. It is highly recommended that the medical status of each student, as determined by a physician, be on file. This information may have diagnostic implications for the selection and/or organization of activities in the curriculum. The medical report should contain data relating to height, weight, and posture. The only area not included is fitness.

Highly related to an individual's success in fundamental locomotor skills and the basic game skills is the level of fitness. Determining this level and relating it to program characteristics may significantly contribute to curriculum analysis and ultimate adjustments. With the growing popularity of aerobic (cardiorespiratory) activities and the research linking aerobic endurance to physiological well-being, a renewed interest has occurred in fitness assessment. As a result, a variety of fitness tests have been developed by physical educators, state departments of education, and colleges and universities (see Table 12.2). Numerous tests measuring so many different components of fitness makes it is easy for the practitioner to become confused.

No group has done more work for the development of a practical fitness test than the American Alliance for Health, Physical Education, Recreation, and Dance (AAHPERD). Their first attempt at developing pertinent fitness material was the Youth Fitness Test published in 1957 with revised norms published in 1965 and again in 1976. In 1980 AAHPERD developed the Health-Related Physical Fitness Test. The emphasis previously placed on sports and motor skill performance in the original test was now being placed on the components of fitness associated with the prevention of disease and the promotion of functional health. The components selected by the task force were:

- Cardio-respiratory endurance
- Body composition
- Abdominal and low back/hamstring musculoskeletal function

As in the Youth Fitness Test, the 1980 Health-Related Physical Fitness Test is norm-referenced. A *norm* is a statistic that describes how a large number of individuals of differing genders, ages, and abilities perform on a specific test. It allows students to compare themselves with a peer group.

In 1988 AAHPERD instituted Physical Best, a comprehensive physical fitness and assessment program designed not only to measure current fitness levels of children, but to also motivate them to participate in physical activity to become their *physical best*. It is further designed to raise student awareness of fitness and help them develop a sense of responsibility for their future health and quality of life. To date, Physical Best has been adopted by hundreds of

TABLE 12.2 Fitness Tests

AAHPERD Youth Fitness Test (1976)

- 50-yard dash
- 600-yard run
- Shuttle run
- Sit ups
- Standing broad jump
- Pull ups (boys)/flexed arm hang (girls)

AAHPERD Health-Related Physical Fitness Test (1980)

- Modified sit ups
- One mile/one-and-one-half mile run
- Sit and reach
- Sum of skinfolds

AAHPERD Physical Best (1988)

- Modified sit ups
- One mile walk/run
- Pull ups
- Sit and reach
- Sum of skinfolds

Alabama Youth Fitness Test (1990)

- Curl ups
- One mile walk/run
- Pull ups
- Shuttle run
- V-sits

Chrysler Fund–Amateur Union Physical Fitness Test (1991)

Required
- Distance run
- Pull ups (boys)/flexed arm hang (girls)
- Modified sit ups

Optional
- Isometric push up (boys)/modified push ups (girls)
- Phantom chair
- Shuttle run
- Sprint 50/100 yards
- Standing broad jump

Fit Youth Today (1986)

- Twenty minute steady state jog
- Curl ups
- Sit and reach
- Sum of skinfolds

President's Challenge (1991)

- Curl ups
- One mile walk/run
- Pull ups
- Shuttle run
- V-sit reach

Prudential FITNESSGRAM (1994)

- One mile walk/run or pacer
- Sum of skinfolds or body mass index
- Trunk lift
- Back-saver sit and reach or shoulder stretch
- Curl up
- Push ups, pull ups, modified pull ups, or flexed arm hang

YMCA Physical Fitness Test

- Bench press
- Sit ups
- Sit and reach
- Sum of skinfolds
- Bryde ergometer ride of three minute step test

---

schools and organizations throughout the United States. The complete program contains:

- A health-related fitness assessment
- An educational component
- An awards system

The educational component contains a kit that is designed to help the physical educator:

- Learn how to motivate students to develop good fitness habits.
- Design specific activities, both in and out of school, to help students improve.
- Teach students to set individualized fitness goals based on their current fitness levels and their unique capabilities for improvement.
- Monitor students' progress and keep fitness records.
- Share results with parents by using report cards and letters.

The kit contains an instructor's manual with guidelines for developing effective fitness education and information needed to plan and implement the program. Computer software is available to aid in the storage and reporting of fitness data. Physical Best does not contain normative data but rather is a criterion-referenced test. Therefore, student performance is compared not to a peer group but rather to a preestablished criterion (score).

In 1994 AAHPERD formulated a partnership with the Prudential FITNESSGRAM. This comprehensive fitness program consists of (a) a health-related fitness assessment; (b) a computerized reporting program; (c) a behavioral oriented recognition system; and (d) educational materials. AAHPERD has maintained the Physical Best educational component and awards system but has replaced its assessment system with that contained in the FITNESSGRAM.

Assessing students to determine progress

The Psychomotor Domain

Assessment in this domain deals with the acquisition of skills and can be accomplished both objectively and subjectively. *Objective assessment* involves the measurement of the product, for example, how many baskets the student made, how fast the student completed the dribble maze, and how far the student threw the ball. It yields a *quantitative* score. *Subjective assessment* involves the measurement of the process—that is, how well the student performed the skill while shooting, dribbling, and throwing. It yields a *qualitative* score.

There are a number of standardized, product-oriented skills tests available. AAHPERD currently has skills tests manuals available for archery, basketball, football, softball, tennis, and volleyball. These tests are most appropriate for secondary students in grades 7–12. Suggested sources for a variety of skills tests are shown in Table 12.3.

TABLE 12.3   Skills Tests Sources

Source	Address
American Alliance for Health, Physical Education, Recreation, and Dance	AAHPERD 1900 Association Drive Reston, VA 22091
Barrow H. M., McGee, R., & Thritschler, K. A. (1989). *Practical measurement in physical education and sport*	Lea & Febiger 600 Washington Square Philadelphia, PA 19106
Baumgartner, T. A., & Jackson, A. S. (1991). *Measurement for evaluation in physical education and exercise science*	William C. Brown Publishers 2460 Kerper Boulevard Dubuque, IA 52001
Dunham, P. (1994). *Evaluation for physical education*	Morton Publishing Company 925 West Kenyon, Unit 12 Englewood, CO 80110
Hastad, D. N., & Lacy, A. C. (1994). *Measurement and evaluation in physical education and exercise science*	Gorsuch Scarisbrick Publishers 8233 Via Paseo del Norte, F400 Scottsdale, AZ 85258
Johnson, B. L., & Nelson, J. K. (1986). *Practical measurement for evaluation in physical education*	Burgess Publishing Company 7110 Ohms Lane Edina, MN 55435
Kirkendall, D. R. Gruber, J. J. & Johnson, R. E. (1987). *Measurement and evaluation for physical education*	Human Kinetics Publishers Box 5076 Champaign, IL 61820
Miller, D. K. (1994). *Measurement by the physical educator: why and how*	Brown & Benchmark Publishers 2460 Kerper Boulevard Dubuque, IA 52001
Morrow, J. R., Jackson, A. W., Disch, J. G., & Mood, D. P. (1995). *Measurement and evaluation in human performance*	Human Kinetics Publishers Box 5076 Champaign, IL 61820

TABLE 12.4 Checklist for Overhand Throw

Name: _____

Grade: _____

Date: _____

Directions: While viewing the student perform the overhand throw, place a check (✓) in the appropriate space.

1. Steps with the proper foot	Yes_____	No_____
2. Leads with the elbow	Yes_____	No_____
3. Rotates at the trunk	Yes_____	No_____
4. Has complete follow through	Yes_____	No_____
5. Has smooth, continuous movement	Yes_____	No_____

Evaluation of students in the elementary program (grades K–6) should be more process oriented. However, standardized skills tests can still be used with younger students if the tests are modified to meet their characteristics. Process assessment is done primarily by way of observing students as they perform the skills. To make the observation somewhat objective, a checklist or rating scale may be used such as the examples shown in Tables 12.4 and 12.5.

The Cognitive Domain

Assessment in this domain deals with the development and application of knowledge including the history, rules, terminology, techniques, and strategy of selected activities, fitness and wellness concepts, and safety concerns.

TABLE 12.5 Rating Scale for Overhand Throw

Name: _____

Grade: _____

Date: _____

Total rating: 1 = Does only one of five steps
2 = Does only two of five steps
3 = Does four of five steps
4 = Has a smooth, continuous, mature movement, doing all five steps

Directions: After viewing the student perform the overhand throw two or more times, circle the appropriate rating.

Action	Scoring
1. Ball held with the fingers	1 2 3 4
2. Steps with the opposite foot	1 2 3 4
3. Rotates at the hip	1 2 3 4
4. Leads with the elbow	1 2 3 4
5. Ends with a follow through	1 2 3 4

Knowledge assessment is just as important as the assessment of both fitness and skills, but too often is ignored. It can be accomplished either formally or informally. Formal assessment involves the use a teacher-made, paper and pencil test and is most appropriate for grades 4–12 when students have developed reading and writing skills. When constructing a formal test, it is important that the test meet the criteria of validity, reliability, objectivity, and administrative feasibility.

For grades K–3 informal assessment in the form of oral questioning is recommended. Asking questions relating to the numerous concepts being taught allows the teacher to determine whether the students are both learning and understanding. This approach may be done as a review at the end of each day's lesson or during the lesson when appropriate.

The Affective Domain

Assessment in this domain deals with the development of appropriate attitudes, values, and social behavior. It involves the interests, appreciation, and emotional biases of a student. More specifically, the affective domain envelops the development of sportsmanship, cooperation, teamwork, self restraint, and leadership.

Miller (1994) states that many physical educators list affective objectives for students. However, teachers sometimes feel uncomfortable measuring students and therefore make no attempt at determining if these affective objectives have been attained. In addition, many physical educators think that if the cognitive and psychomotor objectives are attained the affective objectives will also be pertinent. Even though the affective domain is the most difficult domain to measure objectively, an attempt should be made to determine the feelings and appreciation that students take with them after an exposure to physical education.

Affective development can be measured by (a) teacher observation of student behavior, or (b) a self appraisal inventory. Table 12.6 is an example of a form for the assessment of affective behavior. A list of available, appraisal inventories is shown in Table 12.7.

Several physical education professionals question whether teachers should undertake affective evaluation. Mood (1982) claims that the physical educator does not have enough time to devote to this area and that the teaching of motor skills is more important. In addition, the availability and the reliability of appropriate measuring instruments is questionable. Furthermore, Miller (1994) asks why physical education should assume responsibility for developing and assessing affective behavior when other disciplines like English, mathematics, and so on, in the school curriculum rarely do.

On the other hand, Griffin (1982) states that affective learning and behavior should be evaluated. The affective development that results from varied experiences offered in a physical education program is important. Kirkendall,

TABLE 12.6 Student Behavior Checklist

Name: _____

Grade: _____   Check one: _____ Midterm assessment

Date: _____   _____ Final assessment

Directions: After viewing the student's behavior, place a check (✓) in the appropriate space.

1. Assists classmates   Yes____   No____
2. Arrives promptly for class   Yes____   No____
3. Follows directions   Yes____   No____
4. Accepts criticism   Yes____   No____
5. Uses self control   Yes____   No____
6. Cooperates with others   Yes____   No____
7. Shows respect for others   Yes____   No____
8. Obeys class rules   Yes____   No____
9. Works hard to complete each task. Yes____ No____
10. Works independently   Yes____   No____

TABLE 12.7 Instruments for Affective Assessment

Adams Physical Education Attitude Scale (Adams, 1963)
Blanchard Behavior Rating Scale (Blanchard, 1936)
Carr Physical Education Attitude Scale (Carr, 1945)
Children's Attitude toward Physical Activity Inventory (Simon & Smoll, 1974)
Cowell Social Adjustment Index (Cowell, 1958)
Cratty Self-Concept Scale (Cratty et al., 1970)
Johnson Sportsmanship Attitude Scale (Johnson, 1969)
Kenyon Attitude Scale (Kenyon, 1968)
Lakie Attitude toward Athletic Competition Scale (Lakie, 1964)
Martinek-Zaichkowsky Self-Concept Scale (Martinek & Zaichkowsky, 1977)
Nelson Sports Leadership Questionnaire (Nelson, 1966)
Piers-Harris Children's Self-Concept Scale (Piers & Harris, 1964)
Toulmin Elementary Physical Education Attitude Scale (Toulmin, 1973)
Wear Attitude Scale (Wear, 1955)
Wise Student Inventory toward Athletic Competition (Wise, 1976)

Gruber, and Johnson (1987) further state that the feelings and appreciation derived from physical education participation shape a student's attitude. These attitudes will partly determine if the students will continue to participate after leaving school.

EVALUATION OF STUDENTS WITH DISABILITIES

As previously stated, student evaluation is an essential responsibility of today's teachers. Perhaps nowhere in the curriculum is this more essential

TABLE 12.8 Assessment Tests for Students with Disabilities

AAHPERD Motor Fitness Testing Manual for the Moderately Mentally Retarded (Johnson & Londeree, 1976)
Andover Perceptual-Motor Test (Nichols, Arsenault, & Giuffre, 1980)
Ayres Southern California Perceptual-Motor Tests (Miller & Sullivan, 1982)
Basic Motor Ability Tests (Arnheim & Sinclair, 1979)
Brigance Diagnostic Inventory of Early Development (Brigance, 1978)
Bruininks-Oseretsky Test of Motor Proficiency (Bruininks, 1978)
Denver Developmental Screening Test (Frankenburg & Dodds, 1967)
Fait Physical Fitness Test for Mildly and Moderately Mentally Retarded Students (Dunn & Fait, 1989)
Hughes Basic Gross Motor Assessment (Hughes, 1979)
I CAN Fundamental Skills Test (Wessel, 1979)
Kansas Adapted/Special Physical Education Test Manual (Johnson & Lavay, 1988)
Ohio State University Scale of Intra-Gross Motor Assessment (Loovis & Ersing, 1979)
President's Challenge for Students with Special Needs (President's Council on Physical Fitness and Sports, 1991)
Project ACTIVE Motor Ability Test (Vodola, 1976)
Projective Unique Physical Fitness Test (Winnick & Short, 1985)
Prudential FITNESSGRAM Modifications for Special Populations (Cooper Institute for Aerobics Research, 1992)
Purdue Perceptual-Motor Survey (Roach & Kephart, 1966)
Special Fitness Test Manual for Mildly Mentally Retarded (AAHPERD, 1976)
Test of Gross Motor Development (Ulrich, 1986)

than in the adapted physical education program. Assessment in the adapted program serves the following purposes:

- *Screening*—To determine which students are in need of special help.
- *Placement*—To assure that each student needing special help is in the proper environment.
- *Diagnosis*—To determine the present level of performance of each student to guide both the selection of activities and instruction.
- *Progress*—To determine if the behavioral objectives have been met.

Existing tests in the four domains should be used for assessing students in the adapted program whenever possible. However, these tests may not always be appropriate. A list of the tests most frequently used by physical educators for the screening, placement, diagnosis, and progress assessment of students with disabilities is shown in Table 12.8.

PORTFOLIO ASSESSMENT

A current attempt to provide a broader, more genuine view of what a student has learned is called *portfolio assessment* (Zessoules & Garner, 1991). It is a move away from the more traditional evaluation process cognitive-knowledge test, psychomotor-skills test, or affective-teacher rating scale approach for evaluating students.

Portfolio assessment is a process for documenting what Perrone (1991) calls authentic learning—that is, learning that occurs in the natural setting. This alternative approach stems from the notion that assessment should relate directly to the outcomes deemed important and relevant. Siedentop (1994) provides the following example. In assessing how well a student can write, rather than have the student complete a multiple choice exam on writing, the authentic assessment movement requires the student to write an essay. In physical education, rather than record the number or tennis strokes a student can successfully do against a rebound board in thirty seconds, the student is judged on the forehand and backhand techniques during game play. However, skills testing is not inappropriate for a portfolio, but beyond skills testing, a variety of other assessment items exist that may be used to make up a portfolio (see Table 12.9).

The specific assessment items selected for a portfolio may be determined by school policy, but Defina (1992) argues that this determination should be made, in part, by the student. Allowing students to make decisions on what they want to learn and how they will know if they have learned it is an important component of portfolio assessment.

Melograno (1994) indicates that portfolios provide a nonstigmatizing, motivational, effective means for reporting student learning. When used correctly, portfolios can:

- Capitalize on student work.
- Enhance both teacher and student involvement in evaluation.
- Satisfy the accountability need prompted by school reform (Chittenden, 1991).

TABLE 12.9 Portfolio Assessment Items

Activity diaries
Attitude inventories
Entry-level skills tests
In-class assignments
Independent study contracts
Knowledge tests
Parental questionnaires
Quizzes
Research papers
Self-assessment checklists
Student reflection reports
Task sheets
Teacher/peer rating forms
Unit logs

TEACHER EVALUATION

The teaching profession is scrutinized more closely today than ever before in history. With increased emphasis on teacher accountability, a greater effort to evaluate those responsible for educating our youth exists.

Barrow, McGee, and Tritschler (1989) stress that in order to improve the program educators need to focus on improving the instructional process. Teacher evaluation is the best means of determining the value of the instructional process in physical education. Beyond this purpose, Castetter (1971) lists the following reasons for the ongoing evaluation of teachers:

- To improve instruction
- To determine teacher potential
- To determine teacher strengths and weaknesses
- To promote self development
- For the assignment of teacher responsibilities
- To determine salary increases
- For retention determination

Perhaps the first step in a meaningful teacher evaluation is the development of a valid assessment procedure. The more common, traditional procedures for teacher evaluation are (a) self appraisal; (b) administrator checklist/rating; and (c) student ratings. A fourth and relatively new technique is systematic observation. Self appraisal requires the teacher to analyze his/her teaching behavior. Thomas (1980) indicates that self appraisal is necessary for improvement in instruction and that a simple reflection about course objectives, student interest, and student participation can reveal much for teaching improvement. An example of a teacher self appraisal form is shown in Table 12.10.

Administrator checklist/rating is, perhaps, the most frequently used procedure for evaluating teachers. A checklist or rating form contains a group of statements about which the administrator gives his/her opinion relating to the teaching-learning environment. With a checklist, the judgment usually contains yes or no answer. With a rating form, the range of responses is greater. An example of an administrative rating form is shown in Table 12.11.

Student ratings of teacher effectiveness are widely used, especially in higher education. Their use should be guarded because of the extraneous variables that may affect how a student responds to the selected components of teaching. Among these variables are class size, class composition (coeducational/non-coeducational), and whether or not the class is required or an elective. Kerlinger's 1971 caution against the use of student ratings for teacher evaluation is still pertinent today. He contends that regardless of age, students are not mature enough to make valid judgments of good teaching.

TABLE 12.10 Teacher Self-Evaluation Checklist

Name: _____

Date: _____

Check one: ____End of first grading period

____Mid-semester

____End of semester

Directions: Answer each question with either Yes or No. Five points are allotted for each Yes. A score of sixty (twelve of fifteen) is needed for an above-average teacher.

_____ 1. Do I know the names of all my students?
_____ 2. Do I get my students to think instead of giving back rote memory of what I say?
_____ 3. Do I analyze my own classroom or gymnasium teaching?
_____ 4. Do I find myself available for student conferences?
_____ 5. Do I listen attentively to what students are saying?
_____ 6. Am I intuitive to the varying needs of students, such as hypertense?
_____ 7. Do I know my subject matter well enough to be challenged by questions in class?
_____ 8. Do I really try to develop a positive teaching-learning climate in my classes?
_____ 9. Do I give individual attention to the excellent, the moderate, and the slow learner, and not concentrate just on the talented ones?
_____ 10. Do students talk to me freely inside and outside of class?
_____ 11. Are my students sleeping in class or getting restless?
_____ 12. Am I tolerant of students' mistakes as well as my own?
_____ 13. Do I keep up to date with my professional reading?
_____ 14. Do I grade fairly on learning objectives rather than on likes and dislikes?
_____ 15. Do I really care about students and let them know it?

TABLE 12.11 Teacher Behavior Rating Form

Directions: While or after viewing the educator in a teaching setting, score each of the items below accordingly.

Scoring: 5 = Superior
4 = Acceptable
3 = Needs improvement
2 = Unsatisfactory
1 = No opportunity to observe

Characteristic	*Score*	*Characteristic*	*Score*
Personality	_____	Knowledge of subject matter	_____
Appearance	_____	Ethical behavior	_____
Health	_____	Punctual and dependable	_____
Enthusiasm	_____	Teaching	_____
Initiative	_____	Planning and organization	_____
Flexibility	_____	Voice level and modulation	_____
Poise and self confidence	_____	Nonverbal communication	_____
Professionalism	_____	Motivation of students	_____
Ability to work with others	_____	Attention to individual needs	_____
Understanding of youth	_____	Discipline	_____

An additional concern is that if students are used for assessing teaching behavior, a teacher may seek popularity at the expense of effective teaching. An example of a student rating form is shown in Table 12.12.

Systematic observation has been popular in recent years. It requires both observation and documentation by another individual, usually an administrator or a colleague. To promote its use, Darst, Zakrajsek, and Mancini (1989) state that systematic observation allows an individual, while following stated guidelines and procedures, to observe, record, and analyze interactions with the assurance that others viewing the same events would agree with this recorded data. A list of instruments for systematic observation is shown in Table 12.13.

TABLE 12.12 Instructor Rating Form

Name: _____

Course: _____

Date: _____

Directions: This evaluation is made at the instructor's request for determining teaching effectiveness. Listed below are qualities that describe aspects of instructor performance. Please rate the instructor on each of these items by circling your honest response.

Scoring: 5 = Excellent
4 = Very good
3 = Good
2 = Fair
1 = Poor

The instructor:
1. Clearly presented course objectives.   5 4 3 2 1
2. Used appropriate evaluative procedures.   5 4 3 2 1
3. Stimulated my interest in the subject matter.   5 4 3 2 1
4. Used resource materials well.   5 4 3 2 1
5. Broadened my interest in the subject matter.   5 4 3 2 1
6. Displayed enthusiasm for teaching.   5 4 3 2 1
7. Communicated effectively.   5 4 3 2 1
8. Made appropriate examples of content.   5 4 3 2 1
9. Taught to the level of skill and/or knowledge
   of the class.   5 4 3 2 1
10. Was willing to give advice and attention
    according to my individual needs.   5 4 3 2 1
11. Inspired confidence in me relating to course
    content and its application.   5 4 3 2 1
12. Motivated me to apply the subject matter
    to my own life.   5 4 3 2 1
13. Required too much work for the credit.   5 4 3 2 1
14. Used lecture and discussion well.   5 4 3 2 1
15. Is recommended to my friends.   5 4 3 2 1

TABLE 12.13 Systematic Observation Instruments

Academic Learning Time-Physical Education (ALT-PE)
Cheffer's Adaptation of the Flanders's Interaction Analysis System (CAFIAS)
Flanders's Interaction Analysis System (FIAS)
Observational Recording Record of Physical Educator's Teaching Behavior (ORRPETB)
Ohio State University Teacher Behavior Rating Scale (OSUTBRS)
Rankin Interaction Analysis System (RIAS)

Regardless of the technique used, Bucher and Koenig (1983) provide the following guidelines for teacher evaluation. The evaluation should:

- Involve the teacher personally. Since evaluation is a cooperative venture, the teacher should not only understand the process but should also be involved in developing the evaluative criteria.
- Focus on teacher performance.
- Be concerned with helping the teacher grow professionally.
- Look to the future and be concerned with improvement of the program.
- Be well organized and administered. The procedure should be clearly outlined with a step-by-step approach.

PROGRAM EVALUATION

The purpose of this book has been to examine the total physical education curriculum. Although its parts have been discussed, the overall objective has been to relate specific aspects to the whole program and to effect a proper balance between grade level progression, developmental and adapted class instruction, intramurals, and interscholastic athletics. No one area has been singled out as the most important because they are all important.

The primary purpose of program evaluation is program effectiveness. School administrators and directors of physical education frequently want to know how well their programs are working and how they compare with others in neighboring communities, in neighboring states, or on a national level. Program effectiveness may be determined by (a) student performance; and (b) a self appraisal checklist or inventory.

According to Dougherty and Bonanno (1979), measuring student performance to determine program effectiveness is an accountability system. The use of a student's data in the areas of fitness, skill, knowledge, and attitude (a) allows for curriculum revision to better attain stated objectives; (b) allows for identification and elimination of undesirable outcomes; and (c) serves as an effective means for both the administration and the community to monitor schools. In general, student data allows for quality control which is important to any educational program. Quality control is a way of telling whether or not the program is executed well and whether or not it remains as effective over time as it was when first implemented.

Bloom, Hastings, and Madaus (1971) state that evaluation practices have barely contributed to teaching and learning. They call for more quality control (the tremble factor)—a necessity in today's business world. Since new programs frequently deteriorate, individuals must measure this deterioration by comparing baseline data with current achievement results. Scores relating to fitness, skills, knowledge, and attitudes toward the program may be compared with scores obtained after the implementation stage. Signs of program deterioration frequently relate to a weak implementation practice because of variables such as poor teacher morale, teacher indifference, inadequacy of facilities and equipment, and school learning climate in general.

Using a self appraisal checklist or inventory allows individuals to compare the component parts of the curriculum to recognized, acceptable standards. Self examination is often a good practice since it encourages soul searching and an honest attitude toward what the program should be. When an administrator or faculty member appraises the total curriculum, they have basically opened their minds and humbled themselves just enough to be able to see the changes needed. Therefore, the simple act of deciding to appraise a program is significant. It is the first step to program modifications in a changing society.

A number of self appraisal instruments designed for the physical education program exist, several are standardized and have had widespread use. Many states including California, Florida, Idaho, Illinois, Indiana, Kansas, Ohio, Texas, and Wisconsin have taken the lead in developing instruments for this kind of appraisal.

The *LaPorte Health and Physical Education Score Card I, II* (1951) has been in use longer than any other similar instrument. It is intended to measure all aspects of the health, safety, recreation, and physical education program. Attention is focused on the characteristics of a good program. Ten program elements exist that can be rated from one to thirty, with a perfect score totaling three hundred. If two hundred points are scored, the program is considered fair to good. If one hundred points are scored, the program is considered poor.

Bucher (1977) developed the lengthy but complete Checklist and Rating Scale for the Evaluation of the Physical Education Program. It combines both the standards required by several state departments of education and standards recommended by leading authorities in the field. This instrument is properly suited for the appraisal of a total school program. Not all of Bucher's scale needs to be used for a particular school. Ample items exist in each of the following sections to enable a school to appraise a part of its program:

- *General administrative considerations*—Including philosophy, objectives, and the general curriculum.
- *Considerations in the administration of physical education program*—Including attendance, excuses, required classes per week, length of class, time provisions for shower and dressing, class size, student-to-teacher ratio, public relations, athletic standards, supervision of intramural and extramural activities, teacher scheduling, coeducational instruction, and supervision.

- *Components of the physical education program*—Including program design, activities offered in the instructional, intramural, and interscholastic athletic programs.
- *Staff*—Including status, tenure, and background preparation.
- *Facilities and equipment*—Including general standards, equipment, indoor and outdoor facilities, faculty offices, locker rooms, and showers.
- *Measurement and evaluation techniques*—Including student status and progress, and staff evaluation.

The Illinois Association of Health, Physical Education, and Recreation published the *Criteria for Evaluating Elementary Physical Education in Illinois Schools* in 1980 and the *Criteria for Evaluating Physical Education Programs in Illinois Schools (Form 7-12)* in 1984. These instruments were developed to provide a basis for improving the quality of physical education in Illinois schools and to stimulate self-study and self-evaluation. Each instrument contains approximately one hundred evaluative criteria statements dealing with the (a) instructional program; (b) enrichment program; (c) evaluation of students; and (d) organization.

An instrument for assessing the total program is the revised version of the *Indiana Physical Education Score Card for Elementary and Secondary Schools*. It was developed to improve the quality of physical education programs. It is primarily a self evaluation instrument that encourages follow-up studies. The score card contains four areas—class management and instruction, program activities, facilities and equipment, and administration. The scorecard is separated into three levels: elementary grades 1–3, elementary grades 4–6, and secondary grades 7–12. Each level is scored in each of the areas after several questions have been answered.

At the national level, AAHPERD (1977) published the *Assessment Guide for Secondary School Physical Education Programs*. Its purpose was to provide a functional, easily administered, comprehensive tool that would allow for:

- Self-study and self-evaluation
- Identification of problem areas
- Improvement of the program

The instrument is composed of statements relating to administration, the athletic program, the instructional program, and the intramural program. A *yes* or *no* response is required for each of the forty-six statements. A negative response for an item may indicate that additional self-study is needed or may be justified with an acceptable rationale based on the philosophy of the individual department.

In 1994 AAHPERD published the Checklist for Elementary School Physical Education, developed by NASPE's Council on Physical Education for Children. It is comprised of ninety-four items that are divided into the following seven categories:

- Teacher
- Teacher preparation/staff development
- The instructional program
- Assessment
- Organization/administration
- Equipment and facilities
- School-related programs

Evaluative criteria are presented in the form of statements describing desirable attributes. The evaluator is supposed to determine the extent to which each statement describes the program in question. The eighteen items dealing with the instructional program are shown in Table 12.14.

TABLE 12.14 The Instructional Program

Read each statement carefully and circle the letter that is appropriate.

A—If the attribute is in consistent agreement with what is present in the physical education program.
B—If the attribute is in general agreement but the need may exist for improvement in this area.
C—If you are undecided as to whether or not the item describes the physical education program.
D—If you definitely disagree that the attribute describes what is actually present in the physical education program and a definite need exists for improvement in this area.
E—If no basis for evaluation exists.

The physical education program:

1. Is an integral part of, and consistent with, the total educational philosophy of the school. A B C D E
2. Serves the diverse needs of all students A B C D E
3. Is based on an established written curriculum. A B C D E
4. Is of sufficient breadth and depth to be challenging to all. A B C D E
5. Is developmentally based and progressively sequenced from year to year. A B C D E
6. Is regularly updated and revised. A B C D E
7. Has well defined objectives for progressive learning. A B C D E
8. Is built around the development of efficient, effective, and expressive movement abilities. A B C D E
9. Provides opportunities for the development of fundamental movement patterns and specific movement skills. A B C D E
10. Provides experiences to enhance the development of physical fitness. A B C D E
11. Provides opportunities for students to develop skills in games/sports, dance/rhythms, and gymnastics. A B C D E
12. Provides opportunities for students to enhance their knowledge and understanding of human movement in a variety of physical activities. A B C D E

Continued.

TABLE 12.14 *Continued*

13. Promotes safe behavior by incorporating proper safety practices into physical education lessons.	A B C D E
14. Fosters creativity.	A B C D E
15. Promotes self-understanding and acceptance.	A B C D E
16. Promotes positive social interaction and self-control.	A B C D E
17. Recognizes and provides for learning enjoyment and fun.	A B C D E
18. Helps each student learn how to manage risk-taking and other challenges.	A B C D E

From NASPE's *Checklist for elementary school physical education;* available from AAHPERD by calling 1-800-321-0789. Reprinted by permission.

The Idaho State Department of Education published a self-appraisal checklist in 1982. It was developed by a statewide physical education curriculum committee and contains 116 criterion items against which a program can be judged. The checklist is contained in the appendix.

A number of worthwhile instruments available for the assessment of the total physical education program exist today. Regardless of the technique or instrument used, Annarino, Cowell, and Hazelton (1986) warn that the data should allow an individual to determine the:

- Extent to which student needs are met
- Degree of student achievement
- Strengths and weaknesses of the program objectives
- Quality of instruction
- Extent of faculty, facility, and equipment utilization

In addition, it is recommended that if self appraisal is used, school administrators and the entire physical education staff should participate in the assessment.

SUMMARY

1. Evaluation is the means by which the physical educator demonstrates accountability.
2. Evaluation is a three-step process involving (a) data collection (measurement); (b) judging the value of the data; and (c) making a decision.
3. Beyond determining the status, progress, and/or achievement of students, evaluation serves other purposes that include classification, prediction, and motivation.
4. Evaluation in the school setting involves the student, the teacher, and the program.
5. Student evaluation occurs in four areas: physical, psychomotor, cognitive, and affective.

6. Teacher evaluation, primarily designed to improve instruction, has been traditionally accomplished by self appraisal, professional rating, and/or student ratings. Systematic observation has gained recent popularity.
7. Program evaluation, designed to determine program effectiveness, may be accomplished by student performance and self appraisal.

QUESTIONS AND LEARNING ACTIVITIES

1. Visit a local industry and inquire about quality control practices. How do these efforts compare with these ones employed in public schools?
2. Physical education philosophers have written about the place and importance of measurement in the program. What seems to be the prevailing viewpoint today?
3. How do you feel about setting up outcomes for boys and girls in grades K–12? Are such outcomes readily acceptable by students as worthy of in-class and out-of-class activity?
4. At what point in the evaluation process do measurement activities become *too* time consuming? Explain your viewpoint and illustrate it with an example.
5. Explain how you may use the results of measurement in a secondary school to revise a given curriculum.
6. Examine curriculum guides from various states and/or from other communities. Do you find that measurement and evaluation are considered part of the total program? How do your findings compare with those of your classmates?
7. Obtain a copy of one of the program evaluation instruments referred to in this chapter. Use this instrument to critically evaluate an existing program. Provide a list of strengths and weaknesses of the program, as well as recommendations to improve the program.
8. Develop a short statement relating to the significant relationship between educational aims and objectives and evaluation practices. Before doing this, read what various authors have said about this topic.
9. Select an imaginary school system in a city of 50,000 people. Assume you are going to revise the curriculum partly on the basis of measurement findings. What procedures would you follow? Illustrate a plan for relating evaluation results to curriculum revision.
10. Prepare a proposed plan for grading a seventh grade physical education class. Include the components (skill, knowledge, and so on) and how each will be measured.

REFERENCES

Adams, R. S. (1963). Two scales for measuring attitude toward physical education. *Research Quarterly, 34,* 91–94.

Alabama Governor's Commission on Physical Fitness. (1990). *Youth fitness test manual.* Montgomery, AL: Governor's Commission on Physical Fitness.

American Alliance for Health, Physical Education, Recreation, and Dance. (1976). *Special fitness test manual for the mildly mentally retarded* (2nd ed.). Reston, VA: AAHPERD.

American Alliance for Health, Physical Education, Recreation, and Dance. (1976). *Youth fitness test manual.* Reston, VA: AAHPERD.

American Alliance for Health, Physical Education, Recreation, and Dance. (1977). *Assessment guide for secondary school physical education programs.* Reston, VA: AAHPERD.

American Alliance for Health, Physical Education, Recreation, and Dance. (1980). *Health-related physical fitness test manual.* Reston, VA: AAHPERD.

American Alliance for Health, Physical Education, Recreation, and Dance. (1988). *Physical best.* Reston, VA: AAHPERD.

American Alliance for Health, Physical Education, Recreation, and Dance. (1987). *Program appraisal checklist for elementary school physical education programs.* Reston, VA: AAHPERD.

American Council on Education. (1980). *The evaluative criteria, national study of secondary school evaluation.* Washington, DC: American Council on Education.

American Health and Fitness Foundation. (1986). *FTY program manual.* Austin, TX: American Health and Fitness Foundation.

Annarino, A. A., Cowell, C. C., & Hazelton, H. W. (1986). *Curriculum theory and design in physical education.* Prospect Heights, IL: Waveland Press.

Arizona Department of Education. (1990). *Comprehensive health essential skills.* Phoenix, AZ: Arizona Department of Education.

Arnheim, D. D., & Sinclair, W. A. (1985). *Physical education for special populations: A developmental, adapted, and remedial approach.* Englewood Cliffs, NJ: Prentice-Hall.

Barrow, H. M., McGee, R., & Tritschler, K. A. (1989). *Practical measurement in physical education and sport.* Philadelphia: Lea & Febiger.

Baumgartner, T. A., & Jackson, A. S. (1991). *Measurement for evaluation in physical education and exercise science.* Dubuque, IA: Wm C. Brown Publishers.

Blanchard, B. E. (1936). A behavior frequency rating scale for the measurement of character and personality traits in a physical education classroom situation. *Research Quarterly, 7,* 56–66.

Bloom, B. S., Hastings, J. T., & Madaus, G. F. (1971). *Handbook on formative and summative evaluation of student learning.* New York: McGraw-Hill.

Brigance, A. (1978). *The Brigance diagnostic inventory of early development.* Worburn, MA: Curriculum Associates.

Bruininks, R. H. (1978). *Bruininks-Oseretsky test of motor proficiency: Examiner's manual.* Circle Pines, MN: American Guidance Service.

Bucher, C. A. (1977). *Administration of school and college health and physical education programs.* St. Louis, MO: Mosby.

Bucher, C. A., & Koenig, C. R. (1983). *Methods and materials for secondary school physical education.* St. Louis, MO: Mosby.

Carr, M. G. (1945). The relationship between success in physical education and selected attitudes expressed by high school freshman girls. *Research Quarterly, 16,* 176–191.

Castetter, W. B. (1971). *The personnel function in public administration.* New York: Macmillan Publishing Company.

Cheffers, J., & Keilty, G. C. (1980). Developing valid instrumentation for measuring teacher effectiveness. *International Journal of Physical Education, 17,* 15–23.

Chittenden, E. (1991). Authentic assessment, evaluation, and documentation of student performance. In V. Perrone (Ed.), *Expanding student assessment.* Alexandria, VA: Association for Supervision and Curriculum Development.

Chrysler Fund–Amateur Athletic Union. (1991). *Chrysler Fund–AAU Physical Fitness Program.* Bloomington, IN: Chrysler–Amateur Athletic Union.

Combs, A. W. (1979). *Myths in education.* Boston: Allyn & Bacon.

Cooper Institute for Aerobics Research. (1992). *Prudential FITNESSGRAM.* Dallas, TX: Cooper Institute for Aerobics Research.

Cowell, C. C. (1958). Validating an index of social adjustment for high school use. *Research Quarterly, 29,* 7–10.

Cratty, B., Ikedo, N., Martin, M., Jennett, C., & Morris, M. (1970). *Movement activities,* motor ability, and the education of children. Springfield, IL: Charles C. Thomas.

Darst, P. W., Mancini, V. H., & Zakrajsek, D. B. (1983). *Systematic observation instrumentation for physical education.* West Point, NY: Leisure Press.

Darst, P. W., Zakrajsek, D. B., & Mancini, V. H. (1989). *Analyzing physical education and sport instruction.* Champaign, IL: Human Kinetics.

Defina, A. A. (1992). *Portfolio assessment: Getting started.* New York: Scholastic Professional Books.

Dougherty, N. J., & Bonanno, D. (1979). *Contemporary approaches to the teaching of physical education.* Minneapolis, MN: Burgess.

Dunham, P. (1994). *Evaluation for physical education.* Englewood, CO: Morton Publishing Company.

Dunn, J. M., & Fait, H. F. (1989). *Special physical education: Adapted, individualized, and developmental.* Dubuque, IA: Brown & Benchmark.

Flanders, N. A. (1965). *Teacher influence, pupil attitudes, and achievement.* (Cooperative Monograph No. 12). Washington, DC: U.S. Office of Education.

Frankenburg, W., & Dodds, J. (1967). The Denver developmental screening test. *Journal of Pediatrics, 71,* 181–191.

Golding, L. A., Myers, C. R., & Sinning, W. E. (1989). *The Y's way to physical fitness.* Champaign, IL: Human Kinetics.

Griffin, P. S. (1982). Second thoughts on affective evaluation. *Journal of Physical Education, Recreation, and Dance, 53*(2), 25–26.

Hawaii Department of Education. (1979). *Physical education program guide.* Honolulu, HI: Hawaii Department of Education.

Hughes, J. (1979). *Hughes basic gross motor assessment manual.* Yonkers, NY: G. E. Miller.

Idaho Department of Education. (1982). *Nuts and bolts and climbing ropes: Physical education for Idaho schools K–6.* Boise, ID: Idaho Department of Education.

Illinois Association for Health, Physical Education, and Recreation. (1984). Criteria for evaluating elementary physical education in Illinois schools. *Illinois Journal of Health, Physical Education, and Recreation,* 39–43.

Illinois Association for Health, Physical Education, and Recreation. (1984). Criteria for evaluating physical education programs in Illinois schools. (Form 7–12). *Illinois Journal of Health, Physical Education, and Recreation,* 34–38.

Indiana Department of Education. (1969). *Indiana physical education score card for elementary and secondary schools.* Indianapolis, IN: Indiana Department of Education.

Johnson, B. L., & Nelson, J. K. (1986). *Practical measurements for evaluation in physical education.* Minneapolis, MN: Burgess.

Johnson, L. & Londeree, B. (1976). *Motor fitness testing manual for the moderately mentally retarded.* Reston, VA: AAHPERD.

Johnson, M. L. (1969). Construction of sportsmanship attitude scales. *Research Quarterly, 40,* 312–316.

Johnson, R. E., & Lavay, B. (1988). *Kansas adapted/special physical education test manual.* Topeka, KS: Kansas State Department of Education.

Kenyon, G. S. (1968a). A conceptual model for characterizing physical activity. *Research Quarterly, 39,* 96–105.

Kenyon, G. S. (1968b). Six scales for assessing attitude toward physical activity. *Research Quarterly, 39,* 566–574.

Kerlinger, F. (1971). Student evaluation of university professors. *School and Society, 99,* 353–356.

Kirkendall, D. R., Gruber, J. J., & Johnson, R. E. (1987). *Measurement and evaluation for physical educators.* Champaign, IL: Human Kinetics.

Lakie, W. L. (1964). Expressed attitudes of various groups of athletes toward athletic competition. *Research Quarterly, 35,* 497–503.

LaPorte, W. R. (1951). *LaPorte health and physical education score card I, II.* Los Angeles: Parker & Company.

LaPorte, W. R. (1968). *The physical education curriculum, a national program.* Los Angeles: College Book Store.

Loovis, M., & Ersing, W. F. (1979). *Assessing and programming gross motor development for children.* Loudonville, OH: Mohican.

Martinek, T., & Zaichkowsky, L. D. (1977). *Manual for the Martinek-Zaichkowsky*

Self-Concept Scale for Children. Jacksonville, IL: Psychologists & Educators.

Melograno, V. J. (1994). Portfolio assessment: Documenting authentic student learning. *Journal of Physical Education, Recreation, and Dance, 65*(8), 50–55, 58–61.

Merriam-Webster's Collegiate Dictionary (1993). Springfield, Massachusetts: Merriam-Websters, Inc.

Miller, A. G., & Sullivan, J. V. (1982). *Teaching physical activities to impaired youth: An approach to mainstreaming.* New York: John Wiley & Sons.

Miller, D. K. (1994). *Measurement by the physical educator: Why and how.* Dubuque, IA: Brown & Benchmark.

Mood, D. (1982). Evaluation in the affective domain? *Journal of Physical Education, Recreation, and Dance, 53*(2), 18–20.

Nelson, D. O. (1966). Leadership in sports. *Research Quarterly, 37,* 268–275.

Nichols, D. B., Arsenault, D. R., & Giuffre, D. L. (1980). *Motor activities for the underachiever.* Springfield, IL: Charles C. Thomas, Publisher.

Pennsylvania Department of Education. (1983). *Physical education competencies.* Harrisburg, PA: Pennsylvania Department of Education.

Perrone, V. (Ed.). (1991). *Expanding student assessment.* Alexandria, VA: Association for Supervision and Curriculum Development.

Piers, E., & Harris D. (1964). Age and other correlates of self-concept in children. *Journal of Educational Psychology, 55,* 91–95.

President's Council on Physical Fitness and Sports. (1991). *The President's Challenge Physical Fitness Program.* Washington, DC: President's Council on Physical Fitness and Sports.

Prudential Insurance Company of America. (1994). *Prudential FITNESSGRAM.* Dallas, TX: The Cooper Institute for Aerobics Research.

Rankin, K. D. (1975). *Verbal and non-verbal interaction analysis of student teachers with students in elementary physical education.* Lawrence, KS: University of Kansas.

Rhode Island Department of Education. (1991). *Suggested outcomes in physical education K–12.* Providence, RI: Rhode Island Department of Education.

Rink, J. E. (1979). *Development of an observation system for content development in physical education.* Unpublished doctoral dissertation. Columbus: OH: The Ohio State University.

Roach, E., & Kephart, N. (1966). *The Purdue perceptual-motor survey.* Columbus, OH: Merrill Publishing Company.

Siedentop, D. (1994). *Introduction to physical education, fitness, and sport.* Mountain View, CA: Mayfield.

Siedentop, D., Tousignant, M., & Parker, M. (1982). *Academic learning time-physical education: 1982 revision coding manual.* Columbus, OH: The Ohio State University.

Simon, J. A., & Smoll, F. L. (1974). An instrument for assessing children's attitude toward physical activity. *Research Quarterly, 45,* 407–415.

Thomas, N. (1980). Thoughts on teacher evaluation. *The Physical Educator, 37*(4), 176–178.

Toulmin, M. L. B. (1973). *The development of an original instrument to measure the expressed attitudes of children toward the elementary school program of physical education.* Denton, TX: Texas Woman's University.

Ulrich, D. A. (1986). *Test of gross motor development.* Austin, TX: Pro-ed.

Vodola, T. M. (1976). *Project ACTIVE maxi-model kit.* Oakhurst, NJ: Township of Ocean Park.

Wear, C. L. (1955). Construction of equivalent forms of an attitude scale. *Research Quarterly, 26,* 113–119.

Wessel, J. (1979). *I CAN: Locomotor and rhythmic skills.* Northbrook, IL: Hubbard Scientific.

Winnick, J. P., & Short, F. X. (1985). *Physical fitness testing of the disabled.* Champaign, IL: Human Kinetics.

Wise, M. K. (1976). *A comparison of attitudes of children and their parents toward athletic competition at the elementary school level.* Lincoln, NE: University of Nebraska.

Zessoules, R., & Garner, H. (1991). Authentic assessment: Beyond the buzzword and into the classroom. In V. Perrone (Ed.), *Expanding student assessment.* Alexandria, VA: Association for Supervision and Curriculum Development.

APPENDIX

SELF-APPRAISAL CHECKLIST FOR PHYSICAL EDUCATION IN IDAHO ELEMENTARY SCHOOLS

This self-appraisal checklist contains 116 items. Each item represents a criterion against which a school's program can be judged. Evaluation criteria are presented in the form of statements that describe attributes of school physical education programs. Each item states a condition that is regarded as highly desirable for a quality program. The evaluator should carefully read each statement and objectively determine the extent to which the statement describes the school's program. This is indicated by checking:

4—If the evaluator strongly agrees that the statement describes the program.
3—If the evaluator agrees that the statement describes the program.
2—If the evaluator is undecided.
1—If the evaluator disagrees that the statement describes the program.
0—If the evaluator strongly disagrees that the statement describes the program.

The rating of 4 for an item suggests that the stated attributes of the school's program is very satisfactory; a 3 indicates that the attribute is satisfactory; a 2 may identify that an aspect of the program is borderline between satisfactory and unsatisfactory; a 1 rating suggests that a need for program improvement exists; and a 0 indicates that a stated attribute is missing from the program.

A possible score is given for each category and for the total program, based on a rating for each statement. The *actual score* is the total of the rating given by the evaluator and should be compared to the *possible score* to determine the status of each category and the overall program. The *Summary of Scores* at the end of the checklist should be used to make these comparisons.

When the checklist has been completed, program improvements that are necessary should be identified on the basis of discrepancies between actual scores and possible scores. Needed improvements should be listed by categories. The list may then contribute to continuing the efforts toward improving the quality of the physical education program.

INTRODUCTION

A. *Philosophical Statement*—Physical education subscribes to the widely accepted concept of the unity of mind over body which is formulated on sound physiological, psychological, and sociological principles. The overall aim of physical education is to maximize opportunities for attaining motor skills, physical fitness, knowledge, understandings, and values through participating in movement experiences and the application of movement principles.

B. *Accountability Challenge*—You, the classroom teacher or specialist, are accountable for the development and teaching of the sequential skills of the students in your grade level.

C. *Legal and Professional Challenge*—Physical education on the elementary level should be taught a hundred fifty minutes per week or thirty minutes a day. As the educator responsible for teaching both the mental and physical education of students, you should have some training in elementary physical education. Excellent classes are available through state universities. In-service opportunities are also available through the Idaho State Department of Education, the Idaho Education Association Mobile Lab, and through local promotion of in-service programs.

I. PHILOSOPHY

Possible score = 112 points
Actual score = ___ points

Circle the appropriate response.
4 = Strongly agree
3 = Agree
2 = Undecided
1 = Disagree
0 = Strongly disagree

Item   **Rating**

1. A clear, written statement of the philosophy and principles on which the physical education program is based exists and is available to all staff members.   4 3 2 1 0

2. The physical education program is regarded as an integral part of
   the school's total education program.   4 3 2 1 0
3. The objectives of the physical education program include well
   defined outcomes for each learning experience which contributes
   to the development of the whole student. These objectives include
   specific outcomes in the areas of:
   (a) Knowledge and understanding (cognitive).   4 3 2 1 0
   (b) Motor skills (psychomotor).   4 3 2 1 0
   (c) Feelings, self success, and appreciation (affective).   4 3 2 1 0
4. The planned learning experiences in the physical education program
   are based on the principles of student growth and development.   4 3 2 1 0
5. The characteristics (abilities, interests, and needs) of elementary
   school students are considered when determining the scope and
   sequence of the program.   4 3 2 1 0
6. The program provides learning experiences that help the student.   4 3 2 1 0

Cognitive

(a) Understand the body in relation to the elements of movement
    (force, flow, time, and space), laws of motion, and principles of
    movement.   4 3 2 1 0
(b) Understand the role of physical activity in improving and
    maintaining strength, flexibility, and endurance.   4 3 2 1 0
(c) Understand the role of physical activity in promoting,
    maintaining, and improving emotional and physical health.   4 3 2 1 0
(d) Understand the fundamentals of movement patterns, stunts and
    tumbling, rhythms, and dance, and the skills of games and sports.   4 3 2 1 0
(e) Understand the rules involved in games and sports.   4 3 2 1 0
(f) Understand the techniques and strategies of games and sports.   4 3 2 1 0
(g) Understand the safety aspects involved in physical activity.   4 3 2 1 0

Psychomotor

(a) Be able to effectively perform movement patterns and skills of
    sports, games, and dance.   4 3 2 1 0
(b) Engage in activities that will improve and maintain agility.   4 3 2 1 0
(c) Engage in physical activities that help develop an individual's
    physical, mental, social, and emotional well-being.   4 3 2 1 0
(d) Follow rules in games and sports.   4 3 2 1 0
(e) Demonstrate the understanding of techniques in sports.   4 3 2 1 0
(f) Follow safety principles in all activities.   4 3 2 1 0

Affective

(a) Appreciate the human body in movement.   4 3 2 1 0
(b) Develop desirable attitudes toward physical fitness.   4 3 2 1 0
(c) Appreciate the role of physical activity in promoting, maintaining,
    and improving emotional and physical health.   4 3 2 1 0
(d) Appreciate skilled performance.   4 3 2 1 0
(e) Appreciate the need for rules.   4 3 2 1 0
(f) Appreciate the strategy and techniques of game play.   4 3 2 1 0
(g) Show regard for the safety of all participants in activity.   4 3 2 1 0

II. ORGANIZATION AND ADMINISTRATION

Possible score = 76 points
Actual score = ___ points

Circle the appropriate response.
4 = Strongly agree
3 = Agree
2 = Undecided
1 = Disagree
0 = Strongly disagree

Item	Rating
1. All students are enrolled in physical education classes and participate regularly in an instructional program of activity.	4 3 2 1 0
2. Physical activity is neither denied nor imposed as a punishment by any teacher.	4 3 2 1 0
3. Modified experiences are provided for students who are temporarily restricted from participating in a regular program of physical education.	4 3 2 1 0
4. Exclusion from the physical education program is allowed only on a physician's request. This request includes a statement about the student's condition and denotes a specific period of time for exclusion. The student's case must be reviewed by the physician and school personnel before the student is permitted to return to class.	4 3 2 1 0
5. A student's adapted program has been approved by a physician.	4 3 2 1 0
6. Students are scheduled for physical education in a manner that is not detrimental to their development and that takes into account their needs, interests, and abilities.	4 3 2 1 0
7. Students are provided coeducational experiences at all levels.	4 3 2 1 0
8. Instructional activities are planned in a developmental progression according to an accepted curriculum guide.	4 3 2 1 0
9. Lesson plans for daily instruction are readily available.	4 3 2 1 0
10. The specific objectives of the daily activities are clearly stated.	4 3 2 1 0
11. A system of evaluation is used to report student progress.	4 3 2 1 0
12. The evaluation is consistent with objectives of the program.	4 3 2 1 0
13. Hazards relating to the following areas have been eliminated:	
(a) Facilities.	4 3 2 1 0
(b) Equipment.	4 3 2 1 0
(c) Activities.	4 3 2 1 0
(d) Teaching methods.	4 3 2 1 0
14. An accident policy has been developed that includes procedures for the following:	
(a) Accident prevention.	4 3 2 1 0
(b) First aid.	4 3 2 1 0
(c) Reporting plan.	4 3 2 1 0

III. CLASS MANAGEMENT

Possible score = 40 points
Actual score = ___ points

Circle the appropriate response.
4 = Strongly agree
3 = Agree
2 = Undecided
1 = Disagree
0 = Strongly disagree

Item	Rating
1. Class sizes are kept to a minimum with no more than thirty to thirty-five students assigned to one teacher.	4 3 2 1 0
2. Teacher load, including class instruction and extra-curricular responsibilities, does not exceed six and a half hours per day or three hundred students per day.	4 3 2 1 0
3. The daily class period arrangement includes the following:	
(a) Adequate time for changing clothes.	4 3 2 1 0
(b) Instructional program of twenty minutes minimum for grades K–1.	4 3 2 1 0
(c) Instructional program of thirty minutes minimum for grades 2–4.	4 3 2 1 0
(d) Instructional program of thirty minutes minimum for grades 5–6.	4 3 2 1 0
4. Students share in planning activities.	4 3 2 1 0
5. Appropriate teaching aids (films, slides, charts, and models) are used when applicable.	4 3 2 1 0
6. Students and instructors are appropriately attired for all class work. (Wearing apparel is suitable for physical and psychological freedom of movement.)	4 3 2 1 0
7. Student leadership is developed and utilized by providing opportunities for leading, coaching, planning, and managing.	4 3 2 1 0

IV. THE STAFF

Possible score = 40 points
Actual score = ___ points

Circle the appropriate response.
4 = Strongly agree
3 = Agree
2 = Undecided
1 = Disagree
0 = Strongly disagree

Item	Rating
1. The teacher in charge of the physical education program accepts responsibility for the following:	
(a) Planning.	4 3 2 1 0
(b) Establishing and maintaining positive student-teacher relationships.	4 3 2 1 0
(c) Developing and implementing the physical education program.	4 3 2 1 0
(d) Using a variety of teaching methods.	4 3 2 1 0
(e) Maintaining positive relationships with other teachers, administrators, and parents.	4 3 2 1 0

    (f) Participating in school and community events.   4 3 2 1 0
    (g) Correlating physical education with other events.   4 3 2 1 0
2. The teacher follows a plan for personal and professional growth through participation in graduate work, workshops, and conferences.   4 3 2 1 0
3. The school or school system has a definite, well organized, in-service education program for improving the quality of instruction in physical education classes.   4 3 2 1 0
4. Teachers show great concern for the work and dignity of all students.   4 3 2 1 0

V. THE CURRICULUM

Possible score = 32 points
Actual score = ___ points

Circle the appropriate response.
4 = Strongly agree
3 = Agree
2 = Undecided
1 = Disagree
0 = Strongly disagree

Item	Rating
1. The physical education curriculum includes basic movement, fundamental motor skills, stunts and tumbling, rhythms and dance, and games and sports.	4 3 2 1 0
2. The curriculum includes the effects of activity on the human organism.	4 3 2 1 0
3. The program is specifically structured around the needs, interests, and abilities of the students.	4 3 2 1 0
4. The program is as broad in scope as the facilities will permit.	4 3 2 1 0
5. An annual evaluation of the instructional program will be reviewed using current data and criteria.	4 3 2 1 0
6. A course of study committee gives annual consideration to needed revisions in the program and makes appropriate adjustments.	4 3 2 1 0
7. The course of study is formally revised at least every five years.	4 3 2 1 0
8. A definite sequential program exists from year to year and progression is indicated in each year's program.	4 3 2 1 0

VI. FACILITIES AND EQUIPMENT

Possible score = 88 points
Actual score = ___ points

Circle the appropriate response.
4 = Strongly agree
3 = Agree
2 = Undecided
1 = Disagree
0 = Strongly disagree

Item	Rating
1. Indoor and outdoor facilities are designed to be used by school, community, and recreation groups.	4 3 2 1 0
2. The outdoor area is properly lined, surfaced, graded, drained, enclosed, and free from hazards.	4 3 2 1 0
3. The outdoor area is adjacent to the school building and is large enough to provide for the program.	4 3 2 1 0
4. The gymnasium and auxiliary indoor teaching stations meet the following criteria: floors are properly painted with lines; area is free of safety and health hazards; ceilings are at least twenty feet high; and sufficient adjacent storage space is available.	4 3 2 1 0
5. The gymnasium is used primarily as a physical education facility.	4 3 2 1 0
6. Sufficient gymnasium space is provided to enable the school to schedule physical education for a minimum of two periods per week per student.	4 3 2 1 0
7. Adequate equipment is available, such as the following:	
(a) Climbing apparatus.	4 3 2 1 0
(b) Balancing apparatus.	4 3 2 1 0
(c) Vaulting apparatus.	4 3 2 1 0
(d) Mats.	4 3 2 1 0
(e) Standards or attachments for nets.	4 3 2 1 0
(f) Cabinets for storing supplies.	4 3 2 1 0
(g) Record players or tape recorders.	4 3 2 1 0
8. Supplies are available in quantities that permit active participation of all students. Available supplies include the following:	
(a) Jump ropes.	4 3 2 1 0
(b) Phonograph records.	4 3 2 1 0
(c) Balls (playground, soccer, volleyball, football, and basketball).	4 3 2 1 0
(d) Paddles.	4 3 2 1 0
(e) Clubs.	4 3 2 1 0
(f) Bats.	4 3 2 1 0
(g) Bean bags.	4 3 2 1 0
(h) Hoops.	4 3 2 1 0
(i) Other equipment.	4 3 2 1 0

VII. CO-CURRICULAR ACTIVITIES

        Possible score = 16 points   Circle the appropriate response.
        Actual score   = ___ points   4 = Strongly agree
                                                   3 = Agree
                                                   2 = Undecided
                                                   1 = Disagree
                                                   0 = Strongly disagree

Item	Rating
1. Extracurricular activities are an outgrowth of the instructional program.	4 3 2 1 0
2. A comprehensive program of intramural activities is provided for all students.	4 3 2 1 0
3. Opportunities are provided for participation in non-competitive intramural activities such as rhythms and dance, and rope jumping.	4 3 2 1 0
4. Demonstrations, play days, and sport days are correlated with other school activities.	4 3 2 1 0

VIII. EVALUATION

        Possible score = 56 points   Circle the appropriate response.
        Actual score   = ___ points   4 = Strongly agree
                                                   3 = Agree
                                                   2 = Undecided
                                                   1 = Disagree
                                                   0 = Strongly disagree

Item	Rating
Student	
1. A system for reporting student progress exists.	4 3 2 1 0
2. The report of student progress is consistent with the objectives of the physical education program and the total program.	4 3 2 1 0
3. A variety of tests and instruments are used to evaluate students formally and informally.	4 3 2 1 0
These include:	
(a) Tests—Skill, fitness, and knowledge (subjective or objective).	4 3 2 1 0
(b) Conferences with students.	4 3 2 1 0
(c) Observation of changes in behavior in areas of knowledge and understanding, motor skills, and feeling states.	4 3 2 1 0
4. The system of evaluation and grading is understood by all students.	4 3 2 1 0
Curriculum	
1. An annual evaluation of the instructional program exists.	4 3 2 1 0
2. Students, administrators, faculty, and parents share in the evaluation of curriculum.	4 3 2 1 0

3. The school is making continuous efforts to update its program by striving for the following:
   (a) Daily instruction in physical education. 4 3 2 1 0
   (b) Adequate facilities and equipment. 4 3 2 1 0
   (c) Certified staff in physical education. 4 3 2 1 0

Teacher

1. Periodic formal evaluation of the teacher exists. 4 3 2 1 0
2. The purpose of the teacher evaluation is to aid in the improvement of instruction. 4 3 2 1 0

SUMMARY OF SCORES

Part	Area	Possible Points	Actual Points
I.	Philosophy	112	_____
II.	Organization and Administration	76	_____
III.	Class Management	40	_____
IV.	The Staff	40	_____
V.	The Curriculum	32	_____
VI.	Facilities and Equipment	88	_____
VII.	Co-Curricular Activities	16	_____
VIII.	Evaluation	56	_____
Total		**460**	_____

REFERENCES

Adams, R. S. (1963). Two scales for measuring attitude toward physical education. *Research Quarterly, 34,* 91–94.

Adams, T. M., Kandt, G. K., Throgmartin, D., & Waldrop, P. B. (1991). Computer-assisted instruction vs. lecture methods in teaching the rules of golf. *Physical Educator, 48*(3), 146–150.

Alabama Governor's Commission on Physical Fitness. (1990). *Youth fitness test manual.* Montgomery, AL: Governor's Commission on Physical Fitness.

Aldana, S. G., & Stone, W. J. (1991). Changing physical activity preferences of American adults. *Journal of Physical Education, Recreation, and Dance, 62*(4), 67–71, 73.

Alexander, W. (1971). How fares the middle school? *National Elementary Principal, 51,* 8–11.

Alighieri, D. (1948). *The divine comedy, the inferno, purgatorio, and paradiso.* New York: Pantheon Books.

Almond, L. (1983). Games making. *Bulletin of Physical Education, 19*(1), 25–32.

American Alliance for Health, Physical Education, and Recreation. (1981). *Basic stuff series I.* Washington, DC: AAHPERD.

American Alliance for Health, Physical Education, and Recreation. (1981). *Basic stuff series II.* Washington, DC: AAHPERD.

American Alliance for Health, Physical Education, and Recreation. (1987). *Basic stuff series I.* Washington, DC: AAHPERD.

American Alliance for Health, Physical Education, and Recreation. (1987). *Basic stuff series II.* Washington, DC: AAHPERD.

American Alliance for Health, Physical Education, Recreation, and Dance. (1976). *Special fitness test manual for the mildly mentally retarded* (2nd ed.). Reston, VA: AAHPERD.

American Alliance for Health, Physical Education, Recreation, and Dance. (1976). *Youth fitness test manual.* Reston, VA: AAHPERD.

American Alliance for Health, Physical Education, Recreation, and Dance. (1977). *Assessment guide for secondary school physical education programs.* Reston, VA: AAHPERD.

American Alliance for Health, Physical Education, Recreation, and Dance. (1980). *Health-related physical fitness test manual.* Reston, VA: AAHPERD.

American Alliance for Health, Physical Education, Recreation, and Dance. (1987). *Program appraisal checklist for elementary school physical education programs.* Reston, VA: AAHPERD.

American Alliance for Health, Physical Education, Recreation, and Dance. (1988). *Physical best.* Reston, VA: AAHPERD.

American Cancer Society. (1990). *Cancer facts and figures—1989.* New York: The Society.

American College of Sports Medicine. (1993). *Resource manual for guidelines for exercise test-*

ing and prescription. Philadelphia: Lea & Febiger.

American Council on Education. (1980). *The evaluative criteria, national study of secondary school evaluation.* Washington, DC: American Council on Education.

American Health and Fitness Foundation. (1986). *FTY program manual.* Austin, TX: American Health and Fitness Foundation.

American Sport Education Program. (1996). *Raising the standard: The 1996 national interscholastic coaching requirements report.* Champaign, IL: Human Kinetics.

Anderson, W. G. (1989). Curriculum and program research in physical education: Selected approaches. *Journal of Teaching in Physical Education, 8,* 112–114.

Annarino, A. A., Cowell, C. C., & Hazelton, H. W. (1986). *Curriculum theory and design in physical education.* Prospect Heights, IL: Waveland Press.

Arizona Department of Education. (1990). *Comprehensive health essential skills.* Phoenix, AZ: Arizona Department of Education.

Arnheim, D. D., & Sinclair, W. A. (1985). *Physical education for special populations: A developmental, adapted, and remedial approach.* Englewood Cliffs, NJ: Prentice-Hall.

Arnold, P. J. (1980). Values of being in sport. The Academy Papers. Reston, VA: AAHPERD, *(14),* 31–33.

Austin, S., & Meister, G. (1990). *Responding to children at risk: A guide to recent reports.* Philadelphia: Research for Better Schools.

Auxter, D., & Pyfer, J. (1989). *Principles and methods of adapted physical education and recreation.* St. Louis, MO: Mosby.

Bain, L. L. (1975). The hidden curriculum in physical education. *Quest, 24,* 92–101.

Bain, L. L. (1976). Description of the hidden curriculum in secondary physical education. *Research Quarterly, 47,* 154–160.

Bain, L. L. (1979). Perceived characteristics of selected movement activities. *Research Quarterly, 50,* 565–573.

Baldwin, J. (1989). A talk to teachers. In R. Simonson, S. Walker (eds.), *The graywolf annual five: Multicultural literacy.* St. Paul, MN: Graywolf Press.

Banks, J. A. (1992). Creating multicultural learner-centered schools. In A. Lieberman, *Building learner-centered schools: Three perspectives.* New York: National Center for Restructuring Education, Schools, and Teaching.

Barrow, H. M., McGee, R., & Tritschler, K. A. (1989). *Practical measurement in physical education and sport.* Philadelphia: Lea & Febiger.

Baumgartner, T. A., & Jackson, A. S. (1991). *Measurement for evaluation in physical education and exercise science.* Dubuque, IA: Brown.

Beach, B. (1982). Why do you run? *Journal of Physical Education, Recreation, and Dance, 53*(3), 25.

Bennett, C. I. (1990). *Comprehensive multicultural education: Theory and practice.* Boston: Allyn & Bacon.

Berryman, D., Lefebve, C., Kinney, W., & Dickason, J. (1974). *Systems utilization for comprehensive modular planning of therapeutic recreation services for disabled children and youth.* New York: New York University.

Berryman-Miller, S. (1991). Multicultural dance: The spirit of cultural tradition. *Journal of Physical Education, Recreation, and Dance, 62*(2), 33.

Birch, D. A. (1992). Improving leadership skills in curriculum development. *Journal of School Health, 62*(1), 27–28.

Blanchard, B. E. (1936). A behavior frequency rating scale for the measurement of character and personality traits in a physical education classroom situation. *Research Quarterly, 7,* 56–66.

Block, M. E. (1994). Why all students with disabilities should be included in regular physical education. *Palaestra, 10*(3), 17–24.

Block, M. E., & Vogler, E. W. (1994). Inclusion in regular physical education: The research base. *Journal of Physical Education, Recreation, and Dance, 45*(1), 40–44.

Block, M. E., & Vogler, E. W. (1994). Innovative and adaptive curriculum models for full inclusion. *Teaching Elementary Physical Education, 5*(5), 6–7.

Bloom, B. S., Hastings, J. T., & Madaus, G. F. (1971). *Handbook of formative and summative evaluation of student learning*. New York: McGraw-Hill.

Bookwalter, K. W. (1964). *Physical education in secondary schools*. New York: The Center for Applied Research in Education.

Bredikamp, S. (1992). What is developmentally appropriate and why is it important? *Journal of Health, Physical Education, Recreation, and Dance, 63*(6), 31–32.

Brigance, A. (1978). *The Brigance diagnostic inventory of early development*. Worburn, MA: Curriculum Associates.

Bruininks, R. H. (1978). *Bruininks-Oseretsky test of motor proficiency: Examiner's manual*. Circle Pines, MN: American Guidance Service.

Bruner, J. (1974). *The process of education*. New York: Vintage Books.

Brustad, R. J., & Zehrung, D. A. (1994). Effects of daily vs. every-other day physical education instruction upon indices of physical fitness, motor skill, and psychological characteristics of third grade children. *Research Quarterly for Exercise and Sport, 65*, A73.

Bucher, C. A. (1977). *Administration of school and college health and physical education programs*. St. Louis, MO: Mosby.

Bucher, C. A., & Koenig, C. R. (1983). *Methods and materials for secondary school physical education*. St. Louis, MO: Mosby.

Bucher, C. A., & Thaxton, N. A. (1979). *Physical education for children: Movement foundations and experiences*. New York: Macmillan Publishing Company.

Bunker, D., & Thorpe, R. (1982). A model for the teaching of games in secondary schools. *Bulletin of Physical Education, 18*, 5–8.

Butt, K. L., & Pahnos, M. L. (1995). Why we need a multicultural focus in our schools. *Journal of Physical Education, Recreation, and Dance, 66*(1), 48–53.

Caldwell, S. F. (1972). Toward a humanistic physical education. *Journal of Health, Physical Education, and Recreation, 43*(3), 31–32.

Carr, M. G. (1945). The relationship between success in physical education and selected attitudes expressed by high school freshman girls. *Research Quarterly, 16*, 176–191.

Carroll, R. (1981). CSE in physical education: An evaluation. *Bulletin of Physical Education, 17*, 5–15.

Castetter, W. B. (1971). *The personnel function in public administration*. New York: Macmillan Publishing Company.

Cawelti, G. (1990). How will students be different in the 21st century? *Interchange: Alliance for Arts Education*. Washington, DC: The John F. Kennedy Center for the Performing Arts.

Centers for Disease Control. (1987). Bicycle-related injuries: Data from the national electronic injury surveillance system. *Mortality and Morbidity Weekly Reports, 36*, 269–271.

Chambers, R. L. (1988). Legal and practical issues for grouping students in physical education classes. *The Physical Educator, 45*(4), 180–185.

Cheffers, J., & Evaul, T. (1978). *Introduction to physical education: Concepts of human movement*. Englewood Cliffs, NJ: Prentice-Hall.

Cheffers, J., & Keilty, G. C. (1980). Developing valid instrumentation for measuring teacher effectiveness. *International Journal of Physical Education, 17*, 15–23.

Chepyator-Thomson, J. R. (1994). Multicultural education: Culturally responsive teaching. *Journal of Physical Education, Recreation, and Dance, 65*(9), 31.

Child Advocacy Center. (1991). *Mainstreaming . . . integration . . . inclusion: What does it mean and how can we make it happen?* Cincinnati, OH: Child Advocacy Center.

Children's Defense Fund. (1992). *The state of America's children*. Washington, DC.

Chittenden, E. (1991). Authentic assessment, evaluation, and documentation of student performance. In V. Perrone (Ed.), *Expanding student assessment*. Alexandria, VA: Association for Supervision and Curriculum Development.

Chrysler Fund–Amateur Athletic Union. (1991). *Chrysler Fund–AAU Physical Fitness Program*. Bloomington, IN: Chrysler–Amateur Athletic Union.

Combs, A. W. (1979). *Myths in education.* Boston: Allyn & Bacon.

Commission of the Reorganization of Secondary Education. (1918). *Cardinal principles of secondary education.* Washington, DC: Bureau of Education, Bulletin 35.

Committee on Trauma Research, Commission on Life Sciences, National Research Council, and Institute of Medicine. (1988). *Injury in America: A continuing public health problem.* Washington, DC: National Academy Press.

Conant, J. F. (1961). *Slums and suburbs.* New York: McGraw-Hill.

Conrad, H. L., & Meister, J. F. (1938). *Teaching procedures in health education.* Philadelphia: Saunders.

Cooper Institute for Aerobics Research. (1992). *Prudential FITNESSGRAM.* Dallas, TX: Cooper Institute for Aerobics Research.

Cooper, K. (1978). *The aerobics way.* New York: Bantam Books.

Corbin, C., & Lindsey, R. (1994). *Concepts of physical fitness with laboratories.* Dubuque, IA: Brown & Benchmark.

Cowell, C. C. (1958). Validating an index of social adjustment for high school use. *Research Quarterly, 29,* 7–10.

Cowell, C. C., & France, W. L. (1963). *Philosophy and principles of physical education.* Englewood Cliffs, NJ: Prentice-Hall.

Craft, D. (1994). Strategies for teaching inclusively. *Teaching Elementary Physical Education, 5*(5), 8–9.

Cratty, B. J. (1967). *Social dimensions of physical activity.* Englewood Cliffs, NJ: Prentice-Hall.

Cratty, B. J. (1986). *Perceptual and motor development in infants and children* Englewood Cliffs, NJ: Prentice-Hall.

Cratty, B. J. (1989). *Adapted physical education in the mainstream.* Denver, CO: Love Publishing Company.

Cratty, B. J., Ikedo, N., Martin, M., Jennett, C., & Morris, M. (1970). *Movement activities, motor ability, and the education of children.* Springfield, IL: Charles C. Thomas Publisher.

Csikszentmihalyi, M., & McCormack, J. (1986). The influence of teachers. *Phi Delta Kappan, 67,* 415–419.

Culkin, D., & Davis, H. (1992). Basic data analysis for non-researchers. *Journal of Physical Education, Recreation, and Dance, 63*(8), 29–31, 57.

Daniels, A. S., & Davies, E. (1982). *Adapted physical education.* New York: Harper & Row.

Darst, P. W., & Armstrong, G. P. (1991). *Outdoor adventure activities for school and recreation programs.* Prospect Heights, IL: Waveland Press.

Darst, P. W., Mancini, V. H., & Zakrajsek, D. B. (1983). *Systematic observation instrumentation for physical education.* West Point, NY: Leisure Press.

Darst, P. W., Zakrajsek, D. B., & Mancini, V. H. (1989). *Analyzing physical education and sport instruction.* Champaign, IL: Human Kinetics.

Daughtrey, G., & Lewis, C. (1979). *Effective teaching strategies in secondary physical education.* Philadelphia: Saunders.

Davis, R., & Davis, T. (1994). Inclusion and least restrictive environments. *Teaching Elementary Physical Education, 5*(5), 1, 4–5.

Defina, A. A. (1992). *Portfolio assessment: Getting started.* New York: Scholastic Professional Books.

Dewey, J. (1970). *The way out of educational confusion.* Westport, CT: Greenwood Press.

Dodds, P. (1983). *Consciousness raising in curriculum: A teachers' model for analysis.* Paper presented at the Third Physical Education Curriculum Theory Conference, Athens, GA, February 10–12.

Dougherty, N. J., & Bonanno, D. (1986). *Contemporary approaches to the teaching of physical education.* Minneapolis, MN: Burgess.

Dubos, R. (1981). *Celebrations of life.* New York: McGraw-Hill.

Dulaney, N. M., & Corbin, C. B. (1993). Effects of flexibility training on school children. *Research Quarterly for Exercise and Sport, 64,* A40.

Dunham, P. (1994). *Evaluation for physical education.* Englewood, CO: Morton Publishing Company.

Dunn, J. M., & Fait, H. F. (1989). *Special physical education: Adapted, individualized, and developmental*. Dubuque, IA: Brown & Benchmark.

Durrant, S. M. (1992). Title IX: Its power and its limitations. *Journal of Physical Education, Recreation, and Dance, 63*(3), 60–64.

Eddy, J. M., & Beltz, S. M. (1989). Health-related outcomes of participation in CIGNA's preventive medical program. *Fitness in Business*, April, 164–170.

Educational Policies Commission, (1961). *Policies for education in American democracy: The central purpose of American education*. Washington, DC: National Education Association.

Ehrlich, P. R., & Ehrlich, A. H. (1972). *Population resources, environment: Issues in human ecology*. San Francisco: W. H. Freeman & Company Publishers.

Ellis, M. (1983). *Similarities and differences in games: A system for classification*. Paper presented at the International AIESEP Congress.

Engelman, S. (1969). *Conceptual learning*. Sioux Falls, SD: Adapt Press.

Engh, F. (1992). National youth sports coaches association (NYSCA): More than just a certification program. *Journal of Physical Education, Recreation, and Dance, 63*(7), 43–45.

Ersing, W. F. (1974). The nature of physical education programming for the mentally retarded and physically handicapped. *Journal of Health, Physical Education, and Recreation, 45*(2), 89–91.

Ewing, M. E., & Seefeldt, V. (1990). *American youth and sports participation*. North Palm Beach, FL: Athletic Footwear Association.

Fagles, R. (1990). *Homer's the iliad*. New York: Viking.

Fait, H. (1976). *Experiences in movement: Physical education for the elementary school child*. Philadelphia: Saunders.

Fallon, D. (1977). A man unchained. *Journal of Physical Education and Recreation, 48*(5), 43–45.

Falls, H. B. (1980). *Essentials of fitness*. Philadelphia: Saunders.

Fast, B. (1971). Contingency contracting. *Journal of Health, Physical Education, Recreation, and Dance, 42*(8), 31–32.

Felshin, J. (1974). Cultural considerations for physical education. In G. H. McGlynn (ed.), *Issues in physical education and sports*. Palo Alto, CA: National Press Books.

Fielding, L. W. (1977). Marcus Tullius Cicero: A social critic of sport. *Canadian Journal of History of Sports and Physical Education, 8*, 16–27.

Figone, A. J. (1994). Teacher-coach role conflict: Its impact on students and student-athletes. *The Physical Educator, 51*(1), 29–34.

Fisher, I. (1946). *How to live: Rules for healthful living based on modern science*. New York: Funk & Wagnalls Company.

Flanders, N. A. (1965). *Teacher influence, pupil attitudes, and achievement*. (Cooperative Monograph No. 12). Washington, DC: U.S. Office of Education.

Fluegelman, A. (1976). *The new games book*. Garden City, NY: Dolphin Books.

Fluegelman, A. (1981). *More new games*. Garden City, NY: Dolphin Books.

Frankenburg, W., & Dodds, J. (1967). The Denver developmental screening test. *Journal of Pediatrics, 71*, 181–191.

Frith, G. H. (1982). *The role of the special education paraprofessional. An introductory text*. Springfield, IL: Charles C. Thomas, Publisher.

Gabbard, C. (1996). *Lifelong motor development*. Dubuque, IA: Brown & Benchmark.

Gabbard, C., LeBlanc, E., & Lowy, S. (1987). *Physical education for children: Building the foundation*. Englewood Cliffs, NJ: Prentice-Hall.

Gallahue, D. L. (1996). *Developmental physical education for today's children*. Dubuque, IA: Brown & Benchmark.

Gibran, K. (1923). *The prophet*. New York: Alfred A. Knopf.

Girls participation reaches all-time high. (1994). *National Federation News*, November/December, *12* (3) 12–13.

Glasser, W. (1976). *Positive addiction*. New York: Harper & Row.

Goldberger, L., & Breznitz, S. (eds.). (1982). *Handbook of stress: Theoretical and clinical aspects*. New York: The Free Press.

Golding, L. A., Myers, C. R., & Sinning, W. E. (1989). *The Y's way to physical fitness.* Champaign, IL: Human Kinetics.

Graham, G. (1977). Helping students design their own games. *Journal of Physical Education, Recreation, and Dance, 48*(7), 35.

Graham, G., Holt/Hale, S., McEwen, T., & Parker, M. (1987). *Children moving: A reflective approach to teaching physical education.* Palo Alto, CA: Mayfield.

Gray, J. A. (1992). Creating and navigating a dance research database. *Journal of Physical Education, and Recreation, and Dance, 63*(8), 29–31, 57.

Greene, L. (1989). *Sport specific aerobic routines.* Dubuque, IA: Eddie Bowers Publishing Company.

Griffin, P. S. (1982). Second thoughts on affective evaluation. *Journal of Physical Education, Recreation, and Dance, 53*(2), 25–26.

Gustafson, J. (1973). Making programmed instruction practical. *The Physical Educator, 30*(2), 91–92.

Hall, G. S. (1965). *Health, growth, and heredity.* New York: Teachers College Press.

Hammersley, C. H. (1992). If we win, I win: Adventure education in physical education and recreation. *Journal of Physical Education, Recreation, and Dance, 63*(9), 63–67, 72.

Hankin, T. (1992). Presenting creative dance activities to children: Guidelines for the nondancer. *Journal of Physical Education, Recreation, and Dance, 63*(2), 22–24.

Hardman, M. L., Drew, C. J., & Egan, M. W. (1987). *Human exceptionality, society, school and family.* Boston: Allyn & Bacon.

Harris, J. A., Pittman, A. M., & Waller, M. S. (1988). *Dance a while: Handbook of folk, square, contra, and social dance.* New York: Macmillan Publishing Company.

Harrow, A. J. (1972). *A taxonomy of the psychomotor domain.* New York: David McKay.

Hass, G. (1987). *Curriculum planning: A new approach.* Boston: Allyn & Bacon.

Haubenstricker, J. L. (1982). Motor development in children with learning disabilities. *Journal of Physical Education, Recreation, and Dance, 53*(5), 41–43.

Hawaii Department of Education. (1979). *Physical education program guide.* Honolulu, HI: Hawaii Department of Education.

Health Education and Public Law 93.641. (1977). *Focal points.* Atlanta, GA: Bureau of Health Education, July, 2–4.

Heitmann, H. M., & Kneer, M. E. (1976). *Physical education instructional techniques: An individualized humanistic approach.* Englewood Cliffs, NJ: Prentice-Hall.

Helion, J. G., & Fry, F. F. (1995). Modifying activities for developmental appropriateness. *Journal of Physical Education, Recreation, and Dance, 66*(7), 57–59.

Hellison, D. R. (1973). *Humanistic physical education.* Englewood Cliffs, NJ: Prentice-Hall.

Hellison, D. R. (1978). *Beyond balls and bats.* Washington, DC: AAHPERD.

Hellison, D. R. (1982). Attitude and behavior change in the gym: The Oregon story. *The Physical Educator, 34*(2), 67–70.

Hellison, D. R. (1983). Teaching self-responsibility (and more). *Journal of Physical Education, Recreation, and Dance, 54*(8), 23.

Hellison, D. R. (1985). *Goals and strategies for teaching physical education.* Champaign, IL: Human Kinetics.

Hellison, D. R., & Templin, T. J. (1991). *A reflective approach to teaching physical education.* Champaign, IL: Human Kinetics.

Higgins, R. J. (1979). American athletic mentality: Identities and conflict. In A. Yiannakis (Ed.), *Sport sociology: Contemporary themes.* Dubuque, IA: Kendall/Hunt Publishing Company.

Hopkins, C. T. (1941). *Interaction: The democratic process.* Lexington, MA: Heath.

Howe, C. Z. (1981). From leisure ethic to reindustrialization. *Journal of Physical Education, Recreation, and Dance, 52*(9), 38–39.

Hughes, J. (1979). *Hughes basic gross motor assessment manual.* Yonkers, NY: G. E. Miller.

Idaho Department of Education. (1982). *Nuts and bolts and climbing ropes: Physical education for Idaho schools K–6.* Boise, ID: Idaho Department of Education.

Illinois Association for Health, Physical Education, and Recreation. (1984). 1980 Criteria for evaluating elementary physical education in Illinois schools. *Illinois Journal of Health, Physical Education, and Recreation,* 39–43.

Illinois Association for Health, Physical Education, and Recreation. (1984). Criteria for evaluating physical education programs in Illinois schools. (Form 7–12). *Illinois Journal of Health, Physical Education, and Recreation,* 34–38.

Indiana Department of Education. (1969). *Indiana physical education score card for elementary and secondary schools.* Indianapolis, IN: Indiana Department of Education.

Information Please Almanac. (1994). New York: Houghton Mifflin Company.

Jagger, B. (1977). A characterization of physical education and human movement. In J. E. Kane (Ed.), *Movement studies and physical education.* London: Routledge & Kegan Paul.

Jansma, P. (1977). Get ready for mainstreaming. *Journal of Physical Education and Recreation,* 48(7), 15–16.

Jay, D. (1991). Effect of a dance program on the creativity of preschool handicapped children. *Adapted Physical Activity Quarterly,* 8, 305–316.

Jewett, A. E., & Bain, L. L., Ennis, C. D. (1995). *The curriculum process in physical education.* Dubuque, IA: Brown & Benchmark.

Jewett, A. E., & Miller, M. E. (1977). *Curriculum design: Purposes and processes in physical education teaching-learning.* Washington, DC: AAHPERD.

Jewett, A. E., Bain, L. L., & Ennis, C. D. (1995). *The curriculum process in physical education.* Dubuque, IA: Brown & Benchmark.

Johnson, B. L., & Nelson, J. K. (1986). *Practical measurements for evaluation in physical education.* Minneapolis, MN: Burgess.

Johnson, L. & Londeree, B. (1976). *Motor fitness testing manual for the moderately mentally retarded.* Reston, VA: AAHPERD.

Johnson, M. L. (1969). Construction of sportsmanship attitude scales. *Research Quarterly,* 40, 312–316.

Johnson, R. E., & Lavay, B. (1988). *Kansas adapted/special physical education test manual.* Topeka, KS: Kansas State Department of Education.

Johnson, W. S., & Morris, D. C. (1981). Students as active participants: The case for student oriented research. *Educational Research Quarterly,* 6, 38–45.

Justen, J. E., Adams, T. M., & Waldrop, P. B. (1988). Effects of small group versus individual user computer-assisted instruction on student achievement. *Educational Technology,* 28(2), 50–52.

Kanters, M. A., & Montelpare, W. J. (1994). Enabling healthy lives through leisure. *Journal of Physical Education, Recreation, and Dance,* 65(4), 27.

Karper, W. B. & Martinek, T. J. (1983). Motor performance and self-concepts of handicapped children and nonhandicapped children in integrated physical education classes. *American Corrective Therapy Journal,* 37(3), 91–95.

Katz, A., Branch, L., Branson, M., Papsidero, J., Beck, J., & Greer, D. (1983). Active life expectancy. *New England Journal of Medicine,* 309, 1218–1224.

Keeney, G. L., & Sunnarborg, K. R. (1992). Strategies for identifying health information: One practitioner's experience. *Journal of Physical Education, Recreation, and Dance,* 63(10), 26–28.

Kelly, B., & Kelly, N. (1990). *Physical education for the middle school.* Springfield, IL: Charles C. Thomas.

Kelly, L. J. (1987). Computer assisted instruction: Applications for physical education. *Journal of Physical Education, Recreation and Dance,* 58(4), 74–79.

Kelly, L. J., & Vergason, G. A. (1978). *Dictionary of special education and rehabilitation.* Denver, CO: Love Publishing Company.

Kennedy, J. F. (1960). The soft American. *Sports Illustrated,* December 26, 15–17.

Kenyon, G. S. (1968a). A conceptual model for characterizing physical activity. *Research Quarterly,* 39, 96–105.

Kenyon, G. S. (1968b). Six scales for assessing attitude toward physical activity. *Research Quarterly,* 39, 566–574.

Kerlinger, F. (1971). Student evaluation of university professors. *School and Society, 99,* 353–356.

Kerns, M. M. (1989). The effectiveness of computer-assisted instruction in teaching tennis rules and strategies. *Journal of Teaching in Physical Education, 8,* 170–176.

King, C. S. (Ed.). (1987). *The words of Martin Luther King, Jr.* New York: Newmarket Press.

Kirchner, G., & Fishburne, G. (1995). *Physical education for elementary school children.* Dubuque, IA: Brown & Benchmark.

Kirkendall, D. R., Gruber, J. J., & Johnson, R. E. (1987). *Measurement and evaluation for physical educators.* Champaign, IL: Human Kinetics.

Kleiber, D. A., & Fiscella, J. (1982). Leisure as interlude. *Journal of Physical Education, Recreation, and Dance, 54*(9), 46.

Kliebaard, H. (1968). The curriculum field in retrospect. In Paul W. F. Witt, (Ed.), *Technology and the curriculum.* New York: Teachers College Press.

Kneer, M. E. (1982). Ability grouping in physical education. *Journal of Physical Education, Recreation, and Dance, 53*(9), 10–13.

Knott, E. S. (1991). Working with culturally diverse learners. *Journal of Developmental Education, 13*(2), 14–18.

Kovich, M. (1971). Sports as an art form. *Journal of Physical Education and Recreation, 42*(8), 42.

Krawthwohl, D. R., Bloom, B. S., & Masia, B. B. (1964). *Taxonomy of educational objectives: Handbook II affective domain.* New York: David McKay.

Kraus, R. G. (1977). *Recreation today: Program planning and leadership.* Santa Monica, CA: Goodyear.

Kruger, H., & Kruger, J. (1982). *Movement education in physical education.* Dubuque, IA: Wm. C. Brown Company Publishers.

Laban, R. (1948). *Modern educational dance.* London: McDonald & Evans.

Laban, R., & Ullmann, L. (1960). *The mastery of movement.* London: McDonald & Evans.

Lakie, W. L. (1964). Expressed attitudes of various groups of athletes toward athletic competition. *Research Quarterly, 35,* 497–503.

Lambdin, D. D., & Steinhardt, M. A. (1991). Elementary and secondary physical education teachers' perceptions of their goals, expertise, curriculum, and students' achievement. *Journal of Teaching in Physical Education, 11,* 103–111.

LaPorte, W. R. (1951). *LaPorte health and physical education score card I, II.* Los Angeles: Parker & Company.

LaPorte, W. R. (1968). *The physical education curriculum, a national program.* Los Angeles: College Book Store.

Lawson, H. A. (1992). Why don't practitioners use research? Explanations and selected implications. *Journal of Physical Education, Recreation, and Dance, 63*(8), 36, 53–57.

Lawson, H. A., Bosel, V., & Belka, D. (1992). *Paradoxes in the work orientations and epistemologies of physical education teachers.* Paper presented at the American Educational Research Association Meeting, San Francisco.

Lawson, H. A., & Placek, J. H. (1981). *Physical education in the secondary schools.* Boston: Allyn & Bacon.

Lawton, S. U., & Rogers, F. R. (1937). *Educational paths to virtue, I.* Newton, MA: Pleides Company.

Leonard, G. B. (1975). *The ultimate athlete: Revisioning sports, physical education, and the body.* New York: Viking Press.

Levine, D. U. (1988). Teaching thinking to at-risk students: Generalizations and speculation. In B. A. Presseisen, (Ed.), *At-risk students and thinking: Perspectives from research.* Washington, DC: NEA/RBS.

Lincoln, S. M. (1992). Sports injury risk management and the keys to safety: Coalition of Americans to protect sports (CAPS). *Journal of Physical Education, Recreation, and Dance, 63*(7), 40–42, 63.

Locke, L. F. (1969). *Research in physical education: A critical view.* New York: Teachers College Press.

Locke, L., & Massengale, J. (1978). Role conflict in teacher/coaches. *Research Quarterly, 49,* 162–174.

Lockhart, A. S. (1977). *Modern dance: Building and teaching lessons.* Dubuque, IA: Wm. C. Brown Company Publishers.

Lockhart, A. S., & Mott, J. (1981). An experiment in homogeneous grouping and the effect on achievement in sports fundamentals. *Research Quarterly, 22,* 58–62.

Logsdon, B., Barrett, K., Ammons, M., Broer, M., Helverson, L., McKee, R., & Robertson, M. (1984). *Physical education for children: A focus on the teaching process.* Philadelphia: Lea & Febiger.

Loovis, M., & Ersing, W. F. (1979). *Assessing and programming gross motor development for children.* Loudonville, OH: Mohican.

Loy, J. W., & Kenyon, G. S. (1981). *Sport, culture, and society: A reader on the sociology of sport.* Philadelphia: Lea & Febiger.

Luke, M. D., & Sinclair, G. D. (1991). Gender differences in adolescents' attitudes toward school physical education. *Journal of Teaching in Physical Education, 11,* 31–46.

MacDonald, D. (1990). The relationship between sex composition of physical education classes and teacher/pupil verbal interaction. *Journal of Teaching in Physical Education, 9,* 152–163.

Mager, R. F. (1984). *Preparing instructional objectives.* Belmont, CA: Lake Publishing Company.

Maheu, R. (1963). Sport and culture. *Journal of Health, Physical Education, and Recreation, 39*(8), 18–21.

Mahon, D. A., Ignico, A. A., & Marsh, M. L. (1993). The effects of daily physical education on health-related physical fitness in first-grade children. *Research Quarterly for Exercise and Sport, 63,* A81.

Mandell, B. R., & Schram, B. (1983). *Human services: An introduction.* New York: John Wiley & Sons.

Martin, F. W. (1976). Leisure, culture, and the continuing search for meaning. *Journal of Physical Education, Recreation, and Dance, 54*(8), 46.

Martinek, T., & Zaichkowsky, L. D. (1977). *Manual for the Martinek-Zaichkowsky Self-Concept Scale for Children.* Jacksonville, IL: Psychologists & Educators.

Maslow, A. (1962). *Toward a psychology of being.* New York: Van Nostrand.

Masser, L. (1990). Teaching for affective learning in elementary physical education. *Journal of Physical Education, Recreation, and Dance, 62*(8), 18–19.

May, R. (1953). *Man's search for himself.* New York: Dell Publishing Company.

McCarthy, C. (1990). Race and education in the United States: The multicultural solution. *Interchange, 21,* 45–55.

McCarville, R. E. (1993). Keys to quality leisure programming. *Journal of Physical Education, Recreation, and Dance, 64*(8), 34–36, 46–47.

McGinnis, J. M. (1987). The national children and youth fitness study II: Introduction. *Journal of Physical Education, Recreation, and Dance, 58*(10), 46.

Mead, M. (1967). *The changing patterns of work and leisure.* Washington, DC: U.S. Department of Labor.

Melograno, V. J. (1996). *Designing the physical education curriculum.* Champaign, IL: Human Kinetics.

Melograno, V. J. (1994). Portfolio assessment: Documenting authentic student learning. *Journal of Physical Education, Recreation, and Dance, 65*(8), 50–55, 58–61.

Mero, E. B. (1909). *American playgrounds: Their construction, equipment, maintenance, and utility.* Boston: The Dale Association.

Miles, J., & Priest, S. (1990). *Adventure education.* State College, PA: Venture Publishing.

Miller, A. G., & Sullivan, J. V. (1982). *Teaching physical activities to impaired youth: An approach to mainstreaming.* New York: John Wiley & Sons.

Miller, D. K. (1994). *Measurement by the physical educator: Why and how.* Dubuque, IA: Brown & Benchmark.

Miller, S. E. (1994). Inclusion of children with disabilities: Can we meet the challenge? *The Physical Educator, 51*(1), 47–52.

Montague, M. E. (1972). Dance is affective and therefore effective education. *Journal of Health, Physical Education, and Recreation, 43*(3), 87–88.

Mood, D. (1982). Evaluation in the affective domain? *Journal of Physical Education, Recreation, and Dance, 53*(2), 18–20.

Morris, G. S. D. (1976). *How to change the games children play.* Minneapolis, MN: Burgess.

Morris, G. S. D. (1980). *How to change the games children play.* Minneapolis, MN: Burgess.

Morris, G. S. D., & Stiehl, J. (1989). *Changing kids games.* Champaign, IL: Human Kinetics.

Mosston, M., & Ashworth, S. (1986). *Teaching physical education.* Columbus, OH: Merrill Publishing Company.

Mueller, R. (1976). *Personalized learning in physical education.* Washington, DC: AAHPERD.

Nash, J. B. (1953). *Recreation: Pertinent readings.* St. Louis, MO: Mosby.

Nash, J. B. (1965). *Philosophy of recreation and leisure.* Dubuque, IA: Wm. C. Brown Company Publishers.

National Association for Sport and Physical Education. (1992). *Outcomes of quality physical education programs.* Reston, VA: AAHPERD.

National Association for Sport and Physical Education. (1993). *Shape of the nation 1993: A survey of state physical education requirements.* Reston, VA: AAHPERD.

National Association for Sport and Physical Education. (1994). *National standards for physical education: A guide to content and assessment.* St. Louis, MO: Mosby.

National Association for Sport and Physical Education. (1995). *National standards for athletic coaches.* Washington, DC: AAHPERD.

National Cancer Institute. (1986). *National Cancer Institute monographs 2.* Bethesda, MD: U.S. Department of Health and Human Services.

National Center for Education Statistics. (1995). *The condition of education, 1994.* Washington, DC: U.S. Department of Education.

National Center for Health Statistics. (1975). *Vital and health statistics: Exercise and participation in sports among persons 20 years of age and over.* Washington, DC: U.S. Government Printing Office.

National Dance Association. (1988). *Dance curricula guidelines K–12.* Reston, VA: AAHPERD.

National Institute on Aging. (1986). *Age pages.* Washington, DC: U.S. Department of Health and Human Services.

National Institute on Drug Abuse. (1989). *National household survey on drug abuse: Population estimates 1988.* Washington, DC: U.S. Department of Health and Human Services.

National Safety Council. (1991). *Accident facts.* Chicago: National Safety Council.

National Sporting Goods Association. (1994). *Sports participation in 1994.* Mount Prospect, IL: National Sporting Goods Association.

Nelson, D. O. (1966). Leadership in sports. *Research Quarterly, 37,* 268–275.

Nichols, D. B., Arsenault, D. R., & Giuffre, D. L. (1980). *Motor activities for the underachiever.* Springfield, IL: Charles C. Thomas, Publisher.

Nixon, J.E., & Jewett, A. E. (1980). *An introduction to physical education.* Philadelphia: Saunders.

Oberteuffer, D. (1965). *Background readings for physical education.* New York: Holt, Rinehart & Winston.

Office of Disease Prevention and Health Promotion. (1987). *National survey of worksite health promotion activities: A summary.* Washington, DC: U.S. Department of Health and Human Services.

Orlick, T. (1977). *Winning through cooperation: Competitive insanity.* Washington, DC: Hawkins & Associates.

Orlick, T. (1978). *The cooperative sports and games book: Challenge with competition.* New York: Pantheon Books.

Orlick, T. (1982). *The second cooperative sports and games book.* New York: Pantheon Books.

Ornstein, R., & Ehrlich, P. (1989). *New world—new mind: Moving toward conscious evolution.* New York: Doubleday.

Page, R. M. (1992). Lonely children: A special concern for exercise science professionals. *Research Quarterly for Exercise and Sport, 63,* A81.

Pangrazi, R. P., & Darst, P. W. (1991). *Dynamic physical education for secondary school students:*

Curriculum and instruction. New York: Macmillan Publishing Company.

Parker, J. (1995). Teacher and student beliefs about physical education. *Research Quarterly for Exercise and Sport, 66,* A67.

Partlow, K. (1992). American coaching effectiveness program (ACEP): Educating America's coaches. *Journal of Physical Education, Recreation, and Dance, 63*(7), 36–39.

Pennsylvania Department of Education. (1983). *Physical education competencies.* Harrisburg, PA: Pennsylvania Department of Education.

PEOPEL Project Materials. 3839 West Camelback Road, Phoenix, AZ, 85091.

Perrier. (1979). *The Perrier study: Fitness in America.* New York: Perrier.

Perrone, V. (Ed.). (1991). *Expanding student assessment.* Alexandria, VA: Association for Supervision and Curriculum Development.

Peterson, N. L. (1987). *Early intervention for handicapped and at-risk children.* Denver, CO: Love Publishing Company.

Pickett, A. L. (1981). *Paragraphs in special education: The state of the art.* New York: New Careers Training Laboratory.

Piers, E., & Harris D. (1964). Age and other correlates of self-concept in children. *Journal of Educational Psychology, 55,* 91–95.

Pizarro, D. C. (1990). Reliability of the health-related fitness test for mainstreamed educable and trainable mentally handicapped adolescents. *Adapted Physical Activity Quarterly, 7,* 240–248.

President's Council on Physical Fitness and Sports. (1973). National adult physical fitness survey. *Newsletter,* 1–27.

President's Council on Physical Fitness and Sports. (1991). *The President's Challenge Physical Fitness Program.* Washington, DC: President's Council on Physical Fitness and Sports.

President's Council on Physical Fitness and Sports. (1994). American attitudes toward physical activity and fitness. *Journal of Health, Physical Education, Recreation, and Dance, 65*(1), 15.

Prudential Insurance Company of America. (1994). *Prudential FITNESSGRAM.* Dallas, TX: The Cooper Institute for Aerobics Research.

Rand, J., & English, F. (1968). Towards a differentiated teaching staff. *Phi Delta Kappan, 49,* 264–268.

Rankin, K. D. (1975). *Verbal and non-verbal interaction analysis of student teachers with students in elementary physical education.* Lawrence, KS: University of Kansas.

Read, H. (1945). *Education through art.* New York: Pantheon Books.

Rhode Island Department of Education. (1991). *Suggested outcomes in physical education K–12.* Providence, RI: Rhode Island Department of Education.

Rink, J. E. (1979). *Development of an observation system for content development in physical education.* Unpublished doctoral dissertation. Columbus: OH: The Ohio State University.

Rink, J. E. (1993). *Teaching physical education for learning.* St. Louis, MO: Mosby.

Rizzo, T. L., & Vispoel, W. P. (1992). Changing attitudes about teaching students with handicaps. *Adapted Physical Education Quarterly, 9*(1), 54–63.

Roach, E., & Kephart, N. (1966). *The Purdue perceptual-motor survey.* Columbus, OH: Merrill Publishing Company.

Rogers, C. (1969). *Freedom to learn: A view of what education might become.* Columbus, OH: Merrill Publishing Company.

Rogers, F. R. (1941). *Dance: A basic educational technique.* New York: Macmillan Publishing Company.

Rohnke, K. (1977). *Cowstails and cobras.* Hamilton, MA: Project Adventure.

Ross, J. G., & Gilbert, G. G. (1985). The national children and youth fitness study: A summary of findings. *Journal of Physical Education, Recreation, and Dance, 56*(1), 45–50.

Ross, J. G., & Pate, R. R. (1987). The national children and youth fitness study II. *Journal of Physical Education, Recreation, and Dance, 58*(9), 51–56.

Ross, S. (1981). The epistemic geography of physical education: Addressing the problem of theory and practice. *Quest, 33,* 42–54.

Rothstein, A. (1973). Practitioners and the scholarly enterprise. *Quest, 20,* 56–60.

Sadler, W. C., Tentinger, L. G., & Wiedon, G. A. (1993). America 2000: Implications for physical education. *The Physical Educator, 50*(2), 77–86.

Sage, G. H. (1987). The social world of high school athletic coaches: Multiple role demands and their consequences. *Sociology of Sports Journal, 4,* 213–228.

Sage, G. H. (1990). High school and college sports in the United States. *Journal of Physical Education, Recreation, and Dance, 61*(2), 59–63.

Schurr, E. L. (1980). *Movement experiences for children.* Englewood Cliffs, NJ: Prentice-Hall.

Seaman, J. A., & DePauw, K. P. (1989). *The new adapted physical education: A developmental approach.* Mountain View, CA: Mayfield.

Seefeldt, V. D., & Milligan, M. J. (1992). Program for athletic coaches education (PACE): Educating America's public and private school coaches. *Journal of Physical Education, Recreation, and Dance, 63*(7), 46–49.

Selye, H. (1978). *The stress of life.* New York: McGraw-Hill.

Seneca, L. A. (1908). *Selected essays of Seneca and the satire on the deification of Claudius.* New York: Macmillan Publishing Company.

Shuker, V. B. (1993). Dance education K–12: Theory into practice (part II). *Journal of Physical Education, Recreation, and Dance, 64*(5), 41.

Siedentop, D. (1971). Differences between Greek and Hebrew views of man. *Canadian Journal of History of Sport and Physical Education,* 30–49.

Siedentop, D. (1974). *The humanistic education movement: Some questions and issues in physical education and sports.* Mountain View, CA: National Press Books.

Siedentop, D. (1994). *Introduction to physical education, fitness, and sport.* Mountain View, CA: Mayfield.

Siedentop, D., Herkowitz, J., & Rink, J. E. (1984). *Elementary physical education methods.* Englewood Cliffs, NJ: Prentice-Hall.

Siedentop, D., Mand, C., & Taggart, A. (1986). *Physical education: Teaching and curriculum strategies for grades 5–12.* Mountain View, CA: Mayfield.

Siedentop, D., Tousignant, M., & Parker, M. (1982). *Academic learning time-physical education: 1982 revision coding manual.* Columbus, OH: The Ohio State University.

Simon, J. A., & Smoll, F. L. (1974). An instrument for assessing children's attitude toward physical activity. *Research Quarterly, 45,* 407–415.

Sisley, B., & Wiese, D. (1987). Current status: Requirements for interscholastic coaches. *Journal of Physical Education, Recreation, and Dance, 58*(7), 73–85.

Smith, D. S. (1982). Drownproofing and the water safety spectrum. *Journal of Physical Education, Recreation, and Dance, 53*(5), 56–58.

Smith, J. W., Carlson, R. E., Donaldson, G. W., & Masters, H. B. (1972). *Outdoor education.* Englewood Cliffs, NJ: Prentice-Hall.

Smith, M. D. (1990). Enhancing self-responsibility through a humanistic approach to physical education. *Bulletin of Physical Education, 26*(3), 27–31.

Smith, M. D. (1992). Utilizing the games for understanding curriculum model at the elementary school level. *The Physical Educator, 48*(4), 184–187.

Smith, M. D. (1993). Utilizing different curriculum models to achieve the objectives of physical education. *Bulletin of Physical Education, 29*(1), 15–22.

Spencer, H. (1860). *Education: Intellectual, moral and physical.* New York: Appleton-Century-Crofts.

Stainback, W., & Stainback, S. (1990). *Support networks for inclusive schooling: Interdependent integrated education.* Baltimore, MD: Paul H. Brookes.

Steffen, J., & Hansen, G. (1987). Effect of computer-assisted instruction on development of cognitive and psychomotor learning in bowling. *Journal of Teaching in Physical Education, 6,* 183–191.

Stevens, D. A. (1994). Movement concepts: Stimulating cognitive development in elementary students. *Journal of Physical Education, Recreation, and Dance, 65*(8), 16–23.

Stewart, C., & Sweet, L. (1992). Professional preparation of high school coaches: The problem continues. *Journal of Physical Education, Recreation, and Dance, 63*(6), 75–79.

Stillwell, J. L., & Reneau, P. (1992). A survey of state agency physical education curriculum material. *The Physical Educator, 49*(4), 170–173.

Stillwell, J. L., & Stockard, J. R. (1988). *More fitness exercises for children.* Durham, NC: Great Activities Publishing Company.

Stone, W. J. (1990). *Fitness for you: A guide to wellness.* St. Paul, MN: West Publishing Company.

Straub, W. B. (1976). *The lifetime sports-oriented physical education program.* Englewood Cliffs, NJ: Prentice-Hall.

Swanson, M. S. (1991). *At-risk students in elementary education.* Springfield, IL: Charles C. Thomas.

Swift, E. M. (1991). Why Johnny can't play. *Sports Illustrated, 75*(13), 60–64, 66–68, 70–72.

Taylor, J., & Chiogioji, E. (1987). Implications of educational reform on high school programs. *Journal of Physical Education, Recreation, and Dance, 58*(2), 22–23.

Templin, T. J. (1992). Research for and by practitioners. *Journal of Physical Education, Recreation, and Dance, 63*(8), 11, 16.

Tenoschok, M. (1995). Adventures in supermurals. *Teaching Middle School Physical Education, 1*(4), 13.

Thomas, J. R., Lee, A. M., & Thomas, K. T. (1988). *Physical education for children: Concepts into practice.* Champaign, IL: Human Kinetics.

Thomas, N. (1980). Thoughts on teacher evaluation. *The Physical Educator, 37*(4), 176–178.

Tiedt, A. L., & Tiedt, I. M. (1990). *Multicultural teaching: A handbook of activities, information, and resources.* Boston: Allyn & Bacon.

Tillotson, J. (1970). A brief theory of movement education. In R. T. Sweeney (Ed.), *Selected readings in movement education.* Reading, MA: Addison-Wesley.

Toulmin, M. L. B. (1973). *The development of an original instrument to measure the expressed attitudes of children toward the elementary school program of physical education.* Denton, TX: Texas Woman's University.

Trump, J. L., & Baynham, D. (1961). *Guide to better schools: Focus on change.* Chicago: Rand McNally.

Twine, J., & Martinek, T. (1992). Teachers as researchers: An application of a collaborative action research model. *Journal of Physical Education, Recreation, and Dance, 63*(8), 22–25.

Tyler, R. W. (1949). *Basic principles of curriculum and instruction.* Chicago: University of Chicago Press.

Tyler, R. W. (1981). Curriculum development since 1900. *Educational Leadership, 35,* 598–601.

Ulrich, D. A. (1986). *Test of gross motor development.* Austin, TX: Pro-ed.

United Nations Preparatory Educational, Scientific, and Cultural Commission. (1947). *Fundamental education, common ground for all peoples.* A report to the United Nations Educational, Scientific, and Cultural Organization. New York: Macmillan Publishing Company.

U.S. Department of Education. (1991). *America 2000: An educational strategy.* (ED/0s91-13). Washington, DC.

U.S. Department of Health and Human Services. (1992). *Healthy people 2000: National health promotion and disease prevention objectives.* Washington, DC: U.S. Department of Health and Human Services.

U.S. National Heart Institute. (1968). *The Framingham study: An epidemiological investigation of cardiovascular disease.* Bethesda, MD.

U. S. 94th Congress. (1975). *Public Law 94.142.*

Updyke, W. F. (1994). Fitness trends in a large population of 6–10-year-old children. *Summary Report of the Chrysler-AAU Physical Fitness Testing Program.* Poplars Building, Bloomington, IN: Amateur Athletic Union.

Updyke, W. F. (1994). Fitness trends in a large population of 6–10 year old children. *Summary Report of the Chrysler-AAU Physical Fitness Testing Program.* Bloomington, IN: Amateur Athletic Union.

Vodola, T. M. (1973). *Individualized physical education program for the handicapped child.* Englewood Cliffs, NJ: Prentice-Hall.

Vodola, T. M. (1976). *Project ACTIVE maxi-model kit.* Oakhurst, NJ: Township of Ocean Park.

Vogler, E. W., French, R., & Bishop, P. (1989). Paraprofessional: Implications for adapted physical education. *The Physical Educator, 46*(2), 69–76.

Wall, J., & Murray, N. (1994). *Children and movement: Physical education in the elementary school.* Dubuque, IA: Brown & Benchmark.

Watson, G. (1972). Resistance to change. In G. Zaltman, P. Kotler, & I. Kaufman, (Ed.), *Creating social change.* New York: Holt, Rinehart & Winston.

Wear, C. L. (1955). Construction of equivalent forms of an attitude scale. *Research Quarterly, 26,* 113–119.

Werner, P., & Almond, L. (1990). Models of games education. *Journal of Physical Education, Recreation, and Dance, 61*(7), 23–27.

Wessel, J. (1979). *I CAN: Locomotor and rhythmic skills.* Northbrook, IL: Hubbard Scientific.

Wessinger, N. P. (1992). Demystifying research for the practitioner: How do I find out what I want to know? *Journal of Physical Education, Recreation, and Dance, 63*(8), 12–16.

White, F. A. (1989). *The complete life of Homer.* London: Bell & Sons.

Whitehead, A. N. (1932). *The aims of education: And other essays.* London: Williams & Northgate.

Williams, C., Varnes, J., Smith, C., Mack, C., Harageones, M., Holton, T., & Holyoak, O. (1983). Physical education requirement: FAHPERD recommendations for content specificity. *Florida Journal, 21*(3), 10–11, 20.

Williams, Ted, & Underwood, J. (1969). *My Turn at Bat: The Story of my life.* New York: Simon & Schuster.

Williamson, K. M. (1992). Relevance or rigor: A case for teacher as researcher. *Journal of Physical Education, Recreation, and Dance, 63*(8), 17–21, 25.

Winnick, J. P. (1996). *Adapted physical education and sport.* Champaign, IL: Human Kinetics.

Winnick, J. P., & Short, F. X. (1985). *Physical fitness testing of the disabled.* Champaign, IL: Human Kinetics.

Wise, M. K. (1976). *A comparison of attitudes of children and their parents toward athletic competition at the elementary school level.* Lincoln, NE: University of Nebraska.

Woodward, W. H. (1963). *Vittorino da Feltre and other humanist educators.* New York: Teachers College Press, Columbia University.

Wuest, D. A., & Bucher, C. A. (1995). *Foundations of physical education and sport.* St. Louis, MO: Mosby.

Zessoules, R., & Garner, H. (1991). Authentic assessment: Beyond the buzzword and into the classroom. In V. Perrone (Ed.), *Expanding student assessment.* Alexandria, VA: Association for Supervision and Curriculum Development.

INDEX

A
ability grouping, 151–152
academic discipline curriculum model, 71
accidental occupation, 283
activity curriculum, 68
Adapted Physical Activity Quarterly, 116, 119
adapted physical education
 benefits of, 240–241
 classification and organization in, 247–250
 mandate for, 241–242
 scheduling for, 258
 terminology for, 239–240
adapted physical educator, 239
adapted program, 253, 254, 255
adventure education curriculum model, 74
aerobic endurance, 37
aerobic exercise, 225
aging American, 15–17
aimless play, 215
Aldana, S. G., 22
Alexander, W., 210
Almond, L., 76
America 2000: An Educational Strategy, 45–46
American Alliance for Health, Physical Education, Recreation, and Dance (AAHPERD), 3, 15, 71, 119, 120–122, 300, 302, 303, 314
American Association of Active Lifestyles and Fitness (AAALF), 121
American Association for Leisure and Recreation (AALR), 121–122
American Cancer Society, 13
American Coaching Effectiveness Program (ACEP), 284
American College of Sports Medicine (ACSM), 5, 123
American Medical Association, 151, 250
American Sport Education Program, 283
Ammons, M., 70
Anderson, W. G., 113, 114
Annarino, A. A., 54, 87, 140, 141, 144, 168, 187, 234, 274, 281, 316
aquatics for secondary school students, 224–225
Arizona Department of Education, 296, 297
Armstrong, G. P., 233
Arnold, P. J., 268
Assessment Guide for Secondary School Physical Education Programs, 314
Association for the Advancement of Health Education (AAHE), 122
at-risk students, 52
Austin, S., 52
authentic learning, 308

B
Bain, L. L., 78, 79, 90, 91, 94, 103, 178, 220, 280
Baldwin, J., 9
Banks, J. A., 9
Barrett, K., 70
Barrow, H. M., 309
Basic Stuff, 71
Baynham, D., 140–142, 145

Beach, B., 32
benchmarks, 61
  for second grade, 62
  for sixth grade, 63
  for tenth grade, 64
Bennett, C. I., 9
Berryman, D., 253
Birch, D. A., 87
Bishop, P., 151
Block, M. E., 251, 252
Bloom, B. S., 54, 313
body awareness, 201
body composition, 37
Bonano, D., 312
Bookwalter, K. W., 130, 136, 271, 277
breach of duty, 102
Breznitz, S., 14
broad fields curriculum model, 67
Broer, M., 70
Bruner, J., 51
Brustad, J. R., 116
Bucher, C. A., 69, 70, 153, 200, 206, 268, 281, 312, 313
Bunker, D., 76
Bureau of Health Education, 5
Butt, K. L., 8

C
Caldwell, S. F., 68
California Human Population Laboratory, 11, 12
capacity for activity, 225
Cardinal Athletic Principles, 279
Cardinal Principles of Secondary Education, 34
Carlson, R. E., 233
Carroll, R., 71
Castetter, W. B., 309
Cawelti, G., 8
change, 112
Checklist for Elementary School Physical Education, 314
Cheffers, J., 54
Chepyator-Thomson, J. R., 8
Child Advocacy Center, 252
Children's Defense Fund, 52
circuit training, 225
Clarke, H. H., 4
coaching certification, 283–286
Coalition of Americans to Protect Sports (CAPS), 284

collective scoring games, 194
Combs, A. W., 292
Commission on the Reorganization of Secondary Education, 34
Committee on Trauma Research, 13
community resource inventory, 98–99
Comprehensive Health Essential Skills, 296, 297
computer-assisted instruction (CAI), 156
computer-based instruction (CBI), 156, 158, 160–161
Conant, J. F., 10
conditioning for secondary school students, 225–228
Conrad, H. L., 38
contracting, 153, 154, 155, 156, 157
Cooper, K., 39
Corbin, C. B., 38–39, 116
Council on Physical Education for Children, 314
Cowell, C. C., 42–43, 54, 87, 91, 94, 140, 141, 144, 168, 187, 234, 274, 281, 316
Craft, D., 252
Cratty, B. J., 42, 182, 247
Csikszentmihalyi, M., 52
Culkin, D., 115–116
culture, 44–45
curriculum
  hidden, 78–79
  nature of, 61–62, 64–65
  scheduling of, 138, 140–146
curriculum content
  for elementary schools, 183, 187–209
  for secondary schools, 220–234
curriculum coordinating committee, 171–172
curriculum development, 87–88
  concept approach to, 102–104
curriculum evaluation, 312–316
  definitions of, 292–293
  guidelines for, 294
  and measurement, 293–294
  overview of, 294–299
curriculum guide
  administrator's role in developing, 171
  construction of, 174–178
  definitions of, 168
  faculty involvement in developing, 174
  preliminary considerations for, 168–170
curriculum materials, state agency, 174, 175, 176

curriculum models, 65–79
  academic discipline, 71
  adventure education, 74
  broad fields, 67
  developmental, 69–70
  eclectic, 78
  fitness, 71
  games for understanding, 76–78
  humanistic, 68–69
  movement education, 70–71
  multi-activity, 74, 76
  personal-social developmental, 71–72
  separate subjects, 66–67
  sport education, 72–74
  and teacher effectiveness, 79
curriculum planning
  cooperative, 246–247
  factors affecting, 89, 90
  non-school factors affecting, 95–97, 98–99
  school factors affecting, 91, 94–95
  structuring for quality in, 106
  variety and scope of, 104–106
curriculum reform, 112–113
  and interaction, 129
curriculum research, 113–119
  external influences affecting, 119–124
curriculum subcommittees, 172–173
cycle plan, 145–146

D
daily physical education (DPE), 116, 118
damage, 102
dance
  in America, 21
  for elementary school students, 206, 207
  for secondary school students, 229–232
    ballroom/social, 230
    contra, 230
    folk, 230–231
    modern, 231
    square, 232
Darst, P. W., 228, 233, 311
Daugherty, N. J., 312
Daughtry, G., 147, 272
Davis, H., 115–116
Davis, R., 246
Davis, T., 246
Defina, A. A., 308
developmental curriculum model, 69–70
developmental program, 253

Dewey, J., 32, 35
Dickason, J., 253
differentiated staffing, 148–149
discipline-centered curriculum model, 66–67
Dobos, R., 35
Donaldson, G. W., 233
double oppression, 91
drill and practice programs, 158
Dubos, R., 3
Dulaney, N. M., 116
Dunham, P., 294
Dunn, J. M., 247
Durrant, S. M., 97

E
eclectic curriculum model, 78
Eddy, J. M., 7
educable mentally handicapped (EMH), 119
education. *See* physical education.
Education for All Handicapped Children Act, 100, 241, 242, 244, 248–249
Educational Policies Commission, 34
Ehrlich, A. H., 10
Ehrlich, P. R., 10, 12
Eisenhower, D. D., 5, 122–123
Ellis, M., 77
emerging curriculum, 68
Engelman, S., 102–103
English, F., 148, 149
Ennis, C. D., 91, 103, 178, 280
ERIC Clearinghouse on Teacher Education, 174, 177
Ersing, W. F., 255
established duty, 102
ethical behavior, 267–268
Evanl, T., 54
exercise movement, 22–23
existential curriculum model, 68–69
extracurricular programs
  balance in, 268–269
  need for planning in, 270

F
Fait, H., 200, 247
Fallon, D., 230
Felshin, J., 68
Fielding, L. W., 266–267
Figone, A. J., 280
Fiscella, J., 18
Fishburne, G., 71, 250

fitness
  for elementary school students, 188, 190
  health-related, 37–39
fitness curriculum model, 71
fitness programs, work-site, 7–8
flexibility, 37, 116
flexible scheduling, 140–143
Fluegelman, A., 194
Ford, G., 242
France, W. L., 42–43, 91, 94
free exercise, 226
freedom, 19–20
French, R., 151
Frith, G. H., 149, 150
Fry, F. F., 252
full inclusion, 251

G
Gabbard, C., 196–197, 228
Gallahue, D. L., 198, 199, 200, 204, 206, 253
games for elementary school students, 189, 190–200
  cooperative, 194–196
  creative, 196–197
  lead-up, 198–199
  low organized, 190–192
  relays, 192–194
  sports, 199–200
games for understanding curriculum model, 76–78
games without losers, 194
Gibran, K., 54
Glasser, W., 35, 36
Goldberger, L., 14
Graham, G., 197
Gray, J. A., 115–116
Greene, L., 228
Griffin, P. S., 305
Gruber, J. J., 305–306
guide. *See* curriculum guide.
A Guide for Instruction in Physical Education, 224
gymnastics
  for elementary school students, 189
  for secondary school students, 228

H
Handbook for Physical Education, 223
Hankin, T., 205
Harris, J. A., 230, 231

Harrow, A. J., 54
Hass, G., 87
Hastings, J. T., 55, 313
Haubenstricker, J. L., 256
Hazelton, H. W., 54, 87, 140, 141, 144, 168, 187, 234, 274, 281, 316
health promotion programs, 7
health-related fitness, 37–39
Health-Related Physical Fitness Test (HRPFT), 119, 300
Healthy People 2000, 6, 11–14
Helion, J. G., 252
Hellison, D. R., 51, 71, 72, 73, 74, 152
Helverson, L., 70
Herbert, J. F., 87
Herkowitz, J., 224, 233, 234
hidden curriculum, 78–79
Higgins, R. J., 266
Hopkins, C. T., 51
Howe, C. Z., 17
humanistic curriculum model, 68–69

I
I CAN program, 254–255
Ignico, A. A., 118
Illinois Association of Health, Physical Education, and Recreation, 314
Illinois Journal of Health, Physical Education, and Recreation, 314
IMP program, 255
implicit curriculum, 78–79
inclusion, 240, 250–253
Indiana Physical Education Score Card for Elementary and Secondary Schools, 314
Individualized Education Program (IEP), 244–246, 251
innovative programs, 254–257
intellectual competency, 43–44
interactive video instruction, (IAV), 156, 158
International Association for Physical Education in Higher Education (AIESEP), 24
International Council for Health, Physical Education, Recreation, Sport, and Dance (ICHPERSD), 24
International Federation for Physical Education (FIEP), 24
interscholastic athletic program, 276–286
intramural program, 271–276

J

Jagger, B., 71
Jay, D., 116
Jewett, A. E., 54, 78, 79, 91, 94, 103, 178, 220, 280
Johnson, R. E., 305–306
Johnson, W. S., 156
Journal of Physical Education, Recreation, and Dance (JOPERD), 114–115, 116
Journal of Teaching in Physical Education, 117–118

K

Kanters, M. A., 12
Keeney, G. L., 115–116
Kelly, B., 209
Kelly, L. J., 156
Kelly, N., 209
Kennedy, J. F., 5
Kenyon, G. S., 42
Kerlinger, F., 309
Kinney, W., 253
Kirchner, G., 71, 250
Kirkendall, D. R., 305–306
Kleiber, D. A., 18
Kneer, M. E., 152
Koenig, C. R., 268, 281, 312
Kovich, M., 20
Krathwohl, D. R., 54
Kraus, K. G., 21
Kraus Curriculum Development Library (KCDL), 174, 178
Kruger, H., 70, 89
Kruger, J., 70, 89

L

Laban, R., 70, 71, 116, 200
Lambdin, D. D., 117
LaPorte Health and Physical Education Score Card I, II (LaPorte), 313
Lawson, H. A., 71, 114
LeBlanc, E., 196–197, 228
Lee, A. M., 89, 187, 250
Lefebve, C., 253
leisure, 17–20
Leisure-Time Pursuits, 16
Leonard, G. B., 23
Lewis, C., 147, 272
liability, 100–102
Life Extension Institute, 16
lifestyles, 35–36
Lindsey, R., 38–39
Lockhart, A. S., 231
Logsdon, B., 70
Loovis, E. M., 255
Lowy, S., 196–197, 228
Loy, J. W., 42
Luke, M. D., 117

M

MacDonald, D., 117–118
Madaus, G. F., 55, 313
Mager, R. F., 59
Maheu, R., 44
Mahon, D. A., 118
mainstreaming, 240, 250–253
malfeasance, 101
Man's Search for Himself (May), 4
Mancini, V. H., 311
Mand, C., 79
Marshe, M. L., 118
Martin, F. W., 17–18
Martinek, T., 115
Masia, B. B., 54
Maslow, A., 4, 68
Masters, H. B., 233
May, R., 4
McCarthy, C., 91
McCarville, R. E., 19
McCloy, C. H., 4
McCormack, J., 52
McGee, R., 309
McKee, R., 70
McKenzie, R. T., 4
Mead, M., 19
Meister, G., 52
Meister, J. F., 38
Melograno, V. J., 78, 168, 308
middle schools, 209–210
Miles, J., 233
Miller, D. K., 305
Miller, M. E., 54
Miller, S. E., 251
misfeasance, 101
modular scheduling, 143–144
Montague, M. E., 229
Montana in Action: Physical Education Curriculum Guide Grades K–12, 223

Montelpare, W. J., 12
Mood, D., 305
moral behavior, 267–268
More Fitness Exercises for Children (Stillwell and Stockton), 190
Morris, D. C., 156
Morris, G. S. D., 196, 252
movement, 182–183
movement education curriculum model, 70–71
movement exploration for elementary school students, 200–203
movement qualities, 201
multi-activity curriculum model, 74, 76
muscular endurance, 37

N
Nash, J. B., 4, 8, 19
National Association for the Education of Young Children (NAEYC), 123
National Association of Girls and Women in Sports (NAGWS), 122
National Association of Secondary School Principals (NASSP), 123, 140–142
National Association for Sport and Physical Education (NASPE), 61, 97, 122, 284, 314
National Cancer Institute, 13
National Dance Association (NDA), 122, 229
National Federation of State High School Athletic Associations, 277, 279, 286
National Institute on Aging, 15, 17
National Standards for Athletic Coaches, 284
National Standards for Physical Education: A Guide to Content and Assessment, 61
National Youth Sports Coaches Association (NYSCA), 285
negligence
  elements of, 101–102
  types of, 100–101
Nixon, J. E., 54
nonfeasance, 101

O
Oberteuffer, D., 35
obesity, 39
Office of Disease Prevention and Health Promotion, 6
Office of Special Education, 245
Orlick, T., 194

Ornstein, R., 12
outcomes-based physical education, 60–61
outdoor education for secondary school students, 233–234

P
Page, R. M., 118
Pahnos, M. L., 8
Pangrazi, R. P., 228
paraprofessionals, 149–151
Parent Teacher Association (PTA), 172
Parker, J., 118–119
participation philosophy, 4–6
passive lecture methodology, 160
pay-to-play, 286
peer teaching, 161, 162
perceptual-motor program, 255–256
performance contracts, 153, 154, 155, 156, 157
Perrone, V., 308
personal factors approach, 91
personal-social developmental curriculum model, 71–72
Peterson, N. L., 52
physical activity, benefits of, 38–39
Physical Best, 300, 302
physical education
  aspects of, 53–58
  international, 24
  leisure and freedom in, 19–20
  objectives of, 32, 34–37
    behavioral, 58–60
    developmental, 54, 56–57
    pecific, 58
    raditional, 54, 55
  outcomes-based, 60–61
  potential of, 53
  state requirements for, 97
physical education activity interest inventory, 91, 92–93
physical education curriculum. *See.* curriculum.
physically educated person, 32, 33
Pickett, A. L., 151
Pittman, A. M., 230, 231
Pizarro, D. C., 119
Placek, J. H., 71
play, 42–43
population density, 9–10

PREP play program, 257
President's Council on Physical Fitness and Sports, 5, 14, 122–123
Priest, S., 233
program. *See* curriculum.
Program for Athletic Coaches Education (PACE), 285
programmed instruction, 153, 158, 159, 160
project ACTIVE, 257
project adventure, 257
project PEOPEL, 257
proximate cause, 102
Prudential FITNESSGRAM, 302
Public Law 87.276, 242, 243
Public Law 94.142, 100, 241, 242, 244, 248–249
Purpose Process Curriculum Framework (PPCF), 54

R
Rand, J., 148
Read, H., 200
recreational competency, 39–41
Rehabilitation Act, 242
remedial program, 253
Reneau, P., 174
Research Quarterly for Exercise and Sport, 116, 118–119
reversal games, 194, 196
rhythmic activities
  for elementary school students, 189, 203–207
    basic, 204–205
    creative, 205–206
    singing, 206
    traditional and contemporary dance, 206–207
  for secondary school students, 229–232
Rink, J. E., 147, 161, 168, 224, 227, 228, 233, 234
Robertson, M., 70
Rogers, C., 79
Rogers, F. R., 4, 215
role conflict, 280

S
Sadler, W. C., 45
Sage, G. H., 276, 286
Schurr, E. L., 152, 200–201
scope, 130–137
secondary schools
  organization of, 216
  practical considerations for, 219–220
selective program, 151
self testing for elementary school students, 207–208
Selye, H., 40
Seneca, L. A., 39
separate subjects curriculum model, 66–67
sequencing, 130–137, 138, 139
sex role stereotyping, 117–118
Shuker, V.B., 22
Siedentop, D., 22, 36, 60, 68, 69, 72, 78, 79, 100, 113, 215, 224, 233, 234, 266, 271, 276, 280, 308
simulation programs, 158
Sinclair, G. D., 117
Smith, J. W., 233
Smith, M. D., 71, 72, 76–77
social efficiency, 41–43, 233
society
  free, 3–4
  multicultural, 8–9
  technological, 6–8
spatial awareness, 201
special education, 240
Special Education Act, 242, 243
specialization, 286
Spencer, H., 34
sport(s)
  as art form, 20–21
  as entertainment, 286
  international, 24
  for secondary school students, 232–233
sport education curriculum model, 72–74
sport sociology, 42
Sport Specific Aerobic Routines (Greene), 228
staff organization, 147–149
Steinhardt, M. A., 117
Stiehl, J., 196, 252
Stillwell, J. L., 174, 190
Stockard, J. R., 190
Stone, W. J., 22
Straub, W. B., 97, 98–99
strength, 37
S-T-R-E-T-C-H, 275
student assistants, 161
student evaluation, 299–306

affective domain, 305–306
cognitive domain, 304–305
physical domain, 300–302
portfolio assessment for, 307–308
psychomotor domain, 303–304
students
  at-risk, 52
  attitudes and beliefs of, 117, 118
  disabled, 240
  elementary school, 183, 184–187
    dance and rhythmic activities for, 189, 203–207
    fitness for, 188, 190
    games for, 189, 190–200
    gymnastics for, 189
    movement exploration for, 200–203
    self-testing for, 207–208
  environmental factors affecting, 51–53
  exceptional, 240
  handicapped, 116, 119, 240
    evaluation of, 306–307
  impaired, 240
  instructional strategies using, 161, 162
  motivations of, 91, 94
  personal factors affecting, 89–91
  secondary school, 216–218
    aquatics for, 224–225
    conditioning for, 225–228
    dance and rhythmic activities for, 229–232
    gymnastics for, 228
    individual and dual activities for, 228–229
    outdoor education for, 233–234
    team sports for, 232–233
Sunnarborg, K. R., 115–116
Swanson, M. S., 52

T
Taggert, A., 79
teachable moments, 216
teacher evaluation, 309–312
teachers, attitudes and beliefs of, 117, 118
teaching stations, 146–147
team teaching, 147–148
Templin, T. J., 51, 72, 74, 114–115, 116, 152
Tentinger, L. G., 45–46

Thaxton, N. A., 153, 200, 206
Thomas, J. R., 89, 187, 250
Thomas, K. T., 89, 187, 250
Thomas, N., 309
Thorpe, R., 76
Tillotson, J., 200
Title IX, 97, 100
trainable mentally handicapped (TMH), 119
Tritschler, K. A., 309
Trump, J. L., 140–142, 145
tutorial programs, 158
twice weekly physical education, (TWPE), 118
Twine, J., 115
Tyler, R. W., 88

U
U.S. Department of Education, 45–46
U.S. Department of Health and Human Services, 6, 11–14
Ullman, L., 70, 71
United Nations Educational, Scientific and Cultural Organization (UNESCO), 24

V
value illness, 11
Vodola, T., 257
Vogler, E. W., 151, 251, 252

W
Waller, M. S., 230, 231
Watson, G., 112
weight lifting, 226
Wessel, J., 254
Wessinger, N. P., 115
Whitehead, A. N., 129
Wiedon, G. A., 45–46
Williams, J. F., 4, 35
Williams, T., 86
Williamson, K. M., 115
work-site fitness programs, 7–8
Wuest, D. A., 69, 70

Z
Zakrajsek, D. B., 311
Zehrung, D. A., 116